Women's Writing in
Middle English

Longman Annotated Texts

General Editors:

Charlotte Brewer, Hertford College, Oxford
H.R. Woudhuysen, University College London
Daniel Karlin, University College London

Published Titles:

Michael Mason, *Lyrical Ballads*
Alexandra Barratt, *Women's Writing in Middle English*

Women's Writing in Middle English

Edited by
Alexandra Barratt

LONGMAN
London and New York

Longman Group UK Limited,
Longman House, Burnt Mill, Harlow,
Essex CM20 2JE, England
and Associated Companies throughout the world.

*Published in the United States of America
by Longman Publishing, New York*

© Longman Group UK Limited 1992

First published 1992

British Library Cataloguing-in-Publication Data
A catalogue record for this book is available from the British Library

ISBN 0 582 06193 8 CSD
ISBN 0 582 06192 X PPR

Library of Congress Cataloging-in-Publication Data
Women's writing in Middle English / edited by Alexandra Barratt.
       p.   cm. — (Longman annotated texts)
    Includes bibliographical references and index.
    ISBN 0–582–06193–8 — ISBN 0–582–06192–X (pbk.)
    1. English literature—Middle English, 1100–1500. 2. Literature,
Medieval—Women authors—Translations into English (Middle)
3. Women—England—History—Middle Ages, 500–1500—Sources.
4. English literature—Women authors. 5. Women and literature—
England. I. Barratt, Alexandra. II. Series.
PR1120.W66 1992
808.8′99287′0902—dc20   91–23904
                                                          CIP

Set by 8FF in 10/11pt Ehrhardt Roman

Produced by Longman Singapore Publishers (Pte) Ltd.
Printed in Singapore

Contents

Acknowledgements

No one can compile an anthology without asking other scholars for their help and advice. I should particularly like to thank the following, who provided not only information but also encouragement: Sister Ritamary Bradley; Ms Sheila Cornard; Dr Ian Doyle; Dr Roger Ellis; Professor Douglas Gray; Professor Monica Green; Dr Lotte Hellinga; Dr Anne Hutchison; Professor George Keiser; Ms Sarah McNamer; S. J. Ogilvie-Thomson; Professor Linda Voigts; and Ms Jocelyn Wogan-Browne. For the deficiencies that remain in spite of their efforts, I am myself responsible.

I owe a debt of gratitude to the Committee for Women's Studies (now the Centre for Women's Studies) of the University of Waikato Te Whare Wānanga o Te Waikato, without whom this anthology would never have been conceived; and also to the Council of the University who granted me extended special leave, during which the project came to fruition.

I should also like to thank Dr Charlotte Brewer, one of the General Editors of the Longman Annotated Texts, for her support and assistance.

As for the contribution of Professor Don McKenzie: (αὐτοσχεδιάζει τὰ δέοντα), like Mechtild of Hackeborn, 'be no waye sche cowth ne myght nought schewe itt in wordes'.

Alexandra Barratt
Oxford and Kirikiriroa

List of abbreviations

AISP	*Archivio Italiano per la Storia della Pietà*
BJRL	*Bulletin of the John Rylands Library*
BL	British Library
CCCM	Corpus Christianorum Continuatio Mediaeualis, Turnholt, 1971–.
CT	*Canterbury Tales.*
CUL	Cambridge University Library
DNB	*Dictionary of National Biography*
EETS os	Early English Text Society, Original Series, 1864–.
EETS es	Early English Text Society, Extra Series, 1867–.
EHR	*English Historical Review*
F.	French
IPMEP	*Index of Printed Middle English Prose*, ed. by R.E. Lewis, N.F. Blake and A.S.G. Edwards, New York and London, 1985.
IMEV	*The Index of Middle English Verse*, ed. by C. Brown and R.H. Robbins, New York, 1942.
IMEV Suppl.	*Supplement to the Index of Middle English Verse*, ed. by R.H. Robbins and J.L. Cutler, Lexington, 1965.
L.	Latin
ME	Middle English
MED	*The Middle English Dictionary*, Ann Arbor, 1956–.
MET	Middle English Texts, Heidelberg, 1975–.
MS	manuscript
OED	*The Oxford English Dictionary*, 1st edn, 12 vols, 1933.
OF	Old French
PL	*Patrologiae cursus completus: Series Latina*, ed. by J.-P. Migne, 212 vols, Paris, 1844–65.
PMLA	*Publications of the Modern Language Association of America*

STC   *A Short-Title Catalogue of Books Printed in England,*
                     Scotland and Ireland and of English Books Printed
                     Abroad 1475–1640, 2nd edn, London, 2 vols,
                     1976–86.

Chronology

1380	Catherine of Siena, *Il Dialogo*; Catherine d.
1384	[Wycliffe d.]
c. 1385–7	[Chaucer, *Troilus and Criseyde*]
c. 1387–1400	[*Canterbury Tales*] ✳
1390–3	[Gower, *Confessio Amantis*]
c. 1393	Julian of Norwich, Long Version of *A Revelation of Love*
c. 1394	Eleanor Malet (later Hull) b.
1400	[Geoffrey Chaucer d.] ✳
c. 1400	Christine de Pisan, *L'Epître d'Othéa la déese à Hector*
c. 1405	————, *Livre du Corps de Policie*
c. 1406	————, *Livre des Fais d'Armes et de Chevalerie*
c. 1410	Eleanor Malet m. John Hull
1413	Julian of Norwich 'yet on life'
1415	Syon Abbey founded
?c. 1420	Eleanor Hull tr. *Meditations on the Days of the Week*
1422	*A Revelation Showed to a Holy Woman*
c. 1429	Christine de Pisan d.
1436–38	*The Book of Margery Kempe* ✳
?1437	Elizabeth Woodville b.
c. 1439	Margery Kempe d. ✳
c. 1440	John Paston I m. Margaret Mautby
1443	Lady Margaret Beaufort b.
1449	[Lydgate d.]
?c. 1450	Eleanor Hull tr. *The Seven Psalms*; *The Faits and the Passion of Our Lord Jesu Christ*
1455	Lady Margaret Beaufort m. Edmund Tudor
1456	John Shirley d.
1460	Eleanor Hull d.
c. 1460	Juliana Berners, *The Book of Hunting*
1464	Elizabeth Woodville m. Edward IV
1465	Elizabeth of York b.
1469	Margery Paston m. Richard Calle
c. 1470	Anthony Woodville(?) tr. *The Body of Policy*
1477	John Paston III m. Margery Brews
1478	Caxton publ. *The Moral Proverbs of Christine*, tr. by Anthony Woodville
1483	Anthony Woodville ex.
1484	Margaret Paston d.
1486	'The Schoolmaster of St Albans' publ. *The Book of St Albans*; Elizabeth of York m. Henry VII
1489	Caxton tr. and publ. *The Book of Faits of Arms and of Chivalry*

Editorial procedure

All the texts have been prepared from the manuscripts cited in the Headnotes. Conjectural emendations, which are generally few, are recorded in the Textual Notes but are not indicated in the text. The editor's aim has been to reproduce the manuscript forms as accurately as possible but obsolete letter forms have been replaced with the modern equivalent. Thorn is transcribed as *th* and yogh as *y* or *gh* as appropriate (occasionally as final *z*). Initial *ff* is usually transcribed as *F* or *f*. Flourishes have been ignored and all abbreviations and contractions have been expanded without notice, as appropriate to the individual manuscript. Roman numerals have been translated into their equivalent ME verbal forms. *I/J*, *i/j*, *U/V* and *u/v* have been normalised according to modern practice. Word division, capitalisation, punctuation and paragraphing are editorial.

The principal aim of the glosses is to help the reader to understand the text. They indicate the most likely meaning of the word glossed in its context, but should not be regarded as substitutes for reference to *MED* or *OED*. Words are glossed on their first appearance in each passage; if they appear again in another selection from the same text or author they are glossed again, so that each passage is self-sufficient.

The selections have been chosen both for their intrinsic interest and for their representative nature. They offer a mix of longer and shorter passages, all of which have their own unity. On the rare occasions when lines are omitted within a passage, this is indicated by [. . . .] and, if necessary, a brief summary of the material omitted.

Biblical references are to the text of the Vulgate, and all English Biblical quotations are from the Douai Rheims translation.

Introduction

1 Women's writing in Middle English?

When Margery Kempe asked the Vicar of St Stephen's, Norwich, to spare her an hour or two to speak with him about the love of God, the saintly Richard of Caister expressed incredulity that a woman could occupy so long in speaking about the love of Our Lord (*Book of Margery Kempe*, p. 38). Some people may well harbour similar doubts about an anthology of Middle English women's texts. How can a selection of women's writing in Middle English fill a whole book, when only two names of medieval English women writers immediately come to mind – those of Julian of Norwich and Margery Kempe?

It is true that there is a lamentable dearth of Middle English women writers, though we do now know the names of more than two. Indeed, a statistical study has shown that between the introduction of printing in 1475 and 1640 women's writings made up 0.5 per cent of all publications and that even in the period 1640–1700, when women began to publish in significant numbers, their output constitutes a mere 1.2 per cent (Crawford 1985: 212, 266). A recent bibliography of pre–1900 women's personal writings found that less than 10 per cent of the texts came from the period before 1800 (Davis and Joyce 1989: x). It is therefore not surprising that initial interest in women's writing in English has centred on the nineteenth and twentieth centuries, though recently there has been a growing interest in the sixteenth and seventeenth centuries. The pre-Renaissance period, however, has been neglected, except for the virtual canonisation, both literary and religious, of Margery Kempe and Julian of Norwich.

In contrast, the aim of this anthology is to illustrate the full range of Middle English writing from the period 1300–1530 in whose production we know, or can reasonably assume, that women were involved in one way or another. Some of the texts, therefore, are original compositions in Middle English; some are translations (probably made by men) of texts composed by women in Latin or the European vernaculars; and others are translations of originally male texts made by fifteenth-century Englishwomen into Middle English. The complex issues raised by the inclusion of the latter group of texts, in particular the vital role that translators, both medieval and modern, play in the production and transmission of texts, are discussed later in this Introduction (see pp. 12–15).

Certainly a search for Middle English women's texts, sustained by a conviction that they did indeed exist, can itself be productive. A number of the texts represented here have not been edited at all before – the Trotula translations, one version of the *Revelations of Saint Elizabeth*, Eleanor Hull's translations, an anonymous nun's *The Faits and the Passion of Our Lord Jesu Christ*, and Eleanor Percy's hymn to the Virgin – while Lady Margaret Beaufort's translation of *A Golden Mirror* has not been reprinted since the early sixteenth century. Others, such as lyrics from the Rawlinson and Findern manuscripts, a second version of the *Revelations of Saint Elizabeth*, and *A Revelation Vision Showed to a Holy Woman*, though they have long been available in print, have never received much critical or scholarly attention. But it remains true that even after our best endeavours, only a tiny percentage of the surviving body of writings in Middle English is in any sense 'women's writing'. Why should this be so?

2 Women's education and culture in the Middle Ages

One apparent reason for the dearth of medieval women's writing is the restricted access that medieval women had to literacy. Not much is known about the education of medieval women in England; the standard work on English schools in the Middle Ages devotes a mere three pages to women's education (Orme 1973: 52–5) and most of the evidence is anecdotal, impressionistic, can be gleaned only incidentally and must be treated with caution. However, the outlines of the general situation are clear enough.

Until the thirteenth century, the education of noblewomen in Europe was not much inferior to that of noblemen, if only because in the earlier Middle Ages lay people in general did not often learn how to read and almost never how to write. From the thirteenth century onwards, the education of men, both lay and clerical, improved, especially with the rise of the universities and the growing practical importance in legal and business matters of literacy; but that of women did not (Shahar 1983: 158–9). In later medieval England, the possibilities for women were limited. They might be educated privately, or in one of the very few public elementary schools, or in convents (Power 1922: 260–84, 568–81; Orme 1973: 54–5).

Noblewomen could be educated at home or in another noble household, perhaps by the family chaplain, to whatever level their families deemed necessary (Orme 1984: 156–60). It is significant that the two most learned women represented in this anthology – Dame Eleanor Hull in the early fifteenth and the Lady Margaret Beaufort in the later fifteenth century – were only daughters and heiresses, so no doubt their superior education was related to their quasi-masculine roles. The elementary schools might have provided basic literacy but their impact was insignificant; and not much could be expected of convent education, as the nuns' own intellectual resources were meagre and they could not teach what they themselves did not know (Power 1922: 276–7).

Indeed, the learning and literacy of nuns in England actually deteriorated during the Middle Ages. Anglo-Saxon convents, which were populated exclusively by noblewomen, had a reputation for scholarship (Power 1922: 237). Some abbesses both received and sent letters in Latin; treatises were written for the nuns in both Latin and Old English; there is evidence of determined if somewhat unsuccessful efforts to improve the Latin language skills of the nuns of Nunnaminster in Winchester (see *A Pre-Conquest English Prayer Book*, p. xiv); and Muriel, a nun at Wilton, wrote Latin verse (Tatlock 1933: 317–21).

After the Conquest standards fell, though in the latter half of the twelfth century Clemence, a nun of the Benedictine abbey of Barking, translated a Latin life of St Catherine of Alexandria into Anglo-Norman verse, and another nun of Barking translated Aelred of Rievaulx's Latin life of St Edward the Confessor (Legge 1963: 60–66), while a certain Marie, who was either a nun or an Augustinian canoness, wrote a life of St Audrey based on a Latin source (Legge 1963: 369, Barratt 1987a: 478–9). Most notably, Marie de France who wrote some very popular *lais* in Anglo-Norman, may have been a Benedictine (see p. 40). This represents a collective achievement greater than that of the Continental French nuns, but there is nothing to match the Latin learning of Heloise in France in the twelfth century or of the Helfta nuns in Germany in the thirteenth (see pp. 49–60).

In the fourteenth and fifteenth centuries it was a commonplace that English nuns did not understand Latin, only French or English (see p. 15), but they wrote hardly anything in either language. Of the women represented in this anthology, a nun wrote *The Faits and the Passion of Our Lord Jesu Christ* and Juliana Berners – if indeed she put together *The Book of Hunting* – may have been a Benedictine nun, but all the writers about whom we have any definite information were laywomen or anchoresses (that is, led a solitary religious life enclosed in a cell attached to a church). It looks as if the convents of later medieval England were not conducive to literary activity.

We should not forget that 'education' and 'literacy' are complex concepts, and their connection with 'writing' and composition problematic. 'Education' covers everything from the most basic literacy in one's mother tongue to the knowledge of other languages and a high literary culture, while 'literacy' includes both reading and writing. Unlike today, in the Middle Ages the two skills did not necessarily go together. They do involve quite different mental and physical processes and it was quite common to be able to read but not to write. Writing required a specialised set of tools, a suitable working space, and access to expensive raw materials such as parchment. It was a complex manual skill best left to professionals and not necessarily appropriate for upper-class women who, like the Pastons or the Abbess of Denny, could always employ a clerk to do their writing for them (see below, p. 239).

But when the motivation was there, some medieval women did manage to acquire the level of linguistic and literate skills they felt necessary. So as an adult Catherine of Siena learned to read but not to write; Bridget of Sweden could not write but could read a little Latin; Gertrude of Helfta not only read Latin but could compose at length in that language; clearly Julian of Norwich could read and write English, though whether she could read Latin is disputed. The fifteenth-century translators Dame Eleanor Hull and Lady Margaret Beaufort were fully literate in both English and French. The former, a laywomen and a member of the gentry, who wrote her will 'in her own hand', knew some Latin as well.

In spite of their frequent lack of formal skills, medieval women – at least those who had adopted a religious life (nuns, canonesses and anchoresses) and members of the upper bourgeoisie, the gentry and the nobility – were not without education. Certainly they were part of a literate as well as an oral culture, even if not always fully literate themselves, and in many ways their position – living 'at least on the edges of a literate tradition' – was similar to that of members of so-called 'primitive' cultures today (see Finnegan 1977: 48). Their mentality was as literate as that of their male counterparts: they assumed that writing was valuable and could influence events; that it could function, in the delightful seventeenth-century phrase, as 'a restitution of decayed intelligence' (the title of a book by one Richard Verstegan, published in 1605: STC 21361); and that it was a substitute for human presence (see Ong 1967: 295–304; Webster 1990: 102).

Medieval women knew written texts were useful and so they used them, vicariously if need be. In *The Revelations of Saint Elizabeth* the Virgin uses St John the Evangelist to draw up a written contract between herself and the visionary; similarly Catherine of Siena, Bridget of Sweden and Margery Kempe used others (usually men) to write down their own compositions. Catherine dictated her letters and her treatise *Il Dialogo* (translated into English as *The Orchard of Syon*) to various men and women, both clerics and lay. Bridget of Sweden dictated her revelations in Old Swedish to her confessor, who wrote them down and translated them into Latin. Margery Kempe, whose social status was much lower, could neither read nor write; while she had practical problems in finding a suitable amanuensis (see *Book of Margery Kempe*, pp. 3–5, 6), they were not insuperable, given her own determination.

Women were certainly consumers of the products of others' literacy, or there would not be so many books, such as *Ancrene Wisse* and the associated texts of the Katherine group, specifically directed at women (see Millett and Wogan-Browne 1990). We also know that women particularly enjoyed recreational reading such as romances; a contemporary tells us that the *lais* of Marie de France were especially popular with court ladies, and later collections of Middle English romances such as the early fourteenth-century Auchinleck Manuscript (see below, p. 41) catered for bourgeois women as much as men. Chaucer in *Troilus and Criseyde* presents a memorable picture of Criseyde and her ladies – no men are present – listening to a maiden reading aloud 'the geste / Of the siege of Thebes' (2.81–4).

Why then did not more women write, or compose, themselves? Clearly, inadequate literacy was no bar to those who genuinely wanted to have their experiences recorded, as Margery Kempe demonstrates. There were other barriers to women authors, none the less formidable for being less tangible than the lack of a carrel (the medieval equivalent of a room of one's own), of pens and parchment, of peace and quiet. The real obstacles were as much psychological as practical: Margery Kempe instinctively shrank from the idea of having her experiences recorded when Bishop Repingdon first suggested it; Mechtild of Helfta, finding herself encoded in a text by a woman disciple, was genuinely distressed (see below, p. 50). For the written text both carried and created 'authority' and it was a tacit assumption that 'authority', and therefore authorship, were incompatible with femininity. It is probably this attitude – an attitude with which medieval women tacitly collaborated – that is responsible both for the lack of educational opportunities and for the relative paucity of women's texts.

3 Women, authority and authorship

The concept of authority (*auctoritas*), in its theological, political and literary senses, was thoroughly male. The supreme and highest *auctor* (the Latin word from which 'author' ultimately derives), the creator of the universe, the First Cause, was God Himself who in the Middle Ages was indisputably male. Medieval devotion to 'Jesus our mother' (see Bynum 1982) and Julian of Norwich's heroic effort to overturn more than a thousand years of tradition by redesigning the Holy Trinity on a Father–Mother rather than Father–Son model (see below, p. 109) made no real difference.

In medieval Latin *auctor* also means 'writer' (see Minnis 1984: 10). But without exception, all the written *auctores* of medieval culture were male. That ultimate repository of written *auctoritas*, the Bible, was regarded as divinely inspired, but it was never suggested that its human authors were anything other than male, in spite of the fact that three of its books (Esther, Ruth and Judith) bear women's names. The Vulgate (Latin) translation, which the Western Middle Ages regarded as virtually synonymous with the original text, was made by St Jerome, but the medieval world was not aware that he had been greatly helped by the noble Roman ladies Paula and Eustochium, who learned Hebrew and emigrated to Palestine for that very purpose and to whom he dedicated his translations of many of the individual books (see Hardesty 1982: 17–19). Jerome himself, a notorious anti-feminist, was one of the Fathers of the Church; there was no tradition of Mothers, although Bridget of Sweden was to see the Virgin Mary in that role (see below, p. 92). In philosophy Plato and Aristotle were the *auctores*; in theology (as well as the Church Fathers) Peter Lombard, the Master of the Sentences, or Peter Comestor, the Master of the Histories; and in poetry, Virgil, Homer and Ovid.

On the other hand, female figures, however exalted, were not represented in art or literature as engaging in literary composition. According to the Gospels, as *Ancrene Wisse* (following Bernard of Clairvaux) points out, the Blessed Virgin Mary only ever spoke on four occasions (*Ancrene Riwle*, pp. 33–4). She is often depicted in art as praying or even reading, but never as writing, though in the Renaissance Botticelli was to paint the Madonna writing out the Magnificat, helped by five youthful angels and her infant son. Holy Mother Church might issue pronouncements but did not write, and though she was female for the purposes of grammar, Scriptural exegesis, literary allegory and the visual arts, on earth she was mediated solely through men.

Women's relations with Holy Mother Church, as with their human mothers, have always been equivocal (on this controversial topic see, for instance, Armstrong 1986). The Church both nurtured and frustrated women's potential. Christianity in its primitive form gave women a freedom and status hitherto unparalleled in either Judaic or Hellenistic culture. It preached an incarnate Christ with no human father whose humanity, therefore, must have been wholly transmitted through his mother. It granted to that mother, the Virgin Mary, quasi-divine honours. Women were prominent in the Gospel narratives as special objects of Christ's loving attention and as his most faithful followers; indeed, a woman was the first witness to the resurrected Christ. In the primitive Church women continued to be the equals of men and St Paul, although he would not allow a woman to teach and preached the wife's subjection to her husband, made the revolutionary declaration that in Christ there was neither Jew nor Greek, slave nor free, male nor female. Women were not exempt from persecution or martyrdom on the grounds of their sex; the martyr St Felicitas, for instance, met her fate two days after giving birth (see Petroff 1986: 75). Moreover the early Fathers had little time for marriage and the family, with their potential to subordinate and oppress women, but promoted an ascetic ideal which offered women the same challenge of heroic sanctity as men.

But simultaneously the Church stressed that in Christ a male God had become not only human but also specifically male rather than female, and proceeded to use this as the principal argument against admitting women to the priest-hood. Only priests, however, were granted the authority or spiritual power to celebrate Mass and to absolve sins, and thus to administer and control the two sacraments of the Church without which salvation was deemed impossible. So yet again, to be a woman was necessarily identified with powerlessness and a lack of authority.

4 Three strategies for dealing with male authority

Since medieval women were socialised to see themselves as subordinate to all forms of male authority, they were inevitably resistant to the idea of authoring texts. Even to attempt to write might be seen as a bid to arrogate to themselves an 'authoritative' didactic role; as Julian of Norwich puts it, in the Short Version of *A Revelation of Love*:

> Botte God forbede that ye schulde saye or take it so that I am a techere, for I meene nought so, no, I mente nevere so. For I am a woman: leued [uneducated], febille and freyll. (BL Add. MS 37790, f. 101ʳ)

How then could women write, become 'authors', without offending their societal norms and appearing to infringe male prerogatives? In practice, medieval women evolved a range of strategies. They could substitute an alternative for earthly authority, derived from their own religious experience; they could give up the unequal struggle altogether and lapse into silence; or they could appropriate authority as translators, adaptors and compilers.

4.1 The authority of experience

First, the Church could not deny women direct access to the divine, through mystical experience unmediated by a human priesthood. Visionary women could bypass the human, male, authority of the Church on earth, and claim to be the instruments of a higher, divine authority. In this way, relying like their secular and fictional sister the Wife of Bath on 'experience' rather than 'auctorite' (*CT* III(D): 1–2), they could validate their activity as writers. The fact that so much medieval women's writing (two-thirds of this anthology) is hagio-autobiographical – that is, consists of first-person or pseudo third-person accounts of spiritual experience – shows that they enthusiastically seized the opportunity this strategy offered. (Similar theories have been propounded by Petroff 1986: 32–35, and, with specific application to Hildegard of Bingen, by Flanagan 1989: 55–6, 158–78.)

Each visionary woman writer had to negotiate her own accommodation with the institutional Church, a delicate process in which some were more successful than others. Marguerite Porete was burnt at the stake; Margery Kempe was ostracised by society; the nuns of Helfta, Elizabeth of Hungary and Julian of Norwich lived obscure but unmolested lives; while Catherine of Siena and Bridget of Sweden achieved vast influence and canonisation.

In the hagio-autobiographical texts themselves we find personal experience again and again endowed with the status of authority. Sometimes this comes close to a declared preference for personal revelation that elevates its authority above that of the Church on earth. For instance, when Elizabeth is in a state of spiritual dryness and desolation and about to seek the advice of a friar, the Blessed Virgin appears and claims for herself a superior authority, declaring, in the version published by Wynkyn de Worde:

> ther is noo brother in the worlde that may better enforme the of thy
> spouse than I may . . . . If thou wylt be my doughter, dyscyple and
> servant, I wolde be thy moder, lady and maystresse. (f. 91[va–b]: cf. p. 73)

Julian, too, finds a life built simply on the acceptance of the authority of the Church unsatisfying and at the beginning of the Short Version of *A Revelation of Love* she explains her desire to share in Christ's sufferings for herself through mystical experience (see p. 111).

Bridget of Sweden, less subtle, comes at times very close to saying that the Church is wrong and she is right. One English version of her famous vision of Christ's birth is headed, 'Off the very trewe maner off the byrth and natyvyte off Our Lord Jhesu Cryste'. Where does this leave the Gospel account? Not only does Bridget know, by virtue of her visionary experience, what the Virgin did with the infant Jesus's foreskin after the Circumcision (see below, p. 90), she is also well informed – rather more so than the evangelists – about Christ's post-Resurrection appearances. The Virgin claims that:

> though yt be so that for my grete mekenes this ys not written in the holy evangelys or gospel, yet thys is the very trewth, that when he was rysen from deth, fyrst he aperyd unto me before he aperyd to any other. (Oxford Bodley MS Rawlinson C. 41, f. 39^v)

A controversial figure, Bridget was attacked for this very reliance on her personal revelations. The anonymous English nun who wrote, at the request of another nun, *The Faits and the Passion of Our Lord Jesu Christ* is more conciliatory about her use of material gleaned from such 'authoritative' private revelations:

> Alle the evangelistes witnessin weel in here writing that ther was more of oure Lord Crist Jhesu than thei wretin of him and therfore it may leeffuli [lawfully] been seide or wretin, thing that hath be schewid be Godes goodnesse, although it be not in the Gospel. (p. 215)

Almost all these women visionaries stress that they wrote down their experiences, or had them written down, with great reluctance and only under obedience to some superior authority. Most texts give at least one explanation, if not apology, for the circumstances that led to their composition. The story of how Margery Kempe's book came to be written is well known, but her practical difficulties have obscured the psychological block she had to overcome before she even set about finding an amanuensis. Julian says with characteristic simplicity:

> Botte sothelye, charyte styres me to telle yowe it . . . . Botte for I am a woman, schulde I therfore leve [leave off] that I schulde nought telle yowe the goodenes of God, syne that I sawe in that same tyme that [it] is his wille that it be knawen? (MS Add. 37790, f. 101^r)

In this way the visionary's act of writing represents itself not as an arrogant assumption of power but as an act of submission in keeping with the female ideal of obedience.

Another facet of that ideal is the exaltation of self-effacement. Again, the literary mystic who presents herself as merely a passive vehicle for her experiences and for the edifying message of God's love conforms to this. Losing oneself in God should lead to a thinning out, even a disappearance, of the writer's personality and Julian explicitly says this is her aim:

> this that I saye, I hafe it of the schewynge of hym tha[t] es soverayne techare . . . . Than schalle ye sone forgette me that am a wrecche and dos[t]e, so that I lette [hinder] yowe nought, and behalde Jesu, that ys techare of alle (MS Add. 37790, f. 101ʳ)

The writer, in other words, hopes to write herself out of her text. Marguerite Porete, the only medieval woman known to have been put to death for writing a book, carries this ideal of self-effacement to its logical conclusion, that of self-annihilation, becoming 'pure nought' (see p. 62). While all mystics strive for union with the divine which must involve a giving-up of self, medieval women were perhaps predisposed by their socialisation to embark on a form of mysticism with that as its goal. But those same cultural factors (as well as the approval granted orthodox mystics both by the masses, who often looked on them as wonder-workers, and by the Church, which sometimes elevated them to sainthood) contribute to the dearth of women secular writers, for to encourage the annihilation of self must positively discourage self-expression if it cannot claim an edifying purpose.

4.2 Submission and silence

It has been argued that medieval women's lack of education did not cause the dearth of medieval women's writing but that both phenomena are symptoms of an underlying attitude that disempowered women. Indeed, a medieval literary education, because of some prevailing attitudes that were hostile to women, could actually perpetuate their subordination, as Christine de Pisan discovered. The opening of her *Book of the City of Ladies* neatly captures the dilemma of the literate, educated medieval woman who might want to write as well as read, and demonstrates how education was not in itself enough to empower women but could be a positive disadvantage. Christine presents herself as chancing upon a minor classic of anti-feminist literature, the *Liber Lamentationum* of Matheolus. (On this literature, a genre that attempted to dissuade men from marriage by stressing the supposed vices of women, see Miller 1977: 397–402.) Even though she despises it as untruthful, immoral and badly written, it touches a raw nerve:

the sight of this book, even though it was of no authority, made me wonder how it happened that so many different men . . . all concur in one conclusion: that the behaviour of women is inclined to and full of every vice. (*Book of the City of Ladies*, pp. 3–4)

The universal consensus of authority has to command the respect of someone who is herself striving to be part of a literary and learned tradition, for Christine cannot react like the Roman goddess and queen of the underworld, Proserpine, in her argument with her husband Pluto in Chaucer's *Merchant's Tale*, with her indignant cry, 'What rekketh me [what do I care] of youre auctoritees?' (*CT* IV(E): 2276), but must try to reconcile this authority with her own conflicting experience. Can she trust that personal experience? If she does, what dangerous consequences might follow?

I could not see or realize how their claims could be true when compared to the natural behaviour and character of women. Yet I still argued vehemently against women, saying that it would be impossible [that] . . . so many famous men – such solemn scholars . . . could have spoken so falsely on so many occasions . . . . And so I relied more on the judgment of others than on what I myself felt and knew. (p. 4)

But this heroic act of submission does not bring peace: on the contrary Christine, who decides that 'God formed a vile creature when he made woman', is filled with a debilitating self-hatred. Fortunately she is rescued by the timely arrival of Lady Reason. She encourages Christine to construct a rival, 'authoritative' tradition of virtuous, learned, noble and heroic women, to offset the bedraggled procession of Eve, Delilah, Bathsheba and Solomon's concubines, who so often parade through anti-feminist texts as dreadful examples of wicked women who had ruined virtuous men.

Christine de Pisan is a moral and didactic writer, but her strategy here for circumventing male authority is analogous to that of many women mystics: she sets up an alternative authority which derives from her own experience. We cannot know how many potential women writers were not rescued by Lady Reason but paralysed at the stage of submission to authority – an authority which said women were vile, their opinions of no value and the idea of their writing quite unthinkable.

The only obvious example of the strategy of submission is that of Heloise (*c.* 1100–63), mistress and later wife of the medieval theologian and philosopher Abelard, but inevitably this reaction is invisible except in rare and notorious cases; it must have been more common than we realise. Perhaps because Heloise was brought up by her uncle (a cleric) in a cathedral close, she was thoroughly socialised into anti-feminist attitudes, which were primarily clerical. Her arguments – at least as recorded by Abelard in his *Historia Calamitatum* – against his suggestion that they should marry as she was carrying their child are depressingly perverse, for they regurgitate, with passionate conviction, all the commonplaces of anti-feminism used to discourage clerics from marriage (*Letters*, pp. 70–4). Her exaltation of, and submission to, male authority survived Abelard's castration and her own unwilling profession as a nun, so that when she herself became an abbess it was to her husband that she turned for advice on a suitable Rule for her nuns (*Letters*, pp. 159–79). Her correspondence betrays a low opinion of women in general, in spite of her own exceptional educational achievements, obvious competence and strength of character.

Although Heloise was undoubtedly the most highly educated woman of the time in the whole of Europe, she left no writings except her letters to Abelard. Even of these some scholars have industriously done their best to deprive her, arguing that they were later forgeries or that Abelard wrote them for her (Dronke 1976: 1–14; 1984: 140–3). But European tradition, which until recently presented Christine de Pisan as a prolix bore while it idealised Heloise as the heroine of an archetypal love story, has failed to see that her real tragedy was not that her Latin teacher seduced her, with all the ensuing disasters, but that she was learning Latin at all. Such an education was likely to demoralise unless one could transcend it as a mystic (as Gertrude of Helfta was to do) or had the compelling economic motives of Christine de Pisan. Christine lived in the fifteenth century, when literary activity was beginning to be a way to make money; her responsibility for a mother, three children and other assorted dependants must have helped her overcome any reluctance to become a writer. She was merely the first of many women to discover that writing was one of the few respectable ways in which an educated woman could support a family.

4.3 Appropriation and assimilation

A third strategy is that of appropriation: women writers can attach themselves to male authority as translators or in some other ancillary literary role. In one sense all medieval writers – as 'moderns' rather than 'ancients' – dared set their claims no higher than that of scribe, compiler or commentator (Minnis 1984: 94, 101), for only the classical writers of the ancient world, the divine and human authors of the Bible and the Fathers of the Church had any real claim to true authority and therefore authorship. But it is significant that, of the five women whose names we know who wrote in Middle English – Julian of Norwich, Margery Kempe, Juliana

Berners, Eleanor Hull and Margaret Beaufort – three were translators. Chaucer, who made his Second Nun a translator (*CT* VIII(G): 22–8), sensed that this was an appropriate female role, for translation could function as a more intellectual version of embroidery (Parker 1984: 74; cf. Lamb 1985: 124), similarly designed to keep female minds and fingers occupied and out of mischief by eschewing 'ydelnesse, / That cause is of so greet confusioun'.

The sixteenth-century writer John Florio also detected that there was something intrinsically feminine about translation. In his 1603 translation of Montaigne's *Essays*, he refers to his previous publication, *The World of Words* (a dictionary), as 'my last Birth, which I held masculine (as are all mens conceipts that are their owne though but by their collecting)'. He contrasts his dictionary with 'this defective edition (since all translations are reputed femalls), delivered at second hand' (Lamb 1985: 115–16).

Medieval translators, if they draw any attention at all to their contribution to text production, usually claim to be merely transmitters of authority, and their self-effacing role in relation to their original is remarkably similar to that of the mystics in relation to God, *their* Great Original. Translators claim no authority in their own right but would no doubt agree that, as Florio says, their translations are 'delivered at second hand'. In the Middle Ages, at least ostensibly, the translator functions simply as a 'site of interchange' – the original is fed in, out comes the translation. Medieval theories of translation were not so crude but popular, unexamined assumptions were quite as simplistic.

Paradoxically, translators may profess extreme subservience to, and reverence for, the original while in fact knowing full well that they are in control. It is the translator who often takes the initiative in choosing to translate one text rather than another – for instance, it is unlikely that Juliana Berners made her translation of *The Book of Hunting* under compulsion – even though some may claim merely to be acting in obedience to a patron or a religious superior. And having chosen a text, the translator can influence its transmission by selecting one part rather than another to augment or omit, and can also influence its reception by the way in which it is rendered into English.

Illustrations of these points do not come from the medieval women translators, as both Lady Margaret Beaufort and Eleanor Hull are too self-effacing to emerge from behind their work. But the male translator of a collection of women saints' lives, found in Bodley MS Douce 114, expresses particularly well the complexity, in practice, of translation. In his initial 'Apology of the Compiler' he admits to concentrating on the overall sense of his text rather than the meaning of every word, while simultaneously he explains that he left out anything *he* judged unnecessary or unhelpfully obscure:

> the wryter [i.e. translator], that is but symple letterd [uneducated], neither can ne purposis to folowe the wordes, but unnethis and with harde [barely and with difficulty] the sens [sense, gist], neither puttynge to [adding] nor doynge awaye any clauses that schulde chaunge the substaunce of the story; but otherwhile levyng [sometimes omitting] legeauns [the citing of authorities in support of a doctrine or opinion] and auctorites of Holy Writt that wold be ful dymme [obscure] to undirstonde, if they were turnyd into Englissh withoute more declarynge of glose [explanation]. (Oxford Bodley MS Douce 114, f. 1)

On these grounds, he tells us, he chose not to translate the 'proheme' or prologue at all!

Another confused translator was the Carthusian monk who rendered Marguerite Porete's *The Mirror of Simple Souls* into English. He little knew that his original was composed by a heretic, and a woman into the bargain, but he did sense that there was something amiss and complained that his original was 'yvel writen' or corrupt. Nevertheless he was determined to press on regardless, relying on the correction of the learned and devout.

> I wil folwe the sentence [sense] acordynge to the matiere [subject matter], as nigh [closely] as God wol yive me grace, obeyeng me ever to the correccioun of Holi Chirche, preyng goostli lyvers and clerkis that thei wol fouchesauf to correcte and amend there that I do amys. (Oxford MS Bodley 505, f. 95)

His translation boasts an agitated sub-text, a series of notes framed by his own initials 'M.N.', which intervene from time to time to explicate, explain away or even criticise some of the more theologically dubious passages. This nervous and apologetic attitude is not unlike that ironically adopted by Chaucer's Narrator in *Troilus and Criseyde* towards his (purely fictitious) original, 'Lollius'. (On the critical literature surrounding the vexed question of the identity of Lollius, see *Riverside Chaucer*, p. 1022.)

Medieval translators, then, are not mindless hacks; they tinker with their originals and even occasionally intrude their own opinions (see, e.g., below p. 59). Margaret Beaufort and Eleanor Hull were, given their status, less explicit about their role, but they are likely to have been equally sensitive to the practical problems of their work. To this degree, translations by women were creative acts and would have been perceived, perhaps grudgingly, as such by their more discerning readers. By the same token, men who translated texts originally by women, whether or not they realised the fact of female authorship, may adapt the original either consciously or unconsciously. Where it is possible to discern this process at work (for instance in *The Mirror of Simple Souls* and *The Book of Ghostly Grace*), it has been pointed out in the Notes.

Translations are also of practical utility, as one Middle English Trotula text stresses (see below, p. 30), and it is women in particular, educationally underprivileged as they are, who need them. Indeed, it is so often said that a work has been translated from Latin for the benefit of women, who commonly read English but not Latin (for instance in *The English Register of Godstow Abbey*, p. 25, and *The Myroure of Oure Ladye*, p. 2), that the statement comes to have the air of a topos or literary commonplace.

In several ways, therefore, translation offered women an involvement in literary culture, as both producer and consumer, that did not directly challenge male control of that culture. It provided a camouflage for involvement in text production and an opportunity for some degree of creativity. Moreover, the fact of translation, and the skills demonstrated, illustrate the level of literacy and education some women could deploy, while the freedom to choose texts to be translated, and the choice of texts themselves, are of significance in furthering our understanding of both the translators and their audience.

Another way unobtrusively to appropriate male authority is to be a compiler. This may have been the role of the mysterious Dame Juliana Berners (possibly Prioress of Sopwell, a Benedictine convent where Dame Eleanor Hull spent a great deal of time) in *The Book of St Albans*, though that text combines elements of translation as well as compilation. Christine de Pisan, too, sometimes adopts the role of compiler, though her contributions are in fact more active than she concedes. In her Prologue to the treatise translated into English as *The Book of Fayttes of Armes and of Chiualrye*, she has to confront the obvious problem of her 'hardynes' in writing on such a subject, given the 'lytelhed' of her person. She presents herself merely as a compiler, rewriting the material she has collected in a deliberately simple style suited to the mentality of military men. This is something of a fiction. The editor of the Middle English translation, who has investigated her use of source material, comments:

> Christine deserves credit not only for the skill with which she marshals such a mass of most unfeminine material, but also for the numerous original passages which she inserts. (*Book of Fayttes of Armes*, p. xi)

Christine wrote far more, and in a greater variety of genres, than any other medieval woman. Cliché though it is, she really is the first professional woman writer. A study of her work as a whole would show a chameleon-like ability to switch from one role to another in her negotiations with male authority. Here she is a translator; elsewhere, a compiler; in *The Book of the City of Ladies* she combines an apparent submission to authority with its reinterpretation in the light of experience and its radical reconstruction. She was not known in all these roles in late medieval England, but it is appropriate that hers is the first woman's text to be printed in England, by Caxton in 1478 (Anthony Woodville's translation *The Moral Proverbs of Christine*). This text also contains the first appearance recorded by *OED* of our English word 'authoress' in the sense 'a female literary composer', which the translator applies to Christine.

> Of these sayynges Cristyne was aucteuresse
> Whiche in makyng hadde suche Intelligence
> That therof she was mireur & maistresse;
> Hire werkes testify th'experience.

> *(Moral Proverbes, f. 4ᵛ)*

Hoccleve, no doubt in jest, had applied a somewhat similar term in 1422 to Chaucer's Wife of Bath in his 'Dialog'.

> The wyf of Bathe, take I for auctrice. *(Works, p. 135)*

(See *OED*, s.v. authoress, and *MED*, s.v. auctrice.) Though both women had to grapple with the anti-feminist tradition, the Wife of Bath (a rhetorical construct of a male author) could do no more than tear three pages out of the offensively authoritative *Book of Wicked Wives* and then make her husband burn it. Christine took a leaf out of the tradition of male authority in another sense and wrote her own books. If only more women had emulated her, this anthology would be even larger.

5 Anonymous texts and poetry

Or were there more women writers than we know? A great deal of Middle English writing is anonymous and it is usually assumed that, just as almost all medieval writers whose names we know were men, so almost all anonymous writing must also have been written by men. Perhaps we should be more cautious in our assumptions. Much of the devotional prose of the fifteenth century is translated specifically for women from French or Latin. Sometimes translators make it clear that they are male; but when they do not we should bear in mind the possibility, based on the activities of Dame Eleanor

Hull and Lady Margaret Beaufort, that some of the translations (at least those from the French) were made by women. We know about the Lady Margaret's translations because as the mother of King Henry VII she was a great lady and a patroness of learning and literature who had a faithful and articulate spiritual adviser, John Fisher, eager to tell the world about her accomplishments. As for Dame Eleanor, it is sheer chance that Richard Fox, who compiled the manuscript in which her translations are preserved, happened to mention, 'Alyanore Hulle drowe out of Frensche alle this before-wreten in this lytylle booke' (Barratt 1989: 87). Other translators were perhaps not so lucky.

Anonymous poetry includes some of the highest achievements of Middle English literature, such as 'The Owl and the Nightingale', 'Sir Gawain and the Green Knight' and 'Pearl'. It is not impossible that some poems were written by women, in particular those whose persona is presented as female, and quite likely that if women did write poetry they would do so anonymously. The usefulness of the distinction between the poet and the poet's persona is perhaps put under strain when poems such as 'The Assembly of Ladies' or 'The Flower and the Leaf', with female narrators who are presented quite without irony, are held to be the work of men, with only a cursory consideration of the possibility of female authorship (see further below, p. 262, and Barratt 1987b).

The problem of anonymity does raise the question, why is there apparently no writing by later medieval Englishwomen that we today would call creative or imaginative? This anthology contains accounts of personal religious experience; letters (written with practical ends in view, not as vehicles for self-expression); and utilitarian writings on gynaecology and hunting (though nothing on cooking or household management, perhaps because they were male preserves in most large houses). But there is no imaginative fiction except for *Lai le Freine*, translated from Marie de France's poem of the same name. Any attempt to explain this absence must be speculative, but here are a few suggestions.

First, there was no tradition of women poets. There was a tradition of women's writing about religious experience and also a tradition of Latin texts on gynaecological subjects attributed (however dubiously) to a woman, Trotula. Indeed, the mysterious Trotula, one of the few women who approaches the status of *auctor*, may have provided some validation for women's attempting other types of utilitarian writing. There may also have been a tradition of women translators, given the Anglo-Norman precedents of Clemence of Barking and Marie (see above, p. 3).

In contrast there were virtually no women poets whose writings were known. Sappho of Lesbos, to whom Christine de Pisan refers in *The Body of Policy* (see below, p. 153) – ironically confusing her with the male writer Sophron – was just a name to the Middle Ages, the subject of one of Ovid's *Heroides*. The Sibill, another authoritative female figure used by Christine, was credited with some cryptic verse in Greek that had been translated into Latin (see Kirshner and Wemple 1985: 7–25), but she was more of a prophet than a poet and consequently part of the female visionary tradition. The verses were forgeries anyway.

Moreover, in the Middle Ages poetry, more so than prose, was a learned genre. It was governed by rhetoric, and rhetoric was one of the Seven Liberal Arts studied through the medium of Latin in the schools and the exclusively male universities. Poetry was seen as the product of education as much as of inspiration, for it was made mainly out of other poems, not out of personal experience. As Chaucer puts it in *The Parliament of Fowls*:

> For out of olde feldes, as men seyth,
> Cometh al this newe corn from yer to yere,
> And out of olde bokes, in good feyth,
> Cometh al this newe science . . . .

> (*PF* 22–5)

Thus it was of all literary genres the least hospitable to women.

Paradoxically, the 'subject' *par excellence* of most secular poetry was women. But women no more wrote poetry than lions painted their own portraits. 'Who painted the lion?' as the Wife of Bath trenchantly asked (*CT* III(D): 692); the answer, of course, is 'Not the lion but the lionhunter'. To use a distinction favoured by some French literary theorists, women were the *sujets de l'énoncé*, not the *sujets de l'énonciation* (Belsey 1980: 30–1); their literary role was passive rather than active. But it is hard to believe that medieval Englishwomen wrote no poetry. In the later fifteenth and early sixteenth centuries there is clear evidence that they did, for there are three poems attributed in the manuscripts to specific women – a Hymn to the Virgin attributed to 'an holy anchoress of Mansfield', another hymn (a translation from the Latin) attributed to Eleanor Percy, Duchess of Buckingham, and a Hymn to Venus attributed to 'Queen Elizabeth' (either the wife of Edward IV or her daughter, wife of Henry VII).

In the earlier period the picture is harder to interpret. There are certainly some anonymous fragments with female personae, such as

> Weilawei [alas] that ich ne span [did not spin]
> Tho [when] ich into wude [the wood] ran!

> (Tübingen, Prüssische Staatsbibliothek MS
> Lat. theol. fol. 249, f. 132ᵛ)

and

> He may cume to mi lef [love] bute [only] by the watere:
> Wanne me lust [I desire] slepen, thanne motie [must I] wakie.
> Wnder is that Hi [I] livie!

> > (Worcester Cathedral MS F. 64, f. 8)

and

> Atte ston-castinges my lemman [leman] I ches [chose]
> And atte wrastlinges sone I hym les [lost].
> Allas that he so sone fel!
> Wy nadde [had not] he stonde better, vile gorel [pig]?

> > (CUL MS Ii. 3. 8, f. 87)

As well as an apparently unique celebration of happy love,

> Janekyn of Londone,
> Is [his] love is al myn!

> > (Oxford Merton College MS 248)

there are a few *chansons de mal mariée*, songs of unhappily married
wives, such as

> Alas, hou shold Y syng?
> Yloren [lost] is my playinge.
> How shold Y with that olde man
> To leven [live] and let my leman [abandon my lover]
> Swettist of al thinge?

> > (Red Book of Ossory, f. 71ᵛ)

and

> I am Rose, wo is me,
> Sutere [cobbler], that I snete the [wipe your nose].
> That I wacs [grew], weylawey [alas]!
> Cherles [a churl's] hand me thristet ay [constantly torments me].

> > (CUL MS Hh VI. 11, f. 67)

But these snatches of verse, which are all preserved in passing,
never recorded for their own sake, may well not be the authentic
cries of women. In fact, 'I am Rose' translates a Latin couplet,
presumably written by a cleric, that is written above it in the

manuscript (see Barratt 1990). Such poems probably form part of an anti-feminist tradition of *frauenklagen*, or women's laments. These poems, which purport to be the laments of seduced, betrayed and abandoned young women, are found in all the European languages. While they may call down imprecations on the heads of heartless seducers, they often implicitly invite scorn and condemnation as much as pity for the women's misfortunes and are therefore unlikely to have been written by women themselves, who would hardly wish to advertise their humiliation (see Utley 1944; Plummer 1981).

However women from all levels of society must have composed oral poetry – songs to sing while they worked in the fields, washed their clothes in the river, wove at the loom, rocked the cradle, or danced together in their rare leisure time – as they still do today in many different cultures (see Finnegan 1977: 92, 215). A few such poems have perhaps survived, such as

> Ic chule bere to wasscen [I shall carry to wash] doun i' the toun.
> That was blac and that was broun [what was black and brown].

> (Cambridge Trinity College MS 323, f.27ᵛ)

and the famous lyric, whose speaker is clearly female

> Ich am of Yrlaunde
> Ant [and] of the holy londe of Irlande.
> Gode sire, pray Ich ye
> For of Saynte Charite
> Come ant daunce wyt me in Yrlaunde.

> (Oxford Bodley MS Rawlinson D. 913, f. 1ᵛ)

Some other fragments may also have been preserved, embedded in the refrains or burdens of carols, for instance in the Corpus Christi Carol:

> Lully, lulley, lully, lulley,
> The fawcon [falcon] hath born my mak [mate] away
> He bare him up, he bare him down,
> He bare him into an orchard brown.

> (*Medieval English Lyrics*, p. 272)

or in the Coventry Carol, preserved in a mystery play:

> Lulla, lulla, thou little tiny child,
> By, by, lully, lullay, thou little tiny child,
> By, by, lully, lullay.
>
> (*Medieval English Lyrics*, p. 292)

There are twelve other surviving carols with 'lullaby' refrains, most of which represent the Virgin lulling the infant Christ (see *Early English Carols*, p. clxix). No genuine lullabies survive from the Middle Ages, perhaps because they were essentially ephemeral poetry that no one would think worth preserving, but Finnegan's comment is worth pondering: 'Mothers in countless societies sing lullabies to their babies – and these are not necessarily derivative or simplified' (1977: 199).

6 Women's writing: a continuing tradition?

Finally, is there any evidence for a distinctive women's tradition of writing in medieval England ? It is so fragmentary that no confident conclusions can be drawn. Of the five Continental women visionaries whose writings were available in Middle English translation, only Bridget of Sweden became at all popular. Her success is undoubtedly connected with the fame of Syon Abbey, the sole house in England of the religious order that she had founded. Marguerite Porete, whose treatise was in any case anonymous, had a highly restricted circulation among the élite group of Carthusian monks. Catherine of Siena's *The Orchard of Syon* was originally translated specifically for the Bridgettine nuns to read, though later (in 1519) it was printed by Wynkyn de Worde. Mechtild and Elizabeth probably were also read mainly by nuns and survive in one or two manuscripts only. Indeed, apart from the many versions of Bridget's revelations, the small number of surviving manuscripts of all these texts also points to their limited circulation.

Of the two native women visionaries, Julian of Norwich never refers to the writings of any other woman. Her only reference to a spiritual 'foremother' is to the early Christian martyr St Cecilia (see below, p. 112). There is no evidence that her own writings were widely known, and only one pre-Reformation manuscript, of the Short Text, survives, thanks to the indefatigable Carthusians. Margery Kempe is aware of a women's visionary tradition, in which she energetically tries to situate herself, but her own book survived in only one manuscript (itself undiscovered until this century) although Wynkyn de Worde published an unrepresentative selection from it in 1501. However, *The Faits and the Passion of Our Lord Jesu Christ, A Revelation Showed to a Holy Woman* and the translations of Dame Eleanor Hull and Lady Margaret Beaufort are evidence for a continuing tradition of some sort of women's devotional, as distinct from visionary or mystical, prose. It is to be hoped that future research will uncover other women's writing in this same tradition.

In complete contrast, the Trotula texts in their various forms had a wider circulation but a more ambiguous reputation, which allowed Chaucer, or rather the Wife of Bath's fourth husband Jankyn, to cite Trotula in the same line as Heloise as anti-feminist *auctores* and contributors to his *Book of Wicked Wives* (*CT* III(D): 677).

No pattern can be discerned in the case of the other women represented here. Marie de France received no credit for *Lai le Freine*, as her authorship is not mentioned in the Middle English translation, and although women were avid readers of romances there is no evidence at present that they wrote them (though perhaps the verdict on such anonymous writers as the author of 'Sir Gawain and the Green Knight' should remain open). The only woman writer who made a significant impact in England was Christine de Pisan. 'Dame Christine' is accorded great respect by her translators, but she was known mainly for her educational treatises rather than her proto-feminist polemical writings or her poems.

7 The arrangement and selection of texts

The texts in this anthology are arranged chronologically, so that it is possible to discern some sort of a 'history' of women's texts in Middle English. Texts by women translated into Middle English are placed according to the date of the composition of the original, even though many of them were not available in Middle English until much later. Translations made by women are placed according to the date of translation. Thus it is the point at which a woman writer, compiler or translator becomes involved which determines the dating and therefore the position in the anthology.

While the originals of the women's texts translated into Middle English date from the twelfth century (Trotula and Marie de France) to the early fifteenth century (Christine de Pisan), most of the translations themselves belong to the late fourteenth or fifteenth centuries. The only women's texts available in Middle English before 1400 were *Lai le Freine* (*c.* 1330) and Julian of Norwich's Short Version of *A Revelation of Love* (*c.* 1373). The scholarly commonplace, therefore, that Julian of Norwich was the first known woman writer in English turns out to be true, at least as far as prose is concerned.

The heyday of Middle English women writers is un-doubtedly the fifteenth century, for apart from Julian's Short Version, all the original writings or translations by women are post–1400. Perhaps coincidentally, none of the women's texts translated into English, apart from those by Christine de Pisan, is so late. To a certain extent the increased production by women after 1400 merely reflects the general literary situation, since comparatively little material survives from the early Middle English period (1100–1350) and the bulk of Middle English literature is no earlier than the late fourteenth century – the age of Chaucer, Langland and the 'Pearl'-poet. In terms of quantity if not quality, the fifteenth century far surpasses anything that had gone before. But the texts represented here do suggest that women in England began to write more prolifically and with greater confidence in the fifteenth century than ever before.

Far more work is needed to clarify and expand our – as yet meagre and hazy – picture of the development of women's writing in English. It may well emerge in due course that women's writing did not grow steadily and inexorably but rather proceeded in a series of quantum leaps, the first taking place some time after 1400, another after 1640, and another at the end of the eighteenth century. But as yet we can sketch merely a tentative outline, in the hope that even this will encourage others to join in the task of putting women writers of the past in their place.

The Texts

The fourteenth century and earlier

1 Middle English Trotula texts

There are several Middle English translations of texts associated with the name of Trotula, three of which are represented here. Although her existence has sometimes been questioned, Trota, or Trotula, did indeed exist. She was a woman physician who practised in Salerno, Italy, which was a great centre of medieval medicine, in the late eleventh or twelfth century. ('Trota' is a genuine name found in records of the period and is probably a diminutive of Gertrude, rather like 'Trudy'.) But the only genuine work that can be attributed to her is the very rare *Practica secundum Trotam* (*The Practice according to Trotula*), which was never translated out of Latin (see Green 1989: 442; Benton 1985: 30–53).

From the thirteenth century onwards, however, her name was associated with several Latin treatises that circulated throughout Europe and were translated into many vernacular languages, including English. Whatever the sex of the authors, compilers or translators, these texts were seen in the Middle Ages as written by a woman, and their very existence must have influenced common perceptions of the range, status and role of women's writing. Furthermore, they do clearly seem to be based on, and sympathetic towards, women's experience of sexuality and childbirth.

'Trotula' was often cited in other texts as an authority on obstetrics and gynaecology. Ironically, some anti-feminist writings also claimed her as an authority because she appeared to endorse the idea that women are physically inferior to men (see above, Introduction, p. 22 and below, p. 30 note to ll. 11–14).

The Knowing of Woman's Kind in Childing (the title given it in one manuscript) is a Middle English translation of a compilation that derives in part from the Latin twelfth- or thirteenth-century text the *Cum auctor*, sometimes known as the *Trotula major*. From the number of surviving manuscripts it seems to have circulated quite widely in the late fourteenth and fifteenth centuries. The other two texts were less popular. The *Liber Trotuli* ('Book of Trotulus') is strangely named as one would expect the feminine form *Trotulae* rather than the masculine *Trotuli*. In spite of its Latin title it is an English translation of the *Trotula minor*, the most notorious of Trotula's supposed works as it includes recipes for cosmetics – universally deplored by medieval moralists – and for lotions to create an illusion of virginity. *The Book of Rota* has no title but begins, 'This boke mad a woman named Rota'; some of its material, including the passage printed here, derives from the *Trotula major* and 'Rota' is presumably a corruption of 'Trota'. Its immediate original has yet to be identified but was possibly written in French (see p. 38 note to l. 184).

Comment: The first passage strikingly juxtaposes sexual and gender difference; that is, it considers the biological, sexual differences between men and women but within this frame exposes the social construction of gender through women's exclusion from knowledge, even in an area of intimate concern to them. The translator claims to write specifically for a female audience with their welfare in mind, and has in fact chosen a text generally friendly to women, originally composed from a female perspective. For instance, it treats women's genitals as objects in their own right, not merely defective versions of men's, as Aristotle had implied by his remark, 'we should look upon the female state as being as it were a deformity, though one which occurs in the ordinary course of nature' (*Generation of Animals*, 4, 6). It also displays a positive attitude towards menstruation, which it does not regard as unclean or as a punishment for original sin, as it so often was throughout the Middle Ages, but as necessary for childbearing, even though the causal relationship is misunderstood. Indeed, the implication is that female saints, including presumably the Virgin Mary whom many believed to have been conceived immaculately, i.e. exempt from original sin, were biologically like all other women in menstruating. The second passage, on obstacles to easy childbirth, includes much acute observation but has no practical solutions to offer other than herbal remedies. Unlike seventeenth-century and later obstetrical texts, it does not imply that difficult labours were a mark of refinement and high social status (see Eccles 1982: 86).

The passage from the *Liber Trotuli* shows how women's insecurities about sex made them vulnerable to pseudo-medical, possibly dangerous manipulation. The recipe for restoring virginity consists largely of various gums to constrict the vagina and therefore make intercourse more difficult. It cannot have been good for the female body, even if it worked. But the text is also notable for its non-judgemental, even encouraging attitude towards sexual activity. Generally, all the Trotula texts pay only the most cursory lip-service to Christianity, and none to the ideal of celibacy. Rather, they belong to a tradition springing from Greek scientific thought and regard sexual relations, whether in or out of marriage, as desirable, and indeed necessary for health. Unsympathetic towards virginity, they reserve their only condemnation for abortion and infanticide (however, as they regard regular menstruation as essential to women's health, their numerous recipes to provoke menstruation could possibly have been used to induce abortion).

The passage from *The Book of Rota* includes an explicit recognition that infertility, that disaster for a medieval woman, is not always her fault. It offers a would-be scientific, though no doubt ineffectual, method of diagnosis, which is in fact extremely ancient and goes back to the Greek physician Galen. The suggested cures have strong overtones of sympathetic magic, though one could act as a dietary supplement which might well have aided conception.

Manuscripts: The Knowing of Woman's Kind in Childing is extant in five fifteenth-century manuscripts, the textual relationships of which are confused. The extracts here are edited from Oxford Bodley MS Douce 37. The *Liber Trotuli* is found only in BL MS Add. 34111, and the *Book of Rota* in CUL MS Ii. vi. 33, and Glasgow University Library, MS Hunter 403. None of these texts has been previously edited.

Further Reading (for full details see Bibliography): For the history of the Latin Trotula texts and their vernacular translations and derivatives, see Green 1989; on medieval theories of embryology see Hewson 1975 and Needham 1959. *Medieval Women's Guide to Health* (ed. Rowland), though an edition of a non-Trotula text, contains a useful introduction and a comprehensive bibliography on medieval gynaecology and obstetrics and associated texts.

From *The Knowing of Woman's Kind in Childing*

a) *The Differences between Men and Women* (Oxford MS Douce 37, ff. 1–5ᵛ)

Oure lorde God, whan he had storid the worlde of all creaturs, he made manne and woman a resonabull creature, and badde hem wexe and multiply, and ordende that of them two schulde cume the thurde and that of the man, that is made of hote and drye mature, schulde come the sede and 5
that the woman, that ys made of cold matyre and moyste, schulde receyve the sede, so that by the tempure of hote and colde, moyste and dry, the chylde schulde be engendyrde, ryht as we seen treys, cornys and herbys mou not growe withoute resonabyll tempure of the foure. 10

---

1. storid: stocked.   *of*: with.
2. resonabull: rational.
3. wexe: wax, grow.   *ordende*: provided, decreed.
5. mature: matter, substance.   *sede*: seed, semen.
7. tempure: balance, appropriate mixture.
8. engendyrde: conceived.   *ryht*: just.
9. treys: trees.   *cornys*: corn, cereals.   *mou*: may.
10. the foure: i.e. the elements of the hot, cold, moist and dry; in ancient scientific tradition going back to the Greeks, the four elements that constituted all matter were reflected in the human body by the four 'humours', or bodily fluids, of blood, choler, melancholy (black choler) and phlegm, the correct balance of which maintained good health.

And forasmoche as whomen ben more febull and colde be
nature than men been and have grete travell in chyldynge,
ther fall oftyn to hem mo diverse sykenes than to men, and
namly to the membrys that ben longynge to gendrynge.
Wherfore, in the worschyp of Oure Lady and of all sayntys, I   15
thynke to do myn ententyffe bysynes forto drau oute of Latyn
into Englysch dyverse causis of here maladyes, the synes that
they schall knou hem by, and the curys helpynge to hem,
afture the tretys of dyverse mastrys that have translatyde hem
oute of Grek into Latyn. And because whomen of oure tonge   20
cunne bettyre rede and undyrstande thys langage than eny
other, and every whoman lettyrde may rede hit to other
unlettyrd and help hem and conceyle hem in here maledyes,
withowtyn scheuynge here dysese to man, I have thys drauyn
and wryttyn in Englysch.   25
And yf hit fall any man to rede hit, I pray hym and scharge

11–14. And . . . gendrynge: this assertion of women's physical inferiority
may be one reason why Chaucer included 'Trotula' among the texts that
made up Jankyn's *Book of Wicked Wives* in the *Wife of Bath's Tale* (CT
III(D): 677). In context, however, women's physical weakness is mentioned
to evoke compassion, not contempt.

11. febull . . . colde: weak and cold; women's 'cold and damp' constitution
was believed to be inhospitable to intellectual activity.

12. travell: toil, labour.   *chyldynge*: giving birth.

13. ther . . . hem: they often suffer from.   *mo*: more.

14. namly: particularly.   *membrys*: parts of the body.

          that . . . gendrynge: which appertain to conception.

16. do . . . bysynes: try diligently.

16–17. drau . . . Englysch: translate from Latin into English (this is the
translator's comment, not the original text).

17. here: their.   *synes*: signs, symptoms.

19. afture: according to.

          dyverse mastrys: various masters; the treatise draws partly on the Greek
medical writers Muscio and Soranus (early second century).

20–5. And . . . unlettryd: it was a medieval commonplace (which like most
commonplaces had a strong element of truth) that women were ignorant of
Latin and that if they could read at all they could read only their mother
tongue; consequently translations of all sorts are often explicitly said to have
been made for women, or at women's request (see Introduction, p. 15).

20. whomen . . . tonge: i.e. English-speaking women.

21. cunne: know how to.

22. whoman lettyrde: literate woman.

23. unlettyrd: illiterate.   *conceyle*: advise.

24. scheuynge: showing, disclosing.

26. yf . . . man: if any man chances.   *scharge*: charge, enjoin.

hym in Oure Lady behalve that he rede hit not in no dyspyte
ne sclaundure of no woman, ne for no cause but for the hele
and helpe of hem, dredynge that vengauns myht fall to hym as
hit hath do to other that have scheuyd here prevytees in   30
sclaundyr of hem; undyrstondynge in certeyne that they have
no other evylys that nou be alyve than thoo women hade that
nou be seyntys in hevyn.

Ryht as the makere of all thyngys ordende treys forto
burjone and floure and than aftyrwarde forto beere froyte, in   35
the same manere he hath ordeynde to all whomen an
esporgymente, the whyche ys calde the flourys, witoutyn
whyche may no chylde be engendryde ne conceyvyde. For
befoore that hit ys comyn ne afture hit ys gonne may no
woman conceyve. For ryht as polucyon be superhabundance   40
of humors fallyth to a man, so dothe the flourys to a woman,
as I shall tell yow hereaftyre.

But furste ye shall undyrstonde that ther be fyve dyversyteys
betuen man and woman. The fyrste dyversyte ys above here
fronte, for ther be summe men ballyd and so be not women   45
but seldyn. The seconde dyversyte ys on here berde, for ther

27. *in . . . behalve*: on Our Lady's behalf.
27–8. *no . . . woman*: any contempt or slander of any woman; the fictional
Jankyn's use of a Trotula text, among other anti-feminist writings, to
control the Wife of Bath (see above) suggests that the translator's anxiety
was not unfounded. It is significant, though, that the translator here
condemns such contempt as uncharitable, suggesting that the debate was
not always one-sided.
28–9. *ne . . . hem*: nor for any reason except their healing and help.
29. *vengauns*: vengeance, punishment.
30. *other . . . prevytees*: others who have revealed their (i.e. women's)
secrets.
31. *in certeyne*: certainly.
32. *evylys*: diseases, troubles.   *nou*: now.   *thoo*: those.
35. *burjone*: flourish.   *froyte*: fruit
37. *esporgymente*: purgation.   *flourys*: menstrual flow.
40. *polucyon*: pollution, i.e. nocturnal emissions.   *be*: by.
     superhabundance: excess.
41. *humors*: bodily fluids. *fallyth to*: occurs in.
43. *dyversyteys*: differences. These primary and secondary sexual characteristics are here listed objectively and even-handedly in terms of what men
have and women lack, and what women have and men lack. They carry no
moral overtones, unlike the earlier, more general comments about women's
feebler constitution (see ll. 11–14).
45. *fronte*: forehead.   *ballyd*: bald.
46. *but seldyn*: except seldom.

be men thyke heryde and ther be women smoth. The thurde
diversite ys on here brestys, for ther hath men but lytyll vertis
and ther hath women long pappis and hangynge. The ferthe
diversite ys bytuene here leggis, for ther have men a yerde   50
with other portynauns and ther hathe women an opynynge
wyche ys calde in Frenche a 'bele chose', or ellys a wykket of
the wombe. The fifte dyversite is that in the body of the
woman betuene here navyll and here wyket, for ther hath sche
a vessyll that no man hath, the wych ys callyde the maryce.   55
And because hit ys within the woman, that no man may se
what hit ys, reson wolde that I schulde telle yow fyrst how hit
ys schapyn and formyde and where-of hit is formyde.

The matrice ys a vesell made of thyn leddyr, rowgh within
and playn withowt and slydynge, thykly fretyde and enterlacyde   60
with small synouys all about, and hath a longe nekke and
strayte and large mowthe and a large entre and a plenere, evyn
schapp lyck an urinall, the bottum therof to the navyll of the
woman and the two sydys to the two sydys of the woman. And
hit ys partyde into seven vesellys, of the wyche thre lyth in the   65
party touarde the ryght syde, and thre in the party touarde the
lyfte syde, and the seventh evyn in the myddys betuene the
navyll and the wykket. The whyche matrice ys ordende to
receyve and holde the sede of man, and the chylde to

47. *heryde*: haired.
48. *vertis*: nipples.
49. *pappis*: breasts.
50. *yerde*: penis.
51. *portynauns*: appurtenances, adjuncts.
52. *bele chose*: 'beautiful thing'. Chaucer's Wife of Bath also uses this
phrase as a euphemism (*CT* III(D): 447).
52. *wykket*: wicket, small opening.
54. *navyll*: navel.
55. *vessyll*: organ.   *maryce*: uterus, womb.
59. *matrice*: womb.   *leddyr*: leather, skin.   *rowgh*: rough.
60. *playn*: smooth.   *slydynge*: slippery.
fretyde: interwoven, bound.   *enterlacyde*: interlaced.
61. *synouys*: sinews.
62. *strayte*: narrow.   *entre*: entrance.   *plenere*: open.
63. *urinall*: urinal, i.e. flask used for examining urine.   *to*: against.
64–76. *And ... maydyn schyld*: the theory of the seven-chambered womb,
and of the child's sex being determined by whether the foetus grew in the
right or the left side, was widespread.
65. *partyde*: divided.   *vesellys*: sections.
66. *party*: part.
67. *evyn*: exactly.
68. *ordende*: designed.

conceyve, forme and norsche unto convenabyll tyme of hys   70
byrth. And so hit ys rowgh withynne forto hold the sede, that
hit goyth not oute and peryche.

And yf hit so be that the sede fall into eny of the chambyrs
of the ryght syde, hit schall be a man chylde yf hit therin
abyde and be conceyvydde; and yf hit fall into eny of the   75
vesels of the lyfte syde, hit schall be a maydyn schyld. And yf
hit fall into the vesyll that ys in the myddes, hit fallyth owt and
perysch fro the place of creacyon. And yf hit abyde, hit fallith
to corrupcion of the superfluite of hote, cold, drynesse and
moysture, and other corrupcions that passun out by the wyket   80
withoutyn resistens to the sede rotyth hyt; and yf hit so befall
that hit be conceyvyde ther, hit schall have the tokyn bothe of
man and of woman, that ys, bothe yerde and wikket, as hit
hath be seynne heere-before in many cuntreys. And therfor a
woman that wolde conceyve a man childe, let heere dresse in   85
suche a manere wise here deduyt that here lefte hyppe ly
more herere than here ryght, for so schall sche make the
seede of here hosbonde to fall on here ryght syde where that
the man ys conceyvydde. And in the contrarii maner workyth
for the femall.   90

Nou have I told yow what is the matryce and how hit lyes in
a womans body. And nou I wol tell yow the anguysch that
dysesyth hit. Ye schall know fyrst that ther been thre anguysch
that principally dysesyn woman be here marys. The fyrst ys

70. norsche: nourish.   *unto*: until.   *convenabyll*: suitable.
72. peryche: perish.
76. maydyn schyld: maid-child, girl.
78. perysch: perishes.
78–9. fallith to corrupcion: i.e. rots.
79. of: from.   *superfluite*: excess.
80. passun: pass, flow.
81. withoutyn . . . sede: i.e. without trying to retain the embryo.
81–3. yf . . . wikket: hermaphroditism was rare but not unknown in the
Middle Ages. *OED* cites the first recorded appearance of *hermaphrodite*, in
Bk 3 Cap. 9 of the ME translation of Lanfranc's *Science of Cirurgie*, as
'*c. 1400*'.
82. tokyn: mark.
84. seynne: seen.   *cuntreys*: countries.
85–6. dresse . . . deduyt: conduct her love-making in such a way that.
87. more herere: higher.
89. workyth: act (imperative).
91. matryce: uterus.
92. anguysch: pain.
93. dysesyth: distresses, afflicts.
94. be . . . marys: with respect to their womb.

travelynge of chylde. The seconde ys suffocacyon, precipitacion,   95
or prefocacion of the marys. The thurde ys retencion, defaute,
or superfluite of flourys.

[A brief discussion of the two latter follows.]

The fyrst anguysch that I spake of ys travelynge of chylde and
that commyth of the sede of man, the wyche woman receyvyth
and in here body the chylde conceyvyth, and so muste sche   100
nedys have travill in delyverance, for the wyche I can no
medycyne writt. But sche that wol have no travyll in
chyldynge, let kepe here fro the receyvynge of sede of man
and, oon my parell, sche schall nevyre drede the travelynge of
chylde!   105

b) *Complications of Childbirth*
(ff. 11ᵛ–12ᵛ)

Now woll I tell yow what may lette a woman with chylde of
ryght delyverance. Sche may be dystroubelyd yf sche be
angury or prowde or schamfull; or ellys that hit be here fyrst
chylde; or ellys that sche be small and megyr of body or ellys
over-fatt; or that the matryce be febyll or in ovyre-gret het; or   110
elys that chylde be dysturbyde with sume knot in the nek of

95. travelynge of chylde: labour (in childbirth).
   precipitacion: falling, i.e. prolapse.
96. prefocacion: smothering.   *defaute*: lack.
101. nedys: necessarily.   *delyverance*: child-bearing.
   for ... wyche: i.e. to prevent conception; in fact, the Latin *Trotula
major* does contain some contraceptive remedies and it is interesting that
these are excluded from the vernacular versions, which were far more likely
to be read by women themselves. Medieval moral theologians usually
deplored artificial methods of contraception and induced abortion, as
analogous to murder.
101–2. can ... writt: do not know how to write down any remedies.
102–3. But ... man: abstinence from conjugal relations was the only
method of birth control acceptable to the medieval Church.
103. kepe here: guard herself.
104. oon my parell: upon peril of my soul.
106. lette: hinder.   *with chylde*: i.e. pregnant.
107. ryght delyverance: safe delivery.   *dystroubelyd*: troubled, disturbed.
108. angury: angry.   *schamfull*: embarrassed.
109. megyr: slight.
110. in ... het: i.e. excessively hot (women were supposed to be cold and
wet rather than hot and dry like men).

the matrice; or els that the mouthe of the marys be to clos, or
tornyde in the on syde or on the othyre; or ellys yf sche have
the stoune; or ellys yf here bouelle be over-replet of the gret
urynne for defaute of dygestyon; or ellys yf the chylde have   115
over-gret a hede or body, or yf hit hathe dropsy or other evyls,
or dede or turnyde agayn kynde. Now have I tolde yow the
lettynge of redy and tymfull delyverance of chylde.

Now woll I wryth to yow medycynys for redy delyverance, yf
hit be here tyme, whan a woman travelyth and here throwys   120
commyth. Take the rotys of polypodye that groweth on the
oke, and stampe hem and bynde hem undyre the solys of here
fete, and the chyld schall be borne, allthow he be dede.

From the *Liber Trotuli*

c) *Some Recipes*
(BL MS Add. 34111, ff. 211–12ᵛ)

Now it is to touche of some wyman that han thair prive
membre so large and so eville-smellyng, where-thorow their   125
hosebondes forsaken hem because of largenes and be the
wykked smel, ne han no wille to come nere hem.

For this vice of the woman, do mak a water strictive that
wille mak come togyder in this maner. Tak the bark of the
poumegarnet and the galles and the bark of hem and the   130

112. *to clos*: too narrow.
114. *the stoune*: gallstones.   *bouelle*: bowel.   *over-replet*: excessively
full.
114–15. *gret urynne*: i.e. bodily waste in general.
115. *defaute*: failure.
116. *dropsy*: oedema.   *evyls*: problems.
117. *or dede . . . kynde*: either dead or turned against nature, i.e. abnormal.
118. *tymfull*: prompt.
119. *wryth*: write.
120. *throwys*: contractions.
121. *rotys*: roots.   *polypodye*: polipody (oak fern).
122. *oke*: oak.   *stampe*: pound.   *soly*: soles
123. *allthow*: even though.
124–5. *prive membre*: genitals.
125. *where-thorow*: because of which.
126. *be*: because of.
127. *wille* desire.
128. *vice*: physical defect, blemish.   *do mak*: have made.
     water strictive: astringent liquid.
130. *poumegarnet*: pomegranate.

braunches of lentisci and the leves of vivelef and the rotes of
the two consoudes, the more and the lesse, and the leves of
the lorer and of the rosemarin, and sethe alle thes in reyny
water or in aqua rosacea, in whiche water do boile mastik and
frauncensens, galbanum, sagapium, that bien gummes, and   135
gumma arabica and parchemyn of a calfe, and whan thes bien
wel ysothe, do streyn thes and do to the leves of the lorere and
of rosen, that it smel sote.

   Yif that thow wille so wassh hem with this water, have it
redy and make hem, whan that thei gothe to bed with man, do   140
hem wassh thair instrument with this same water with thaire
fynggers within with wolle iwet in this water; and also wassh
welle withoute, for it clensith and maketh swote the humours,
bothe within and withoute, and than do hem dry with a lynnen
clothe iput within and also do dry withoute and than she may   145
stride and lete passe the moisture within benethe. And than
another tyme do hir putte in and dry it with a dry lynnen
cloute.

   And whan that she wille go slepe with any man, do hir take
thes poudres ymade of dry roses, of clowes and of   150
notemugges, of galyngale and of the leves of the lorer, and of
this poudre do tak a lytel porcion bitwix thin hondes and do
frote the brest and the teten and the prive menbre and other
that longgeth therto and than do wassh the face with aqua

131. lentisci: mastic tree.　　*vivelef*: five-leaf, quintfoil.
132. the(1) . . . *lesse*: the consound is a kind of herb, the 'lesser' being the
daisy, the 'greater' being comfrey.
133. lorer: laurel.　　*rosemarin*: rosemary.　　*sethe*: simmer.
　　reyny: rain.
134. aqua rosacea: rose water.　　*do boile*: have boiled.
135. frauncensens: frankincense.　　*galbanum*: gum resin.
　　sagapium: gum resin, concrete juice of *Ferula persica*.
136. gumma arabica: gum from certain species of acacia.　　*parchemyn*: skin.
137. ysothe: seethed, simmered.　　*do streyn*: have sieved.　　*do to*: add.
138. rosen: roses.
140–1. make . . . *wassh*: make them have washed.
141. instrument: genitals.
142. within: internally.　　*wolle*: wool.
143. withoute: externally.　　*swote*: sweet.　　*humours*: secretions.
146. stride: walk around.
　　lete . . . *benethe*: allow the moisture within to flow out.
147. another: i.e. a second.
149. do hir take: let her take.
150. poudres: powders.　　*clowes*: cloves.
151. notemugges: nutmegs.　　*galyngale*: galingale.
152. thin: thy.
153. frote rub.　　*teten*: nipples.
153–4. other . . . *therto*: the other parts of the body in that area.

rosacea and than do touche the man; and at she do frote hir   155
under the armeoles and in other places where she see that it
be do.

A pouder yproved for staunchyng of the blode ate the nose
and of the prive floures. Take saunk de dragoune and bolum
armenicum and canel and the rynd of the poumegarnet, of   160
alum and mastik of galles ana unces too, and mak poudre of
alle thes other ana, and do hem in a litel water ichaufyd and
do this togyder and sithen put in the hole that gothe to the
marice.

Forto mak streyt the prive membre. Tak a stone that is   165
yclepyd omathistos and gallas and bollum armenicum and
saunk de dragoune and stamp hem wonder smalle that thei
may be sarcid thorow a lynnen cloute, and tempre thes
poudres with the juse of plantayne, and than do dry it ate sone
and than tak a lytel of this pouder with the juse forsayd and do   170
it in be a tent and do mak the woman somdel lige wyddopyn,
strechyng oute the legges, and this pouder is gode for woman
that hathe han part of man and wolde be holde for a mayden.

For woman that hathe the prive membre large, to beo made
streyt. Tak gallas and sethe hem in water, and with this water   175

155. *at . . . hir*: that she may, i.e. let her, rub herself.
156. *armeoles*: armpits.
158. *yproved*: tested.
159. *prive floures*: menstruation.
    saunk de dragoune: san-dragoun, red juice or the resin of the dragon-tree (*Dracaena Draco*).
159–60. *bolum armenicum*: Armenian bole (red earth).
160. *canel*: cinnamon.
161. *ana unces too*: two ounces of each.
162. *other ana*: each of these.
162. *do . . . ichaufyd*: have them warmed in a little water.
163. *sithen*: then.
165. *streyt*: narrow.
166. *yclepyd*: called.
167. *wonder*: extraordinarily.
168. *sarcid*: sieved.   *cloute*: piece of cloth.   *tempre*: mix.
169. *juse*: juice.   *ate sone*: quickly.
170–1. *do . . . tent*: put it in by means of a linen plug.
171. *somdel*: to a certain extent.   *lige*: lie.
    wyddopyn: i.e. with her legs apart.
173. *han part*: had experience.
    wolde . . . mayden: wants to be thought a virgin; presumably the various gums served to create adhesions and make intercourse difficult.

do wassh the prive membre, and than take the pouder of boli
armenici and of thes gallas and strew thes poudres ther-upon,
and it shalle mak streyt.

From *The Book of Rota*

d) *Infertility: Diagnosis and Cure*
(CUL MS Ii. vi. 33, ff. 11ᵛ–13)

Another infirmite ther ys of the matrice of a woman, that is
they may nott conceave children as they wold. And this may   180
be sumtyme thorowe the defaute of the man, and sumtyme it
may be the defaute of the woman, and sumtyme thorow bothe.
But to knowe in whether the faute is, take this medicyne:
    Take a lytyll erthen pott newe and put therin the mans uryn
and cast therto an handfull of bran and stere it fast with a   185
sticke about and take annother newe erthen pott and put
therin the womans uryne and put bran therto and ster it as the
other, and let it stande so nine dayes or ten and loke than in
whether pott that yow fynde wormes in. Ther ys the defaute
that is baren, be yt the man or the woman, for the baren wyl   190
be full of wormes. The vessell that the baren uryn is in wyll
stynke. And yf nether vessell be with wormes, than is neyther
of them baren. And than they may be holpen with medicynes,
of the which sum I wyll speke of, to make a woman to conceve
with childe.   195
    Take woll well tosed and roste it well in asse mylke and

---

177. *strew*: sprinkle; this recipe probably worked by acting as a constrictive.
179. *infirmite*: disease, disorder.   *matrice*: uterus.
180. *conceave*: conceive.
181. *defaute*: deficiency, fault.
184. *lytyll . . . newe*: small, new, earthen pot; the position of 'newe' after the
noun suggests that the translator's original might be French.
184. *uryn*: urine.
185. *cast therto*: throw into it.
185–6. *stere . . . about*: stir it round thoroughly with a stick.
188. *than*: then.
189. *whether*: which.
190. *baren*: barren, infertile.   *be yt*: whether it is.
193. *holpen*: helped.
196. *woll*: wool.   *tosed*: combed, carded.
      roste: cook, boil.   *asse mylke*: ass's milk.

bynd it uppon the womans navell and let hit lye soo tyll she
have done with her husband for that journey, and she shall
conceave.

Take the lyver and the stones of a gryse that a sowe hath　　200
noo moo of that lytter but one, and drye that and make it in
powder, and gyffe it to the woman to drynke and she shall
conceve. And geve a man the pouder to drynke and sone after
he shall engender. Sum men seye yt ys no forse whether ther
be no moo of that varow or no. And sum men saye yt were　　205
good inogh yf the stones of the grysse were bakyn in a pye by
hemselfe, without any other fleshe. And make a woman to
eate of that pye, and the same nyght let it be knowen to her
husbande, and than company with hym, and she shall
conceve, as it hath byn proved in dede.　　210

Textual notes

2. a] and.
7. by] be.
8. be engendyrde] engendyrde.
22. may rede] rede.
63. an] and.
81. sede rotyth (1)] sede and rotyth.
122. hem] hym.
186. annother] annothe.
207. hemselfe] hymselfe.

197. bynd: tie.
198. have done: has had intercourse.
198. journey: day (compare F. *journée*).
200. lyver: liver.　　*stones*: testicles.　　*gryse*: piglet.
200–1. that . . . one: i.e. that is the only product of a sow's litter.
202. gyffe: give.
203. geve: give.　　*pouder*: powder.
204. engender: father a child.　　*ys no forse*: makes no difference.
204–5. whether . . . no: whether or not there are any more (piglets) in that
litter; a litter of a single piglet would be extremely rare.
206. inogh: enough.　　*bakyn*: baked.
206–7. by hemselfe: i.e. on their own.
207. fleshe: meat, i.e. the pig's liver.
209. company: (let her) have intercourse.
210. byn: been.

2 Marie de France

A woman called Marie identifies herself as the author of at least one of twelve *lais* or short verse romances, written in Anglo-Norman and found in the thirteenth-century manuscript British Library Harley 978. The same manuscript contains a collection of fables in a similar style, also claimed by a Marie 'of (or from) France', while Denis Piramus, an Anglo-Norman poet writing around 1180, refers to the popularity at court, particularly among the ladies, of the *lais* of 'Dame Marie'. Probably all three Maries are the same woman, whom we now know as Marie de France and who is regarded as one of the most accomplished writers of medieval romance.

Marie was active as a poet in the later twelfth century. As she identifies herself as 'of France', and as the earliest manuscript is Anglo-Norman, she presumably lived in England. She was clearly both aristocratic and learned; familiar with the conventions of courtly literature, she read and understood both French and Latin. Possibly she can be identified with Marie, half-sister of Henry II and abbess of the rich and powerful house of Benedictine nuns at Shaftesbury (Fox 1910: 303–6, 1911: 317–26; Bullock-Davies 1965: 314–22).

Marie's best-known works are her *lais*, short narrative poems about courtly love (usually adulterous) and often involving magic, which she claimed to have heard from the 'Bretons'. Two of these made their way into English; there are several later Middle English romances rather distantly derived from her *Lanval*, while *Lai le Freine* was translated in the early fourteenth century, possibly by the same poet who composed, or translated, *Sir Orpheo*.

Comment: The Middle English *Lai le Freine* is a fairly close translation of Marie's original, whose octosyllabic couplets it reproduces. This is one of the few poems of Marie's that ends with the lovers happily married, which may be why it appealed to fourteenth-century English taste. Usually in Marie's *lais* the lady already has a husband but here both Sir Guroun and Freine are free to marry and the only obstacle to their union is the heroine's apparent low birth. The story is basically a folk tale (it has some affinities with Chaucer's *Clerk's Tale*), told with economy and verve. Its female characters – the mother, her maid, the abbess and Freine herself – are far from the passive figures of many courtly romances and actually initiate most of the action.

The poem is unusually tolerant towards the characters' behaviour. The worst sin appears to be against the ideals of courtesy: the narrator criticises the mother's uncourteous speech, later punished by Heaven with the birth of twins, while attempted infanticide and her abandonment of her child go uncastigated. Her daughter Freine's gracious speech and generous behaviour are ultimately rewarded and seem more important than her sexual frailty and her ungrateful treatment of the abbess. Even Sir Guroun, who first seduces the heroine and then plans to displace her by marrying her sister, is rewarded by the discovery that Freine is of noble birth and therefore marriageable, not just beddable.

Manuscript: Unfortunately the only surviving copy of the Middle English, in the Auchinleck Manuscript (Edinburgh National Library of Scotland MS Advocates' 19.2.1), has been extensively mutilated. The missing parts of the text (ll. 121–33 and 341–408) were skilfully reconstructed in the early nineteenth century by Henry Weber, Sir Walter Scott's literary assistant. The Auchinleck Manuscript is an important collection of verse romances, saints' lives and other didactic poems, dated as 1330–40. It was probably produced by a lay scriptorium or 'bookshop' in London and is indicative of middle-class – including female – tastes in literature (Barron 1987: 54; Loomis 1942: 595–627). Romances seem to have been as popular among the citizens' wives of pre-Chaucerian England as among the ladies of the court of Henry II and his wife Eleanor of Aquitaine.

Further reading (for full details see Bibliography): On Marie's place within the European romance tradition, see Barron 1987: 11–45. On Middle English romances in general, see Barron 1987, Mehl 1968 and Stevens 1973.

From *Lay le Freine*

a) *The Birth of Freine*
(Advocates' MS 19.2.1, ff. 261^{ra-rb})

In the west cuntre woned tvay knightes
And loved hem wele in al rightes;
Riche men in her best liif
And aither of hem hadde wedded wiif.
That o knight made his levedi milde   5
That sche was wonder gret with childe
And when hir time was comen tho
Sche was deliverd out of wo.
The knight thonked God almight
And cleped his messanger an hight.   10

1. *cuntre*: country.   *woned*: dwelt.   *tvay*: two.
2. *hem*: them, i.e. each other.
    in al rightes: as strongly as possible, absolutely.
3. *her*: their.
4. *aither*: each.
5. *o*: one.   *levedi milde*: gentle lady.
6. *wonder*: extraordinarily.
7. *tho*: then.
9. *almight*: almighty.
10. *cleped*: called.   *an hight*: in haste.

'Go', he seyd, 'to mi neighebour swithe
And say y gret him fele sithe
And pray him that he com to me
And say he schal mi gossibbe be.'
The messanger goth and hath nought foryete   15
And fint the knight at his mete.
And fair he gret in the halle
The lord, the levedi, the meyne alle.
And seththen on knes doun him sett
And the Lord ful fair he gret: 20
'He bad that thou schust to him te
And for love his gossibbe be.'
'Is his levedi deliverd with sounde?'
'Ya, sir, ythonked be God the stounde.'
'And whether a maiden child other a knave?'   25
'Tvay sones, sir, God hem save!'
The knight therof was glad and blithe
And thonked Godes sond swithe
And graunted his erand in al thing
And yaf him a palfray for his tiding.   30

Than was the levedi of the hous
A proude dame and an envieous,
Hokerfulliche missegging,
Squeymous and eke scorning.
To ich woman sche hadde envie.   35
Sche spac this wordes of felonie:
'Ich have wonder, thou messanger,
Who was thi lordes conseiler,

11. *swithe*: at once.
12. *fele sithe*: many times.
14. *mi gossibbe*: my sponsor, i.e. godparent of my child.
15. *foryete*: forget.
16. *fint*: found.   *mete*: meal.
17. *fair*: politely.
18. *meyne*: household.
19. *seththen*: then, next.
21. *schust*: shouldst.   *te*: go.
23. *with sounde*: safely.
24. *the stounde*: at this time.
25. *whether . . . knave*: is it a girl or a boy?.
28. *sond*: dispensation.
30. *yaf*: gave.
33. *Hokerfulliche missegging*: scornfully abusing.
34. *Squeymous*: disdainful.
36. *this . . . felonie*: these villainous words.

To teche him about to sende
And telle schame in ich an ende,   40
That his wiif hath to childer ybore!
Wele may ich man wite therfore
That tvay men hir han hadde in bour;
That is hir bothe deshonour.'

The messanger was sore aschamed   45
The knight himself was sore agramed
And rebouked his levedy
To speke ani woman vilaynie.
And ich woman therof might here
Curssed hir alle yfere   50
And bisought God in heven
For his holy name seven
That yif hye ever ani child schuld abide
A wers aventour hir schuld bitide.

Sone therafter bifel a cas   55
That hirself with child was.
When God wild sche was unbounde
And deliverd al with sounde.
To maiden childer sche hadde ybore.
When hye it wist, wo hir was therfore!   60

39. *about*: abroad, far and wide.
40. *in ... ende*: everywhere.
41. *to childer*: two children.   *ybore*: born.
42. *Wele ... wite*: anyone may well know.   *therfore*: from that.
43. *hir ... hadde*: have had (intercourse with) her; this misapprehension about multiple births, still a widespread folk belief, was common in the Middle Ages. Superfetation, i.e. the formation of a second foetus in a uterus already pregnant, does occur in some animals (e.g. cats) and possibly on rare occasions in women.
43. *bour*: chamber.
44. *hir bothe*: to both of them.
46. *agramed*: vexed.
47–8. *rebouked ... vilaynie*: rebuked his lady for speaking discourteously of any woman.
49. *ich ... here*: every women who might hear of this.
50. *yfere*: together.
52. *holy ... seven*: seven holy names, i.e. El, Elohim, Elyon, Jehovah, Yahweh, Adonai and Shaddai.
53. *hye*: she.   *abide*: expect.
54. *wers aventour*: worse chance.
55. *bifel a cas*: it so happened.
57. *wild*: willed.   *unbounde*: delivered.

'Allas,' sche seyd, 'that this hap come.
Ich have y-yoven min owen dome.
Forboden bite ich woman
To speken ani other harm opon!
Falsliche another Y gan deme;   65
The selve happe is on me sene.
Allas', sche seyd, 'that Y was born!
Withouten ende ich am forlorn.
Or ich mot siggen sikerly
That tvay men han yly me by,   70
Or ich mot sigge in al mi liif
That Y bileighe mi neghbours wiif,
Or ich mot, that God it schilde,
Help to sle min owhen child.
On of this thre thinges ich mot nede   75
Sigge other don in dede.
Yif ich say ich hadde a bileman
Than ich leighe meselve opon,
And eke thai wil that me se
Held me wers than comoun be.   80
And yif ich knaweleche to ich man
That ich leighe the levedi opon
Than ich worth of old and yong
Behold leighster and fals of tong.
Yete me is best take mi chaunce,   85
And sle mi childe, and do penaunce.'

61. *come*: should come.
62. *y-yoven*: given.   *dome*: judgement.
63. *Forboden . . . woman*: may every woman be forbidden.
65. *Falsliche*: falsely.   *gan deme*: did judge.
66. *selve happe*: very same chance.   *on me sene*: seen in me.
68. *Withouten ende*: i.e. for ever.   *forlorn*: lost, ruined.
69–71. *Or . . . Or*: either . . . or.
69. *mot*: must.   *siggen*: say.   *sikerly*: surely.
70. *yly by me*: lain with me.
72. *bileighe*: lied about.
73. *that . . . schilde*: God forbid!
74. *owhen*: own.
75. *On*: one.   *nede*: necessarily.
76. *other*: or.   *don . . . dede*: do in fact.
77. *bileman*: lover, paramour.
78. *leighe . . . opon*: slander myself.
80. *Held . . . be*: hold me to be worse than wanton.
81. *knaweleche*: acknowledge.
83. *worth*: will be.
84. *Behold*: considered.   *leghster*: woman liar.
85. *Yete*: yet, still.   *me is best*: it is best for me.

Hir midwiif hye cleped hir to.
'Anon', sche seyd, 'this child fordo
And ever say thou wher thou go
That ich have o child and namo.'   90
The midwiif answerd thurchout al
That hye nil, no hye ne schal.

[A resourceful maidservant suggests that the baby should be abandoned, and leaves her, wrapped in a richly embroidered cloth with a ring tied to her arm, in an ash-tree outside a nearby convent. The nuns take her in, name her Freine (F. = ash-tree) and bring her up.]

b) *The Seduction of Freine*
(ff. 262^{rb–vb})

This Frein thrived fram yer to yer.
The abbesse nece men wend it were.
The abbesse hir gan teche and beld.   95
Bi that hye was of twelve winter eld
In al Inglond ther nas non
A fairer maiden than hye was on.
And when hye couthe ought of manhed
Hye bad the abbesse hir wis and rede   100
Whiche were her kin, on or other,
Fader or moder, soster or brother.
The abbesse hir in conseyl toke
To tellen hir hye nought forsoke,

87. *Hir . . . to*: she summoned her midwife to her.
88. *Anon*: at once.
89. *fordo*: destroy; it would be unwise to treat this romance as a historical document but there is some demographic evidence that infanticide of baby girls was widespread in the Middle Ages. Midwives (who had to be licensed by the local bishop) were often suspected of involvement, but this one behaves impeccably.
89. *wher*: wherever.
90. *namo*: no more.
91. *thurchout al*: all the time.
92. *hye . . . schal*: she neither would nor should.
94. *abbesse nece*: abbess's kinswoman.   *wend*: thought.
95. *beld*: instruct, edify. On women's education see Introduction, pp. 2–5.
96. *Bi*: by (the time).   *hye*: she.   *eld*: old.
97. *nas non*: was no.
99. *couthe . . . manhed*: knew anything about human nature.
100. *wis and rede*: inform and advise.
101. *Whiche . . . other*: who were her relatives, one and all.
102. *soster*: sister.
103. *hir . . . toke*: took her into her confidence.
104. *nought forsoke*: did not omit.

Hou hye was founden in al thing   105
And tok hir the cloth and the ring
And bad hir kepe it in that stede.
And ther whiles sche lived so sche dede.

Than was ther in that cuntre
A riche knight of lond and fe,   110
Proud and yong and jolive
And had nought yete ywedded wive.
He was stout, of gret renoun,
And was ycleped Sir Guroun.
He herd praise that maiden fre   115
And seyd he wald hir se.
He dight him in the way anon
And joliflich thider he come;
And bad his man sigge verrament
He schuld toward a turnament.   120
The abbesse and the nonnes alle
Fair him gret in the gest halle
And damisel Freyn, so hende of mouthe,
Gret him faire as hye wele couthe.
And swithe wele he gan devise   125
Her semblaunt and hir gentrise,
Her lovesum eighen, her rode so bright,
And comced to love hir anon right
And thought hou he might take on
To have hir to his leman.   130

106. *tok*: gave.
107. *stede*: place.
110. *riche . . . fe*: knight rich in landed and movable property.
111. *jolive*: youthful, lusty.
113. *stout*: proud, brave.
115. *herd . . . fre*: heard that noble maiden praised.
116. *wald*: would.
117. *dight him*: prepared himself, got ready.
118. *joliflich*: gladly.
119. *sigge*: say.   *verrament*: truthfully.
120. *schuld . . . turnament*: had to go to a tournament.
122. *gest*: guest.
123. *hende*: courteous.
124. *wele couthe*: knew well.
125. *swithe*: very.   *devise*: observe.
126. *semblaunt*: appearance.   *gentrise*: graciousness.
127. *lovesum*: lovely.   *eighen*: eyes.   *rode*: complexion.
128. *comced*: began.
130. *to . . . leman*: as his love.

He thought, 'Yif ich com hir to
More than ichave ydo,
The abbesse wil souchy gile
And voide hir in a litel while.'
He compast another enchesoun, 135
To be brother of that religioun.
'Madame,' he seyd to the abbesse,
'I lovi wele in al godenisse,
Ichil yive on and other,
Londes and rentes, to bicom your brother, 140
That ye schul ever fare the bet
When Y com to have recet.'
At fewe wordes thai ben at on.
He graythes him and forth is gon.
Oft he come bi day and night 145
To speke with that maiden bright,
So that with his fair bihest
And with his gloseing atte lest,
Hye graunted him to don his wille
When he wil, loude and stille. 150
'Leman,' he seyd, 'thou most lat be
The abbesse, thi nece, and go with me.
For ich am riche, of swiche pouwere,
The finde bet than thou hast here.'
The maiden grant and to him trist, 155
And stale oway that no man wist.

132. *ichave ydo*: I have done.
133. *souchy gile*: suspect a plot.
134. *voide*: dismiss.
135. *compast*: devised.   *enchesoun*: excuse, pretext.
136. *brother ... religioun*: associate of that religious order.
138. *lovi*: love.   *godenisse*: goodness.
139. *Ichil*: I will.   *on and other*: (to) one and all.
141. *bet*: better.
142. *have recet*: take refuge, obtain shelter.
143. *at on*: i.e. agreed.
144. *graythes him*: prepares himself.
147. *bihest*: promises.
148. *gloseing*: flattery.
149. *graunted*: allowed.
150. *loude and stille*: i.e. under all circumstances, at all times.
151. *lat be*: leave.
153. *pouwere*: power.
154. *The ... bet*: to provide for you better.
155. *trist*: trusted.
156. *stale oway*: stole away.

With hir tok hye no thing
Bot hir pel and hir ring.

When the abbesse gan aspie
That hye was with the knight owy,   160
Sche made morning in hir thought
And hir biment and gained nought.
So long sche was in his castel
That al his meyne loved hir wel.
To riche and pouer sche gan hir dresse,   165
That al hir loved, more and lesse.
And thus sche lad with him hir liif
Right as sche hadde ben his wedded wiif.

[But Sir Guroun is persuaded to abandon Freine and to marry her twin
sister. Freine generously decks the nuptial bed with her embroidered cloth,
which is recognised by the bride's mother. All is explained, the wedding is
promptly annulled, and Freine marries Sir Guroun herself.]

Textual notes

123. damisel] damilel.
125. swithe] swhe.

158. Bot: except.   *pel*: mantle.
160. owy: away.
161. morning: mourning.   *thought*: mind.
162. hir biment: lamented.   *gained nought*: did no good.
163. sche: i.e. le Freine.
165. gan . . . dresse: behaved.
168. Right: just as if.

3 Mechtild of Hackeborn and Gertrude the Great

The Book of Ghostly Grace is a fifteenth-century translation of the Latin *Liber Spiritualis* (or *Specialis*) *Gratiae*, an account of the revelations of Mechtild of Hackeborn written between 1291 and 1298 by Gertrude the Great in a fluent and elaborate Latin. Mechtild (commonly known in medieval England as 'Maud' or 'Moll') was born *c.* 1240 and entered the monastery of Helfta in Germany, where her sister was abbess, at the age of seven. She later became the mentor and close friend of the younger Gertrude. Her visions are strongly visual, often schematically allegorical, and partly structured around the feasts of the Church's year. Most took place during the celebration of mass and are often linked to specific liturgical texts.

Helfta in Thuringia (eastern Germany) was a Benedictine foundation, strongly influenced by the Cistercian reform movement and its leader, Bernard of Clairvaux. Unlike most English and French religious houses for women of the time, it was a learned institution. Gertrude and many of the other nuns both read and wrote Latin; the nuns still mainly entered as child 'oblates' (that is, their parents offered them in infancy to the religious life), grew up in a totally female environment and were given a thorough education in the Liberal Arts (which included the reading and writing of Latin) and in theology.

Gertrude, the most literary of all the medieval women visionaries, was a prolific writer. In addition to the *Liber Spiritualis Gratiae*, she wrote an account of her own experiences, now Book II of the *Legatus Divinae Pietatis* (*The Herald of God's Loving-Kindness*). The rest of *The Herald* consists of a biographical sketch of her and three books of Gertrude's visions compiled by another, anonymous Helfta nun, so there was a well-established tradition of women's writing in that monastery.

Some sort of apology for the writing of a book is almost invariably found in women's texts, but the account Gertrude gives of the circumstances of the composition of the *Liber* is particularly revealing as it makes explicit what is often left unsaid by less consciously literary writers. She writes that Mechtild:

> sawe mysteries of hevenlie privetees [secrets] moo [more] than I can nowmbre, ande of here owne lownes [humility] sche helde here so unworthye that sche walde noght tell bott [except] as sche was compellede of thame that were too here famyliere [intimate] in here goostelye counseyls [spiritual secrets], ande yit of that sche tolde in partye [part]. Some sche withdrowe [withheld] ande some sche sayde to the worschepe of Owre Lorde, ande that was whene sche was constreynede be [by] the vertue of obedience. Tho that sche tolde, in the name of Jhesu I schalle wryte als Y have connynge, to the worschepe of the Holye Trynite. (BL MS Egerton 2006, f. 21ʳ)

Gertrude therefore writes purely to edify, to tell the world about Mechtild's spiritual gifts to the glory of God. Through her declared dependence on God's help she implicitly disclaims any authority as a writer. At the same time she absolves Mechtild from any suggestion of the kind of egotism which often goes with literary composition and is considered inappropriate to women. She stresses that, restrained by humility from communicating her own experiences, the visionary consented to do so only under obedience, at the insistence of her spiritual advisers. Indeed, it was only divine intervention that reconciled Mechtild to the dissemination of her visions.

> Botte when sche hadde knowen thare-offe [i.e. about Gertrude's book] be anothere mannys tellynge, sche was so sorye that sche cowth noght be comforthede ... sche sayde to Oure Lorde, 'Lorde, whate schall befall off this booke efter my deth?' Oure Lorde sayde agayne, 'All that sekene [seek] me with a trewe and a faythfull herte schall be mayde gladde in this booke . . . . Ande the booke schall be callede *The Booke off Spyritualle Grace.*' (f. 136ʳ⁻ᵛ)

Finally Gertrude explains that her text is, as it were, merely a fragment of an unwritten book, a text that cannot be fully realised, partly because of the visionary's reluctance but also because her experiences cannot always be reduced to words:

> alle these revelacions that beene written in this booke be off nowmbre botte fewe, havynge rewarde to [considering] alle othere that been lefte unwrytten. For manye moo was schewede of Oure Lorde whiche sche walde noght tell. Also itt was some tyme so spyrituall that sche sawe, that be no waye sche cowth ne myght nought schewe itt in wordes. (f. 136ᵛ)

The axiomatic inadequacy of human language to express the inexpressible is, of course, a problem with all such writing, but it is perhaps rarely made quite so explicit.

The Middle English translator of *The Book of Ghostly Grace* assumed that the author of the original was a man, no doubt because it was written in Latin. This misunderstanding was made possible because Gertrude always refers to herself in the third person as *illa persona* ('that person'), grammatically feminine in Latin; hence any consequent feminine forms are easily explained on grammatical, not natural grounds. Moreover, Latin does not make the use of personal pronouns that English does, and the possessive always agrees, not with the natural gender of the possessor but with the grammatical gender of the thing possessed. Gertrude is thus able to exploit linguistic features of Latin to efface her gender.

Comment: Mechtild's visions of the birth of Christ, in which she cradles, kisses and later even suckles the infant herself, are influenced by the new devotion to Christ's humanity, found from the twelfth century (see, e.g., Southern 1953: 240–50; Bynum 1982: 16–20). But by her choice of detail and its interpretation (e.g. the mountain on which the Virgin sits before giving birth), and her intellectual response to the child in the greeting she is inspired to offer him, she simultaneously stresses the theological significance of the Incarnation. These aspects of her visions form an instructive contrast with Bridget of Sweden's later emphasis on the human, obstetrical aspects of the birth itself (see pp. 87–9), which also reflects the later visionary's wider experience of a life outside the convent.

The second passage illustrates the devotion to the Heart of Jesus with which Helfta became associated (see Bynum 1982: 192–3), which celebrates Christ's parental (almost maternal) love as much as the erotic love more usually associated with medieval mysticism. Divine Love, who dwells in the Heart, recalls the 'Lady Love' of Mechtild's contemporary Marguerite Porete (see p. 62) and suggests a peculiarly female interpretation of love in the experience of widely differing women mystics. By characterising Divine Love as female, both Mechtild and Marguerite implicitly assert the dignity of women, though Mechtild may also have been influenced by the fact that the German word for (courtly) love, *Minne*, is grammatically feminine.

The third passage demonstrates an important role played by the medieval visionary (who was far more likely to be female than male): to act as a link between the living and the dead (compare text 10, *A Revelation Showed to a Holy Woman*). It provides some surprisingly close parallels with the Middle English poem 'Pearl', while incidentally illuminating the domestic tensions caused by child oblation, commonly practised in the earlier Middle Ages but obsolete in fifteenth-century England. The overt intervention of the translator, alarmed by the apparent heterodoxy of his 'authoritative' source, is most unusual.

Manuscript: This selection is edited from BL MS Egerton 2006, which once belonged to Richard III and his wife, Anne of Warwick. *The Book of Ghostly Grace* is also extant in Oxford MS Bodley 220, a manuscript written by John Wells, who may have been a Carthusian monk. The complete text has been edited from MS Egerton 2006 by Theresa A. Halligan (1979).

Further reading: On medieval women visionaries in general see Petroff 1986, and on women's spirituality in the Middle Ages see Bynum 1987. On the nuns of Helfta see Mary Jeremy 1962 and Bynum 1982: 170–262 (Books I and II of Gertrude's *Legatus* have been translated by Barratt 1991). On the ME translation see Halligan 1974.

From *The Book of Ghostly Grace*

a) *Visions of the Birth of Christ*
(BL MS Egerton 2006, ff. 29^r–30^v)

In the holye nyght of Crystes Natyvite, hitt semyde to that holye nunne as sche hadde bene in a stonye hyll or in a mountayne of stone, in whiche mountayne sche sawe Oure Ladye sytte, full nere here tyme of byrth. Ande when the tyme

2. *as*: as if.

was commen, that blesfull modere ande maydene was 5
fulfillede with suche gladnesse that no tonge maye telle, ande
with a plentevous inwarde ande effectuele joye. Ande
sodaynlye sche was becleppede all abowte with a lyght that
come fro God, in so moche that with a manere stonynge ande
anone sche rayse uppe ande with a grete mekenesse sche 10
knelydde downe agayne with lawelye thankkynge to God ande
towarde thee erthe sche enclynede, in dowte whate schulde
befall here, tyll sche hadde sodaynlye that gloriouse childe in
here lappe, whiche passede in speciouste all mennys childre.

Botte when sche sawe hym before here, than toke sche here 15
dere sonne with full fervente love and with suche joye that hitt
may not be spokenne ande kyssede hym full lovynglye,
thorowe whiche kusse sche was oonyde fullye to the blessede
Trinite, as moche as evere hitt was possibile anye manne or
woman to be onyde to God withowtyn personale oonyon. 20

Be that hill or mowntayne es fygurede a gostelye habyte
whiche semys full herde ande scharpe in this worlde, botte
Cryste ande his blessede modere schewyde us furste that hylle
ande gaffe us ensaumple of verrey religious lyffynge. This
religious mayden, sche behelde that holye vysione ande 25
blessede countenaunce betwyxte the modere ande the sonne,
syttynge besyde Oure Ladye, as here semydde; gretlye sche
desyrede to kysse that amyable childe. Anone than that
glorious modere ande maydene toke here sonne ande spake
thareto full mekelye ande beclyppede hym betwyx here aarmys 30

5. *blesfull*: glorious.
7. *plentevous*: plentiful.   *effectuele*: efficacious, powerful.
8. *becleppede*: surrounded.
9. *with ... stonynge*: in a kind of trance.
10. *anone*: immediately.   *rayse*: rose.
11. *lawelye*: lowly, humble.
12. *dowte*: doubt, fear.
14. *passede*: surpassed.   *speciouste*: beauty.
18. *kusse*: kiss.   *oonyde*: united.
19–20. *as*(1) ... *oonyon*: this qualification was probably added to protect
Mechtild from any suspicion of holding the heretical belief that mystical
union could enable a human being to become divine.
20. *personale oonyon*: union of person.
21. *fygurede*: symbolised.   *gostelye*: spiritual.
22. *herde*: hard, harsh.
24. *gaffe*: gave.   *verrey ... lyffynge*: the true religious life.
25. *religious mayden*: i.e. nun.
28. *amyable*: lovely.
30. *thareto*: i.e. to him.   *beclyppede*: embraced.   *betwyx*: between.

full softelye, ande so toke hym to the maydene for sche
schulde halde hym in here aarmys als sche desyrede. That
blessede nunne toke hym of Oure Ladye with a full gret love
ande helde hym betwyx here aarmys ande with here handes
impressede that lorde to here herte ande made to hym   35
reverentlye salutacion sodeynlye, with these manere wordes
whiche sche herde nevere ne thought of thame before that
tyme.

This was his salutacion: 'Hayle,' sche saide, 'the marowgh
of the Faders herte, fulle swete fattenes of a langores sawlle   40
ande a blyssede refeccion; to the I offre the marowe of myne
herte and of myne sawle into thy everelastynge laude ande
glorye.' Sche understode also be Goddys inspyracion howe
Goddys sonne es the marowe of the Faderys herte; ande ryght
als a marowe es comfortatyfe, helynge and full swete in kynde,   45
ryght so God the Fadere hath gyffene us his sonne, whiche es
the vertue ande wysdome of the Fadere ande the full
delectable gostelye swetnesse of hym, for his dere sonne
schulde be to us comforthe, heyle ande swetnesse. Ande the
marowe of the sawle is that thynge that es so swete, whiche a   50
sawle felys inwardelye be infucion of love oonely of Godde,
wharebye hitt dyspyseys verrelye all passynge thyngesse. Also
that swetnes es so joyefulle to a man that, thowh all the joye of
the worlde were putte into one manne, yit schulde hitt nought
be lyke evyn in comparysonne to that othere joye whiche a   55
sawle felys be gostelye swetnes.

In this vysyone this maydene sawe also howe fowre sunne-
bemys schynede bryghtlye fro that childes face, whiche

31. *softelye*: gently.   *toke*: brought.
32. *halde*: hold.   *als*: as.
33. *of*: from.
35. *impressede*: pressed.
39. *his salutacion*: her greeting of him.
    marowgh: marrow, i.e. the innermost part.
40. *fattenes*: fat, i.e. the richest, most nourishing part.
    of(2) . . . *sawlle*: for a yearning soul.
41. *refeccion*: meal, refreshment.
45. *comfortatyfe*: strengthening.
47. *vertue*: power.
48. *for*: so that.
49. *comforthe*: comfort.   *heyle*: salvation.
51. *infucion*: pouring in, inspiration.
52. *wharebye*: by which.   *passynge*: transitory.   *thyngesse*: things.
53. *thowh*: though, even if.
56. *sawle*: soul.
57–8. *sunne-bemys*: sunbeams.

fulfillede the fowre partyes of the werlde, be the whiche
bemys the holye conversacion of Cryste was fygurede ande his　　60
blessede doctrine, whiche lyghttenede all the worlde.

[A lengthy chapter heading has been omitted here.]

Atte the masse in that holye nyght whiche begynnesse
Dominus dixit, whiche es songgen in mynde and reverence of
that privey ande blesfull Crystes byrth, hytt semede to that
holye maydene that sche sawe God the Fadere of hevene ande　　65
myghtfull kynge syttynge within a tente of a full wonderfull
werke in a throne of iverye, ande spake to here thes manere of
wordes: 'Come ande take here the everlastynge ande the
oonelye-borne sonne of my herte ande comwne hym furth to
all tho whiche worschepe nowe his hye generacion of me with　　70
a devoute thankynge.'

And with tho wordes anone sche sawe a wonderfull
bryghtnesse ande schynynge come fro the herte of that kynge,
Almyghttye God, whiche schynynge clevede to the herte of
that maydene in lykenesse of a lytell childe alle fulle of　　75
clerenesse, whome sche reverentlye salutede ande sayde:
Salve, splendor paterne glorie etc., that es to saye, 'Hayle, the
schynynge of the Faderes glorye'. With tho wordys ande
othere that folowys in that same ympne, sche worscheppede
that worthye lorde, Goddys sonne, ande full hyelye behelde　　80
hym inwardlye in here sawle. Ande that same mattere of
contemplacion mowe we haffe in that ympne, for hitt acordys
wele to that feste, all be hitt that hitt be nought songgene than
in Holye Cherche.

59. *fulfillede*: filled.
60. *conversacion*: life.
61. *lyghttenede*: enlightened.
63. *mynde*: remembrance.
64. *privey*: secret, intimate.
66–7. *tente . . . werke*: tent of miraculous workmanship.
67. *iverye*: ivory.
69. *oonelye-borne*: only-begotten.
　　comwne: communicate, share. God's command implicitly assigns
Mechtild a role like that of the priest who distributes the consecrated Host.
70. *hye generacion*: noble birth.
74. *clevede*: attached itself.
76. *clerenesse*: purity, brightness.
79. *ympne*: hymn.
82. *mowe*: may.　　*acordys*: fits, agrees.
83–4. *all . . . Cherche*: the hymn 'Splendor paternae gloriae', composed by
Ambrose of Milan, was sung regularly at dawn and was not specifically a
Christmas hymn.

Botte this maydene, aftere sche hadde worscheppede so   85
that childe, sche bare hym abowte to eche sustere ande gaffe
hym to eche of thame syngulerlye, ande so aboyde with eche
persone. Ande nought withstondynge that yitt sche bare hym
styll abowve here herte, the childe restede abowve the breste
of eche of thame, ande thryes he kyssede eche of thare hertys   90
ande att eche cusse, to here semynge, he sowkede full swetlye.
Atte the furste cusse he sowkede to hym the holye desyre of
thare hertys; ande atte the secounde the goode will that thay
hadde, ande atte the thrydde he sowkede to hym all thare
travayle whiche was profyte to thare sawlys, that es to saye the   95
travayle that thay hadde in synggynge, in enclynynge, in
wakynge, in othere gostelye excercyses.

In this tyme sche hadde knawynge, as God wolde, that hytt
schulde be full acceptable to oure lorde God that menne
schulde make joye togedders with a meke ande holye beleve of   100
that Nativite, ande make hitt hye ande worthie with all
worscheppes ande praysynges that thaye mowe, all be hitt thay
mowe nought in thare felynge comprehende ne atteyne the
Faderys generacion of Goddys sonne. For that was of so hye
myght of the Godhede that hitt may nought be schewyde be   105
no speche.

b) *Union with God*
(ff. 116ᵛ–117ᵛ)

Anothere tyme in here tyme of prayere, when sche desyrede
here love, sodeynlye the vertewe of the Godhede drowe here
sowle sodeynlye to hym, in so moche that to here semynge

86. bare: carried.
87. syngulerlye: individually.   *aboyde*: stayed, remained.
88. yitt: still.
89. abowve: i.e. on.
90. thryes: thrice.
91–7. att . . . excercyses: a medieval audience, who inevitably took breast-feeding for granted, would not have found any erotic overtones in this tender vision of the collective nursing of the Christ-child.
91. cusse: kisse.   *to here semynge*: i.e. it seemed to her.   *sowkede*: sucked.
95. travayle: work, toil.
96. enclynynge: bowing.
97. wakynge: watching, keeping vigil.   *gostelye*: spiritual.
100. beleve: belief.
103. felynge: thinking.   *atteyne*: reach (a full understanding of).
104–5. so . . . myght: such lofty power.
105. schewyde: revealed.
108. vertewe: power.   *drowe*: drew, attracted.

sche sate att the toone syde of Oure Lorde. Oure Lorde than   110
threstede here sore to his herte with a lovyng beclippynge and
fulfyllede here soo plentevoslye with his grace that here
thought that ryvers rennynge flowede ande ranne fro all the
lymes off here bodye into all seyntys, that all thay were
fulfyllede with a newe gostelye joye ande gladnesse, ande   115
thaye helde thare owne hertis in here honddes, als thay hadde
been clere lyght lampys, whiche lampes were fulfyllede with
that nobyll gyfte whiche God hadde putte into that sowle off
the maydene, ande grette thankkynges thay yeldede to God
with grete gladnes ande merthe for the sowle of that maydene.   120
    Aftere that sche sawe in the herte of God als itt hadde bene
a full fayre maydene, havynge a rynge in here handde. In
whiche rynge was a stone whiche men calles an addamantid,
with the whiche stone sche towchede the herte of Oure Lorde
contynuelye withowten any styntynge. This mayde askede that   125
othere fayre maydene in here sowle why sche towchede soo
Owre Lordes herte?
    Sche aunswerde ande sayde, 'I am the devyne Love ande
this stone betokeneth the synne off Adam. Ande as the stone
that es callede ademaunde may nought be brostyn withowtene   130
blode, ryght soo Adam synne myght nought be unbownde
withowten the humanyte ande the blode of Criste. Anone als
Adam hadde synnede, I putte me within that devyne herte

---

110. toone: one.
111. threstede: thrust.   *sore*: forcefully.   *beclippynge*: embrace.
112–13. here thought: it seemed to her.
113–14. ryvers . . . seyntys: that Mechtild should see herself as a source of
sustenance to others is highly significant within the context of the medieval
female piety that stressed the holy woman as feeding others, or exuding
healing liquids; see Bynum 1987: 145–6.
113. rennynge: running.   *fro*: from.
114. lymes: limbs.
116. here honddes: their hands.   *als*: as if.
117. lyght: bright.
119. yeldede: yielded, rendered.
120. merthe: mirth, joy.
122. havynge . . . handde: the ring is very often a symbol of the mystical
marriage of the soul to the divine.
123. addamantid: loadstone, magnet; diamond.
125. styntynge: ceasing.
129. betokeneth: signifies.
130. ademaunde: adamant.   *brostyn*: split.
131. Adam: Adam's.   *unbownde*: absolved.
132. humanyte: i.e. the process of become human, the Incarnation.
    Anone als: as soon as.

ande undertoke for all that synne. Ande so I towchede the
herte off God withowten any cesynge and I suffrede hym   135
nought to reeste to I styrrede hym to pytee, tylle Y putte
Goddes sonne fro the herte of the Fadere in a momente into
the bosome, that es to saye into the wombe, of a maydene
whiche was than bothe modere ande maydene. Aftere that I
layde Goddes sonne in a crach ande wondyn he was in clothes   140
ande fro that tyme I ledde hym into Egipte ande eftere all this
I mayde hym to lowe hymselfe to alle creatures and to all
traveyls ande disese whiche he dyede ande suffrede for man,
into the tyme that Y turmentyde hym into the gybette of the
crosse, ande so I saghthylde the wreth of God the Fadere   145
ande cowplede man to God with a bande of love whiche maye
nowght be unbownden.'

[A half-page discussion of Christ's sufferings on the cross has been
omitted here.]

After thees wordes Love sayde agayne to this maydene: *Intra
in gaudium domini tui*, that es to saye, 'Entre into the joye of
thy lorde'; and with that sche was ravyschede all hoole into   150
God, thatte ryght als a droppe of watere, when itt es pourrede
into wyne, anone itt es chawngede alle into wyne, ryght so
whan the sowle off this blessede maydene passede into the
sowle off oure lorde God, itt was made al oone spyrite with
hym.   155

In this unyon the sawll was nootede in hereselfe, that es to
saye felte noght of hereselfe. Botte Oure Lorde comforthede
here ande sayde, 'I schall powre into the alle goodnes which
evere man maye receyve. Ande I schall multyplye my gyftes in
thee in as moche as itt es possibille any man to haffe.'   160

134. undertoke: took responsibility.
136. to(2): until.   *styrrede*: roused.   *putte*: pushed, expelled.
140. crach: manger.   *wondyn*: wound, swaddled.
142. lowe: humble.
143. traveyls: toils.   *disese*: discomfort.   *dyede*: did, performed.
144. into . . . that: until.   *gybette*: gibbet.
145. saghthylde: assuaged.   *wreth*: wrath.
146. cowplede: linked.   *bande*: bond.
148–9. Intra . . . tui: Matthew 25:21.
150. ravyschede: snatched up.   *all hoole*: completely.
151–2. ryght . . . wyne(2): a common simile used to elucidate the nature of
mystical union.
152. chawngede: changed.
156. nootede: annihilated; cf. Marguerite Porete's teaching, p.62 below.
157. felte . . . hereselfe: was not conscious of herself.

Than sayde Luffe agayne to this maydene, 'Here abyde
ande reste the in the herte of thy lovere, and be noght
unrestede in prosperyte. Here also abyde ande reste the in
remembrawnce of the benefettys of hym that thowe loveste
ande be nevere unrestede in adversytez.'   165

c) *The Spirit of a Dead Child Appears to Maud*
(f. 194^{r-v})

A matrone ande a worschepfull wyfe thare was of this
maydene knowelechynge, whiche wyfe was with childe ande
ordeynede that childe to halowe itt to God, so yif itt were a
dowghttere. When itt were borne sche purposede to wedde
here to Cryste. Botte withyn the secounde yere after the   170
berth the childe dyede. Ande the childe in spyritte apperede to
this holye maydene, in lykenesse of a full fayre maydene, fulle
honestelye cloythede with a cloyth of rede coloure ande abowve
that with a mantelle of golde, wonderefullye embrowdede with
whyte lylyes. Than sayde this maydene to this chylde, 'Howe   175
and for whate cawse came alle this joye ande blys to the?'
    The childe aunswerde ande sayde, 'Owre Lorde gaffe itt
me thorowe his benygnyte. This rede cloythynge betokene

163. *unrestede*: i.e. restless.
164. *benefettys*: benefits, blessings.
165. *adversytez*: adversities, tribulations.
166. *matrone*: married woman.   *worschepfull*: honourable.
167. *maydene knowelechynge*: maiden's acquaintance.
168. *ordeynede . . . itt*: decided to consecrate that child.   *so yif*: if.
171–5. *Ande . . . lylyes*: compare the appearance of the Pearl-maiden to her
bereaved father ('Pearl', ll. 161–240). In both texts, a child less than two
years old at the time of her death appears as a young woman.
173. *honestelye*: honourably.
174. *embrowdede*: embroidered.
175–81. *Than . . . lyffe*: Mechtild's dialogue with the maiden, and her
astonishment that, although she never lived to become a nun, she has been
rewarded in heaven as if she had, parallels the Pearl-narrator's
astonishment that his infant daughter has been so richly rewarded:

> Thou lyfed not two yer in oure thede [land];
> Thou cowthes never God nauther plese ne pray,
> Ne never nawther Pater ne Crede –
> And quen mad on the fyrst day!

('Pearl', ll. 483–6)

176. *cawse*: cause.   *blys*: glory.
178. *benygnyte*: kindness.

that of nature I was luffynge my God. The mantelle of golde
betokene the habyte of religion whiche he gaffe me for als   180
moche als my modere ordeynede me to lyffe a religious lyffe.'

This holye maydene wondrede gretelye of this ande while
sche wondrede Owre Lorde aunswerede to here thowghte
ande sayde, 'Why wonders thowe so of this? Be nowght yonge
chyldrene that bene baptizede savede thorowe othere mens   185
feyth? Ande als a modere, yiffe sche behete a gostelye vowe of
Crystiante for a childe, yif itt happe than that the childe dye,
yitt schalle the childe be saffede be the vowe. Ryghtte so in
thys case I take the hole wille of the modere for the dede, so
that alle the goodnessys in here desyre whiche sche willede to   190
here childe, I wille that thay be rewardede in the childe ande
that the childe haffe the meritte for the moderes wille.'

(Offe this ensaumple before, beware, that es to saye that a
childe be the moderes vowe of Cristiante schalle be savede,
thowe itt deye before, for clerkes holdene the contrarye   195
opynyon. For I trowe the furste wrytere mysunderestode.)

Botte fortheremore than this maydene askede Owre Lorde
ande sayde, 'Ande why, dere beluffede Lorde, haffes thowe
takene that childe so tymelye?' Owre Lorde sayde agayne,
'That childe was so amyable that itt was nowghte spedefulle   200

---

180. habyte of religion: religious dress.
180–1. for als moche: in that.
181. religious: i.e. as a nun
184–6. Be . . . feyth: essentially this is the theme of 'Pearl', expressed by the
reiterated line 'The innocent is ay saf by ryght' (l. 720 etc.).
186. als: (just) as.   *behete*: promises.
186–7. a . . . Crystiante: i.e. the baptismal vow.
188. saffede: saved. It was firmly believed in the Middle Ages that
unbaptised infants were damned.
188. be(2): by.
189. hole: whole, complete.   *dede*: deed, action.
190. to: for.
193–6. Offe . . . mysunderestode: this is the translator's own comment and is
not found in the Latin; possibly he thought Mechtild meant that a child
who died without baptism might be saved if the mother had herself
mentally made the baptismal vows on the child's behalf.
193. ensaumple: exemplum, illustrative story.
195. before: i.e. before baptism.   *clerkes*: clerics, theologians.
196. trowe: think.
      furste: i.e. original; the translator implicitly regards himself as the
'second writer'.
198. beluffede: beloved.
199. tymelye: early.
200. amyable: lovable, attractive.   *spedefulle*: beneficial.

for here to lyve in the worlde. Ande moreovere here fadere
wolde haffe adnullede here moders vowe ande wolde haffe
kepte here stylle in the werlde.'

Textual notes

14. childre] childree.
34. here handes] here a handes.
92. to hym] to.
111. lovyng] lovynglye.
167. knowelechynge] knowlechynne.

202. adnullede: revoked.
203. stylle: continually.

4 Marguerite Porete

Marguerite Porete was a late thirteenth-century béguine from Hainault in Flanders (béguines were laywomen vowed to chastity who were self-supporting and led a disciplined life, either at home, in convents or in béguinages, i.e. settlements or special areas within a town). Some time between 1296 and 1306 she wrote a lengthy and obscure mystical treatise in Old French, *Le Mirouer des Simples Ames*, a dialogue between Lady Love, Lady Reason and the Free Soul, which was condemned by the local bishop as heretical and publicly burnt. The bishop considered that Marguerite's book was associated with the heresy of the Free Spirit, a loosely organised Continental movement whose adherents (many of them women) taught that Free Spirits, i.e. advanced and favoured souls whose wills were united with the Divine, no longer needed to observe the moral law or avail themselves of the Church and the sacraments (see Lerner 1972). In spite of this condemnation, Marguerite Porete continued to circulate copies of *Le Mirouer* and seek approval from theologians of its orthodoxy. She was therefore arrested by the Inquisition, brought to Paris and imprisoned. In 1309 fifteen suspect articles extracted from *Le Mirouer* were examined and condemned by twenty-one prominent Paris theologians. In 1310 she was condemned by the Inquisition as a relapsed heretic and burnt at the stake, having refused to speak in her own defence (see Verdeyen 1986: 47–94).

Of the French original only one late and somewhat corrupt manuscript survives, from the late fifteenth or early sixteenth century. Four manuscripts, three from the fourteenth century, survive of the Latin translation, which may have been made by the Inquisition as part of their investigation, and translations were made into Italian as well as into Middle English. None of the surviving manuscripts of the original or of the translations identifies the author or indicates that the text had been condemned as heretical. It was not until 1965 that an Italian scholar, R. Guarnieri, linked the historical Marguerite Porete, of whose trial and condemnation there are full historical records which do not, however, name her heretical book, with the French, Latin and English versions of *Le Mirouer*. Since then there has been much discussion of whether Porete was indeed a heretic, and much favourable comment on the literary value of her writings, which combine the conventions and language of courtly love with a passionate and exalted mysticism (see Dronke 1984: 217–28).

The Mirror of Simple Souls is a late fourteenth- or fifteenth-century Middle English translation of *Le Mirouer*, probably made by a Carthusian, a member of a strict and austere contemplative order of monks who led the lives of hermits within their monasteries. We do not know his name, only his initials, 'M.N.', with which he signed various editorial comments inserted to explain passages in his translation that he feared might be misunderstood. He tells us that his original version had indeed been poorly received and misinterpreted.

Although the Carthusians avoided all contact with women, they took a great interest in women's mystical texts and we owe to them the preservation of both the Short Version of Julian of Norwich's *A Revelation of*

Love and *The Book of Margery Kempe*. But it is interesting that this translator clearly had no suspicion that his original was composed by a woman who had been condemned as a heretic (see Colledge and Guarnieri 1968). In medieval England, therefore, *The Mirror of Simple Souls* was not perceived as a woman's text, but this very fact is significant for it indicates the difficulty of assigning gender to texts in the absence of external evidence.

Comment: Generally, *The Mirror of Simple Souls* is a difficult and challenging text; as the translator puts it, it is written 'full mistily'. His translation is literal and consequently does not always make obvious sense, nor does it read elegantly; it also contains a number of mistranslations which may be due as much to the corruption of the original as to the translator's shortcomings. And his own translation is further corrupted in the three surviving manuscripts. (Most notably, they all have the garbled phrase 'Far night' for what must have been the translator's original rendering of Marguerite's term for God, OF *loing-pres*, as 'Far-nigh'.) But fortunately these factors still cannot obscure the intellectual daring, spiritual passion and profound originality of Marguerite Porete.

The dialogue form is not in itself unusual in visionary and mystical writings, which often consist largely of exchanges between the visionary and God or the Virgin (cf. *The Revelations of St Elizabeth*, pp. 72–5). In medieval didactic literature, from Boethius's *Consolation of Philosophy* to Christine de Pisan's *Book of the City of Ladies*, dialogues between the narrator and various abstract personifications are also common. But Marguerite's use of the form, with its three female protagonists, is distinctive. Reason when personified in medieval literature is invariably female because L. *ratio* and OF *raison* are grammatically feminine nouns. 'Lady Reason' is usually a direct descendant of Boethius's Lady Philosophy; she is prominent in the great thirteenth-century French allegorical dream poem *Le Roman de la Rose*, and also appears in Christine's *Book of the City of Ladies* (see Introduction, pp. 10–11). But Marguerite's Lady Reason is very different: she is seen as earth-bound and must die before the soul can progress. The figure of Lady Love is also unusual. L. *amor* is masculine, though its OF derivative is usually a feminine noun and Love is more usually personified as a male figure, especially as the God of Love, in medieval literature. However, Marguerite's near-contemporary, Mechtild of Hackeborn, also personifies Divine Love as a female figure (see p. 51). Finally, the soul too, as always in Christian tradition, is female.

The first passage, from the dialogue between Lady Love and Lady Reason, comes from the early part of the text and contains those daringly paradoxical and extravagant statements about the freedom of the 'free', 'surmounted' (i.e. sublime) soul which led ultimately to Porete's condemnation. The second passage comes from very near the end of the book, after the death of the invincibly ignorant and incorrigible Lady Reason, and records a crucial but agonising stage in the soul's progress towards perfection and complete union with the Divine, when she is faced with the need completely to annihilate her own will in order to mature spiritually and finally enter the Country of Freedom. The extreme passivity which this requires, though cultivated by male as well as female mystics, can be seen in part as a logical extension of the role forced on women in the Middle Ages (see Introduction, p. 10).

Manuscript: Oxford MS Bodley 505 (modernised version by Kirchberger, 1927). There are two other manuscripts of the Middle English: BL Add. MS 37790, which also contains the only copy of the Short (Carthusian) Version of *A Revelation of Love* of Julian of Norwich, and Cambridge St John's College MS 71 (edited from this manuscript by Doiron, 1968). Although the dialects are different, the texts are otherwise very close. This suggests that they were copied under strict supervision and that the scribes were instructed not to stray from their copy text. They might well otherwise have been tempted to do so, as the text is often awkwardly worded as well as corrupt. The manuscripts all belonged to Carthusian monasteries or individual Carthusian monks and there is no evidence of circulation outside that somewhat restricted and specialised environment.

Further reading (for full details see Bibliography): On the heresy of the Free Spirit, see Lerner 1972. On Marguerite herself, see Dronke 1984: 217–28; Wilson 1984: 204–26; Petroff 1986: 280–3 (both the latter with bibliographies).

From *The Mirror of Simple Souls*

a) *A Dialogue between Love and Reason*
(Oxford MS Bodley 505, ff. 112ᵛ–114ᵛ)

'A, Love,' seith Reson, 'ye doon oure preier for the actyves
and the contemplatyves. Now I praie you to declare and
expowne to the comune peple these double wordes, that bien
hard to undirstonde to her undirstandyng, that summe bi
aventure may come to this beyng, bi whiche this booke may   5
shewe to alle the verrai light of trouthe and the perfeccioun of
charite of hem that preciousli bien clepid and chosen of God
and soveranli be loved of hym.'

1–2. *ye ... contemplatyves*: you are carrying out our request as to the 'actives' and 'contemplatives'; Love addresses herself in three different ways to three groups – the actives, contemplatives and the common people. Actives are those still actively purging themselves of sin; contemplatives those who have progressed to contemplation of and union with God; the common people the general run of humanity.
3. *expowne*: expound, explain.   *double*: i.e. equivocal, ambiguous.
3. *bien*: be, are.
4. *her*: their.
4–5. *bi aventure*: perhaps.
5. *beyng*: (state of) being of having a 'noughted' (annihilated) will through a complete union of the will with God's.
6. *verrai*: true.
7. *clepid*: called.
8. *soveranli*: supremely.

'Reson,' seith Love, 'to this I wole answere, for the profite
of hem for whom thou makest to us this pitous requeste.   10
Reson,' seith Love, 'where bien these double wordis that thou
preiest me to discusse for the auditours of this booke, that in
wille and in desire dwel, the which book we clepe "The
Mirrour of Symple Soules"?'

'To this I answere, Ladi Love,' seith Reson, 'for this booke   15
seith greete mervailes of this soule, that seith she ne reckith of
shaame ne of worship, ne of povert ne of riches, ne of ease ne
of diseese, ne of love ne of hate, ne of helle ne of paradise.
And also it seith that this soule hath al and she hath nought,
she woteth al and she woteth nought, she willeth al and she   20
willeth nought.'

'Ne she desireth,' seith Reson, 'dispite ne povert ne no
martirdom ne tribulacion ne sermons ne fastynges ne
oreisons. And she giveth to nature al his askynges, withoute
grucchyng of conscience. Withoute faile, Love,' seith Reson,   25
'this may noon undirstonde be myn undirstondyng but if thei
lierne it of you bi youre techyng. For my counsail is, for the
beste that I kan counsaile, that men desire dispite and povert
and al maner of tribulacion, massis, sermons, fastynges and
oreisons, and that men have drede of al maner of loves,   30

10. *hem*: them.   *pitous*: compassionate.
12. *discusse*: define.
        auditours: hearers; books were frequently read aloud to groups in the
Middle Ages, rather than silently studied by individuals.
16. *mervailes*: extraordinary things. Many of the paradoxical statements
which Reason asks Love to clarify are precisely those heretical positions for
which Porete was condemned and executed.
16. *ne reckith*: does not care.
17. *worship*: honour.   *povert*: poverty.
20. *woteth*: knows.
22. *dispite*: contemptuous treatment.
23. *fastynges*: fasting.
24. *oreisons*: (vocal) prayers.
        giveth . . . askynges: grants Nature all his demands (Nature is more
usually personified as female in medieval literature and the choice of
gender here is the translator's, not Porete's). This statement was extracted
and presented to the Inquisition and it was particularly this apparent
antinomianism (the belief that there is no need to observe a moral law)
which undid Porete.
25. *grucchyng*: demur.
26. *be*: by.   *but if*: unless.
27. *counsail*: advice.
28. *kan*: know how to.   *men*: people (F. *on*).
29. *massis*: Masses.
30. *have drede*: should be wary of.

whatever thei be, for perels that might falle, and that men
desire paradise soveranli; and also that men have drede to go
to helle and that thei refuse al maner of wurshippes and
temporel thinges and al eases, in bynemyng nature al that he
askith but oonli that withouten whiche thei myte not lyve, aftir   35
the ensample of suffraunce that Oure Lord Jhesu Crist
suffrid. This is the best that I kan counsaile,' seith Reson, 'to
alle thoo that lyven undir myn obedience. And therfor I seie
that noon shal undirstande this booke be myn undirstondyng
but if thei undirstonde it bi the vertu of Feith and bi the   40
strengthe of Love that ben my mastressis, for I obeie to hem
in al. And yit,' seith Reson, 'thus myche I seie, that who hath
these two cordis in his herte, the light of Feith and the
strengthe of Love, he hath leeve to doo what him likith,
witnesse of God hymsilf that seith to the soule, "Love, loveth   45
and doo what ye wole." '

'Reson,' seith Love, 'thou art ful wise of al thing that
aperteyneth to thee, that woldest have answers to these wordis
aforseide, and that thou askist what it is to seie; it is wele
yasked. And I wole,' seith Love, 'answer thee to alle thine   50
askynges. Reson,' seith Love, 'I certifie thee that these soules
that Fyne Love ledith, thei have as lief schame as worship and
worship as shame, and povert as richesse and richesse as

31. *falle*: happen.
32. *desire*: should desire.
33. *wurshippes*: honours.
34. *temporel*: worldly.   *eases*: comforts, luxuries.   *bynemyng*: depriving.
    he: again, the choice of gender is the translator's (F. *elle*).
35. *but oonli*: except only.   *myte*: could.
36. *ensample*: example.   *suffraunce*: suffering, endurance.
37–8. *This . . . obedience*: Reason's teaching is of course the orthodox
teaching of the Church on self-denial as a means of salvation.
38. *thoo*: those.
39. *be*: in accord with.
41. *mastressis*: mistresses; Reason admits that she is subordinate to Faith
and Love.
42. *myche*: much.   *who*: whoever.
43. *cordis*: strings.   *herte*: a mistranslation of F. *arc* (bow).
44. *leeve*: permission.   *what . . . likith*: whatever pleases him.
45–6. *Love . . . wole*: 'Beloved, love and do what you like', a famous
sententia (saying) from the *Confessions* of St Augustine (*PL* 35: 2033).
48. *aperteyneth*: relates.
49. *what . . . seie*: a literal translation of F. *que c'est à dire* (what it means).
50. *yasked*: asked.
51. *certifie*: inform.
52. *Fyne Love*: pure or refined love, F. *Fine Amour* ('courtly love').
    ledith: leads, conducts.   *lief*: willingly, gladly.

povert, and tormentis of God and of his creatures as
comfortes of God and of his creatures, and to be hated as   55
loved and loved as hated, and helle as paradise and paradise
as helle, and litel estate as grete and grete estate as litel. This
is to seie in sooth that thei ne willen ne unwillen none of these
prosperitees ne noone of these adversites, for these soules
have no wille but thing that God willith in hem, and the divine   60
wille clepith not these surmounted creatures with suche
encombraunces as we have heere devysed. I have,' seith Love,
'afore saide that these soules have as lief alle maner of
adversites of hert, for body and for soule, as prosperites, and
prosperitees as adversitees. This is sooth,' seith Love, 'if it   65
come to hem, sithen her wil is not the cause. The soules wote
not where that the ende lieth, ne for what cause God wole
fynde her savacioun ne the savacion of her evencristen, ne for
what encheson God wole do rightwisnesse or mercy, ne for
what cause God wole yeve to the soule the surmounted yiftis   70
of the goodenesse of his divine noblesse; and for this skile the
fre soule hath no wille to wille ne unwille, but oonli to wille
the wille of God and suffre in pees his divine ordynaunce.'

   'Yet, Love,' seith Reson, 'I am at my demaunde, for this
booke seith that this soule hath al, and sche hath nought.'   75

   'It is sooth,' seith Love, 'for this soule hath God in hir bi
divine grace, and who hath God hath al. And it seith that she

54. *tormentis of God*: tortures from God.
57. *estate*: status, position.
61. *clepith*: calls, summons, but a mistranslation of F. *n'ocuppe* (burdens):
the ME may have originally read *cloggith* or *chargith*.
   surmounted: sublime, elevated.
62. *encombraunces*: encumbrances, hindrances (such as fasting, tribulation,
etc.).
62. *devysed*: described.
66. *come*: happen.   *sithen*: since.
   her ... cause: i.e. they do not actively will it.
67. *where ... lieth*: a mistranslation; the F. here means 'which is better for
them'.
68. *fynde*: provide.   *savacioun*: salvation.   *evencristen*: fellow Christian.
69. *encheson*: reason.   *rightwisnesse*: justice.
70. *yeve*: give.   *yiftis*: gifts.
71. *noblesse*: nobility.   *skile*: reason.
72. *fre soule*: F. *Ame Enfranchie* (liberated soul), a key phrase, dangerously
reminiscent of the 'free spirit' of the heretics.
73. *pees*: peace.   *ordynaunce*: decree.
74. *I ... demaunde*: i.e. I am still asking, but again the phrase is a
mistranslation; the F. means 'I add one thing more to my request'.
74–5. *this booke*: i.e. the *Mirror*.

hath nought, for al that this soule hath of God in hir bi yifte of
divine grace, it semeth hir nought, ne no more it is as in
regarde of that that sche loveth, that is in him whiche he   80
yeveth to noon but to hym. And bi this undirstandyng, this
soule hath al and sche hath nought, sche wote al and sche
wote nought.'

b) *The Simple Soul Abandons Herself to the Will of God* (ff. 212–14ᵛ)

And thanne I seid thus, that if it myght be that I hadde never
be, be so that I had nevere mysdon ayentis his wille: if it   85
plesid him, it were my plesaunce.

And thanne I seid to him, that if it myght be that he wolde
yive me as grete tormentis as he is myghtful, forto avengen
him of my defautis: if it plesid him, it were my plesaunce.

And thanne aftir I seid thus to hym, that if it myght be so   90
that I were right as he is, and shulde be withouten failaunce,
and with this I shulde suffre as moche of povert and of
dispites and tormentis as he hath of bounte, of wisdom and of
myght, be so I had nevere don ayens his wille: if it were his
plesyng, it were my plesaunce.   95

And thanne I seid to him, that if it myght be that I went to
nought right as I cam of nought, forto avenge him of me: if it
plesid him, it were my plesaunce.

And thanne I seide this to him, that if it myght be that I had
of me as moche of worthinesse as he hath of himsilf, so that it   100
myght nat be binome me ne amynused, but if I aloone wolde
it mysilf; I shulde leie al this in him and go to nought, or than

---

80. *regarde*: respect.   *that that*: that which.
84–5. *if . . . be*(1): if it were possible that I should have never existed.
85. *be so that*: as long as.   *mysdon . . . wille*: acted against (God's) will.
86. *him*: i.e. God.   *were*: would be.   *plesaunce*: pleasure.
88. *as*(1) . . . *myghtful*: torments as great as he is powerful.
88–9. *forto . . . defautis*: to take vengeance on my sins.
91. *right . . . is*: exactly as he is.
     shulde . . . failaunce: would be so (in the future), without fail.
92. *with*: i.e. together with.
93. *dispites*: scorns.   *bounte*: goodness.
96–7. *went to nought*: should return to nothingness.
97. *forto . . . me*: so that he could wreak his vengeance on me.
100. *of me*: from myself, in my own right.   *worthinesse*: worth.
101. *binome*: taken away from.   *amynused*: diminished.   *but if*: unless.
102. *leie. . . him*: return this all to him.   *or than*: before.

I might enything withholde that cam not to me from him. And
though it myght be that I mighte have al this biforeseide, I
myght not do it, to holde enything that cam me not from him.   105
    And than I seide this, that if I hadde of my propir condicion
this foreseid, I shulde love bettir and rather chese that it went
to nought withouten recoveryng, than I shulde have it but if it
came of hym. And if I hadde as grete tormentis as he is of
myght, I shulde love bettir these tormentis, if it cam of hym,   110
than I should the glorie that cam not of him, to have it
everlastyngli.
    And thanne I seide to him, rather than I shuld hennes-
forward do thing that were ayens his plesyng, it were more in
my choyse that his manhode suffridde on the crosse as moche   115
as he hath suffred of tormentis for me, if it myght be, I seie,
for this, rather thanne I shuld do thing that were his
displesaunce.
    And thanne I seid him, that if I wist and were thus, that al
that he hath made of nought (I and al othir thing, this is to   120
undirstande) must go to nought but if I mysdide ayens his
wille, it shulde go, to my choys, rathir thanne I mysdide.
    And thanne I seide him, that if I wist that I shuld have as
moche of torment withouten ende as he hath of goodenesse,
but if I mysdede ayens his wille, I shuld chese rather to go   125
suffre tho peynes everlastyngli than I shuld do thing that I wist
shuld displese his wille.
    And thanne this I seide him, that if it myght be that he
myght and wold yive me bi his wille as moche of goodenesse
as he hath of worth everlastyngli, I shuld not love it but for   130
him, and if I loste it I shuld not recke therof but for him; and
if he yildide it me ayen aftir this losse, I shuld not take it but
for him; and if it myght be that it myght betre plese him that I

---

103. withholde: keep.
105. holde: retain.
106. of . . . condicion: as part of my intrinsic nature.
107. rather: sooner.   *chese*: choose.
108. withouten recoveryng: irrecoverably.
109. of hym: from him (i.e. not from herself).
113–14. hennesforward: henceforward, from now on.
114–15. it . . . choyse: I would rather choose.
115. manhode: human nature.
118. displesaunce: displeasure.
119. if . . . thus: if I knew it and it were the case.
126. tho: those.
131. recke therof: care about it.
132. yildide: gave back.

went to nought and had not of beyng than that I shulde take
this yift of him, I shuld love more that I went to nought. And 135
if it myght be that I hadde the same that he hath in him, as
wele as he hath of him, with this that it shuld nevere faile if I
wolde, and I wiste that it myght bettir plese him that I suffride
as moche torment of him as he hath of goodenesse in him; I
shulde love it bettre than forto dwelle in that glorie. 140

And though I wiste that it might be that the swete manhede
of Crist Jhesu and the Virgyne and al the court of hevene
might not suffre that I had the tormentis everlastyngli, but that
I had the beyng that I was come fro, and God seeth this in
hem, if it might be, this pite of hem and this goode wille, thus 145
seith to me, 'If thou wilt, I shal yilde thee that whiche thou art
comen fro bi my wil, for this that my friendis of my court
wolen it; but ne were her wille, thou shuldest not have it.
Wherfore I yilde thee this yifte if thou wolt take it,' it shulde
falle in my choys rather withouten ende to dwelle in torment 150
than I shuld take it, siththe I had it nat of his oonli wille, so I
refusid it at the praiers of the humanite and of seintes and of
the Virgyne Marie. I might not suffre it but if I had it of the
pure love that he hath to me for me, of his pure bounte and of
his alloone wille and love that Loved hath to Lover. 155

And thanne I seide to him that if I wiste it mighte more
plese him that I loved another more than him: heere me failith
wit; thus it goith, that I ne feele myght ne wille to graunte, but
I aunswerd that I shulde counsaile me.

And thanne I seide this, that if it might be that he might 160
love another more than me: heere me failith wit. I kan not
aunswer ne wille ne graunte.

134. *had ... beyng*: had no existence.
137. *with this*: together with this (condition).
138. *wolde*: willed.
143. *suffre*: bear.
143-4. *but ... fro*: but (wished) that I should enjoy the existence I had had
previously.
145. *hem*: them, i.e. the Virgin, Christ and the court of heaven.
148. *ne ... wille*: if it were not for their wish.
149-50. *it(2) ... choys*: I would choose.
151. *siththe*: since.   *nat ... wille*: not from His will alone.
     so: as long as.
152. *humanite*: i.e. the Incarnate Christ.
155. *love ... Lover*: the love that the Beloved has for the Lover.
157-8. *heere ... wit*: here reason fails me, i.e. this is unthinkable.
158. *goith*: happens, transpires.
     ne(1) ... graunte: could not think or desire to grant (it).
159. *counsaile me*: think about it.

And than this I seide to him, that if it might be that he
might wille that anothir loved me more than he loveth me,
here me faileth also witte. I kan not answere no more than   165
afore, but alwei I seide that of al that I shuld counsaile me;
and right so I dide. I counsailed me at himsilf and seide him
that these thre thinges weren right harde forbi the tothir
weren bifore: that I shulde love anothir more thanne him, and
he another more thane me, and that another shuld love me   170
more than he. Witt failid me heere, for I might not to noon of
these thre thinges wille ne graunte, and alwei he assailed me
forto have aunswere. And so moche I loved me with him that I
might not for nothing have maner in this, and thus I was at
distresse, so went I not lightli awei. This wote noon but if he   175
have assaied this poynt and alweies I might have noo pees, but
if I aunswerd to this forsaide.

A, I loved me, this hadde me. Therfor I might not lightli
aunswer and if I hadde not loved me, the aunswer hadde be
swift and light and alweies me bihovide to aunswere, if I   180
wolde not leese of me in him, for whiche myn hert suffrid so
greete distresse.

Textual notes

2. contemplatyves] comtemplatyves.
117. shuld] shud.
145. hem] him.

167. I . . . himsilf: I took advice from him.
168. right harde: really difficult.
168–9. forbi . . . bifore: in comparison with the other (demands) that were
made before.
172. assailed: challenged.
173. so . . . him: I loved myself so much together with him.
173–4. I(2) . . . maner: a literal translation of F. *je ne povoye . . . ne avoir en
moy maniere* (I could not have any moderation in myself).
174. at: in.
175. went . . . awei: I did not get away easily.   *noon*: no one.
176. assaied . . . poynt: tested, experienced, this degree.
178. A . . . me(2): Ah, I loved myself and this love of self possessed me; the
L. here reads *Diligebam me et habebam me* ('I loved myself and had myself'),
while the F. reads *Je me amoye tant avec luy* ('I loved myself so much along
with him').
178. lightli: easily.
180. light: easy.   *me bihovide*: it was incumbent upon me.
180–1. if . . . him: if I was not to lose myself in him; but again, this is a
mistranslation of the F. which means 'if I did not wish to lose both him and
myself'.

5 Elizabeth of Hungary

Two Middle English translations of *The Revelations of Saint Elizabeth* are extant. One (like most of the manuscripts of the Latin) attributes the original to the Elizabeth of Hungary who died in 1231, i.e. to Elizabeth of Thuringia (b. 1207). Elizabeth, who was the widow of the Count of Thuringia and the mother of his three children, was devoted to poverty and to the care of the sick. She never became a nun but was a Franciscan tertiary (i.e. a member of the Third Order of St Francis, lay people who led a disciplined and dedicated life in the world), and there is no authentic early tradition that she was a visionary. Although St Elizabeth of Schönau, a twelfth-century German Benedictine nun and mystic, has been suggested as a more likely candidate for the authorship of the *Revelations* (Oliger 1926: 44–50), a better case can be made for Elizabeth of Toess (*c.* 1294–1336), the great-niece of Elizabeth of Thuringia and also, like her, daughter of a king of Hungary. This Elizabeth was a Dominican nun in the Swiss convent of Toess whose life, together with those of her sisters in religion, was written in Middle High German by Elsbeth Stagel, the close friend and spiritual daughter of the great Rhineland mystic Henry Suso.

As an account of her spiritual experiences, the *Revelations* must have originated with Elizabeth. But she apparently communicated them orally to another person, presumably a fellow nun (probably Elsbeth Stagel), who was responsible for the literary form of the work. The Middle English versions were translated from a Latin text, but the original text of the *Revelations* may not have been in that language. There are two, rather different, Latin versions extant and both may be translations from a now vanished original, possibly composed in Middle High German (see Barratt 1992). In the Middle Ages the *Revelations* also circulated in Italian, French, Spanish and Catalan translations.

The Book of Margery Kempe almost certainly refers to this text when it speaks of 'Saint Elizabeth in her treatise', whose tears were like Margery's. There are many references in the *Revelations* to Elizabeth's noisy and boisterous weeping and other points of contact make it clear that either Margery herself or her scribe knew this text well, in a Latin or Middle English version (see Ellis 1990: 164–8).

Comment: As nine out of the thirteen individual visions consist of dialogues with the Virgin, she is a central figure in Elizabeth's *Revelations*. Generally she both models and validates the visionary's own ecstatic, affective (i.e. emotional) and unrestrained spirituality. In the first passage, which opens the *Revelations*, the Virgin is also presented as a multivalent figure of supreme power: as 'lady' with all its feudal overtones, as mother and as 'maystresse'. (L. *magistra*, like 'mistress', can specifically mean 'teacher' as well as, more generally, 'woman in a position of authority'.) Elizabeth swears allegiance to her with the traditional gesture of feudal submission which establishes a contractual relationship between them. The written charter, which the notably silent St John the Evangelist is later commanded to provide, acts merely as a record. The second extract provides an unusual

71

treatment of the popular Annunciation motif (cf. Eleanor Hull, pp. 227–31 below). The Virgin does not merely react to a completely unexpected announcement from Gabriel but actively cooperates with the divine plan from an early stage. Her life in the Temple also parallels the life of medieval nuns like the visionary: the Virgin studies the law and the prophets, takes a vow of virginity and, once she has been informed that she will become the Mother of God, prepares by praying for the traditional Gifts of the Spirit. Her own original ambition to see and to serve the Virgin prophesied by Isaiah also foreshadows a desire common among women visionaries; compare Margery Kempe and her visions of caring for St Anne and the Virgin (pp. 186–8 below).

Manuscript and copy text: The first passage comes from CUL MS Hh. 1. 11, ff. 122–7, early or mid fifteenth century, which contains the only copy of this version; it is unpublished. The manuscript seems to have belonged to a convent of nuns, possibly the Franciscans at Bruisyard in Suffolk, and some of its many scribes may be nuns. The second passage comes from the early printed version, *The Revelacions of Saynt Elysabeth the kynges doughter of hungarye*, in *Lyf of Saint Katherin of Senis* printed by Wynkyn de Worde (1492?, *STC* 24766, ff.91ʳ–6). De Worde reprinted his version, with a few minor changes, *c.* 1500 (*STC* 24766.3).

Both versions have become somewhat corrupt in transmission. The extracts printed here have been collated with the Latin version in Magdalene College Cambridge MS F. 4. 14, and sometimes corrected where the translator's original reading is obvious.

Further reading (for full details see Bibliography): On the text and authorship of the *Revelations*, see Oliger 1926 (this article is written in Latin) and Barratt 1992; on Elizabeth of Toess, see Ancelet-Hustache 1928 and Riehle 1981: 31; on the text's spirituality, see Barratt (forthcoming); on the connections with Margery Kempe, see Ellis 1990.

From *The Revelations of Saint Elizabeth*

a) *Elizabeth Enters the Service of the Virgin Mary* (CUL MS Hh. 1. 11, f. 122ʳ⁻ᵛ)

On a day as Seynt Elyzabeth, beynge in devowt preyowr, wyt a dewouth mende and anoied spirite sought here spouse Jhesu Cryst and myte not fyndyn hym as sche was wont forto do,

---

1. *beynge . . . preyowr*: being in devout prayer.
2. *dewouth*: devout.   *mende*: (state of) mind.   *anoied*: troubled, anxious.
   here: her.
3. *myte*: might.   *wont*: accustomed.

sche began forto thenk and styr in here sowle qwat schulde be
the cause that here spouse visited here nawt be insendynge of 5
swete comfortes as he was wonht to done. And as sche
dysposyd hyr in here prevy thowt forto gon to sum gostely
brothyr forto have cunseyl of thys thynge, Owre Lady Seynte
Marye apperede to here and seyde, 'Elizabeth, yyf thou wyth
be my disceple, I schal be thy maystresse and yyf thow wyth 10
be myn handmaydyn, I schal be thy lady.' To qwom sche
sayde, 'What be ye, lady, that woldyn han me to yow discyple
and andmaydyn?' And Owr Lady answerde, 'I am the modyr
of Goddys sone lyvyng, swych thou ast chosyn to thy lord and
to thy spouse.' And sche seyde everemor, 'Ther ys no brother 15
in thys word that of thy spouse kan betere enforme the than I.'
Thanne Seynt Elyzabeth, fallynge doun to the erthe,
worschepyd here and stondynge vp ayen, bowhede here knes
and puth here hondys joynede to the hondys of Owre Lady.
And Owre Lady eft seyde to here, 'Yyf thou wyth be my 20
dowtyr, my discyple and myn handmaydyn, I schal be thy
modyr, thy lady and thy maystresse. And qwanne thou art
suffysly tawt and reformyd of me, I schal brynge the to my
sone thy spouse, the qwech schal resseyve the into ys hondys,
as I ave take the now.' And thanne sche began to amoneste 25

4. *thenk . . . sowle*: think and consider in her soul. *qwat*: what.
5. *nawt*: not. *insendynge*: infusion (L. *inmissione*).
6. *wonth*: wont, accustomed.
7. *prevy*: privy, secret. *thowt*: thought, heart.
7–8. *gostely brothyr*: spiritual brother, i.e. friar.
8. *cunseyl*: counsel, advice.
9. *wyth*: wilt.
10. *disceple*: disciple, follower. *maystresse*: mistress, teacher.
11. *qwom*: whom.
12. *woldyn*: would, wish. *han*: have. *to yow*: i.e. as your.
13. *andmaydyn*: handmaiden, servant.
14. *swych*: such, i.e. whom. *ast*: hast.
15. *everemor*: in addition.
16. *word*: world. *kan . . . the*: knows how to instruct you better.
18. *worschepyd*: worshipped, honoured.
   bowhede . . . knes: bowed, bent her knees.
19. *puth*: put, placed. *hondys joynede*: joined hands. *to*: into.
20. *eft*: after.
21. *dowtyr*: daughter.
22. *qwanne*: when.
23. *suffysly*: sufficiently. *tawt*: taught, instructed.
   reformyd: re-formed. *of*: by.
24. *qwech*: which. *resseyve*: receive. *ys*: his.
25. *ave take*: have taken. *amoneste*: admonish.

here, seyinge, 'Flee debatys and stryvis and bakbytyngys and
gruchyngys, and to gruchynge made of the, yyf thou nowt thyn
ere ne thyn herte. Be not turmentyd for hem and thynke that
so manye evylle may be not seyd of the, that ne yyt ther ys
mykyl more in the than may be seyd.'   30
Another tyme aftyr the Feste of Owr Lady, qwan the
handmaydyn of Cryst, Elizabeth, was in preowr and wepte
byttyrly, she dreddit that sche adde not fulleke kept the
forseyde observaunce of the Virgyne; sodeynleche apperede to
here, nowt in slep buth wakynge, the blessyd Virgine, wyt   35
swete speche clepynge here be hyr name, and seyde,
'Elizabeth my swete dowttyr, tormente the nowt so mykyl for
thou ast nawt alle fully don my bedyngys and my comowndementys. For why thou begynnyst now to go perfectly in the
weye of Gode. Buth thow ast nowt yyt atteyned to the hyghnes   40
of perfeccyown. Buth fyth stable ayen vicys and sey oones the
gretynge of the awngyl with the wech Gabriel, Goddys

26. *debatys*: arguments.   *stryvis*: strife, argument.
    bakbytyngys: backbiting, slanders.
27. *gruchyngys*: grudging, complaining.   *of the*: about you.   *yyf*: give.
28. *ere*: ear.   *turmentyd*: tormented, distressed.
29. *evylle*: evil (things).   *that ne yyt*: but that still.
30. *mykyl*: much.   *more*: i.e. more evil.   *seyd*: said.
31. *qwan*: when.
33. *dreddit*: dreaded, feared.   *adde*: hadde.   *fulleke*: fully.
34. *forseyde observaunce*: aforesaid practice.   *sodeynleche*: suddenly.
35. *nowt ... wakynge*: not in sleep but waking, i.e. this was a corporeal
vision, not a dream; this text is quite specific about the various types of
vision Elizabeth experiences.
35. *wyt*: with.
36. *clepynge*: calling.
37. *dowttyr*: daughter.
38. *alle fully*: i.e. completely.   *bedyngys*: biddings.
38–9. *comowndementys*: commandments.
39–41. *For ....perfeccyown*: the *Revelations* are insistent that spiritual
perfection can be achieved only gradually, with God's grace and the
subject's earnest cooperation, and that sin cannot be totally eliminated.
39. *For why*: for.   *go*: walk.
40. *Buth*: but.   *yyt*: yet.   *atteyned*: attained, reached.
    hyghnes: height, peak.
41. *perfeccyown*: perfection.
    fyth: fight: the MS here reads 'felth' and has been emended to bring it
closer to the L. reading *dimica*, 'fight'.
41. *stable*: constantly.   *vicys*: vices.   *oones*: once.
42–3. *gretynge .... me*: i.e. the Hail Mary.
42. *gretynge*: greeting, salutation.   *awngyl*: angel.   *wech*: which.

messager, grette me, and alle thy trespasyn schal be frely
foryevyn to the of my sone.'

Afftyr thys in the day of Seynte Scolast, Crystys handmaydyn   45
Elizabeth was in preyer and preyende sche wepte wondyr
bytterly so that sche myte nawt wytholdyn here from
owtwardys sobbynge and clamor of voys. Sodanly thanne the
Blessyd Virgine Marye apperede to here, havynge wyt here
Seyn Jon the wangelyst, and seyde, 'Elyzabeth, thou ast chose   50
me to thy modyr, thy lady and thy maystresse, buth o thys
chesynge and o thys wylfully be-etynge I wele that thou make
me a chartere so that thou may not goo abak fro thy purpos.
Werfore I ave browt wyt me the belovyd discyple of my sone,
Jon the wangelyst, that yyf thou consent he may make an opyn   55
wytenessynge.'

Thanne blessyd Elizabeth fel down on here kneys, and
handes joyned, on the erthe and worchypt here and seyde, 'Of
me, my lady, as of yowr andmaydyn, dooth qwat ye wyln.' And
thys yevynge sche confyrmede wyt an hoot and Seynt Jon the   60
wangelyste at the comowndement of the blessyd Virgyne
Marye wrot therof a chartere.

43. grette: greeted.   *trespasyn*: trespasses.   *frely*: freely, generously.
44. foryevyn: forgiven.
45. day . . . Scolast: i.e. 10 February. St Scholastica was St Benedict's sister
and traditionally regarded as the foundress of the religious life for women
in the West.
46. preyende: praying (present participle).
47–8. sche . . . . voys: typical of the references to Elizabeth's weeping which
consoled Margery Kempe's amanuensis.
47. wytholdyn here: restrain herself.
48. owtwardys: outward, external.   *voys*: voice.   *Sodanly*: suddenly.
50. Seyn . . . wangelyst: Saint John the Evangelist, traditionally regarded as
the protector of religious women as Christ on the cross had entrusted his
mother to him (see John 19:26–7).
51–2. o . . . be-etynge: of this choosing and of this voluntary promising.
52. wele: will, wish.
53. chartere: charter, legal document.   *goo abak*: retreat.
54. Werfore: wherefore, for which reason.   *browt*: brought.
55–6. opyn wytenessynge: a patent, rather than closed, legal document.
58. erthe: earth; the MS here reads *herte* but as the Latin has *terram*, 'earth,
ground', it is probably a mistake.
59. dooth: do.   *qwat ye wyln*: what you wish.
60. yevynge: giving, gift.   *hoot*: oath.
62. wrot: wrote.

b) *The Virgin Prepares to be the Mother of God*
(ff. 92ᵛ–93ᵛ, 94)

Over that in a nyght whyles Elysabeth, Crystis servaunt, began
to thynke how God the gloryous Fader was plesid in the
gloryous mayde Marye yet whyles she lyved, for that he wolde   65
his sone toke flesshe of her, the blessyd mayden answerde to
her, 'Of me, my lovely doughter, God wrought as he that kan
touche the harpe or the fydele. For why fyrst he temperyth it
that it maketh a swete sowne and acordyng sowne, and
afterward ledyng and touchyng he syngeth somme thynge   70
wyth the sowne of it. Ryght soo God the Fader, first he
ordeyned and tempered in me all my steringes and all my
wyttes, as well of the soule as of the body; after that he
touched and ordeyned with the fynger of his ghost all my
sawes and my werkes to the plesaunce of him and ofte sythes   75
he reysed me wyth companye of angels to beholde the courte
of heven. Wherfore I founde soo moche comforte and echeing
of grete and ghostely swetenesse that after, whan I come
agayn to myself, I was soo fulfylled in love of that contree that
I desyred forto halse stones, trees, bestys and other creatures   80
for love of hym that them formyd. I coveted also forto doo

63. Over that: a literal translation of L. *insuper*, 'moreover'.
64. Fader: father.
65. yet . . . lyved: while she was still alive.   *for that*: because.
65–6. wolde . . . her: willed that his son should take flesh from her.
67. wrought: worked, acted.   *kan*: knows how to.
68. fydele: viol.   *For why*: for.   *temperyth*: tunes, adjusts.
69. that: so that.   *sowne*: sound.   *acordyng*: harmonious.
70. ledyng: singing.   *touchyng*: plucking.
72. ordeyned: regulated.
　　steringes: impulses: the text here has 'stringes' which makes good sense
given the metaphor of the viol, but the L. reads *motus*, 'movements,
stirrings'.
73. wyttes: senses.
74. ghost: spirit.
75. sawes: sayings, words.   *werkes*: works, deeds.
　　to . . . him: to his pleasure.   *ofte sythes*: many times.
76. reysed: raised, elevated.
77. echeing: increase.
78–9. come agayn: returned.
79. fulfylled in: filled with.   *contree*: (heavenly) country.
80. halse: embrace.   *bestys*: beasts, animals.
81. formyd: created.

servyse to all the ladyes that came to the Temple, for love of
her maker off whom I tasted suche swetenesse that they may
not be spoken.'

'Therfore, doughter, on that same maner whan God wolde   85
gyve the ony grace or comforte, thou shalt take it mekely and
suffre hym to doo of the what soo be pleseyng to hym. Ne
thou shalt not waxe proude under couler of mekenesse and
saye, "Lord, why doost thou thyse thynges to me? I am not
worthy" and suche odyr. For though thou be alther wysest, he   90
knoweth better what is to doo of the than thyn owne self. And
yf he worketh in the ony wounderfull thynge, the joye is his
and not thyn.'

Thenne it befyll whyle this homely spekynge was drawen on
longe that one of Elysabeth felowes passed forthe where she   95
prayde, whome Saint Elysabeth gretely blamynge sayde full
sharpely to her, 'Wherto gooste thou now hyther and thider
this tyme before my face?' and began as it were to menace her
wyth wordes and sygnes.

Thenne whan she was passed, Our Lady the blessyd mayde   100
sayde to Elysabeth, Crystys servaunt, 'O doughter, loo how
that thou art yet a foole and undescrete, that aplyest thyn
herte to ony worldly thynges whyle thou hast me present wyth
the. Therfore use now my presence this nyght, for of specyall
grace I am sente fro my sonne to the that thou aske sekerly   105
what the lyketh. And I wolde answere in stedfastnesse to the
all thyng that thou askest. Neverthelesse for thou applyed

82. *Temple*: the Virgin has already related how her parents dedicated her to
serve God in the Temple at Jerusalem.
83. *her*: their.   *swetenesse*: sweetnesses.
86. *ony*: any.   *mekely*: meekly, humbly.
88. *waxe*: grow.   *couler . . . mekenesse*: colour (pretence) of humility.
90. *odyr*: other (things).
    For . . . wysest: ironic presumably, but a misunderstanding of the L.
here which means 'since he (i.e. God) is most wise'.
90. *alther wysest*: wisest of all.
92. *joye*: glory.
94–5. *drawen . . . longe*: going on, protracted.
95. *Elysabeth felowes*: Elizabeth's companions.
98. *menace*: threaten.
99. *sygnes*: signs, gestures.
100. *was passed*: had gone.
102. *undescrete*: unwise.   *aplyest*: apply.
104. *use*: enjoy.
105. *sekerly*: securely, confidently.
106. *what . . . lyketh*: what you like.   *stedfastnesse*: steadfastness.
107. *for*: because.

thyne herte to the dede of thy felowe and reproved here
undiscretely, I wolde gyve to the penaunce, that in no wyse
thou go agayn to thy bed this nyght; ne I thynke not to shewe   110
the somme thyng now the whiche I wolde have sayd yf thou
hadde not offended my reverence.'

Whan that nyght was passed and daye was come, Elysabeth
began to make moche sorowe and gretely to be tormented for
the offence she hadde done in the nyght afore to the mageste   115
of the gloryouse Virgyne, as it is sayd above. And she dredde
gretely lest she myght never after recover suche a grace and so
grete a comforte, to whos prevy thought the blessyd mayde
answeryd, aperynge to hyr eftsones, and sayd, 'Drede the not,
doughter, ne tormente the not wyth foly doubtyng for wantyng   120
of me for thy trespas that is passyd, for why thy trespas is now
forgyven to the by thy penaunce and I am now come to the
that thou aske what the lyketh, for I am redy to gyve the
answere of all thynges as I behete the.'

To whome Saynt Elysabeth sayd, 'I praye you, lady, that ye   125
say me what steryd you forto aske of Our Lord that he wold
lette you of hys specyall grace seen that mayde borne, of the
whiche hys sone sholde be borne?' And she answerd, 'On a
daye whan I hadde comforte of God so wonderfull that unto
that tyme I was not experte of none suche, and came ageyne   130
to myself, I beganne to thynke and desyre wyth wylfull
brennyng herte yf I myght doo ony thyng or have in me for the
whiche God wolde lette me never parte from hym. And whan
I thought thus, I rose up and went to a book and beganne to
rede in it. And in the fyrst openyng of the book came before   135
my syght the worde of Esaye the prophete, *Ecce, virgo concipiet*

108. *dede*: deed, action.
115. *afore*: before.   *mageste*: majesty.
116. *dredde*: feared.
118. *prevy*: private, intimate.
119. *eftsones*: afterwards.
120. *foly*: foolish.   *wantyng*: wanting, i.e. lack.
121. *for why*: for.
123. *the lyketh*: pleases you.
124. *behete*: promised.
126. *steryd*: stirred, prompted.
126–7. *wold lette*: would allow.
127. *seen*: to see.
129. *unto*: until.
130. *was . . . experte*: had not experienced.
131–2. *wylfull brennyng*: strong-willed burning.
136. *Esaye*: Isaiah.
136–7. Ecce . . . etc.: Isaiah 7:14.

et pariet filium etc. That is, "Loo, a mayden shall conceyve and
bere a sonne" etc. And as I bethought me, thynkyng that
maydenhode pleased moche to God, sythen he wolde hys
sonne sholde be born of a mayde, thenne I purposed in my   140
herte, for the reverence of hym, to kepe maydenhode and, yf it
befyll me to see hyr, forto serve hyr in maydenhede all my lyf
tyme and, yf it nedyd, forto goo wyth hyr thorugh all the
worlde.'

'After this, the next nyght folowyng, whyles I prayed wyth   145
devocyon of soule and besought God that he wold let me see
the mayde before or I deyed, sodeynly whan I was in
derkenes, soo moche bryghtenesse apperyd to me before my
syght that in comparyson of it the sonne was as nought and fro
that shynyng I herde a voyce clerely seyeng to me, "Mayden of 150
Davyd kynred, thou shalt bere my sonne." And he added
therto, "Wote thou certeynly that the same worshyp and
reverence that thou desyred forto do to another mayden shall
be done to the afore other. I wyll forsothe that thou be that
mayden the whiche shall bere my sonne, the whiche not onely   155
thou shalt have hym by thyself ne in thyself, but by lawe of
matrymonye thou shalt may gyve hym to whome the lyketh;
and he shall not have my grace ne my love, ne he shal not
entre the kyngdome of my sonne, that wyll not love the and
trowe the the moder of my sonne, that shall take flesshe of the 160

138. *bethought me*: thought.
139. *maydenhode*: virginity.   *sythen*: since.
141. *for . . . hym*: in honour of him.   *kepe*: preserve.
142. *befyll me*: happened to me.
    hyr: her, i.e. the 'maiden' of Isaiah's prophecy.
    maydenhede: virginity.
142–4. *serve . . . worlde*: this desire to serve the Mother of God and follow
her anywhere she might go is imitated by Margery Kempe; see below p.
187.
147. *before or*: before.   *deyed*: died.
151. *Davyd kynred*: David's kindred.   *bere*: bear.
152. *Wote*: know.
154. *afore other*: before others.
154–62. *I . . . me*: this passage establishes the Virgin as the only means of
access to Christ and, through Christ, to God the Father.
154. *wyll*: will, desire.
156–7. *lawe of matrymonye*: right of marriage; i.e. Jesus is to be the Virgin's
'jointure', the property settled on a woman at the time of her marriage and
of which she could dispose as she wished.
157. *shalt may*: shall be able to.
160. *trowe*: believe.

for helthe of mankynde. And thou allone shalte may graunte
to other of hys grace the whiche thou shalte receyve of me."
    'And whanne I herde this wordes, I was ravysshed of myself
for moche drede and wonderyng and I fylle doun prostrate on
my face as dede, for I myghte not holde up myself. But   165
sodeynly the aungels of God stood by me, reysyng me fro the
erthe, and comforted me and sayde, "Drede the not, for why
thou arte blyssed above alle wommen and in the restyd
Goddes grace by the whiche all maye lyghtly be fulfylled that
be sayde to the of Oure Lorde." Fro that tyme forwarde I   170
cessyd not to gyve louynges to my creatour daye and nyghte,
wyth herte, mouthe and werke, wyth stable and certeyne
trouth, abydynge the daye and the houre whan tho thynges
sholde be fulfylled that were shewed to me of Oure Lorde.'
    'I sayde also oft sythes wythin myselfe, "O moost benygne   175
lorde, sythen it lyketh the forto gyve soo grete grace to thyne
unworthy handmayden, I beseche the that thou gyve me the
spyryte of wysdom, that I may worthely conceyve thy sonne,
maker of heven and of erthe, and serve hym to paye; the
spyryte of understondyng, by the whiche I may wyth lyghtned 180
soule fulfyll hys mekenes in as moche as is possyble in this
worlde; the spyryte of counseyll, by the whiche I may kepe
and governe hym as it besemeth whyle he is in hys
chyldehode, and wepyng of mannes infyrmyte and not yet
formyng wordes in spekyng; the spyryte of strengthe, by the 185

161. helthe: salvation.
162. of(1): (some) of.
163. ravysshed: ravished, i.e. caught up in ecstasy.
164. fylle doun : fell down.
165. as dede: as if dead.
166. reysyng: raising.
168. restyd: rested.
169. lyghtly: easily.
171. cessyd: ceased.   *louynges*: praises.
173. trouth: trust.   *abydynge*: awaiting.   *tho*: those.
175. oft sythes: many times.   *benygne*: kindly.
177–93. I beseche . . . reverence: the Virgin's prayer is consciously modelled
on Isaiah 11:2, which lists the virtues which came to be known as the Gifts
of the Spirit.
179. to paye: satisfactorily.
180. lyghtned: enlightened, illuminated.
183. as it besemeth: as is suitable.
184. of mannes infyrmyte: (L. *ex humana infirmitate*) out of human weakness,
i.e. the infant Christ will share the weaknesses and incapacities of any
human child.

whiche I may wyth manly herte bere in mynde the name of
hys worthynesse and stedfastely cleve unto hym; the spyryte of
connyng, by the whiche I may enfourme alle thoos that shall
have to do wyth hym and that wyll folowe hym; the spyryte of
pyte, by the whiche I may have compassyon of his swete   190
manhede and of hys tender compleccyon, as it semeth forto
have; and the spyryte of drede of God, by whiche I may serve
him wyth a meke soule and dew reverence. Alle this thynges,
my dere doughter, the whiche I askyd were graunted to me, as
thou mayst understonde, by the angellys salutacyon whiche I   195
was haylled of Gabryell the angell.' [. . . .]

'Whanne I was alle brennyng in Goddes love, and felyd soo
moche swetenes in hym that for hym alle the worlde was vyle
to me, ones whan I was alone wyth devocyon in my prevy
chambre, loo, sodeynly the aungell Gabryell stood by me and,   200
as the gospell seyth, heylled me and sayde *Ave gracia plena etc.*
Off the whiche salutacyon, whanne I herde it fyrst I was ferde,
but afterwarde that I was comforted wyth hys holy and swete
speche and made seker, not doubtyng thyse thynges to be
sothe that he shewed, I fyll to the erthe and, knelynge wyth   205
my hondes joynde, I honoured and sayde *Ecce ancilla domini;
fiat michi secundum verbum tuum.* That is to saye, "Loo here

186. *manly herte*: (L. *virili animo*) i.e. with a specifically masculine, rather
than generally human, mind (contrast previous note); *strengthe*, i.e. fortitude
(l. 185) is usually seen as a masculine virtue in the Middle Ages.
188. *connyng*: knowledge.
    enfourme: instruct; another reference to the Virgin's role as teacher.
189. *wyll*: desire.
191. *tender compleccyon*: delicate constitution.   *as . . . semeth*: as it is seemly.
193. *dew*: due, proper.
195–6. *by . . . angell*: i.e. when Gabriel hailed Mary as 'full of grace', she
was endowed with all the spiritual gifts she had requested in this prayer.
195. *salutacyon*: salutation.
196. *haylled*: hailed, greeted.
197. *felyd*: felt, experienced.
198. *for hym*: for his sake.   *vyle*: vile, worthless.
199. *ones*: once.
199–200. *prevy chambre*: private room.
201. *heylled*: hailed, greeted.
    Ave . . . etc.: Hail Mary full of grace (Luke 1:28).
202. *ferde*: afraid.
204. *seker*: confident.
205. *sothe*: true.   *shewed*: revealed.   *fyll*: fell.
206. *honoured*: worshipped.
206–7. Ecce . . . tuum: Behold the handmaid of the Lord; be it unto me
according to thy word (Luke 1:38).

the servaunt of God; be it done to me after thy worde." The whiche worde sayd, anone I was ravysshed and in soo grete fulnesse of Goddes grace enbasshed me that I never felte soo   210 moche swetenesse and comforte in my soule. And in that ravysshyng Goddes sonne took flesshe of my puryst blood wythoute ony wem of me or flesshely delyt.'

'The cause why God dede this grace to me, was feyth and mekenes wyth whiche I trowed in ful feyth the aungellys   215 wordes, and meked me and dressed me all to Goddes wyll. And therfore he wouchesave to gyve me soo moche grace. And soo thou, my doughter, in alle thynges that God heteth or dothe to the, have thou not hym in mistrowyng ne ayenstond hym not, seyeng, "Lord, why doest thou this to me?" But by   220 exsample of me saye: *Ecce ancilla domini etc.* And ony tyme it be not fulfylled as it is hyght to the, or ellys it is taken fro the that was gyven to the of God, blame thy owne self and thynke that thou hast done somme trespas before the syghte of Goddes mageste, for the whiche Goddes sentence is   225 chaunged; for he that hath wyll to purchace the lyf wythouten ende, he nedeth to be buxom of herte to the commaundementes and loue hymself to God by veray mekenesse and obedyence, for the contraryous of tho synnes, pryde and inobedyence of our forefaders Adam and Eve, for the whiche they lost the   230 grace and the dygnyte that they were made in.'

210. *enbasshed me*: abased myself.
212. *ravysshyng*: ecstasy.
213. *wem*: stain.   *flesshely delyt*: physical pleasure.
214–16. *The ... wyll*: for this stress on the Virgin's faith and humility, rather than her purity, cf. Eleanor Hull's *Meditations*, below p. 226.
214. *feyth*: faith.
215. *trowed*: believed.
216. *meked me*: humbled myself.   *dressed me*: submitted myself.
217. *wouchesave*: vouchsafed.
218. *heteth*: promises.
219. *have*: hold.   *mistrowyng*: disbelief, distrust.
    ayenstond: withstand, resist.
222. *fulfylled*: fulfilled, carried out.   *hyght*: promised.   *ellys*: else.
225. *sentence*: decision, judgement.
226. *hath wyll*: desires.   *purchace*: obtain.
227. *buxom*: obedient.
228. *loue*: abase, humble.   *veray*: true.
229. *for*: on account of.   *contraryous*: opposite (L. *propter contraria*).
    inobedyence: disobedience.
230. *forefaders*: ancestors.
231. *dygnyte*: dignity.

Textual notes

1. preyowr] preyowr and.
2. and] as.
19. hondys(1)] hondys and.
35. wakynge] wakyge.
37. tormente the] tormente.
40. hyghnes] hy3est.
41. fyth] felth (L. *dimica*).
43. thy] they.
53. thou] I.
58. joyned] ioned.   *erthe*] herte (L. *terram*).
66. the blessyd mayden] and toke the blessyd mayden.
70. syngeth] synget.
72. steringes] stringes (L. *motus*).
75. sawes] saweys.
101. how] who (L. *quomodo*).
108. felowe] folowed.
112. reverence] presence (L. *reuerenciam*).
124. behete] bete (L. *promiseram*).
135. And in] And.
146. soule and] soule.
155. the whiche(2)] and the whiche.
175. sythes] syghtes.
186. in mynde] mynde.
201. heylled] sheylled.
215. trowed] troweth.
219. not hym] not.   *ayenstond*] yenstond.
221–2. it be] be.
226. he that] he.
229. contraryous] contrayous.

6 Bridget of Sweden

Bridget of Sweden (1302 or 1303–1373) was a devout noblewoman who, before she was widowed, spent much time at the Swedish court attempting to influence King Magnus and his French wife Blanche by her own example and her constant exhortations to moral reformation. A mother of eight, after her husband's death in 1344 she started to experience visions which led her to found a religious order dedicated to the Virgin, whose apotheosis Bridget took to new heights. The Order of the Most Holy Saviour was a double order for nuns and monks, ruled by an abbess; Bridget's own daughter Katherine presided over both the men and women in the mother house at Vadstena in Sweden.

Although Bridget was the first woman in the Western Church to found a religious order, she never herself became a nun. She travelled to Rome to seek papal approval for her new order and stayed to press for the return of the pope from Avignon in France where, for political reasons, all the popes had lived with their courts since 1304. As a result of her efforts Pope Urban V did indeed return in 1367 but, finding conditions intolerable, left again in 1370, only to die a month later. It was left to another woman visionary, Catherine of Siena, to help bring about the permanent resettlement of the papacy in Rome (see below, p. 95) and to accidentally precipitated the election of a rival pope, leading to the crisis known as the Great Schism.

Bridget died in 1373 and, renowned for her holiness, her works of charity and her miracles, was canonised in 1391. But she was as well known for her numerous visions, many of which denounced the corruption of the Church in general and of certain individuals in particular, and stressed apocalyptic themes of the judgemental wrath of God. Other visions were vivid recreations of events in the lives of Christ and the Virgin, which had a strong influence on the representation of the Nativity and the Crucifixion in the later Middle Ages.

Bridget was a very popular saint in fifteenth-century England and in 1415 Henry V founded Syon, the only English Bridgettine house, at Twickenham in Middlesex (it later moved to Isleworth). Until its closure in 1539 it continued to enjoy close ties with the Lancastrians and their descendants, including Lady Margaret Beaufort (see Keiser 1987b: 11–13; below, p. 301). It was renowned for its austerity, its influence at court and its learning. Bridget, who had learnt Latin late in life, encouraged scholarship as much as asceticism among her nuns; her Rule, which otherwise stressed personal poverty, allowed them as many books as they needed for reading. Syon continued its corporate existence abroad after the Reformation and, having returned in the nineteenth century, is the only religious community in England that can claim an unbroken existence since the Middle Ages.

Bridget's revelations, too, were widely known. Indeed, of all the continental women mystics included in this anthology whose writings were translated into English, she is the only one to have achieved real popularity and widespread circulation among layfolk as well as religious. The first set of passages printed below derives from the *Liber Celestis*, the vast collection of Bridget's visions originally dictated by her in Old Swedish, translated and recorded in Latin by her spiritual directors, and then checked by her. The visions were later translated into Middle English in several versions; there are two translations of the complete text and in addition numerous extracts and selections (see Ellis 1982). The passages printed here come from a collection which has extracted and rearranged individual revelations to construct a life of the Virgin, as told by her to Bridget; this forms an interesting parallel with the preference of so many medieval women visionaries for hagio-autobiography (see Introduction, pp. 8–10).

The second set of extracts comes from *The Rule of St Saviour*, the Middle English translation of the Latin Rule that was dictated by Christ himself, Bridget claimed. The translation was one of the official legislative documents of the Bridgettine monastery at Syon and was presumably made for the benefit of the nuns, who could not read the original Latin.

Comment: The first passage is perhaps Bridget's best-known revelation, a vivid and emotional vision of the Nativity which had an immediate and continuing influence on its representation in art (Butkovich 1972: 31–4). It stresses the supernatural, if not anti-natural, aspects of Christ's birth, with a passion for ingenious detail that clearly derives from the visionary's own experience of childbirth (contrast the very different treatment of the subject by the lifelong nun Mechtild; see above, p. 50). Thus it emphasises the status of the Virgin as the Mother of Christ in a way that could not have occurred to male commentators.

The second passage shows Bridget's passion for detail extending to a curiosity that goes beyond what would now be considered the bounds of good taste. It also asserts the Virgin's supremacy as head of the apostles after Christ's Ascension, a position used in the final extract to justify the unusual power structure of the Bridgettine order within which the abbess, elected by the sisters alone, had absolute authority over all the temporal affairs of the monastery.

The third passage shows the same concern for detail finding a practical outlet in prescribing the distinctive, not to say eccentric, habit of the Bridgettine nuns. The good sense of their winter outfit, with its sheepskin cloak, boots and stockings, reminds us that Bridget was not only the first woman but also the first Northern European to draft a religious rule.

Manuscripts: The extracts from the *Revelations* are from the compilation in Oxford Bodley MS Rawlinson C. 41, a late fifteenth-century manuscript; it is unpublished. The extracts from the Bridgettine Rule are from CUL MS Ff. 6. 31 and are available in facsimile, ed. Hogg (1978).

Further reading (for full details see Bibliography): On St Bridget see, e.g., Butkovich 1972; Wilson 1984. On the *Revelations* in English see Ellis 1982; Lagorio and Bradley 1981: 156–7. On the Bridgettines in England see Knowles 1955: 175–81 and Knowles 1961: 212–21; and the Middlesex volume of the *Victoria County Histories*.

From *The Revelations*

a) *Bridget Witnesses the Nativity*
(MS Rawlinson C. 41, ff. 12ᵛ–16)

How the gloryous Vyrgyn ordyrd hyrselfe afore the byrth
off owre savyour Jhesu Cryst in Bethleem.
The XIth chapter. Brygyt speketh.

After thys when I, Brygytt, at the commandement off God
went in pylgrymage to the holy cyte off Jerusalem and frome   5
thens into Bethleem to the crybbe off Owre Lorde, I saw a
vyrgyn ther moost goodly fayer and beauteyus, beyng grete
wyth chylde, clothyd in a whyte mantell and in a fyne kyrtell,
thorow the whych I myght well perceyve and see the clene
whyte flesshe off the Vyrgyn. Her wombe was then very grete   10
and full, for she was redy to the byrth.

There was also wyth her a very honest olde man and they
both had wyth them an oxe and a asse when they intryd into
the denne, the olde man byndyng the oxe and the asse to the
crybbe. When they come owt off the denne he brought to the   15
Vyrgyn a candell brynnyng and made yt fast in the wall and
went owt agayne, lest he shulde be present then at the byrth.
After this the Vyrgyn put off her shoone and layd down her
mantyll frome her that she was clothyd wythall and toke off
the kercher frome her hede and layd yt downe, she beynge   20

4–6. when . . . Lorde: Bridget sees her vision of the Nativity when she is in
Bethlehem, just as Margery Kempe (who had had Bridget's revelations
read to her) receives a vision of the Passion when she is visiting Jerusalem.
6. thens: thence, from there.   *crybbe*: manger, stall.
7. fayer: fair.   *beauteyus*: beauteous.
8. fyne: finely textured.
   kyrtell: gown (worn over a smock and under a mantle).
9–10. thorow. . . Vyrgyn: this acutely physical description (cf. also ll. 19–23)
is surprisingly sensual, particularly in a context designed to emphasise the
Virgin's chastity.
9. clene: pure.
13. intryd: entered.
14. denne: cave.
16. brynnyng: burning.   *made . . . fast*: set.
17. lest . . . byrth: only exceptionally were men present at childbirth in the
Middle Ages.
18. put: took.   *shoone*: shoes.
19. wythall: with.
20. kercher: headcloth, veil.

then oonly in her kyrtyll and her moost fayer and goodly here, shynyng bryght as golde, spred down and lyinge upon her sholders.

Then she toke owte two fayre lynyng clothes and two clene wolen clothes, fyne and sotell, whych she browght wyth her to lay and to wrappe yn the chylde that shulde be born; an also two other fyne lynyng clothes to kevyr and bynd yn the hede off the chylde. Thes clothes she layd down besyde her that she myght occupy and use them at dewe tyme.

Off the very trewe maner off the byrth and natyvyte off   30
Oure Lord Jhesu Cryste. The XIIth chapter.

Thes thyngis doone, the gloryus Vyrgyn knelyd downe with grete reverence, dysposynge herselfe to prayer, havynge her bakke towarde the crybbe and her face lyfte up into hevyn towarde the eest. Then she, holdynge up her handis and eyn   35
into hevyn, knelyd as she had bene frome her bodely wyttis rapt into hye contemplacyon, all fulfyllyd wyth godly swetnes. Then she beyng thus in prayer, I sawe the chylde in her wombe meve and styrre hymselfe and sothenly in a moment and in the twynklynge off an ey she had borne her chylde,   40
from whome there came suche a grete lyght and off so gloryus a bryghtnes that the lyght off the sunne was not to be comparyd therto. And the candell that Joseph faystynd in the wall gave then no maner off lyght for that gloryus lyght and bryghtnes that came owt off the chylde utterly dystroiyde and   45
putt owt the natural lyght off the candell. And that maner off the byrth was so sothenly and so wysely doone that I myght not discerne nor perceyve how or what membyr off her body she had borne her chylde wythall.

21. here: hair.
24. lynyng: linen.
25. sotell: finely woven.
26. an: and.
27–8. clothes: cloths.   *kevyr*: cover.
27. bynd ... chylde: wrap the child's head in.
29. occupy: take.   *dewe*: due, appropriate.
35. eest: east.   *eyn*: eyes.
36–7. knelyd ... contemplacyon: i.e. the birth takes place while the Virgin is in a mystical trance.
36–7. bodely ... rapt: ravished out of her physical senses.
36. as: as if.
39. meve: move.   *sothenly*: suddenly.
44. for: because of.
47. wysely: discreetly.
48–9. what membyr ... wythall: from what part.

Then I sawe that gloryus and blysshyd chylde lyinge upon   50
the harde erth all nakyd, ful fayre, whyte and clene. The
flesshe off hys moost gloryus body was then ful clene and pure
frome al fylth and unclennes. I harde then also a wonderfull
melody and yoyfull syngynge off angellis wyth a mervelus
swetnes and hevynly delyte. Then the wombe of the Vyrgyn   55
that was very grete afore the byrth, yt swagyd and wythdrewe
inwarde agayn to the state that yt was in afore she conceyvyd.
And then her body was off a mervelus and off ryght grete
beuty and fayrnes and ful plesaunt to beholde.

How the blyssyd Vyrgyn worshypte the glorius chylde   60
and lappyd hym in clowthes.
The XIIIth chapter.

After that the Vyrgyn perceyvyd and knewe that she had borne
the chylde, she then beyng styll upon her knees, moost
devowtly she inclyned and bowyd down her hede and wyth   65
bowth her handys yoynyd togyder she honouryd and worshypte
hym with grete honeste and reverence, sayng to hym thes
wordis: 'Welcome, my God, my lord and my son.' Then the
blyssyd chylde, wepyng and tremblynge for coldnes and
hardnes off the pament where apon he lay, turnyd hymselfe   70
then a lyttell, sekynge to fynde sum comforte and the favyour
and socour off hys moder and anon the blyssyd Vyrgyn hys
moder ful loveyngly and reverently toke hym up into her
handis and helde hym to her brest and wyth her pappe and

50. *blysshyd*: blessed.
52–3. *flesshe . . . unclennes*: i.e. there was no need for the Infant Jesus to be
cleansed of blood and vernix and (possibly) there was no afterbirth;
throughout, Bridget stresses the exceptional nature, in every way, of the
Nativity.
53. *harde*: heard.
54. *yoyfull*: joyful.
55–7. *Then . . . conceyvyd*: again, Bridget would know from her own
experience that this is not the case after normal childbirth.
55. *wombe*: belly.
56. *swagyd*: shrank.
61. *lappyd*: wrapped, enveloped.
66. *bowth*: both.   *yoynyd*: joined.
67. *honeste*: honour.
70. *pament*: hard ground.
71–2. *favyour and socour*: help and assistance.
74. *pappe*: breast, nipple.

her brest she made hym warme wyth full grete yoye and 75
gladnes, with a moderly tender compassyon.

Then she satt downe upon the erth and layd her son in her
lappe and ful moderly she layde hym in clowthes, lappyng hym
ful dilygently, fyrst in lynnyn and after in wollen clowthes,
byndyng and swathynge hys lytyl blyssyd body, hys armys and 80
hys leggis, wyth the swathynge bonde whych was sewde in
fowr partis upon the upper wolen clowth. Afterwarde she
bonde hys hede with the two fyne lynyn clowthes whych she
had ordaynd for hym. In thys she nevyr chaunged her colour
nor was anythyng weyke or seyke nor lakkyd anythyng off her 85
bodyly strenght, as other women doo in tyme off byrth, but
oonly that her wombe, that was so grete afore the byrth,
withdrewe ytselfe to the fyrst state that yt was yn before.

b) *The Circumcision*
(ff. 18–19)

Off the Cyrcumcysyon and off the complaynt off
the Vyrgyn upon the cyte off Roome. 90
The XVIth chapter.

In the day off cyrcumcysyon off Cryst, when I, Brygytte, was
in the cyte off Roome, the Vyrgyn Mary aperyd and sayd to
me, 'Doughter, thys day that blysshyd Lambe off God my son
was borne in my armys, that cowde ful wele goo. Thys day the 95

75. *brest*: bosom.
76. *moderly*: maternally.
80. *swathynge*: swaddling.
81. *swathynge bonde*: swaddling-clothes, i.e. 'Clothes consisting of narrow
lengths of bandage wrapped round a new-born infant's limbs to prevent
free movement' (*OED*). These were the accepted way of dressing infants in
Antiquity and the Middle Ages.
81. *sewde*: sewed.
81–2. *in . . . partis*: i.e. one at each corner.
82. *upper*: top, outer.
84. *ordaynd*: prepared.
85. *anythyng . . . seyke*: at all weak or sick.   *lakkyd*: was lacking.
86–8. *but . . . before*: Bridget has already mentioned this point, which
clearly made a great impression on her.
94. *blysshyd*: blessed, glorious.
95. *borne*: carried.
    that . . . goo: who (i.e. the Virgin) was well able to walk. As Jesus was
circumcised according to Jewish custom on the eighth day after birth,
Bridget's point is that the Virgin was fully recovered from childbirth earlier
than other mothers.

styll chylde was cyrcumsycyd that never synnyd. When he was
cyrcumsysyd I kept full derely that skynne that was kutte off
frome hys membyrs with moost grete reverens and worshype
wheresumever I went. How myght I fynde in my hert to bury
yt in the erth, that was begotten off me wythowt synne?   100
Therfore when I shulde depart owt off thys worlde, I
delyverde that precyus tresour to Saynt John Evangelyste, my
keper, wyth the blyssyd blode that remayned in hys woundes
when we toke hym down fro the crosse.

After that Saynt John and hys successours wer departyd   105
owte off the worlde and synne, malyce and infydelyte encresyd
in the worlde, the frendis and lovers off God that had then
that precyous tresour in kepynge hydde yt prevely in the
moost clene and honest place under the erth and yt was there
longe tyme unknown, unto the angell of God shewde yt by   110
revelacyon to the frendis off God.

O Roome, o Roome, yff thou knewyst, thou shuldest yoye
ye sowthly; yf thou cowldest wepe, thow shuldest wepe evyr
more, for thou hast my most dere tresour and doyst not
honour and worshype ytt.'   115

---

96. styll: motionless, silent.

that ... synnyd: the Old Testament sometimes regards circumcision as
a metaphor for spiritual purification (e.g. Deuteronomy 10:16) and is in this
followed by St Paul (e.g. Romans 2:29); it is therefore logically superfluous
for the infant Christ.

97. kept ... derely: preserved with great care.   *skynne:* foreskin.
      kutte: cut.

98. membyrs: (genital) members.

99. wheresumever: wherever.

101. shulde: was about to.

102. precyus tresour: Bridget's devotion to the relic of the Circumcision is
not unique among medieval women visionaries; see Bynum 1987: 377,
n. 135.

103. keper: protector. On St John as protector of the Virgin (and therefore
virgins) cf. *The Revelations of St Elizabeth,* above p. 75.

106. infydelyte: lack of faith.   *encresyd:* increased.

108. prevely: secretly.

109. clene: pure.   *honest:* honourable.

110–11. unto ... God: many places in the Middle Ages claimed to possess
and venerate the Holy Prepuce.

110. unto: until.

112–13. yoye ye: rejoice.

113. sowthly: truly.

From *The Rule of Our Saviour*

c) *The Sisters' Clothes*
(CUL MS Ff. 6. 33, ff. 43–4)

The clothynge of the susterys must be two smokkes of white
burel, oon for cotidian use, anothere for wasshynge; oon
kyrtyll of grey burel and oon couele, whose slevys shall be no
lenger than the ende of the myd fynger, and whan they shall
exercise manual servises, the wydenes of the slevys hangyng   120
downe aboute the handes shall be streynyd togedyr moderatly
to the armes wyth a botyn, to the lykenesse of other sleves.
Oon mantyl they schall have also, of grey burel as the kyrtyl
and couele, which mantyl shal not be fruncyd ne pynchyd
togedyr fro wythoute, nor curyously made, but on party streyte   125
and playne, havyng all thynge of profytte, ryght nought of
vanyte, which mantyl also owyth to be sengyl in somere and
furred in wyntyr, not wyth delicate skynnys but wyth lambys
skynnys or shepys. Of suche skynnys also may be hadde a
pylche in wyntyr. And the mantyl schal not towche the erth   130
from a span and it must be bownde togedyr at the breest wyth
a botoun of tree. And as to hosyn and shoes of there feet, in
somyr they must have shoes to the ankles and hosyn to the
knees and in wyntyr hyghe shoys to the knees, furred wyth
burell, and hosyn as hyghe.   135

116. *smokkes*: smocks, i.e. shifts, undergarments.
117. *burel*: burrel, a coarse woollen cloth.   *cotidian*: everyday.
118. *couele*: garment.   *slevys*: sleeves.
119. *lenger*: longer.
120. *exercise . . . servises*: engage in manual work.   *wydenes*: fullness.
121. *streynyd*: bound, fastened.
122. *botyn*: button.   *to . . . of*: like.
123. *mantyl*: mantle, cloak.
124. *fruncyd*: pleated.   *pynchyd*: gathered, tucked.
125. *curyously*: intricately.   *on party*: in part.   *streyte*: narrow.
127. *owyth*: ought.   *sengyl*: unlined.   *somere*: summer.
130. *pylche*: fur or skin outer garment.
130–1. *schal . . . span*: i.e. must clear the ground by at least a hand's span.
131. *bownde*: fastened.
132. *botoun*: button.   *tree*: wood.   *hosyn*: hose, stockings.
134. *furred*: trimmed.

The araymentys of the hedde shal be a wympyl wyth which the forhede and the chekes must be unbelappyd and the face on party coveryd, whos extremytees wyth a pyn must be joynyd togedyr behynde the hede in the naterel. Upon this wympyll must be put a veyle of blacke clothe, which thre pynnys must 140 fasten togedyr that it flowe not abrode, oon aboute the frounte and tweyn aboute bothe erys.

Farthermor, upon the veyle must be sett a crowne of whyte lynen cloth, to the which must be sowyd fyve smale partyes of redde cloth, as fyve dropys. The first lytel part shal be in the 145 forhede, anothir in the aftir-hedde, the thyrd and fourth aboute the erys, the fyfte in myddes of the hede, in maner of a cros. This crowne shal oon pyn in the myddys of the hede stablyssh and make it apte to the hede. And this crowne shal both wydweys and virgynes bere in signe of continence and 150 chastite.

d) *The Abbess*
(f. 56^r–v)

The Abbes must be chose of the covente and whanne she is chose lawfully, she must be confermyd of the bisshope, whiche for the reverence of the most blessid Virgyn Marie, to whom this ordre ys halwyd, owith to be hedde and ladye. For 155

---

136. araymentys: clothing, covering.
         wympyl: wimple, i.e. a head-dress that covers the head, chin and sides of the face.
137. unbelappyd: enveloped.
138. extremytees: edges.
139. naterel: back of the head.
141. abrode: out.   *aboute*: over.   *frounte*: forehead.
142. tweyn: two.
143–4. crowne . . . cloth: this white 'crown' is the most distinctive part of the Bridgettine nun's habit.
145. dropys: i.e. of blood; the five pieces of red cloth symbolise the Five Wounds of Christ.
146. aftir-hedde: back of the head.
149. stablyssh: hold.   *make . . . apte*: fit it.
150. wydweys: widows; the crown did not symbolise virginity, and widows were eligible to join the Bridgettine Order.
150. bere: wear.   *in signe*: as a symbol.
152. chose of: chosen by.   *covente*: convent, i.e. the community of nuns.
154. whiche: i.e. the abbess.
155. halwyd: consecrated.   *owith*: must, ought.   *hedde*: head

that Virgyn whose stede the Abbes beryth in eerth, Cryst
ascendynge into hevyn, was hedde and qwene of the apostelis
and disciples of Cryst.

The Abbes also oon of the thrittene preestis, in whom she
oon with all the congregacion of susterne and brotheren   160
consentyth, muste chese in confessoure of all. And the bys-
shope must ordeyn and conferme hym Generall Confessoure
of the monastery; to whom (auctorite of bynddyng and losyng,
correctynge and reformyng, plenarly graunted of the bisshope)
all preestys and bretheren, ase the susteris to the Abbes, in all   165
thyngys muste obey, doyng ryght noughte or not the leest thynge
ayens his commaundment; whiche General Confessoure, save
the domys of the brethern and conservacion of the ordre,
withoute councell of the Abbes shall doo ryghte noughte;
whiche, for she is hedde of the monasterye, of the nedys and   170
goodes of the monasterye to be ordeyned ys to be councelid.

156. stede: place.
159–61. The ... all: 'The abbess must choose one of the thirteen priests
... as general confessor'; word-for-word translation of the Latin makes the
sentence awkward.
159. in: on.
160. oon: together.   *susterne*: sisters.
161. consentyth: agree.
162. ordeyn: appoint.
163. to whom: i.e. to the Confessor General; this phrase is governed by 'all
... muste obey'.
163–4. auctorite ... bisshope: this clause, 'authority ... having been fully
granted by the bishop', translates word for word an absolute clause in the
Latin.
163. bynndyng and losyng: binding and loosing. This traditional formula for
supreme religious authority derives from Christ's words to Simon Peter,
'And whatsoever thou shalt bind on earth, it shall be bound also in heaven:
and whatsoever thou shalt loose on earth, it shall be loosed also in heaven'
(Matthew 16:19).
165. ase: (just) as.
166. ryght noughte: absolutely nothing.
167. ayens: against.
167–8. save ... ordre: except for judgements concerning the brothers and
the maintenance of the Order.
169. councell: advice.
170. whiche: i.e. the abbess; she had authority over the men as well as the
women in all except spiritual matters.
170–1. of(2) ... ordeyned: concerning the arrangements to be made for the
needs and the property of the monastery.
171. ys ... councelid: must be consulted.

Textual notes

5. *went*] when.
15. *he*] an.
21. *goodly*] gooly.
49. *chylde wythall*] chylde.
53. *fylth*] fylthy.
60. *blyssyd Vyrgyn*] blyssyd.
80. *swathynge*] swatynge.
81. *swathynge*] swatynge.
105. *successours*] sussessours.
106. *infydelyte*] indefydelyte.
107. *lovers off God*] lovers off off God.
141. *fasten*] fastenyd.

7 Catherine of Siena

Catherine of Siena (1347–80) was the daughter of Jacopo Benincasa, a Sienese dyer, and his wife Lapa. As an adolescent she refused to marry and led a solitary life of piety and mortification for some years in her own home. Her spiritual life became more focused after she became a Mantellata, i.e. a member of the Third Order of St Dominic. In the Middle Ages the Dominican Order or Order of Preachers, which had been founded to combat heresy by preaching and teaching, consisted of the First Order of Friars Preachers, the Second Order of enclosed nuns, sometimes called Dominicanesses, and a Third Order for women who lived under vows but in the world, either at home or in small groups, and engaged in works of mercy, caring for the sick and the poor.

Gradually Catherine gathered around her a group of men and women, religious and secular, who were attracted by her charismatic personality and looked to her as a figure of spiritual authority, calling her 'mother'. She began to travel around Italy, preaching reform and repentance, and wrote many letters (dictated to members of her 'family' as she could read but not write). During the last seven years of her life she took an increasingly active part in public life, influencing Sienese and, later, Italian affairs. A woman of strong and indomitable personality, she urged Pope Gregory XI to return to Rome from Avignon. When he died in 1378, not long after taking her advice, she publicly supported his successor, Pope Urban VI, whose election and subsequent behaviour precipitated the Great Schism (see above, p. 84). Privately she tried to moderate his tactless reforming zeal, although she herself was a reformer who castigated the corruptions of her own society, the papacy and the Dominican Order.

Little of this is evident in her long work *Il Dialogo* (translated into Middle English as *The Orcherd of Syon*). Most of this treatise was dictated in a state of trance during the autumn of 1378, just after the pope had returned to Rome. Although according to her biographers she was an ecstatic and a visionary, the *Dialogo* is a didactic treatise rather than an account of personal religious experience and consists mainly of orthodox moral instruction, delivered to her by God. It demonstrates her acutely analytical intelligence and her respect for learning, in spite of her own lack of formal education.

The early fifteenth-century English translation of *Il Dialogo* was made by a deliberately anonymous cleric, 'unworthi to bere ony name', and his assistant 'Dane [i.e. Dom] James', for the Bridgettine nuns of Syon Abbey (see *The Orcherd of Syon*, pp. 1/7 and 421/14–15 and above, p. 84). It was later printed in 1519 by Wynkyn de Worde and thus acquired a circulation in England beyond the Bridgettine Order. The original connection with the Bridgettines, however, was most appropriate, as in some ways Catherine was Bridget's spiritual successor, though she and her writings were less widely known in England. Both women were uncloistered visionaries who mixed fearlessly with the world and exercised authority over men as well as women, similarities that may have contributed to the English Bridgettines' interest in Catherine.

A link between Catherine and England is provided by William Flete, an originally English Augustinian friar. He lived as a hermit at Lecceto near Siena and was one of Catherine's closest associates. At the time of her death it was to him that she entrusted her spiritual family and he may well have been the channel through which her writings made their way to England. (Another factor that contributed to the circulation of Catherine's writings in England was English support during the Great Schism for Pope Urban.)

Comment: The first passage presents Catherine as the mother of a spiritual family, whose prayer of loving concern for them is closely modelled on Christ's prayer for his disciples on the eve of the Crucifixion. This is a startling ·act of appropriation and the parallel implied between Christ himself and Catherine is daring. The imagery of light and darkness, of vision and blindness, is characteristic of Catherine's deep respect for the enlightened intellect, in which she was influenced by the learned traditions of the Dominican Order.

The second passage is one of the few in *The Orcherd* that records a visionary experience. The vision itself, which a mystical theologian would technically classify as 'intellectual' rather than 'corporeal' or 'imaginative', is subordinated to God's use of it to exemplify the Catholic doctrine of Transubstantiation. However, it also situates Catherine in a tradition of visions and miracles associated with food that centres on the Eucharist. This, specifically female, form of spirituality, which developed from the thirteenth century onwards, has been examined in detail by Bynum 1987.

The third passage, an impassioned call for the reform of the Dominicans, illustrates Catherine's identification as a woman with an order which was predominantly male. After careful examination, the Dominicans had granted her their official approval in 1374 and had provided her with a new spiritual director, Raymond of Capua. As her confessor he was in a good position to influence and protect Catherine (and as her biographer to promote the interests of his spiritual daughter after her death). From then on the sanction of such a powerful international organisation provided Catherine with a validation for her activities which she might not otherwise have enjoyed. As long as she professed submission to the Order, she enjoyed a remarkable freedom of action for a religious woman. In contrast Marguerite Porete, a béguine with no such powerful male backing, was vulnerable to charges of heresy, while Margery Kempe, a bourgeoise and a married woman, was doomed to ineffectuality though she continually, with rather mixed success, sought male support and approval. Only Bridget of Sweden's secular status as a powerful aristocrat allowed her a freedom of action similar to Catherine's.

In return for their protection during her life, after her death the Dominicans tried to promote Catherine as a saint to equal or even outclass Francis of Assisi, the founder of the rival order of Friars Minor. Indeed, Catherine of Siena is still today the only medieval Dominican saint with much popular appeal.

Manuscript: BL MS Harley 3432 (early fifteenth century); the text is also extant in Cambridge, St John's College MS 75 (early fifteenth century) and

New York Public Library, MS Morgan M 162 (second half of the fifteenth century). It was printed by Wynkyn de Worde (STC 4815) and has been critically edited from Harley 3432 and the other manuscripts by P. Hodgson and G.M. Liegey (1966).

Further reading: There are numerous popular and scholarly biographies of Catherine; see for instance Curtayne 1929, Fawtier and Canet 1948. There is a modern translation of *Il Dialogo* by Noffke (1980), and of selected letters by Foster and Ronayne (1980). On Catherine's spirituality see especially Bynum 1987: 165–80. On *The Orcherd of Syon* see Hodgson 1942; Finnegan 1980; Keiser 1987a; Mary Denise 1958. See also Petroff 1986: 238–40, 263–75; Wilson 1984: 252–68.

From *The Orchard of Syon*

a) *Catherine Prays for her Spiritual Family*
(BL MS Harley 3432, ff. 110^{r-v})

O fier of love, thankinge be to thee, eendelees Fadir. I, unparfight and ful of derknesse, and thou, parfight and ful of light, hast schewid me parfeccioun and a cleer schinynge way of doctryne of thin oonly soothfast soone, Jhesu. I was deed and thou hast areisid me. I was seek and thou hast yove me   5 medicyn, and not oonly the medicyne of the blood that thou yavest to mankynde by mediacyoun of thi sones passioun, but thou hast yove me anothir special medycyn ayeins my pryve seeknesse, the which I nevere knewe afore, by the doctryne that thou hast yove me, that in no wise I schulde deeme ony   10 maner resonable creatures, and specialy thi servauntis, of

1. *fier*: fire.   *eendelees*: eternal.
2. *unparfight*: imperfect.
3. *cleer schinynge*: brightly shining.
4. *doctryne*: teaching.   *soothfast*: true.   *deed*: dead.
5. *areisid*: raised.   *seek*: sick.   *yove*: given.
6–7. *blood . . . passioun*: i.e. the sacramental Blood of Christ received in the Eucharist under the form of the consecrated wine. Catherine had a strong devotion to the Precious Blood as a symbol of God's redemptive love and often opened her letters with the phrase, 'the blood of Christ'.
7. *mediacyoun*: mediation.
8. *ayeins*: against.   *pryve*: secret, private.
9. *doctryne*: precept.
10. *deeme*: judge.
10–11. *ony . . . creatures*: any kind of rational beings, i.e. men and women.

whom oftentymes as a blynde wrecche and languorynge in this
seeknesse, undir colour of the honour and worschip of thi
name and heelthe of soulis, I have yeve doomes. Wherfore I
thanke thee, eendeless and infinyte Goodnes, for thou hast   15
maad me knowe by manyfestacioun or schewynge of thi
soothfastnesse bothe disceyt of the feend and also the
infirmyte of myn owne propre passioun.

Wherfore of synguler grace and mercy I biseche thee that
fro this day foreward I go nevere out fro thi doctryne, that thin   20
eendelees goodenesse hath taught me; and also for alle tho
that wolen folowe the same doctryn. And, for withoute thee is
nothing doon, to thee therfore I fle, eendelees Fadir, and I
may not praye for me to thee, but for al the world, and
specialy for the mysterial body, oure modir Holy Chirche, that   25
this truthe of doctrine schyne in the mynystris of Holy
Chirche.

And yit specialy I preye thee for hem alle that thou hast
take me forto love in special love, whom thou hast maad oon
with me; for thei schulen be my refreischyng and comfort   30
whanne I se hem renne by this doctrine undefoulid and
mortified to alle her owne willis, and withoute ony deemynge
or sclaundir or grucchinge of her neighboris, to the worschip

12. *languorynge*: languishing.
13. *colour*: pretext, cover.
14. *heelthe*: salvation.   *yeve doomes*: passed judgement.
17. *soothfastnesse*: truth.   *disceyt*: deception.
18. *infirmyte . . . passioun*: weakness of my very own emotions.
19. *of . . . grace*: out of your unique grace.
20. *go . . . fro*: never stray from.
21. *tho*: those.
22. *wolen*: wish.
23–37. *I(2) . . . labour*: Catherine's prayer for her spiritual family
audaciously recalls Christ's prayer for his disciples the night before the
Crucifixion (John 17: 9–15): 'I pray not for the world, but for them whom
thou hast given me . . . . Holy Father, keep them in thy name whom thou
hast given me; that they may be one, as we also are . . . . Those whom thou
gavest me have I kept; and none of them is lost . . . . I pray not that thou
shouldest take them out of the world, but that thou shouldest keep them
from evil.'
25. *mysterial body*: the mystical body (of Christ).
26–7. *mynystris . . . Chirche*: priests.
29. *take me*: entrusted to me.   *maad oon*: made one, united.
30. *refreischyng*: refreshment.
31. *renne . . . doctrine*: run (their course) according to this precept.
   undefoulid: undefiled.
32. *mortified. . . willis*: dead to their own wills.   *deemynge*: judging.
33. *sclaundir*: slander.   *grucchinge of*: complaining about.

and honour of thin holy name. I praye thee therfore, infinyte
Love, that noon of hem be withdrawe fro thin hondis by the   35
feend of helle, but that thei mowe come to thee that art the
eende of al her labour.

Also I praie thee for two pilers, the whiche ben myn two
goostly fadris, whom thou hast lente to me for my kepyng and
doctryne of me, moost wrecchid and seek, fro the bigynnyng   40
of my lyvynge unto this tyme: that thou make hem bothe oon
and of two bodyes o soule; and that noon of hem take heede
to noon other thing principally than forto fulfille the
mynysterye of her offices, the whiche thou hast put into her
hondis for the heelthe of soulis, to the worschip of thin holy 45
name. And I, unworthi and moost wrecchid servaunt and not
a doughtir, mowe tendirly kepe her doctrine with du
reverence and holy dreede, and that also I mowe dreede hem
reverently for thi love, that it mowe be to thee worschip and to
hem pees and qwyete and edificacioun of her neighbore.   50

b) *God Recalls Catherine's Intellectual Vision of the Eucharist*
(f. 114^{r-v})

'Thanne aftir tyme the prest cam to the tyme of consecracioun,
thou biheldist bisily the preest and whanne he seyde wordis of

35. *withdrawe fro*: taken from.
36. *feend*: fiend.   *mowe*: may.
37. *eende*: object, consummation.
38. *pilers*: pillars.
38–9. *the . . . fadris*: i.e. her two Dominican confessors, Tommaso della
Fonte and Bartolomeo Dominici.
39. *goostly*: spiritual.
39–40. *for . . . me*: i.e. to preserve and instruct me.
41. *lyvynge*: (religious) life.
42. *o*: one, a single.
42–3. *take . . . principally*: pay attention principally to anything other.
44. *mynysterye . . . offices*: the carrying out of their duties.
47. *du*: due, proper.
48. *dreede*: fear.
50. *pees*: peace.   *qwyete*: quiet.
   edificacioun: edification, spiritual benefit.
51. *aftir tyme*: after the time that.
   consecracioun: Consecration (of the bread and wine in the most solemn
part of the Mass).
52. *bisily*: intently, carefully.
52–3. *wordis . . . consecracioun*: i.e. *Hoc est corpus meum*, 'This is my body'.

consecracioun, I made me open to thee. And so thou saygh
comynge out of my breste a light, as it hadde be a sonne-
beem comynge out fro the whele of the sonne and not   55
departynge from the same whele or rondel of the sonne. In
the which light cam a culver and flikeride or smoot hise
wyngis togydere aboute the hoost, ofschewynge joye and
gladnesse for vertu of tho wordis that the prest seyde in tyme
of consecracioun.   60
And so thi bodily iye was not sufficient forto suffre to se
sich a light, but thi sight oonli bilefte in the iye of intellecte,
there thou say and taastist the depnesse of the Trinyte, al God
and al man, hid and keverid undir whightnesse of breed. And
neither the greet light that thou haddist of me, ne the worthi 65
presence of me that thou feldist in thee intellectualy took not
awey the whightnesse of breed. For that oon was no lettyng to
that othir, that is, forto se me intellectualy, verry God and
verry man in that liknesse of breed. Ne also that lyknesse of
breed was nott ilettid, for fro that liknes of breed was not   70

53. *made ... open*: disclosed myself.   *saygh*: saw.
54. *as*: as if.
54–5. *sonne-beem*: sunbeam.
55. *whele*: disc.   *sonne*: sun.
56. *departynge from*: leaving.   *rondel*: circular shape.
57. *culver*: dove (the traditional symbol of the Holy Spirit).
      flikeride: fluttered.
57–8. *smoot ... hoost*: struck his wings together around the Host
(consecrated wafer).
58. *ofschewynge*: manifesting, exhibiting.
59. *for vertu*: because of the power.   *tho*: those.
61. *bodily iye*: physical eye.   *suffre*: bear.
62. *sich*: such.
      but ... intellecte: but your capacity for sight remained in the eye of your
understanding alone, i.e. Catherine was temporarily blinded physically.
63. *there*: where.   *say*: saw.   *taastist*: tasted, experienced.
      depnesse: depth, profundity.
64. *keverid*: covered, concealed.   *whightnesse*: whiteness.
66. *feldist*: felt, experienced.   *intellectualy*: i.e. through the understanding.
67. *lettyng*: hindrance.
68. *verry*: true.
69. *liknesse*: appearance.
70. *ilettid*: hindered.
70–1. *fro ... savour*: i.e. the consecrated Host did not lose its bread-like
attributes, such as whiteness, texture or taste. Catherine is formulating
quite precisely the Catholic doctrine of Transubstantiation, according to
which the 'substance' of the bread is transformed into Christ's body while
the 'accidents' – the attributes perceptible to the physical senses – remain.

withdrawe whitnesse ne touchinge ne savour. This revelacioun
and visyoun was schewid to thee of myn eendelees goodenesse,
the which eendelees goodnes yaf to thin iye of intellecte a
cleer sight with holy feith. Therfore the iye of intellecte
schulde be thi principal sight, and with that sight ye schulden   75
biholde this sacrament of the auter.'

c) *God on the Dominican Order: Its Original Ideals and Present Corruption* (ff. 178ᵛ–180ʳ)

'If thou biholde now the schip of thi fadir Seynt Domynyk, my
blessid chield, thou schalt se how he sett it in a parfight ordir.
And he wolde that sogetis whiche entren into the schip
schulden oonly take heede to my worschip and heelthe of   80
soulis, with the light of kunnyng. And upon that light he made
the principal bigynyng of his religyoun. Yit it was not deprived
fro verry wilful povert, but he had it. And in tokene that he
had it, the contrarie therof displeside him so myche that he
bilefte to hise children in the same religyoun by his testament,   85
for their heritage, his curs and myn, if thei evere kept or

---

74. *cleer sight*: pure vision.

75. *sight*: (means of) seeing; God very often opens his addresses to
Catherine with the injunction, 'Open the eye of thy intellect.'

77. *schip*: ship. The Church itself was often symbolised as a ship,
specifically as Noah's Ark; here the various religious orders are called ships
as they provide safe passage across the stormy seas of life.

77. *thi ... Domynyk*: Catherine was a member of the Third Order of
St Dominic (see Headnotes).

78. *chield*: child.

79. *sogetis*: subjects, i.e. those who owe obedience to another.

80–1. *schulden .... soulis*: should pay attention to the honour of God and
the salvation of souls alone.

81. *kunnyng*: knowledge. Although Dominic founded his order of preachers
primarily to fight heresy, Dominicans quickly became famous for their
learning and prominent in the Universities.

82. *principal bigynyng*: primary foundation.   *religyoun*: religious order.

82–3. *deprived... povert* : i.e. without the additional element of true,
voluntary poverty, the hallmark of the Franciscan Order which God has just
finished praising.

83. *in tokene*: as a symbol.

84. *contrarie therof*: opposite of it (i.e. poverty).

85. *bilefte*: bequeathed, left.   *testament*: will.

86. *heritage*: inheritance.   *curs*: curse.

hadde ony maner of possessiouns in special or in general.
This was a verry tokene that he chees to his spouse the
Qweene of Povert; but for his principal vertu that he sette his
religioun upon, was the light of kunnyng, which he took   90
myghtily upon himsilf, for distriynge of errouris and heresies
whiche regnede in tho dayes. He took upon him the office of
my sone, so that in the world he was worthily clepid apostil,
bycause with right greet truthe he sewe my word, puttinge
awey derknes and yevynge light. He was o light that schinede   95
in the derk world, which light I yaf to the world by mene and
mediacioun of Marye, my sones worthi modir, that was sent
into the mysterial body of Holy Chirche as a distrier of
heresies, for sche yaf him his abyte whanne the office of
preching was comyttid to him by my sone.   100
Why seyde I "by mene and mediacioun of the right blessid
Marye"? For sche praiede that the heresies myghten be
distried in Holy Chirche. Wherfore I chees Domynyk forto
labour thereupon with light of kunnyng, of the which light of
kunnyng he made hise children in the same religioun ete upon   105

87. in(1) ... *general*: either individually or collectively. The Dominicans,
like the Franciscans, were mendicants, i.e. they owned no property except
their houses and churches and begged to support themselves.
88. chees to: chose as.
89. sette: founded, established.
91. distriynge: destroying.   *errouris*: errors.
91–2. heresies ... dayes: St Dominic (*c.* 1170–1221) founded his order to
oppose the Albigensian or Catharist heresy, prevalent in the south of
France in the thirteenth century, by the peaceful means of preaching and
teaching. Cathars were dualists who believed that the physical world,
including the human body, was the work of Satan and the soul alone
created by God.
92. regnede: reigned, held sway.   *office*: function.
93. worthily: rightly.   *clepid*: called.
94. sewe: sowed. Dominic was a preacher, an apostolic function which had
hitherto been seen as the role of bishops rather than of priests.
94. puttinge: driving.
95. o: one.
96. yaf: gave.
96–7. by ... Marye: through the means and mediation of Mary.
97. that: who, i.e. Dominic.
98. mysterial: mystical.   *distrier*: destroyer.
99–100. sche ... sone: traditionally, the Dominicans' white habit had been
given them by the Virgin, whose intercession had brought about the
foundation of the Order.
100. comyttid: entrusted.
104. thereupon: i.e. on that task.
105. ete: eat, i.e. nourish themselves intellectually.   *upon*: at.

the table of the cros, upon the which cros was sett amongis
hem the table of holy desier, where soulis eten for my honour
and worschip. He wolde not that hise children schulde take
hede to ony other bisynes than oonli forto stonde upon this
table with the light of kunnyng, forto seke the glorie and laude   110
of my name and heelthe of soulis. That thei schulden have no
matir forto be lett in othere thingis, he withdrowgh fro hem
the bisynes of temperal goodis, whom he wolde were poore.
He doutide nevere for no liiflode for hem, ne he dredde
nevere that, for he had myghtily arayed him in verry feith and   115
in stidefast hope, and so hopide in my providens.

He wolde also that thei schulden kepe obedyens, and that
thei be obedient forto do that thing to the which thei ben
chose; and also for cause that by unclene lyvyng the iye of
intellecte is blyndid, and not oonli the intellecte but by that   120
wrecchide vyce the bodily sight failith. Wherefore he wil not
that therby their light were lette with the which light thei
wynne the light of kunnyng the betere and the moore
parfightly. Therfore he put to hem the thridde avow, that is of
contynens. And among alle hise children he wolde it were   125
kepte with verri parfight obediens, though it be these dayes
yvel kept.

109. bisynes: occupation.
110. laude: praise.
111. heelthe: salvation.
111–12. That ... thingis: i.e. so that there should be nothing else to
distract them.
112. withdrowgh: withdrew.
113. bisynes ... goodis: preoccupation with worldly possessions.
   whom: the antecedent is *hem* (l. 112).
114. doutide ... hem: he never worried about their means of living.
115–16. he ... hope: he had powerfully arrayed himself in true faith and
steadfast hope.
117. kepe obedyens: keep (a vow of) obedience; Catherine has much to say
about obedience, on which the Dominicans placed a special emphasis: they
put it before chastity and poverty in their vows.
119. for cause: because.   *unclene*: impure, unchaste.
121. bodily: physical.
122. therby: by that (i.e. unchastity).   *were lette*: should be hindered.
123. wynne: win, achieve.
124. put to: enjoined upon.   *thridde avow*: third vow.
125. contynens: continence, chastity.
127. yvel: badly: by the late fourteenth century there was much hostility
toward the mendicant orders, and friars were regularly accused of
unchastity: see for instance, the description of the Friar in the General
Prologue to *The Canterbury Tales* (*CT* I(A): 212–3) and the opening of the
Wife of Bath's Tale (*CT* III(D): 880–1).

For now thei perverte the light of kunnyng into derknes
with the blyndnes of pride – not for this light of kunnyng may
resceyve derknes, but I sey this as for the derknes of her   130
soulis. For where that pride is, there may noon obediens be.
For as I toolde thee late, a verry obediencer is as myche in
mekenes as he is in obediens, and as myche in obediens as he
is in mekenes. Therfore he that breketh the vow of obediens,
seldom it is seen but that he brekith the avow of continens, or   135
mentaly or actualy. And this thou maist knowe and se wel, that
he hath ordeyned forto bynde his religious schip with these
thre coordis, that is, with obediens, contynens and verry
povert. It is al maad rialy, for al deedly synne may be eschewid
thereynne.   140
He was so illumyned of me with verry light and providens,
that he providide to hem which were of lesse parfeccioun than
othere, as wel as he dide for hem that weren parfight in the
same religioun. For though alle that kepen this ordir ben
parfight, yit in that way of lyvynge there may be oon moore   145
parfight than another. And so he providide therfore, that
bothe parfight and unparfight, alle mowe dwelle togydere in
this religious schip. He festnede himsilf myghtily to myn oonly
soothfast sone, Jhesu, sewynge his doctrine, and that he
schewide wel in that he wolde not the deeth of the synners but   150

128. *For now*: Catherine of Siena's biographer, Raymond of Capua, was
elected to reform the Dominican Order after her death.
129. *pride*: the friars were also attacked for their pride, because of their
role as university teachers and their association with aristocratic society.
129. *not for*: not that.
130. *resceyve*: admit.   *as for*: with respect to.
132. *late*: recently.
    verry obediencer: a person who practises true obedience.
    myche: great.
135. *seldom . . . he*: it is very rare if he does not.
135–6. *or . . . actualy*: either in his mind or in fact.
137. *he*: i.e. St Dominic.   *ordeyned*: provided.
    bynde: constrain, tie up firmly.
138. *coordis*: cords, ropes.
139. *rially*: royally.   *deedly*: deadly, mortal.   *eschewid*: avoided.
141. *illumyned of*: illuminated, enlightened, by.   *providens*: foresight.
142. *to*: for.
147. *mowe*: might.
148. *festnede*: fastened, attached.
149. *sewynge*: following.
149–50. *that . . . wel*: he demonstrated this effectively.

that thei weren turnyd and lyveden. He was vertuously al
large, al myrye and jocunde and al swete in vertu as a
delytable viridarie.

But wrecchis siche as kepen not the ordre, but brekeris of
the same, defoulen and enfecten othere whiche ben norischid   155
in the same religioun at the breste of vertu, with the lytil light
of kunnyng that thei have. I sey not of the ordir in itsilf for, as
I seyde, it hath al goostly delectacioun in itsilf. But in the
bigynnyng I seie ther was noon sich infectioun among hem,
for thanne alle were as o flour wel smyllinge. In that tyme men   160
weren of so greet parfeccioun that there was no derknes of
errour ne heresies, but that it was with the light of kunnyng of
hem put away.

Se and biholde Seynt Thomas Alqwyn, which with the light
of his intellecte worthily he bihelde in the myrrour of my   165
truthe, where he wan light above nature and kunnyng infudid
by grace. For booth by praier and mannus studie he wan sich
kunnyng. He was as a brennyng light that yaf light in his ordre
and qwenchide derknes in the mysterial body of Holy
Chirche.   170

150–1. he ... lyveden: quoting Ezekiel 33:11: 'As I live, saith the Lord
God, I desire not the death of the wicked, but that the wicked turn from his
way, and live', but also reminding us that among its other functions the
Dominican Order staffed the Holy Inquisition.
152. large: generous.   *myrye*: joyful.   *jocunde*: gay.
153. delytable viridarie: a delightful pleasure-garden.
154. siche: such.   *kepen ... ordre*: do not keep the (rules of the) order.
   brekeris: breakers, violators.
155. defoulen: defile.   *enfecten*: infect.
158. goostly delectacioun: spiritual delight.
159. seie: say.
160. as ... smyllinge: like one sweet-smelling flower.
162–3. kunnyng ... hem: their knowledge.
164. Seynt ... Alqwyn: St Thomas Aquinas (*c.* 1225–74), the chief
intellectual ornament of the Dominican Order and the leading figure in
Scholasticism, a synthesis of Aristotelian philosophy and Christian theology.
165–6. he ... truthe: he gazed into the mirror of my truth, i.e. engaged in
philosophy and theology.
166. wan: won, achieved.   *light ... nature*: supernatural enlightenment.
   infudid: poured in, infused.
167. mannus studie: man's (i.e. human) intellectual activity.
168. as ... light: like a burning light.
169. qwenchide: extinguished.

Biholde also Seynt Petir of Melan, that virgyn and martir, which with scheding of his blood by marterdom, yaf light in distriynge of manye heresies, whiche heresies he had in so greet hate that he disposide himsilf forto dye rather than forto suffre hem. And al the while he lyvede in erthe, he disposide   175
hym to noon othir thing than forto exercise him in praier, prechinge, disputinge with heretikis, schewinge the truthe, and spredinge the feith overal, withoute ony drede, and that not oonli he wold knowleche it bi his liif but unto the deeth, so ferforth that in the eende of his deeth, whanne his tonge   180
faylide him in resceyvynge of the strook, he wett his fyngur in his blood and bycause he lackid a chartir to write upon, he put his fyngir to the erthe and wroot, knowlechinge his feith and bileeve in this wise: *Credo in Deum*, etc.

His herte brennyde in the forneyce of my charite and   185
therfore in his passioun he turnede not his heed abak, knowynge wel that he schulde dye. For eer than he diede, I schewide him by revelacioun his maner of deeth. Wherfore as a verry knyght withoute ony servyle drede, he stood in the

171. Seynt . . . Melan: the Dominican St Peter Martyr (1205–52), whose parents were Cathars, was in 1234 appointed Inquisitor for the Milan area. His opposition to heresy caused much hostility and he was assassinated, his head split open by an axe. Regarded as the first Dominican martyr, he is also the patron saint of Inquisitors.

172. scheding: shedding.

173. had: held.

174. he . . . dye: he made up his mind to die.

175. suffre: endure, tolerate.

176. exercise him: exert himself.

178. overal: everywhere.

179. knowleche: acknowledge, confess.

180. so ferforth: to such an extent.

181. in(1) . . . strook: i.e. when he had received the blow.

182. chartir: piece of parchment.

183. wroot: wrote.   *knowlechinge*: acknowledging, confessing.

184. Credo . . . Deum: 'I believe in God', the opening words of the Apostles' Creed.

185. brennyde: burned.   *forneyce*: furnace, oven.   *charite*: love.

186. passioun: suffering.   *abak*: back.

187. eer than: before.

188–90. as . . . batel: the image of the monk and, later, religious as a 'knight of Christ' is very ancient, going back to St Paul's injunction (Ephesians 6:11–17), 'Put you on the armour of God . . . .'

189. verry: true.

servyle drede: i.e. the fear of a servant or slave for his master.

stood: i.e. stood firm.

feeld of batel. And thus of manye I may telle thee, that though   190
thei suffriden no marterdom actualy, yit thei suffriden
mentaly, as Seynt Domynyk and othere siche.

Heere now what tiliers I have sent into my vyneyerd forto
pul up thornes of vicis and forto plaunte vertues. Serteyn,
Domynyk and Fraunceis weren tweye pyleris in Holy Chirche: 195
Fraunceys with his povert, which was yoven him principally as
his owne propre vertu, as it is afore rehersid.'

Textual notes

23. fle] fle to the.
29. take me] take.
82. was not] was.
131. obediens] obedienc.
147. togydere] togyde.

190. feeld: field.
193. Heere: Hear.   *tiliers*: cultivators, labourers.
    vyneyerd: recalling the parables of the Lord of the Vineyard (e.g.
Matthew 20:1–16).
194. plaunte: plant.   *Serteyn*: Certainly.
195. tweye: two.
    pyleris: pillars. This recalls the legend that Pope Innocent III, who
later approved the foundation of their Orders, dreamt of two men, Francis
and Dominic, who sprang forward to save the Church from collapse.
197. afore rehersid: repeated before.

8 Julian of Norwich

Very little is known about Julian of Norwich, not even her baptismal name. She was born in 1342. On 8 or 13 May 1373, when aged thirty, she experienced a series of visions as she lay dying, followed by a miraculous recovery. She wrote two accounts of this experience, one almost at once and another up to twenty years later. Before 1413 she became an anchoress at St Julian's Church, Norwich, from which she may have taken her name in religion. She was still alive in 1416, when a will of that year left her a bequest, but was dead by 1426 when another will refers to the male recluse at St Julian's.

Julian was not a nun or an anchoress at the time of her revelations. She mentions that her mother, the parish priest and a small boy were present at her sick-bed, which would have been impossible if she were an enclosed religious. She had probably been married, for unmarried laywomen of thirty were virtually unknown in medieval England, but as there is no mention of her husband we may deduce that she was a widow (like Bridget of Sweden, Christine de Pisan, Eleanor Hull and Lady Margaret Beaufort) and that, if she had borne children, they too were dead by 1373.

Julian has been the object of much ill-informed adulation and dubious interpretation. She was a profound thinker, a difficult writer and an original theologian, not at all the simple, homely and cheerful woman of popular perception. Although one manuscript asserts that 'she did not know a letter', i.e. was illiterate or at least without Latin, and Julian describes herself as 'lewd' (i.e. uneducated), she was clearly literate in English and in the Latin of the Vulgate at least; how much further her learning extended is, like so much about her, a subject of dispute. Perhaps the most original writer in this anthology, she was also ultimately one of the most assured. A passage in the Short Version of *A Revelation of Love* apologising for her temerity in writing as a 'woman, lewd, feeble and frail' has been removed from the later Long Version (see Introduction, p. 7). She was also unlike other women visionaries in her tendency to engage in theological speculations on the most intractable of topics, such as the reality of sin and the constitution of the Trinity, rather than in affective, emotional recreations of events from the life of Christ. Her probing, analytical mind is most like that of her near-contemporary Catherine of Siena.

Comment: The first two passages are from the Short (Carthusian) Version of *A Revelation of Love* (see below, p. 110). The first, which provides the context for Julian's visionary experiences, makes it clear that Julian was originally a medieval pious woman of a not uncommon type who, like many others, desired personal religious experience to enhance her faith based on the authority of the Church. Her longing for a more intense realisation, a 'bodily vision', of Christ's Passion, as if she had herself been present at the Crucifixion, is similar to that of Margery Kempe or Bridget of Sweden. What is slightly unusual, however, is her choice of St Cecilia as a role model; a combative early Christian martyr who converted her husband and his brother, she was popular in the Middle Ages (her legend is told by, among others, Chaucer in his *Second Nun's Tale*) but she represented a type of heroic, apostolic spirituality out of sympathy with late medieval piety. She was a preacher and teacher, a role Julian too ultimately adopted.

The second passage is one of six revelations concerned with Christ's Passion, granted Julian in response to her request for her first 'grace'. The vision is painfully vivid, though not morbid or grotesque as late medieval devotion can so often be: the physical description of the suffering Christ is balanced and ultimately obliterated by her perception that even such physical pain is less than the spiritual pain of Christ's thirst for souls or the anguish of despair. Above all, Christ's love is stronger than his pain, and finally the suffering of Christ, of the visionary and of the whole of creation is transformed into joy.

The third passage, from the Long (Benedictine) Version of the text, is part of Julian's radical attempt to reconstruct the traditional model of the Trinity on a Father–Mother rather than Father–Son basis. The latter part of the argument, in which Julian describes Christ's motherhood as an aspect of the humility of the Incarnation, his Passion as the travail of childbirth, and the Eucharist as his feeding his children with his body and blood as a mother does with her milk, is clear enough. So is her moving description of how Christ deals with the individual soul as a mother relates to her growing child, providing nurture, support and an education in which mistakes and setbacks (i.e. sins) actually play a positive role. No experience is wasted, for sin is not so much something from which we must dissociate ourselves as a part of ourselves through which we grow but which we eventually outgrow. The model is developmental, a very modern idea of fulfilling one's potential, through God's grace, and becoming the ideal, complete person whom God has eternally in mind.

But it would misrepresent the complexity of Julian's thought to omit the earlier part of the passage, difficult and obscure though it is. For the motherhood of God is a truth which operates on more than one level and springs ultimately from a conception of the Trinity as primarily a Father–Mother relationship, and of Christ – who as the Second Person of the Trinity was traditionally both the masculine *logos* or cosmic Reason and the feminine Wisdom or divine creative activity – as God our Mother in relation to God our Father. One cannot consider Julian's teaching on the motherhood of God without remembering that it is complementary to her concept of God's fatherhood, nor can it be fully understood without some knowledge of medieval theories about the biological roles of father and mother. Some medieval physiologists, following Aristotle, gave the mother a subordinate role in reproduction; she retained and nourished the father's seed and in due course produced it, but did not contribute anything herself to the initial conception (Rousselle 1988: 27–32).

The final passage illuminates the compositional history of the texts. In this moving conclusion Julian draws a careful distinction between the visions and their meaning. For all their complexity, she finally sees that their meaning is single: 'Love was Our Lord's meaning.' All that ever can be drawn out of the revelations can neither exceed, nor exhaust, that parameter.

Manuscripts: Julian's textual history is complex (see Glasscoe 1989). She probably wrote the short account of her revelations almost immediately; this is extant in a single manuscript, the mid fifteenth-century BL MS Add. 37790, which belonged to Carthusian monks. (It also contains a copy of the ME translation of Marguerite Porete.) Fifteen or twenty years later she wrote a greatly expanded version (see below, p. 134) but there are no complete mansucripts of this text any earlier than the mid seventeenth century (BL MS Sloane 2499 and Paris, BN Fonds Anglais 40 – both manuscripts that belonged to Continental communities of émigré English Benedictine nuns). However, MS Westminster Treasury 4 (*c.* 1500) contains extracts from this longer version.

Julian's text first appeared in print in 1670, edited by the English Benedictine monk Serenus de Cressy who used the Paris manuscript, which varies in important details from Sloane 2499. There has never been a scholarly consensus as to which manuscript is preferable. Sloane 2499 (S) preserves Middle English forms better, and for that reason is used as the base text for these extracts. The Paris MS (P), though it modernises the language, may preserve Julian's rhetorical figures better, and is preferred by Colledge and Walsh (1978).

Further Reading (for full details see Bibliography): There are many popular and scholarly accounts of Julian and her thought: see in particular Pelphrey 1989. On the textual tradition, see Glasscoe 1989. For further bibliographical references, see Lagorio and Bradley 1981: 105–26; Petroff 1986: 299–301; Wilson 1984: 295–6.

From the Short (Carthusian) Version of *A Revelation of Love*

a) *The Opening*
(British Library MS Add. 37790, f. 97^{r-v})

I desyrede thre graces be the gyfte of God. The fyrst was to have mynde of Cryste-es passion. The seconde was bodelye syekenes. And the thryd was to have of Goddys gyfte thre woundys.

    For the fyrste come to my mynde with devocion. Me   5
thought I hadde grete felynge in the passyon of Cryste. Botte

---

2. mynde: mindfulness, recollection.
2–3. bodelye syekenes: physical sickness.
6. felynge: awareness, insight.

yitte I desyrede to have mare, be the grace of God. Me
thought I wolde have bene that tyme with Mary Mawdeleyne
and with othere that were Crystes loverse, that I myght have
sene bodylye the passion of Oure Lorde that he sufferede for　10
me, that I myght have sufferede with hym as othere dyd that
lovyd hym, not withstandynge that I leevyd sadlye alle the
peynes of Cryste as Halye Kyrke schewys and techys, and also
the payntyngys of crucyfexes that er made be the grace of
God, aftere the techynge of Haly Kyrke, to the lyknes of　15
Crystes passyon, als farfurthe as manys witte maye reche.

And nought withstondynge alle this trewe beleve, I
desyrede a bodylye syght whareyn Y myght have more
knawynge of bodelye paynes of Oure Lorde oure savyoure and
of the compassyon of Oure Ladye and of alle his trewe loverse　20
that were belevande his paynes, that tyme and sythene. For I
wolde have beene one of thame and suffrede with thame.
Othere syght of Gode ne schewynge desyrede I nevere none
tylle atte the sawlle were departyd frome the bodye, for I
trayste sothfastlye that I schulde be safe; and this was my　25
menynge, for I wolde aftyr, becawse of that schewynge, have
the more trewe mynde in the passion of Cryste.

For the seconde come to my mynde with contricion, frelye
withowtyn any sekynge, a wylfulle desyre to hafe of Goddys

7. *mare*: more.　*be*: by.
8. *wolde*: would like.
　Mary Mawdeleyne: Mary Magdalene, the type of the contemplative and
penitent woman; see *The Faits and the Passion of Our Lord Jesu Christ*, below,
p. 208.
9. *Crystes loverse*: lovers of Christ.
12. *leevyd*: believed.　*sadlye*: solemnly.
13. *Halye Kyrke*: Holy Church.
14. *crucyfexes*: Christ crucified.　*er*: are.
15. *aftere*: according to.
16. *als farfurthe*: as far.　*manys witte*: human understanding.
17. *beleve*: belief, faith.
18. *syght*: sight, vision.　*whareyn*: in which.
19. *knawynge*: knowing.
20. *compassyon*: shared suffering.
21. *belevande*: believing.　*sythene*: since.
22. *thame*: them.
23. *schewynge*: revelation.
24. *tylle atte*: until.
25. *trayste*: trusted.　*schulde . . . safe*: was to be saved.
26. *menynge*: intention.　*aftyr*: afterwards.
28. *seconde*: second (grace of bodily sickness).　*frelye*: freely.
29. *sekynge*: (conscious) seeking.　*wylfulle*: wilful, voluntary.

gyfte a bodelye syekenes and I wolde that this bodylye   30
syekenes myght have beene so harde as to the dede, so that I
myght in the sekenes take alle my ryghtynges of Halye Kyrke,
wenande myselfe that I schulde dye, and that alle creatures
that sawe me myght wene the same. For I wolde hafe no
comforth of no fleschlye nothere erthelye lyfe. In this sekenes   35
I desyrede to hafe alle manere of paynes, bodelye and
gastelye, that I schulde have yyf I schulde dye, alle the dredes
and tempestes of feyndys and alle manere of thayre paynes,
safe of the owghte-passynge of the sawlle. For I hoped that it
myght be to me a spede when I schulde dye. For I desyrede   40
sone to be with my God.

This two desyres, of the passyon and of the seekenes, I
desyrede thame with a condicion, for me thought that it
passede the comene course of prayers and therfore I sayde,
'Lorde, thowe woote whate I wolde. Yyf it be thy wille that I   45
have itt, grawnte itt me. And yyf it be nought thy wille, goode
Lorde, be nought dysplesede, for I wille nought, botte as
thowe wille.' This sekenes desyrede I yn my thought that Y
myght have it whene I were in threttye yeere eelde.

For the thirde, I harde a man telle of Haly Kyrke of the   50
storye of Saynte Cecylle, in the whilke schewynge I

31. harde: severe.
    as . . . dede: as if unto death. Julian's desire to experience her own
death is in line with traditional meditative practice; a standard subject of
meditation was one's own death-bed.
32. take: receive.   *ryghtynges*: (last) rites, i.e. extreme unction.
33. wenande: thinking.   *schulde*: was to.
35. nothere: neither.
37. gastelye: spiritual.
38. tempestes: disturbances.   *feyndys*: fiends.
39. safe: except.   *owghte-passynge*: departure, passing away.
    hoped: expected.
40. spede: help.
44. passede: exceeded.   *comene course*: usual run.
45. woote: knowest.
47. botte: except.
49. in . . . eelde: at thirty years old.
50. harde: heard.
51. Cecylle: Cecilia, a legendary early Christian martyr. She was said to
have converted her bridegroom Valerian and his brother to Christianity;
they were martyred and she was condemned to death. An attempt to
suffocate her in her bath failed; an executioner then made three attempts to
behead her but she lingered three days before dying (see above, pp. 108–9
and Farmer 1978: 72).
51. schewynge: exposition.

undyrstode that sche hadde thre woundys with a swerde in the nekke, with the whilke sche pynede to the dede. By the styrrynge of this I conseyvede a myghty desyre, prayande Oure Lorde God that he wolde grawnte me thre woundys in my lyfe-tyme, that es to saye, the wound of contricyon, the wounde of compassyon, and the wounde of wylfulle langgynge to God. Ryght as I askede the othere two with a condyscion, so I askyd the thyrde withowtyn any condyscyon. This two desyres beforesayde passed fro my mynde and the thyrde dwellyd contynuelye.

b) *The Eighth Revelation*
(ff. 103ʳ–104ᵛ)

Aftyr this, Cryste schewyd me a partye of his passyone nere his dyinge. I sawe that swete faace as yt ware drye and bludye-lesse with pale dyinge, sithen mare dede pale langourande; and than turnede more dede to the blewe, and sithene mare blewe, as the flesche turnede mare deepe dede. For alle the paynes that Cryste sufferde in his bodye schewyd to me in the blyssede faace als farfurthe as I sawe it, and namelye in the lyppes, thare I sawe this foure colourse, thaye that I sawe beforehande freschlye and ruddy, lyflye and lykande to my syght.

---

52. swerde: sword.
53. pynede ... dede: suffered unto death.
54. styrrynge: suggestion.   *conseyvede*: conceived.
57. wylfulle langgynge: voluntary desire.
58. to: for.   *Ryght*: just.   *condyscion*: condition.
60. beforesayde: i.e. formerly mentioned.
62. partye: part.   *nere*: near, close to.
63. as yt ware: as if it were.   *drye*: dry, dehydrated.
63–4. bludyelesse: bloodless, drained of blood.
64. sithen ... langourande: then sickening, more deadly pale.
65. than ... blewe: then becoming more dead, transformed to the colour of lead.
66. as ... dede: as the flesh became more profoundly dead.
67. schewyd: were evident.
68. als farfurthe: insofar.   *namelye*: particularly.
69. lyppes: lips.   *thare*: where.
     this ... colourse: these four (gradations of) colours, i.e. the initial pallor and its three stages of intensification towards a livid lead colour.
69. thaye: those, i.e. the lips.
70. freschlye and ruddy: fresh and rosy.   *lyflye*: living, alive.
     lykande: pleasing.

This was a hevy chaunge to see this deepe dyinge, and also
the nese chaungede and dryed to my sight. This lange
pynynge semede to me as he hadde bene a sevennyght dede,
allewaye sufferande payne. And me thought the dryinge of   75
Crystes flesche was the maste payne of his passion, and the
laste. And in this dryhede was brought to my mynde this
worde that Cryste sayde, 'I thryste.' For I sawe in Criste a
doubille thyrste, ane bodylye, ane othere gastelye. This worde
was schewyd to me for the bodylye thirste, and for the gastelye   80
thyrste was schewyd to me als I schalle saye eftyrwarde. And I
undyrstode of bodelye thyrste that the bodye hadde of
faylynge of moystere. For the blessede flesche and banes were
lefte allane withowtyn blode and moystere: the blyssyd bodye
dryede alle ane lange tyme with wryngynge of the nayles and   85
paysynge of the hede and weyght of the bodye, with blawynge
of wynde fra withoutyn that dryed mare and pyned hym with
calde mare than myn herte can thynke, and alle othere paynes.
    Swilke paynes I sawe that alle es to litelle that Y can telle or

72. *hevy chaunge*: wearisome change.   *deepe*: profound.
73. *nese*: nose.
    chaungede: changed. Beer emends to *claungede*, Colledge and Walsh to
clung (both forms of the ME verb *clung*, to congeal, stiffen); but the Middle
Ages recognised the changing of the nose in 'sharpening' as a sign of
imminent death.
73–4. *lange pynynge*: lengthy pining.
74. *as . . . dede*: as if he had been dead (or, as Beer glosses it, on the verge
of death) for a week.
75. *sufferande*: suffering.   *dryinge*: drying-out, dehydration.
76. *maste*: most, i.e. greatest.
77. *dryhede*: dryness.
78. *thryste*: thirst; cf. John 19:28.
79. *doubille*: double, two-fold.
    ane(1) . . . *gastelye*: one physical, the other spiritual.
    worde: saying, locution.
80. *schewyd*: revealed.   *for*: concerning.
81. *als*: as.   *eftyrwarde*: afterwards.
82. *of*: about.
82–3. *of*(2) . . . *moystere*: from lack of moisture.
83. *banes*: bones.
84. *allane*: alone, i.e. deprived, bereft.
85. *wryngynge*: squeezing, pressing.   *nayles*: nails.
86. *paysynge*: heavy hanging.   *blawynge*: blowing.
87. *fra withoutyn*: from outside.   *pyned*: tormented.
88. *calde*: cold.
89. *Swilke*: such.
89–90. *alle . . . saye*: what I can tell or say is completely inadequate.

saye, for itt maye nought be tolde, botte ylke saule, aftere the   90
sayinge of Saynte Pawle, schulde feele in hym that in Criste
Jhesu. This schewynge of Criste paynes fillyd me fulle of
paynes, for I wate weele he suffrede nought botte anez, botte
as he walde schewe yt me and fylle me with mynde as I hadde
desyrede before.   95

My modere, that stode emangys othere and behelde me,
lyftyd uppe hir hande before me face to lokke myn eyen, for
sche wenyd I had bene dede or els I hadde dyede, and this
encresyd mekille my sorowe, for nought withstandynge alle my
paynes, I wolde nought hafe been lettyd, for loove that I   100
hadde in hym. And to whethere, in alle this tyme of Crystes
presence, I felyd no payne botte for Cristes paynes, than
thought me I knewe ful lytylle whate payne it was that I askyd.
For me thought that my paynes passede any bodylye dede; I
thought, 'Es any payne in helle lyke this payne?' And I was   105
aunswerde in my resone that dyspayre ys mare, for that es
gastelye payne. Bot bodilye payne es nane mare than this:
howe myght my payne be more, than to see hym that es alle
my lyfe, alle my blys and alle mye joye suffyrande? Hir felyd I

90. maye: can.   *ylke*: each.
90–1. aftere . . . Pawle: according to St Paul's words.
91–2. schulde . . . Jhesu: a literal translation of Philippians 2:5, *Hoc enim
sentite in vobis, quod et in Christo Iesu* ('For let this mind be in you, which
was also in Christ Jesus'), which suggests that Julian was familiar with the
Latin Vulgate.
93. wate weele: knew well.   *suffrede. . . anez*: only suffered once.
93–4. botte(2) . . . *walde*: except insofar as he would.
94. mynde: mindfulness.
94–5. as . . . before: see above, ll. 1–27.
96. emangys: amongst.
97. me: my.   *lokke*: lock, close.   *eyen*: eyes.
98. wenyd: thought.   *had . . . dyede*: was dead or else had (just) died.
99. encresyd: increased.   *mekille*: much.   *nought*: not.
100–1. I(1) . . . *hym*: I did not want to be prevented, because of the love
that I had for him.
101. to whethere: Beer takes this as a conjunction, a variant of 'though
whether' (nevertheless, however); Colledge and Walsh understand *whethere*
as a pronoun and gloss 'and with regard to either', i.e. 'her own sickness'
and 'the sorrow she feels when she can no longer see Christ'.
102. felyd: felt, experienced.
103. thought me: it seemed to me.
104. passede: surpassed, exceeded.   *bodylye dede*: physical death.
106. resone: intellect, mind.   *dyspayre*: despair.
107. gastelye: spiritual.
   bodilye . . . this: there is no physical pain greater than this.
109. blys: bliss, glory.   *suffyrande*: suffering.   *Hir*: here.

sothfastlye that Y lovede Criste so mekille aboven myselfe that   110
me thought it hadde beene a grete eese to me to hafe dyede
bodylye.

Here-yn I sawe in partye the compassyon of Oure Ladye
Saynte Marye, for Criste and scho ware so anede in loove that
the gretnesse of hir loove was the cause of the mykillehede of   115
hir payne. For so mykille as scho lovyd hym mare than alle
othere, her payne passed alle othere, and so alle his disciples
and alle his trewe lovers suffyrde paynes mare than thare
awne bodelye dying. For I am sekyr be myn awne felynge that
the leste of thame luffed hym mare than thaye dyd thamselfe.   120

Here I sawe a grete anynge betwyx Criste and us, for when
he was in payne, we ware in payne, and alle creatures that
myght suffyr payne soffyrde with hym. And thaye that knewe
hym nought, this was thare payne, that alle creatures, sonne
and the mone, withdrewe thare servyce, and so ware thaye alle   125
lefte in sorowe for the tyme. And thus thaye that lovyd hym
sufferde payne for luffe, and thay that luffyd hym nought
sufferde payne for faylynge of comforthe of alle creatures.

In this tyme I walde hafe lokyd besyde the crosse botte I
durste nought, for I wyste wele whilys I lukyd uppon the   130
crosse I was sekyr and safe. Therfore I walde nought assente
to putte my sawle in perille, for besyde the crosse was na

110. sothfastlye: authentically.   *aboven*: above, i.e. more.
111. hadde: would have.   *eese*: comfort.
113. Here-yn: in this.   *in partye*: partially.
114. scho: she.   *anede*: united.
115. mykillehede: magnitude.
116. so mykille: as much.
118. thare: their.
119. awne: own.   *sekyr*: sure, convinced.
     be . . . felynge: by my own experience.
120. leste: least.   *luffed*: loved.
121. anynge: uniting, union.   *betwyx*: between.
122–3. alle . . . payne: all created beings capable of suffering pain.
123. soffyrde: suffered.
123–4. thaye . . . nought: those who did not recognise him (as Christ).
124–5. alle . . . servyce: a reference to the eclipse at the time of the
Crucifixion: see Matthew 27:45.
128. faylynge . . . creatures: failure of the comfort provided by the created
world.
129. walde . . . lokyd: wanted to have looked.   *besyde*: to one side of.
130. durste: dared.   *wyste*: knew.
131. sekyr and safe: safe and sound.
132. besyde: apart from.

syekernesse, botte uglynesse of feendes. Than hadde I a
profyr in my resone as yyf it hadde beene frendelye. It sayde
to me, 'Luke uppe to Heven to his Fadere.' Than sawe I wele,   135
with the faythe that Y felyd, that thare ware nathynge betwyx
the crosse and heven that myght hafe desesyd me, and othere
me behovyd loke uppe or els aunswere. I answerde and sayde,
'Naye, I may nought. For thowe erte myne heven.' This I
sayde for I walde nought, for I hadde levyr hafe bene in that   140
payne to Domysdaye than hafe commen to Hevene otherewyse
than be hym. For I wyste wele he that bought me so sare
schulde unbynde me when he walde.

Thus chese I Jhesu for my heven, wham I saw onlye in
payne at that tyme. Me lykede no nothere hevene than Jhesu,   145
whilke schalle be my blysse when I am thare. And this has
ever beene a comforthe to me, that I chesyd Jhesu to my
hevene in alle tyme of passyon and of sorowe; and that has
beene a lernynge to me, that I schulde evermare do so and
chese anly hym to my heven, in wele and in wa. And thus   150
sawe I my lorde Jhesu langoure lange tyme, for the anynge of
the Godhede for love gafe strenght to the manhede to suffyr

---

133. syekernesse: safety, security.   *uglynesse of feendes*: the horror of fiends.
133–4. Than . . . frendelye: then I experienced an apparently friendly
proposal in my mind.
136–7. thare . . . me: there was nothing between the cross and heaven
which could have harmed me.
137–8. othere. . . . aunswere: either I must look up or answer.
139. may nought: cannot.   *thowe erte*: thou art.
140. walde nought: did not want to (look up).
140–2. I(2) . . . hym: I would rather have continued in that state of
suffering until Judgement Day than come to heaven except through him
(Christ).
142. bought . . . sare: paid so high a price for me.
143. schulde . . . walde: would release me (from pain) when he wished to.
144. chese: chose.   *wham*: whom.
145. Me . . . Jhesu: no other heaven pleased me except for Jesus.
146. whilke: who.
147. comforthe: (source of) strength.   *chesyd*: chose.   *to*: for.
149. lernynge: lesson, source of instruction.   *evermare*: evermore.
150. in(1) . . . wa: in happiness and in sorrow.
151. langoure: sicken.
151–2. anynge . . . Godhede: union with the Divine Nature.
152. gafe strenght: strengthened, reinforced.   *manhede*: human nature.

mare than alle men myght. I mene nought anly mare payne
anly than alle men myght suffyr, bot also that he suffyrde
mare payne than alle men that ever was fra the fyrste   155
begynnynge to the laste daye.

No tonge maye telle ne herte fully thynke, the paynes that
Oure Savyoure sufferde for us, haffande rewarde to the
worthynes of the hyest, worschipfulle kynge and to the
schamefulle, dyspyttus and paynfulle dede. For he that was   160
hieste and worthyest, was fullyest noghthede and witterlyest
dyspyside. Botte the love that made hym to suffere alle this, itt
passes als fare alle his payns as heven es aboven erthe. For the
paynes was a dede done in a tyme be the wyrkynge of love.
Botte luffe was withowtyn begynnynge, and es and evere   165
schalle be withowtyn any ende.

And sodaynlye, me behaldande in the same crosse, he
chaunchede into blysfulle chere: the chawngynge of his chere
chaungyd myne and I was alle gladde and mery as yt was
possybille. Than brought Oure Lorde merelye to my mynde,   170
whate es any poynte of thy payne or of thy grefe? And I was
fulle merye.

153. *myght*: could.
153–4. *nought ... suffyr*: not only more pain (alone) than all men might
suffer.
158. *haffande rewarde*: having regard.
159. *worthynes*: worth.   *hyest*: highest.   *worschipfulle*: honourable.
160. *dyspyttus*: cruel.   *dede*: death.
161. *fullyest noghthede*: most completely brought to nothing.
161–2. *witterlyest dyspyside*: most surely despised.
163. *als fare*: as far.
164. *paynes ... love*: the pains were a single action which took place on one
occasion through the operation of love.
165. *withowtyn begynnynge*: without beginning, i.e. eternal, in contrast to the
temporal nature of Christ's suffering.
167. *me ... crosse*: while I was contemplating the same cross.
167–8. *he ... chere*(1): his expression was gloriously transformed.
168–9. *the ... myne*: the transformation of his expression transformed
mine.
169. *mery*: joyful.
170. *merelye*: joyfully.
171. *whate ... grefe*: not 'What is the point of your pain or your grief?', an
exclusively twentieth-century idiom. Possibly *poynte* here means 'state,
condition', i.e. 'How is your pain and sorrow (now)?', but more likely is the
sense 'smallest part, the least bit', i.e. 'Are you experiencing (now) the least
bit of pain or grief?'
172. *fulle*: very.

From the Long (Benedictine) Version of *A Revelation of Love*

c) *The Trinity as Father, Mother and Lord* (MS Sloane 2499, ff. 41ᵛ–45)

God was never displesid with his chosin wif; and of thre properties in the Trinite: faderhede, moderhede and lordhede; and how our substance is in every person but our sensualite is in Criste alone: LVIII Capitulum.   175

God the blisful Trinite, which is everlastand beyng, ryte as he is endless from without begynning, ryte so it was in his purpose endles to maken mankynd, which fair kynd first was adyte to his owen son, the second person. And whan he wold,   180 be full accord of all the Trinite, he made us all at onys; and in our makyng he knitt us and onyd us to hymseffe, be which onyng we arn kept as clene and as noble as we were made. Be the vertue of the ilke pretious onyng we loven our maker and liken him, praysen him and thankyn him and endlesly enjoyen   185 in him. And this is the werke which is wrought continuly in every soule that shal be save, which is the godly will afornseid.

173. *his chosin wif*: i.e. the soul.
174. *properties*: attributes, characteristics.   *lordhede*: power, sovereignty.
175. *substance*: existential being.   *every person*: each Person (of the Trinity).
   sensualite: specifically human aspects of our being.
176. *Capitulum*: chapter.
177. *blisful*: glorious.   *everlastand beyng*: eternal being.   *ryte*: just.
178. *endless ... begynning*: i.e. eternal.
179. *purpose endles*: eternal design.   *mankynd*: humanity.
   fair kynd: i.e. human nature in its divinely destined form, when it achieves its full potential.
180. *adyte to*: destined for.   *wold*: willed.
181. *he ... onys*: i.e. God created the whole human race simultaneously (in Adam).
181–2. *in ... hymseffe*: this refers to God's creating human beings 'in his own image and likeness', so that there is a fundamental and essential continuity between the divine and the human.
182. *makyng*: creation.   *onyd*: united.   *hymseffe*: himself.
183. *clene*: pure.
183–4. *Be ... onyng*: by the efficacy of that same precious union.
185. *liken*: please.   *enjoyen*: rejoice.
186. *werke*: working, operation.
187. *godly will afornseid*: the 'divine' (or maybe 'goodly') will in those predestined to salvation which, Julian asserted in Chapter 37, never sins.

And thus in our makeyng God Almigty is our kindely fader, and God al wisdam is our kindly moder, with the love and the goodnes of the Holy Gost: which is al one God, on Lord. And   190 in the knittyng and in the onyng he is our very trew spouse and we his lovid wif and his fair maiden, with which wif he is never displesid. For he seith, 'I love the and thou lovist me and our love shal never be departid onto.'

I beheld the werking of all the blissid Trinite, in which   195 beholdyng I saw and understode these thre properties – the properte of the faderhede, the properte of the moderhede, and the properte of the lordhede – in one God. In our Fader almyty we have our keping and our bliss as anemts our kindly substance, which is to us be our makyng without begynnyng;   200 and in the second person, in witt and wisdam, we have our keping as anempts our sensualite, our restoryng and our savyng. For he is our moder, brother and savior. And in our good lord the Holy Gost we have our rewarding and our yeldyng for our lifyng and our travel, and endless overpassing   205 all that we desiren, in his mervelous curtesy of his hey plentivous grace. For al our life is in thre. In the first we have

188–92. And ... maiden: Julian distinguishes between God's two-fold parental role in the creation of humanity, and the Trinity's role as spouse in uniting humanity with the godhead. Elsewhere she hardly uses the metaphor of the spiritual marriage so common among other women mystics (e.g. Elizabeth of Hungary, p. 72 above; *Book of Margery Kempe*, pp. 86/9–87/26).

188. kindely: natural; beneficent.

190. which: who, i.e. Father, Son and Holy Spirit.   *on*: one.

191. very: real.

192. lovid: beloved.   *fair maiden*: sweetheart.

194. departid onto: separated.

199. keping: preservation.   *bliss*: glorification.
as anemts: with respect to.

199–200. our(3) ... *begynnyng*: our natural being which is ours through our creation in eternity.

201. in(1) ... *wisdam*: the Father is Power (*almyty*), the Son is 'the Wisdom of the Father'.

201–3. we ... savyng: we have our preservation, restoration and salvation with respect to our specifically human aspects.

204. good lord: patron, protector.

205. yeldyng: payment.   *lifyng*: way of life.   *travel*: hard work.

205–6. endless ... desiren: eternal fulfilment, exceeding all we long for.

206. hey: high, lofty.

207. plentivous: fruitful, productive.

207–10. For ... grace: i.e. human life goes through three phases: creation, the work of God the Father and his deputy Nature; growth, through God's mercy (which includes not just preservation from the hazards of life but also the possibility of salvation through Christ's redemptive death); and

our beyng and in the second we have our encresyng and in the
thrid we hav our fulfilling. The first is kinde, the second is
mercy, the thred is grace.   210

For the first: I saw and understod that the hey myte of the
Trinite is our fader, and the depe wisdam of the Trinite is our
moder, and the grete love of the Trinite is our lord, and al
this have we in kynd and in our substantial-makyng.

And ferthermore I saw that the second person, which is our   215
moder substantial, that same derworthy person is become our
moder sensual. For we arn duble of Gods makyng, that is to
say, substantiall and sensual. Our substance is the heyer parte,
which we have in our fader, God Almyty; and the second
person of the Trinite is our moder in kynde in our substantiall   220
makeyng, in whome we arn groundid and rotid, and he is our
moder in mercy, in our sensualite-takyng. And thus our
moder is to us dyvers manner werkyng, in whom our parties
are kepid ondepartid. For in our moder Criste we profitten
and encresin and in mercy he reformith us and restorith and   225
be the vertue of his passion and his deth and uprisyng onyth

finally consummation, the fulfilling of human potential as designed by the
Trinity, through the grace of the Holy Spirit. This formulation is
apparently original to Julian.

211. hey myte: high power, potency.
212. depe: profound.
213. moder: see above, p. 109. The Son is our mother in two senses:
through nature, in that he was traditionally the agent of creation ('our
moder substantial', 'our moder ... in our substantiall-makeyng'); and
through mercy, in that he redeemed humanity through his Incarnation and
Passion ('our moder sensual', 'our moder ... in our sensualite-takyng').
216. derworthy: precious.
217–18. we ... sensual: Julian's concepts of 'substance' and 'sensuality',
vital to a correct understanding of her teaching, are difficult and unusual.
By 'substance' she seems to mean 'the truth of our being, body and soul;
the way we are meant to be, as whole persons' (Pelphrey 1989: 90), or 'the
soul as a spirit existing independently of its function as the soul, the
formative principle and life of the body ... its inmost depth or centre from
which the will and understanding take their rise' (Watkin 1979: 17);
'sensualite' is quite different from modern English 'sensuality' and means
rather 'that human existence which becomes God's in the Incarnation'
(Bradley, forthcoming) or 'the soul as informing the body, its life-principle
and the subject of our psycho-physical experience' (Watkin 1979).
221. groundid: based, established.   *rotid*: rooted.
223–4. our ... ondepartid: i.e. our mother, Christ, in whom we, being
many, are all one body, manifests herself to us in various ways.
226. uprisyng: resurrection.   *onyth*: unites.

us to our substance. Thus werkith our moder in mercy to all
his children which arn to him buxum and obedient.

And grace werkyth with mercy, and namely in too propertes
as it was shewid, which werkyng longyth to the tred person,   230
the Holy Gost. He werkith rewardyng and gifyng. Rewardyng
is a large gevyng of trewth that the Lord doth to hym that hath
travellid; and gevyng is a curtes workyng which he doith frely
of grace fulfill, and overpassand al that is deservid of cretures.

Thus in our fader God Almigty we have our beyng; and in   235
our moder of mercy we have our reformyng and restoryng, in
whome our partes are onyd and all made perfitt man; and be
yeldyng and gevyng in grace of the Holy Gost we arn fulfilled.
And our substance is our fader, God almyty, and our
substance is our moder, God al wisdam; and our substance is   240
in our lord the Holy Gost, God al goodnes. For our substance
is hole in ilke person of the Trinite, which is on God. And our
sensualite is only in the second person, Crist Jesus, in whom
is the Fader and the Holy Gost; and in him and be him we
arn mytyly taken out of helle and out of the wretchidnes in   245
erth, and worshipfully browte up into hevyn and blisfully onyd
to our substance, incresid in riches and noblith, be al the
vertue of Criste and be the grace and werkyng of the Holy
Gost.

Wickednes is turnyd to bliss be mercy and grace in the   250
chosyn, for the properte of God is to do good agayn ille, be
Jesus our moder in kynd grace; and the heyest soule in vertue

228. *buxum*: tractable, responsive.
229. *namely*: in particular.
230. *longyth*: belongs.   *tred*: third.
231. *Holy Gost*: the Holy Spirit is our 'good lord', i.e. the patron or
protector who in medieval society rewarded his loyal vassals with generous
gifts.
232. *gevyng of trewth*: gift of faithfulness; P here reads 'gyfte of trust'.
233. *travellid*: served, toiled.   *curtes*: courteous, gracious.
234. *overpassand*: going beyond.
238. *yeldyng*: rewarding, paying.
242. *hole*: whole, complete.   *ilke*: each.   *on*: one.
244. *be*: by.
245. *mytyly*: powerfully.
246. *worshipfully*: with honour.   *browte*: brought.
246–7. *blisfully ... substance*: i.e. through Christ human *sensualite* is
reunited with our underlying being, which is God, and glorified.
247. *noblith*: nobility.
251. *agayn*: against.
252. *heyest*: highest, most exalted.

is mekest, of which ground we have other vertues: LIX
Capitulum.

And all this bliss we have be mercy and grace, which manner   255
of bliss we myte never had ne knowen but if that propertes of
goodness which is God had ben contraried, wherby we have
this bliss. For wickednes hath ben suffrid to rysen contrarye to
the goodnes, and the goodnes of mercy and grace contraried
ageyn the wickidnes, and turnyd al to goodness and to worship   260
to al these that shal be savid. For it is the propere in God
which doith good agen evil.

Thus Jesus Criste that doith good agen evill is our very
moder: we have our beyng of him wher the ground of
moderhed begynnyth, with al the swete kepyng of love that   265
endlessly folowith. As veryly as God is our fader, as verily
God is our moder; and that shewid he in all, and namely in
these swete words where he seith 'I it am', that is to seyen: I it
am, the myte and the goodness of the faderhed. I it am: the
wisdam of the moderhede. I it am: the lyte and the grace that   270
is all blissid love. I it am, the Trinite. I it am, the unite. I am
the sovereyne goodness of all manner of thyngs. I am that
makyth the to loven. I am that makyth the to longen. I it am,
the endles fulfilling of al trew desires.

For then the soule is heyest, noblest and worthyest when it   275
is lowest, mekest and myldhest; and of this substantial ground
we have al our vertues, and our sensualite be geft of kynd and

253. *mekest*: most humble.
    of which ground: i.e. based on this virtue of humility.
256-7. *but ... contraried*: had not those characteristics of goodness which
constitute God been resisted (i.e. if human beings had not fallen and Christ
had not been crucified).
258. *suffrid*: permitted.   *contrarye*: in opposition.
260-1. *turnyd ... savid*: transformed everything to the profit and honour of
those predestined to salvation; this is a restatement of God's words in
Chapter 27, 'Sin is behoveli [necessary, expedient or inevitable]; but all shal
be well and all shal be wel and al maner of thing shal be well'.
262. *doith ... evil*: opposes good to evil.
264. *ground*: foundation, basis.
267. *shewid ... all*: he revealed in all (the revelations).
268. *I it am*: It is I, I am.
269. *myte*: power.
270. *lyte*: light.   *that*: he who.
273. *longen*: long, desire.
274. *endles fulfilling*: eternal fulfilment.
275. *worthyest*: of greatest worth.
276. *myldhest*: most gentle.   *substantial ground*: foundation of our being.
277. *geft*: gift.

be helpyng and spedyng of mercy and grace, without the
which we may not profitten. Our hey fader, God almyty,
which is beyng, he knew us and lovid us fro aforn any tyme; of   280
which knoweing, in his mervelous depe charite be the forseing
endless councel of all the blissid Trinite, he wold that the
second person shuld becom our moder, our brother and our
savior. Wherof it folowith that as verily as God is our fader, as
verily God is our moder. Our fader wyllyth, our moder   285
werkyth, our good lord the Holy Gost confirmith. And
therfore it longyth to us to loven our God in whom we have
our being, him reverently thankyng and praiseyng of our
makyng, mytily prayeng to our moder of mercy and pite, and
to our lord the Holy Gost of helpe and grace. For in these   290
thre is all our life: kynde, mercy and grace; whereof we have
mekehede, myldhede, patiens, and pite, and hatyng of synne
and wickidnes, for it longith properly to vertues to haten synne
and wickidness.

I understode thre manner of beholdyng of moderhede in
And thus is Jesus our very moder in kynde, of our first   295
makyng, and he is our very moder in grace be takyng of our
kynde made. All the fair werkyng and all the swete kindly
office of dereworthy moderhede is impropried to the second
person; for in him we have this godly will hole and save
without ende, both in kinde and in grace, of his owne proper   300
goodnes.

I understode thre manner of beholdyng of moderhede in
God: the first is groundid of our kinde makeying; the second
is taken of our kinde, and there begynnyth the moderhede of
grace; the thrid is moderhede of werkyng, and therin is a   305

278. spedyng: encouragement.
279. profitten: prosper.
280. fro aforn: from before.
281–2. be . . . councel: by the providential and eternal secret design.
285. wyllyth: exercises his will.
286. werkyth: carries it out.   *confirmith*: strengthens, consolidates.
287. it . . . us: it is our part.
289. mytily: strenuously.
290. of: for.
292. mekehede: humility.   *myldhede*: gentleness.
293. longith . . . to(1): is the proper function of.
297. kynde made: created (human) nature.
298. office: function, role.   *impropried*: assigned as a prerogative.
299. hole and save: complete and integral.
302. beholdyng: contemplation.
305. moderhede of werkyng: i.e. a manifestation of motherhood through
Christ's dealings with us as individuals.

forth-spreadyng be the same grace of length and bredth and of heyth and of depenes withouten end, and al his own luf. How we be bowte ageyn and forthspred be mercy and grace of our swete, kynde and ever-lovyng moder Jesus; and of the propertes of moderhede; but Jesus is our very moder, not 310 fedyng us with mylke but with himselfe, opening his syde onto us and chalengyng al our love: LX Capitulum.

But now behovyth to sey a litil mor of this forth-spredyng, as I understond in the menyng of Our Lord, how that we be bowte agen be the moderhede of mercy and grace into our kyndly 315 stede wher that we were made be the moderhede of kynd love; which kynd love it never levyth us. Our kynd moder, our gracious moder, for he wold al holy become our moder in al thyng, he toke the ground of his werke full low and ful myldely in the maydens womb. And that he shewid in the first, 320 where he browte that meke mayde aforn the eye of myn understondyng in the simple statur as she was whan she conceivid; that is to sey, our hey God, sovereyn wisdom of all, in this low place he raysid him and dyte him ful redy in our pore flesh, himselfe to don the service and the office of 325 moderhede in all thyng.

The moders service is nerest, redyest and sekirest, for it is most of trueth. This office ne myte, ne couthe, ne never non

306. *forth-spreadyng*: permeation, pervasiveness.
307. *heyth*: height.
308. *bowte agayn*: redeemed (P reads *brought*).   *forthspred*: permeated.
312. *chalengyng*: claiming.
313. *behovyth*: it is appropriate.
313–14. *as . . . Lord*: as far as I understand Our Lord's intention.
315–16. *into . . . stede*: to our natural place.
317. *levyth*: leaves, abandons.
318. *al holy*: completely; the Second Person could not truly become our mother without taking on him our human nature.
319–20. *he . . . myldely*: he laid the foundations of his design very humbly and gently.
320. *first*: i.e. revelation.
322. *simple*: unpretentious; in her First Revelation Julian had seen the Virgin as 'a simple mayde and a meke, young of age and little waxen above a child' (Chapter 4).
324. *raysid him*: set himself up; also continuing the metaphor of constructing a building implicit in 'the ground of his werke'.
324. *dyte him*: dressed himself.
327. *nerest*: closest.   *redyest*: promptest.   *sekirest*: most reliable.
328–9. *This . . . full*: no one was able to, knew how to, or ever did completely achieve the ideal of a mother's service.

don to the full, but he alone. We wetyn that all our moders
beryng is us to peyne and to deyeng; and what is that? But our   330
very moder Jesus, he, al love, beryth us to joye and to endles
lyving, blissid mot he be. Thus he susteynith us within
himselfe in love; and traveled into the full tyme that he wold
suffre the sharpist throwes and the grevousest peynes that
ever were or ever shall be; and dyed at the last. And whan he   335
had don and so born us to bliss, yet myte not al this makyn
aseth to his mervelous love; and that shewid he in these hey
overpassing wordes of love, 'If I myte suffre more, I wold
suffre more.'

He myte ne more dyen, but he wold not stynten of werkyng.   340
Wherfore than him behovyth to fedyn us, for the dereworthy
love of moderhede hath made him dettor to us. The moder
may geven hir child soken her mylke, but our pretious moder
Jesus, he may fedyn us with himselfe; and doith full curtesly
and full tenderly with the blissid sacrament that is pretious   345
fode of very lif. And with al the swete sacraments he
susteynith us ful mercifully and graciously. And so ment he in
this blissid word wher that he seid, 'I it am that Holy Chirch
prechith the and techith the.' That is to sey, 'All the helth and
lif of sacraments, al the vertue and grace of my word, all the   350
godness that is ordeynid in Holy Church for the, I it am.'

329. *wetyn*: know.
330. *beryng*: birthing.
332. *susteynith*: supports, maintains.
333–4. *traveled . . . suffre*: toiled (also laboured) until the time came that he
was to suffer.
334. *throwes*: birth-pangs; in his Crucifixion Christ gives birth like an
ordinary human mother, unlike the Virgin's traditionally painless experience
(see Mechtild, p. 52, and Bridget of Sweden, p. 87).
336–7. *makyn aseth to*: satisfy.
340. *stynten of*: cease from.
341. *Wherfore . . . us*: therefore he must feed us.
342. *dettor*: debtor, one who owes an obligation; this paradox expresses
Julian's insight that Christ, like any mother, can never feel he has done
enough for his children.
343. *may . . . mylke*: can give her child her milk to suck.
345. *blissid sacrament*: Blessed Sacrament of Christ's Body and Blood.
346. *al . . . sacraments*: the medieval Church recognised seven sacraments
in all: baptism, confirmation, marriage, ordination, penance, communion
and extreme unction.
347. *ment*: meant, intended.
348–9. *I . . . the*(1): I am what the Church preaches to you.
349. *helth*: healing power.
351. *ordeynid*: provided.

The moder may leyn the child tenderly to hir brest, but our
tender moder Jesus, he may homley leden us into his blissid
brest be his swete open syde, and shewyn therin party of the
Godhede and the joyes of Hevyn, with gostly sekirnes of   355
endless bliss; and that he shewid in the tenth, gevyng the
same understondyng in this swete word wher he seith, 'Lo
how I lovid the', beholdand into his syde, enjoyand.

This fair lovely word 'moder', it is so swete and so kynd of
the self that it may ne verily be seid of none but of him, and to   360
hir that is very moder of hym and of all. To the properte of
moderhede longyth kinde love, wisdam and knowing, and it is
good; for thow it be so that our bodily forthbrynging be but
litil, low and semple in regard of our gostly forthbringing, yet
it is he that doth it in the creatures be whom that it is done.   365

The kynde, loveand moder that wote and knowith the nede
of hir child, she kepith it ful tenderly as the kind and
condition of moderhede will. And as it wexith in age she
chongith hir werking but not hir love. And whan it is waxen of
more age, she suffrid that it be bristinid in brekyng downe of   370
vices to makyn the child to receivyn vertues and graces. This
werkyng, with al that be fair and good, Our Lord doith it in
hem be whom it is done. Thus he is our moder in kynde by
the werkyng of grace in the lower parte, for love of the heyer
parte. And he will that we know it. For he will have al our love   375

---

352. leyn: lay.

353. homley: intimately, without ceremony.

354. party: part. In her Tenth Revelation (Chapter 24) Julian had received
a vision of the Sacred Heart.

357. understondyng: insight.

358. beholdand: looking.

360–1. to hir: i.e. the Virgin (P reads the more difficult *him*).

363. thow: although.   *bodily forthbrynging*: physical birthing.

364. semple: simple, modest.   *in regard of*: in comparison to.

364–5. yet ... done: i.e. even in physical birth it is Christ who is
responsible for our coming into existence, through the mediation of
creatures (created beings, i.e. our parents).

366. nede: need, necessity.

368. condition: quality, characteristic.   *wexith in age*: grows older.

369. chongith: changes, modifies.   *werking*: practice.

370. bristinid: beaten.

371–3. This ... done: i.e. it is Christ who is training and disciplining the
child through her mother.

373–5. by ... parte: by the operation of grace in training and controlling
the child's (fallen) human nature.

festynyd to him. And in this I saw that al our dett that we owen, be Gods biddyng, be faderhede and moderhede, for Gods faderhede and moderhede, is fulfillid in trew lovyng of God, which blissid love Christ werkyth in us. And this was shewid in all, and namly in the hey plentivous words wher he seith, 'I it am that thou lovest.' 380

Jesus usith more tenderness in our gostly bringing-forth; thow he suffrith us to fallyn in knowing of our wretchidness, he hastily reysith us, not brekyng his love for our trespass, for he may not suffre his child to perish; for he will that we have the properte of a child, fleing to him alway in our necessite: LXI Capitulum. 385

And in our gostly forth-bringyng he usith mor tenderness of keping, without ony likenes, be as mech as our soule is of more price in his syte. He kyndelyth our understondyng, he directith our weys, he esith our consciens, he comfortith our soule, he lightith our herte and gevith us in parte knowyng and lovyng in his blisful Godhede, with gracious mynd in his swete manhede and his blissid passion, with curtes mervelyng in his hey overpassyng goodnes; and makith us to loven al that he loveth for his love, and to ben payd with him and all his werkes. And we fallen, hastily he reysith us be his lovely clepyng and gracious touchyng. And whan we be thus strengthid be his swete werkyng, than we wilfully chesyn him, 390 395

---

376. festynyd: fixed, concentrated.
376–8. al . . . moderhede: i.e. all the obligation we have incurred, at God's command, for God's parental care and which must be paid, either to our own parents or through ourselves taking on the duties of parenthood.
377. be(2) *. . . moderhede*: P reads 'to faderhede and moderhede' here, and omits 'for . . . moderhede', which is clearer but less subtle: see previous note for a possible interpretation of S's reading.
382. usith: exercises.
383. fallyn: fall.   *knowing*: recognition, knowledge.
384. hastily: promptly.   *reysith*: raises.
386. fleing: fleeing, running.
389. ony likenes: any comparison.   *mech*: much.
390. price: value.   *kyndelyth*: stimulates.
392. lightith: enlightens.
393. gracious mynd: mindfulness, by grace.
396. payd: pleased.
397. And: if.
398. clepyng: calling.   *gracious touchyng*: touching by grace.
399. wilfully: voluntarily.   *chesyn*: choose.

be his swete grace, to be his servants and his lovers lestingly   400
without end.

And after this he suffrith sum of us to fallen more hard and
more grevously than ever we diden afore, as us thynkyth. And
than wene we that be not al wyse, that al wer nowte that we
have begun. But it is not so. For it nedith us to fallen, and it   405
nedith us to sen it; for if we felle nowte we should not knowen
how febil and how wretchid we arn of ourselfe; ne also we
shuld not fulsomely so knowen the mervelous love of our
maker. For we shal sen verily in hevyn withouten end that we
have grevously synned in this life and, not withstondyng this,   410
we shal sen that we were never hurt in his love, ne were never
the less of price in his syte. And be the assay of this fallyng we
shall have an hey, mervelous knoweing of love in God without
end; for herd and mervelous is that love which may nowte, ne
will not, be brokin for trespas. And this is one understonding   415
of profite.

Another is the lownes and mekenes that we shal gettyn be
the syte of our fallyng; for therby we shal heyly ben raysid in
hevyn; to which reysing we might never a come withoute that
mekeness. And therfore it nedyth us to sen it, and if we sen it   420
not, thow we fellyn, it should not profitt us. And commenly first
we fallen, and syth we sen it; and both of the mercy of God.
The moder may suffre the child to fallen sumtyme and be
disesid in dyvers manners for the owen profitt, but she may
never suffre that ony maner of peril cum to the child, for love.   425

And thow our erthly moder may suffre hir child to
perishen, our hevynly moder Jesus may not suffre us, that arn
his children, to perishen. For he is almyty, all wisdom and al

---

400. *lestingly*: everlastingly.
402. *hard*: painfully.
403. *us thynkyth*: it seems to us.
404. *nowte*: nothing, of no avail.
406. *sen*: see.   *nowte*: not.
408. *fulsomely*: fully.
411. *hurt*: harmed.
412. *assay*: experience.
414. *herd*: strong.
415–16. *understonding of profite*: useful insight.
417. *lownes*: humility.   *gettyn*: obtain.
419. *might . . . come*: could never have come.
421. *thow*: even though.   *commenly*: usually.
421–2. *first . . . it*: an acute observation of children's reactions.
422. *syth*: then, next.
424. *disesid*: disturbed, upset.   *the owen*: its own.

love, and so is non but he. Blissid mot he ben! But oftentymes
whan our fallyng and our wretchidnes is shewid us, we arn so   430
sore adred and so gretly ashamid of ourselfe that onethys we
wettyn where that we may holden us. But than will not our
curtes moder that we fle awey, for him wer nothing lother.
But he will than that we usen the condition of a child, for
whan it is disesid or dred, it rennith hastely to the moder for   435
helpe with al the myte; so wil he that we don as a meke child,
seyand thus, 'My kind moder, my gracious moder, my
dereworthy moder, have mercy on me! I have made myselfe
foule and onlike to the, and I ne may ne can amenden it but
with prive helpe and grace.'   440
   And if we fele us not than esyd al swithe, be we sekir that
he usith the condition of a wise moder, for if he sen that it be
more profitt to us to morne and to wepen, he suffrith it with
ruth and pite into the best tyme, for love. And he will than
that we usen the propertie of a child that evermor kindly   445
trosteth to the love of the moder in wele and in wo. And he
will that we taken us mytyly to the feith of Holy Church and
fyndyn there our dereworthy moder in solace of trew
understonding with al the blissid common. For on singler
person may often tymes be broken, as it semyth, to selfe, but   450
the hole body of Holy Church was never broken ne never
shall, withouten end.
   And therfore a sekir thing it is, a good and a gracious, to
willen mekely and mytyly ben susteynd and onyd to our
moder, Holy Church, that is Crist Jesus. For the foode of   455

429. *mot*: may.
431. *sore adred*: terribly frightened.
431–2. *onethys . . . us*: we hardly know where to put ourselves (again, an
acute observation).
433. *him . . . lother*: there is nothing he would dislike more.
434. *usen . . . of*: imitate, copy.
435. *dred*: scared.   *rennith*: runs.
439. *foule*: dirty.   *onlike*: unlike.
440. *prive*: private, intimate.
441. *than*: then.   *esyd*: comforted.   *al swithe*: quickly.
   be we sekir: we may be sure.
443. *morne*: mourn.
444. *ruth*: compassion.
445–6. *kindly trosteth*: naturally trusts.
447. *taken us*: entrust ourselves.   *mytyly*: wholeheartedly.
449. *al . . . common*: the whole company of the blessed.   *on singler*: a
single individual.
450. *to selfe*: with respect to herself.
455. *Holy . . . Jesus*: the Church is traditionally the Body of Christ.

mercy, that is his dereworthy blood and pretious water, is
plentious to make us faire and clene. The blessid wound of
our savior ben open and enjoyen to helyn us; the swete
gracious hands of our moder be redy and diligently aboute us.
For he in al this werkyng usith the office of a kinde nurse and   460
hath not ell to don but to entendyn abouten the salvation of
hir child. It is his office to saven us, it is his worship to don
us, and it is his will we knowen it; for he will we loven him
swetely and trosten in him mekely and mytyly. And this
shewid he in these gracious words, 'I kepe the ful sekirly.'   465

The love of God suffrith never his chosen to lose tyme, for all
their troble is turnyd into endless joye; and how we arn al
bownden to God for kindness and for grace. For every kind is
in man and us nedyth not to seke out to know sondry kindes,
but to Holy Church: LXII Capitulum.   470

For in that tyme he shewid our frelte and our fallyngs, our
brekyngs and our nowtyngs, our dispits and our outcastings
and all our wo, so forferth as methowte it myte fallen in this
life. And therwith he shewid his blissid myte, his blissid
wisdam, his blissid love, that he kepyth us in this tyme as   475
tenderly and as swetely to his worship and as sekirly to our

---

457. plentious: fruitful.   *faire*: lovely.
458. enjoyen: rejoice.   *helyn*: heal.
461–2. hath ... child: has nothing to do other than concentrate on her
child's well-being (another remark which shows Julian's shrewd awareness
of the realities of women's domestic life).
462. office: function.   *worship*: honour.
464. trosten: trust.
466. lose: waste.
468. every kind: all species.
471. frelte: both 'physical lack of strength' and 'tendency to sin'; in this
passage many of Julian's terms are ambiguous and continue the metaphor
of the soul as a young child, with the inadequate control of the toddler over
her body symbolising spiritual inadequacies.
471. fallyngs: falls; lapses.
472. brekyngs: fractures (of bones), tears (in clothing); transgressions.
    nowtyngs: disparagements, effacements; possibly also 'naughtiness'.
    dispits: disgraces; acts of disobedience.
    outcastings: vomitings; rejections.
473. so ... fallen: as far as, it seemed to me, it could occur.
474. therwith: simultaneously.
475. in this tyme: i.e. in this time of struggle and apparent failure. Julian's
point is that those predestined to salvation continue to learn and progress
(therefore not 'wasting time') even while they appear to be failing dismally,
just as the young child does eventually learn to walk and control her legs,
bowels and digestion in spite of – or as a result of – numerous accidents.

salvation as he doith whan we are in most solace and comfort. And therto he reysith us gostly and heyly in hevyn, and turnith it al to his worship and to our joye, withoute end. For his love suffrith us never to lose tyme, and al this is of the kind   480
goodness of God be the werkyng of grace.

God is kynde in his being: that is to sey, that goodnes that is kind, it is God. He is the ground, he is the substance, he is the same thing that is kindhede, and he is very fader and very moder of kinde. And all kindes that he hath made to flowen   485
out of him to werkyn his will, it shall be restorid and browte ageyn into him be the salvation of man throw the werking of grace. For of all kyndes that he hath set in dyvers creatures be parte, in man is al the hole in fulhede and in vertue, in fairhede and in goodhede, in rialtie and nobley, in al manner   490
of solemnite of pretioushede and worshipp.

Here may we sen that we arn al bound to God for kinde, and we arn al bound to God for grace. Here may we sen us nedith not gretly to seken fer out to knowen sundry kindes, but to Holy Church, into our moder brest, that is to sey, into   495
our owen soule wher Our Lord wonnyth. And ther shall we fynde all: now in feith and in understondyng, and after verily in himselfe clerely in bliss.

478. gostly: spiritually.
482–98. God . . . bliss: in these two paragraphs the meaning of *kind* and its derivatives constantly changes.
482. kynde: naturally affectionate; but possibly also, 'God contains within him the whole of Nature.'
484. kindhede: natural affection, kindness; also perhaps kinship.
485. kinde: the fullness of the natural world.
485–8. And . . . grace: i.e. the whole of creation will ultimately be redeemed, sanctified and reunited with God through the salvation of humanity.
485. kindes: species.
485–6. flowen out: emanate.
488. kyndes: characteristics.
488–9. be parte: partially.
489. al the hole: the totality.   *fulhede*: plenitude, perfection.
490. fairhede: (spiritual) beauty.   *goodhede*: goodness.
    rialtie: royal power.   *nobley*: nobility.
491. pretioushede: preciousness, value.
492–3. Here . . . grace: i.e. we are dependent on God, our true Father and Mother, through both Nature and Grace.
494. seken fer out: seek far afield.   *kindes*: species, natures.
495–6. our . . . wonnyth: in her Sixteenth Revelation (Chapter 67) Julian sees her soul like a kingdom with Christ enthroned in its midst.
496. wonnyth: dwells.
498. clerely: clearly, not 'through a glass darkly'.

But no man ne woman take this singler to himselfe, for it is
not so, it is general. For it is our pretious Criste and to him   500
was this fair kind dyte for the worship and noblyth of mannys
makyng, and for the joye and the bliss of mannys salvation;
ryte as he saw, wiste and knew from without begynning.

d) *Conclusion: The Cause of This Showing*
(f. 57ʳ⁻ᵛ)

The good Lord shewid this booke shuld be otherwise
performid than at the first writing; and for his werking he will   505
we thus prey, him thankand, trostand and in him enjoyand;
and how he made this shewing because he will have it
knowen, in which knoweing he will give us grace to love him;
for fiftene yeere after it was answerid that the cause of all this
shewing was love, which Jhesus mote grant us. Amen.   510
LXXXVI Capitulum.

This booke is begunne be Gods gift and his grace, but it is
not yet performid, as to my syte. For charite pray we all to
God, with Godds werking thankand, trostand, enjoyand. For
thus will our good lord be prayd, as be the understonding that   515
I tooke in al his owne mening, and in the swete words wher he
seith full merrily, 'I am ground of thi beseking.' For trewly I
saw and understode in Our Lords mening that he shewid it
for he will have it knowen more than it is, in which knowing
he will give us grace to loven him and clevyn to him. For he   520
beholdith his hevenly tresure with so grete love on erth that he
will give us more light and solace in hevenly joy in drawing of
our herts, for sorow and merkness which we arn in.

499. *singler*: specifically.
500. *For . . . Criste*: i.e. salvation and redemption are collective and Christ
is 'ours', not the personal possession of any one individual.
501. *this fair kind*: i.e. redeemed and glorified human nature; cf. ll. 178–80
above.
501. *dyte*: prepared, destined.   *noblyth*: ennoblement.
504. *shewid*: revealed.
505. *performid*: carried out, completed.
     werking: achievement, completion.
506. *trostand*: trusting.
510. *mote*: may.
513. *as . . . syte*: in my opinion.
515. *as be*: according to.
516. *tooke*: received.   *mening*: intention.
517. *ground*: basis, foundation.   *beseking*: beseeching.
520. *clevyn*: cling, adhere.
523. *merkness*: darkness.

And fro that time that it was shewid, I desired often times
to witten what was Our Lords mening. And fiftene yer after   525
and more I was answerid in gostly understonding, seyand
thus: 'Woldst thou wetten thi lords mening in this thing? Wete
it wele, love was his mening. Who shewid it the? Love. What
shewid he the? Love. Wherfore shewid it he? For love. Hold
the therin and thou shalt witten and knowen more in the   530
same. But thou shalt never knowen ne witten therein other
thing, without end.'

Thus was I lerid that love was Our Lords mening. And I
saw full sekirly in this and in all, that ere God made us, he
lovid us: which love was never slakid no never shall. And in   535
this love he hath don all his werke, and in this love he hath
made all things profitable to us. And in this love our life is
everlestand. In our making we had beginning. But the love
wherin he made us, was in him fro withoute begynning, in
which love we have our beginning. And all this shall be seen   540
in God without end, which Jhesus mot grant us. Amen.

Textual notes

56. wound] woundys.
103. ful lytylle] fully tylle.
109. suffyrande] suffyrde.
134. It] I.
154. also] anly.
157. herte fully] hertefully.
185. thankyn] thankyng.
199. kindly] kindy.
238. gevyng] P, vesyng S.
240. our] ou.
241–2. substance is hole] substance is is hole.
285. wyllyth] P, *om.* S.
323. God, sovereyn] God is sovereyn.
329. but] P, *om.* S.
356. tenth] ix.

525. witten: know.
527. wetten: know.
529–30. Hold the: keep yourself.
533. lerid: taught.
534. sekirly: surely.   *ere*: before.
535. slakid: diminished.   *no*: nor.
538. everlestand: everlasting.   *making*: creation.
541. which: i.e. that endless vision of God.   *mot*: may.

390. *kyndelyth*] P, kydelyth S.
396. *ben*] bend.
399. *strengthid*] strenthyd P, stengtid S.
405. *not*] P, no S.
430. *fallyng*] fallyn.
438–9. *myselfe foule*] myselfe my foule.
473. *myte*] myght P, my S.
482. *that is to sey*] that it is to sey.
503. *begynning*] begynnig.

The fifteenth century

9 Christine de Pisan

Christine de Pisan was the first French professional woman writer. A near-contemporary of Catherine of Siena and Julian of Norwich, she was born in Venice *c.* 1365. Her father was a university lecturer in astrology at Bologna but soon moved to France to become physician to Charles V. His daughter received a good education and when she was left a penniless widow in her early twenties, she supported her three small children, mother and niece by working as a copyist. She also began to write courtly lyric verse and engaged in a literary quarrel over the thirteenth-century allegorical dream poem *Le Roman de la Rose*, which she and others regarded as slandering women. Charles's son, Philip the Bold of Burgundy, commissioned her to write a eulogistic biography of his father, and from then on Christine regularly composed works that she presented to members of the French court and for which she was rewarded. In her later years she retired into the royal convent of Poissy, where her daughter was a nun, and she was dead by 1434 (see Willard 1984 and *The Epistle of the Prison of Human Life*, pp. xiii–xviii).

Christine was essentially a skilful compiler and populariser who had an immense respect for learning, though most of hers was derivative. She knew Greek and Roman history largely through digests, such as the *Factorum et dictorum memorabiliorum libri novem* (a handbook of exemplary stories for the use of rhetoricians compiled by the first-century Roman historian Valerius Maximus), and was familiar with classical literature through French translations of such writers as Livy, Cicero and Ovid (see Lucas 1970). The sheer quantity of her writing, on a wide range of mainly didactic and educational subjects including warfare and politics, was prodigious. She always wrote from a strongly moral viewpoint and consistently tried to raise the valuation of women by popularising a knowledge of women's history (some of it invented), in order to oppose the dominant clerical anti-feminism of the later Middle Ages. How far she can be considered an early feminist, however, is a subject of dispute (see Gottlieb in Kirshner and Wemple 1985: 337–64).

Five of her works were translated into English in the fifteenth century (see Campbell 1925). Hoccleve does not acknowledge that his 'Letter of Cupid' is an adaptation of Christine's poem 'L'Epître de Cupid', and

possibly he travesties his source (see Fleming 1971). But all the works of
which she was known to be the author were moral and didactic. The first of
these, an elementary work for children, was translated by Anthony
Woodville, brother of Elizabeth the wife of Edward IV and tutor to Edward
V, as *The Moral Proverbs of Christine* and published by Caxton in 1478;
Woodville may also have made the fifteenth-century translation *The Body of
Policy*. The *Epistle of Othea* was translated twice, by Stephen Scrope for his
uncle Sir John Fastolf (see *Some Paston Letters*, p. 238) and by
Anthony Babington; and in 1489 Caxton translated and printed *The Faits
[Deeds] of Arms and of Chivalry* at the request of Henry VII.

All the prose translations follow their original very closely. Often they do
so to the extent of translating characteristically French constructions word
for word. Sometimes the translators use English words originally borrowed
from French with their original French meanings rather than those they
had acquired in English (examples are signalled in the notes). Consequently
the translations are frequently inelegant and unidiomatic, and can
sometimes be fully understood only by recourse to the French original.

Comment: The first set of passages comes from a translation of Christine's
single most popular and successful work, *L'Epître d'Othéa la déesse à Hector*
(*c.* 1400). This is an educational treatise containing the advice on
knighthood offered by Othea (said to be the Greek goddess of wisdom but
in fact an invention of Christine's) to the young Trojan hero Hector. It
consists of one hundred sections; each is composed of a *Texte*, four lines of
narrative verse putting forward an exemplary model from classical myth or
history; a *Glose*, its gloss or moral interpretation in terms of appropriate
knightly behaviour, citing pagan philosophers; and an *Allegorie*, its
allegorisation or doctrinal interpretation in terms of Christian belief, citing
Scripture or a Church Father. The results seem very strange indeed today,
but medieval readers were more accustomed to such apparently arbitrary
treatment of literary texts, not only in Scriptural commentaries (see below,
p. 219) and in texts, such as *Piers Plowman*, strongly influenced by them,
but also in moralised interpretations of secular literature, such as the *Ovid
moralisé*, a thirteenth-century French moralisation of the *Metamorphoses*.

Christine re-used some of the material on famous and virtuous women in
her *Book of the City of Ladies* (first translated into English in 1521), in which
Minerva, Ceres and Io all reappear as the female inventors of technology,
agriculture and literacy – the foundations of civilisation. The stories of Ceis
and Alcione, and of Troilus and Cresseide, had also attracted Chaucer
(*Book of the Duchess*, ll. 62–230, and *Troilus and Criseyde*) though he handled
them very differently. The last passage offers the final word on the vexed
question of 'Women's Counsel' (i.e. should one take the advice of a
woman?) which preoccupies both Chaunticleer and Melibee in the
Canterbury Tales (*CT* VII:1055–63, 3252–64). Christine's clinching argument for the worth of women's advice is the mysterious figure of the
Sibyll who revealed the birth of Christ to Augustus Caesar. The Sibyll (or
sibylls, for the Middle Ages were never sure if the name was generic or
individual) held a position of authority unique for a woman (see
Introduction, p. 18); Aeneas's guide through the Underworld in Book VI of

Virgil's *Aeneid*, linked with David and the Old Testament prophets in the famous medieval hymn the *Dies Irae* as a prophet of the Day of Judgement, she provided the authentication of a virtuous pagan for the female prophetic role. The Sibyll appears again in Christine's dream vision *Le chemin de longue estude*, where she acts as Christine's other-worldly guide.

The second passage is from *The Body of Policy*, a translation of *Le Livre du Corps de Policie* (*c.* 1405), a political treatise combining the characteristics of a chivalric manual on the duties of knighthood, a mirror for princes, and a treatise on the three estates or social classes (knights, clerks and labourers). This must be the only place in medieval literature where a woman dispenses advice (perhaps a little wistfully) to university students, 'the disciples of study and of wisdom'. Christine argues, demonstrating her early-humanist respect for learning, that the pursuit of knowledge is superior to that of power and money, and preaches the Christian humanist and Platonic doctrine that knowledge leads to virtue. The stories she uses to support her position show her respect for the Greek and Roman past and her wide range of reference, drawing on Seneca, Horace and Valerius Maximus (see above, p. 137). She goes on to show a wider maternal concern for the welfare of students by advising them to temper their zeal for study with physical or mental recreation, promoting the classical educational ideal of 'a healthy mind in a healthy body'.

The third passage, the Prologue to the translation of *Le Livre des Fais d'Armes et de Chevalerie* (1406), is a studied masterpiece of irony. Christine writes a conventionally humble introduction, triply necessary because medieval writers commonly engage in extravagant preliminary gestures of humility (the so-called 'humility *topos*'); women writers on any subject invariably do so; and Christine here is about to engage in a subject peculiarly inappropriate to a woman writer. But the gesture of humility is couched in such lofty language and complex syntax as to be incomprehensible – no doubt deliberately so. Christine's 'style clergial' (see Bornstein 1977), which Caxton faithfully reproduced in his very close and literal translation, is characterised by lengthy sentences whose main clauses are broken up by a succession of subordinate clauses. For instance, the second sentence in the passage has the basic structure 'I . . . am exhorted . . . to entrepryse to speke', but the subject, verb and complement are all separated from each other by at least two subordinate clauses. This style is also marked by the use of 'doublets' (two or more words used to express a single idea), as in 'not digne ne worthy', 'castell or forteresse', 'of armes and of chyvalrye'.

This elaborate prose style entirely subverts the pose of inadequacy, while it implicitly puts at a disadvantage Christine's putative audience, the military men who 'be not comunely clerkys ne instructe in science of langage', by implying that, in contrast, the author (although a woman and therefore ignorant of military matters) is highly educated and rhetorically adept. It also serves to camouflage Christine's arguments, which combine bare-faced effrontery with sheer absurdity. She writes because she has been asked to do so; because she is a successful writer who can present complex material in a way adapted to uneducated knights; and because armour was invented by a woman, Minerva, who, like Christine, was an Italian!

Manuscripts: *The Epistle of Othea* is found in Cambridge St John's College MS H. 5 (mid fifteenth century); this translation is also extant in New York Pierpont Morgan Library MS 775 and Longleat MS 253. The unique manuscript of *The Body of Policy* is CUL MS Kk. 1. 5 (third quarter of the fifteenth century), ff. 1–79ᵛ. *The Book of Faits of Arms and of Chivalry* was printed by Caxton in 1489. The extract here is taken from Oxford Bodl. Douce 180.

Further reading (for full details see Bibliography): The most comprehensive general introduction to Christine in English, with bibliography, is Willard 1984; for further bibliographical information see also Petroff 1986: 303–7; Wilson 1984: 64–89; *The Epistle of the Prison of Human Life*, pp. xxxiii–xlii. On Christine's prose style and its influence, see Bornstein 1977; on Christine's writings in England, see Campbell 1925; Fleming 1971.

From *The Epistle of Othea*

a) *Women Found Civilisation*
Minerva, Founder of Technology
(Cambridge St John's College MS H. 5, f. 14ʳ)

Texte

Of alle maner soortes of armure
Forto arme the with, bothe wel and sure,
Be thi moder nowe signed schall be –
Minerve, the which is not bitter to the.   5

Glose

Minerve was a ladi of grete connynge and fonde the crafte to make armure. For afoore the pepill armed them not but with cuirboille. And for the grete wisedome that was in this ladi,

---

1. Texte: passage for comment.
2. soortes: sorts, kinds.   *armure*: armour, arms.
3. sure: surely.
4. Be: by.   *signed*: assigned.
5. the which: who.
6. Glose: gloss, interpretation (see above, p. 138).
7. connynge: wisdom.   *fonde . . . crafte*: invented the technique.
8. afoore: formerly.   *but*: except.
9. cuirboille: quir-boili, 'leather boiled in water and then moulded to the required form and hardened by drying' (*MED*).

thei called here a goddes. And because that Hector couthe 10
sette armure wel a-werke and that it was his ryghte crafte,
Othea callid him the sone of Minerve, not withstandyng he
was sone to Quene Echuba of Troy. And in the same wise alle
that loveth armes may be named. And to this purpoos an
auctor seith that knyghtes yoven to armes be sugettes to the 15
same.

Ceres, Founder of Agriculture
(f. 20^{r-v})

Texte

Be thou like to the goddes Ceres,
That took fro noon, but yaf to corn encrees.
In such wise abandoned schulde be 20
The good knyghte, wel sette in his degre.

Glose

Ceres was a ladi that fonde the crafte to ere lande, for afore
gaineryes sewe withoute laboure; and because that the lande
bare the more plenteuouslye after that it was eried, they seide 25
that sche was a goddes of cornys; and thei callid the lande
after here name. Wherefore it wolde be seide that, as the
lande is habundaunte and large yevere of alle goodes, on the

10. here: her.
    Hector: son of Priam, king of Troy, and his wife Hecuba; brother of
Menelaus, whose abduction of Helen caused the Trojan War and the
ultimate fall of Troy.
10–11. couthe ... a-werke: knew how to use arms well.
11. ryghte crafte: proper art.
13. Echuba: i.e. Hecuba.
    in ... wise: in the same way, i.e. as 'sons of Minerva'.
15. auctor: author, authority.   *yoven*: given, i.e. devoted.
    sugettes: subjects.
15–16. the same: i.e. Minerva. The brief 'Allegorie' that follows has been
omitted.
19. noon: no-one.   *yaf*: gave.   *encrees*: growth.
20. abandoned: abundant, lavish.
21. sette: established.
23. ere: plough.
24. gaineryes: farmers.   *sewe*: sowed, planted.
25. bare: bore, produced.   *plenteuouslye*: plentifully.
26. cornys: cereals.
28. habundaunte: fertile, productive.   *large yevere*: generous giver.
    goodes: good things.

same wise schulde a good knyghte be habundaunte to alle
persones and to yeve his helpe and comforte aftir his powere.   30
And Aristotill seith, 'Be a liberal yevere and thou schalte have
frendes.'

Io, Founder of Learning
(f. 22ᵛ)

Texte

Delite the greteli in the connynge
Of Yoo, more than good or othir thinge;   35
For bi that thou maist lerne ful gretli
And of good therinne take largeli.

Glose

Yoo was a yonge jentil womman and doughter to Kynge
Ynacus, the which was righte connynge and fonde many   40
maneres of lettres that had not be seen afoore, though that
som fablis sey that Yoo was Jubiteris love and that sche
become a cowe and aftir a womman as sche was. But as that
poetis hath hidde trouthe under coverture of fable, it may be
that Jubiter loved hire, that is to understande, be the vertues   45
the which were in hire sche become a cowe. For as a cowe
yeveth mylke, the which is swete and norisschynge, sche, be the

29. *habundaunte*: lavish, generous.
30. *aftir his powere*: according to his ability.
31. *Aristotill*: Aristotle.
34. *Delite the*: take pleasure.   *connynge*: knowledge.
35. *Yoo*: Io, daughter of Inacus, king of Argos; Jupiter fell in love with her
and Juno turned her into a heifer. Her story is told by the Greek historian
Herodotus and the Roman poet Ovid.
35. *good*: property.
36. *bi that*: i.e. by means of wisdom ('connynge').
39. *jentil*: noble.
40. *Ynacus*: Inacus.   *the which*: i.e. Io.
41. *maneres*: kinds.
42. *fablis*: fables, myths.   *Jubiteris*: Jupiter's.
43. *aftir*: afterwards.
     woman . . . was: i.e. formerly. The F. here says Io was a *femme
commune*, i.e. prostitute; possibly the translator misread *commune* as *comme
une*.
43. *as that*: since.
44. *under coverture*: in the manner.
45. *be*: because of.
47. *norisschynge*: nourishing.

lettres that sche fonde, yaf noryshschynge to understandynge.
And in that sche was a comon womman, may be understanden
that hire witte was comon to alle, as lettres be comon to alle   50
pepill. Therfore it is seide that the good knyghte schulde ful
muche love Yoo, the which may be understanden be lettres
and scriptures and stories of good pepill, the which the good
knyghte scholde here tolde gladlye and redde. The example of
the which may be vaylable to him. To this purpos Hermes   55
seith, 'Whoso enforceth him to gete connynge and good
condicions, he fyndith that the which schall please him in this
worlde and in that othere.'

b) *Two Chaucerian Tales*
Ciys and Alcione
(f. 50^{r-v})

Texte

Be the see yf thou wilt undertake   60
Perlious viagis forto make,
Of Alchion beleve the counceill:
Ceys therof the soothe may the tell.

Glose

Ceys was a king, a ful good man, and loved wel Alchion his   65
wiif. The king took a devocion forto goo a perlious passage on

---

49–51. And . . . . pepill: this revealing remark indicates one reason women were reluctant to write in the Middle Ages: that public utterance was associated with unchastity.
49. comon womman: prostitute.
50. witte: intelligence.
52. the . . . lettres: who may be understood as writing.
53. scriptures: writings.
54. here: hear.
55. vaylable: valuable, advantageous.
     Hermes: Hermes Trismegistus, the supposed writer of the Greek philosophico-religious treatises known as the *Hermetica*; this reference comes from the *Dits moraux des philosophes*, a medieval French translation of an originally Arabic compilation of philosophical sayings, later translated into English as *The Dicts and Sayings of the Philosophers*.
56. Whoso: anyone who.   *enforceth him*: strives.
57. condicions: character, morals.   *fyndith . . . which*: finds the thing that.
58. othere: the following 'Allegorie' has been omitted.
66. took a devocion: desired.   *perlious passage*: perilous voyage.

the see. He took the see in a tempest, but Alchion his wiif, the
which loved him right hertily, dide greetly hir bisines to meve
him fro that viage and with greete teeres of weping praid him
ful bisily; but it myght not be remedied be hir, ne he wolde   70
not suffre hir to go with him, standing that she wolde algatis a
goon with him; and at the departing she stirte into the shippe.
But Ceys the king confortid hir and with forse made hir to
abide, for the which she was ful anguishous and hevi and in
right greet woo.   75

    Nevertheleees Colus, the god of wyndes, meved them so
greetly upon the see that the king Ceys with-ynne fewe daies
perishid on the see, for the which, whan Alchion knewe that
aventure, she kest hirsilf into the see. The fabill seith that the
goddes had pite therof and chaungid the bodies of the two   80
lovers into two birdis, to the entent that theire greet love
myght be had in perpetuel mynde. And yit the same birdis fle
upon the see-side, the which be callid 'alchiones' and theire
fedris be white and whanne the maryners see theim come,
than be thei sikir of a tempest.   85

    The ryght exposicion here-of may be that, in mariage, two
lovers loved togidir in liche wise, the which poetis likneth to

67. *tooke the see*: i.e. set sail.   *see*: sea.
68. *dide . . . bisines*: did her utmost.   *meve*: dissuade.
69. *viage*: voyage.
70. *bisily*: earnestly.   *remedied*: put right.   *be*(2): by.
71. *standing*: understanding.   *algatis*: by any means.
71–2. *a goon*: have gone.
72. *departing*: departure.   *stirte*: started, rushed.
73. *forse*: force.
74. *abide*: remain, stay.   *anguishous*: apprehensive.   *hevi*: unhappy.
75. *woo*: woe.
76. *Colus*: a misreading of F. *Eolus*, i.e. Aeolus, ruler of the winds.
    meved: moved.   *them*: i.e. the winds; the style here is very awkward.
79. *aventure*: event.   *kest*: cast, threw.
    fabill: fable, myth (possibly here referring specifically to the best-known
version of the story in Ovid's *Metamorphoses*).
80. *goddes*: gods.   *therof*: i.e. on them.
81. *to the entent*: for the purpose.
82. *had . . . mynde*: held in perpetual remembrance.   *yit*: still.   *fle*: fly.
83. *alchiones*: halcyons, 'A bird of which the ancients fabled that it bred
about the time of the winter solstice in a nest floating on the sea, and that it
charmed the wind and waves so that the sea was specially calm during the
period' (*OED*).
84. *fedris*: feathers.   *maryners*: sailors.
85. *sikir of*: secure from.
86. *ryght exposicion*: correct interpretation.
87. *liche wise*: similar fashion.   *likneth*: compare.

the two birdis that had such a caas and aventure. Therefore it
is seid that the good knyght schoulde not put him in no
perlious passage ayens the counceil of his good freendes. And   90
Assaron seith that the wise man enforcith him to drawe him
from hurtys, and the fool doith his diligence to finde hurtis.

Allegorie

Forto beleve Alchion, it is to undirstande that the good spirit
be some yvil temptacion is empechid with some errour or   95
doute in his thought, in the which he shoulde reporte him to
the oppinion of the Chirche. For Seint Ambrose seith, in the
secunde book of Offices, that he is from himsilf that dispiseth
the counceil of the Chirche, for Joseph helpid Kinge Pharaoo
more profitabli with the counceil of his prudence than though   100
he hadde yoven him eithir goold or silver. For silver myght
not a purveid for the famyn of Egipte the space of seven yere,
and therfore it is concludid: 'Trust counceil and thou shalte
not repente the.' To this purpos the wiseman seith in his
Proverbis to the persone of Holichirche: *Custodi legem meam*   105
atque consilium et erit vita anime tue. Proverbiorum tertio capitulo.

---

88. caas: accident.
89–90. put ... passage: undertake any dangerous voyage.
90. ayens: against.
91. Assaron: again, Christine takes this reference to an otherwise unknown
philosopher from the *Dits moraux* (see note to l. 55).
91–2. drawe ... hurtys: withdraw from what is hurtful.
92. doith his diligence: does his best.
93. Allegorie: allegorical (i.e. doctrinal) interpretation; see p. 138 above.
94. good spirit: virtuous soul.
95. empechid: hindered.
96. reporte him: submit himself.
97. Seint Ambrose: Ambrose of Milan (*c.* 339–97), one of the four Fathers
of the Church.
97–8. seith ... Offices: *De Officiis Ministrorum* II, xv (*PL* 16: 122–3).
98. from himsilf: out of his wits.
99. counceil: advice.
99–102. Joseph ... yere: the story is told in Genesis 41.
100. counceil ... prudence: his wise advice.   *though*: if.
101. yoven: given.
102. a purveid: have provided.   *famyn*: famine.
104. repente the: repent (the verb is reflexive in ME).
105. persone ... Holichirche: Holy Church personified.
105–6. Custodi ... tue: 'Keep the law and counsel: And there shall be life
to thy soul', Proverbs 3: 21–2.
106. Proverbiorum ... capitulo: 'in the third chapter of Proverbs'.

Cresseide
(ff. 52ᵛ–53ʳ)

Texte

If thou wilt yeve the to Cupido,
Thin hert and all abaundon hir-to,
Thinke on Cresseidis newfangilnes,   110
For hir herte hadde to myche doubilnes.

Glose

Cresseide was a gentilwoman of grete beaute, and yit she was
more queint and sotill to drawe peopill to hir. Troilus, the
yongist of Priantys sones, was ful of grete gentilnes, of beaute   115
and of worthines, loved hir right hertily, and she hadde yoven
him hir love and promissid to him that it shoulde nevir to
faile. Calcas, fadir to the gentilwoman, the whiche knewe be
science that Troye should be distroied, dide so myche that his
doughtir was delyverid to him and brought oute of the cite   120
and ledde to the sege among the Grekis, where hir fadir was.
    Greet was the sorowe and ful pitous the compleintis of the
two lovers at theire departing. Nevirthelesse, within a while
aftir, Diomede, the which was a high baron and a ful worthi
knyght, aqueinted him with Cresseide and labored so sore to   125

108. *yeve the*: devote yourself.   *Cupido*: Cupid.
109. *abaundon hir-to*: surrender to it (i.e. love).
110. *Cresseidis newfangilnes*: Cresseide's tendency towards novelties.
    Cresseidis: the F. text has the original form 'Brisseide', derived from
the accusative case of the Greek name 'Briseis'. In the *Iliad* Briseis was the
beautiful captive woman whom Agamemnon took away from Achilles, thus
provoking his wrath, his withdrawal from the Trojan War, and the death of
his friend Patrocles.
111. *to ... doubilnes*: too much duplicity.
113. *gentilwoman*: lady.
114. *queint*: clever.   *sotill*: subtle.   *drawe*: attract.
    Troilus: Troilus, a son of Priam king of Troy and his wife Hecuba,
and brother of Hector and Menelaus, does not appear in classical myth. He
is first mentioned in early medieval (fifth-century) Latin accounts of the
Trojan War.
115. *Priantys*: Priam's.   *gentilnes*: nobility.
118. *Calcas*: Calchas, Cresseide's father, was a Trojan priest who, knowing
Troy was doomed, had deserted to the Greeks.
118–19. *be science*: by astrology.
119. *dide ... myche*: acted in such a way (*myche* = much).
121. *sege*: besieging force.
123. *departing*: separation.
124. *Diomede*: Diomedes, in the *Iliad* king of Argos and the son of Tydeus.
125. *aqueinted ... with*: made himself known to.
125–6. *labored ... hire*: wooed her so energetically.

hire that she loved him and holly foryate hir trewe love, Troylus. And because that Cresseide had so light a corage, it is seide to the good knyght that, yif he wil sette his herte in any place, lete him beware that he aqueinte him not with such a lady as Cresseide was. And Hermes seith, 'Kepe the from   130
yvil feleship, that thou be not oon of theim.'

Allegorie

Cresseide, of whom a man shoulde bewarre to aqueinte him, is veinglorie, with the which the good spirit shoulde not aqueinte him, but fle it unto his power, for it is to light and   135
cometh to sodeinly. And Sent Austin upon the Psaulter seith that he, the which hath wel lerned and assaied be experience to overgoo the degrees of vices, he is comen to the knoulech that the synne of veinglorie is holli or mooste specialli to eschewe of parfit men. For among all other synnes it is hardist   140
to overcome. Therfore the apostle Seint Paul seith: *Qui gloriatur, in Domino glorietur. Secunde ad Corinthios.*

c) *A Last Word on Women's Counsel* (ff. 59ᵛ–60ʳ)

Texte
Autoritees Y have writen to thee
An hundrith; lete them be take a-gree.   145
For a womman lerned Augustus
To be worshipid, and taught him thus.

---

126. *holly*: wholly.   *foryate*: forgot.   *trewe*: faithful, loyal.
127. *light*: frivolous, wanton.   *corage*: heart.
131. *yvil feleship*: evil fellowship.   *oon of theim*: one of them.
133. *bewarre*: beware.
134. *veinglorie*: vain glory, vanity.
135. *unto ... power*: as far as he can.   *to light*: too fickle.
136. *Sent... seith*: St Augustine, *Enarratio in Ps. VII* (PL 36: 100).
   upon ... Psaulter: (in his commentary) on the Book of Psalms.
137. *assaied*: tested.
138. *overgoo*: surmount.   *degrees*: stages of development.
   is comen: has come.   *knoulech*: knowledge.
140. *eschewe of*: be shunned by.   *parfit*: perfect.
141–2. *Qui ... glorietur*: 'he that glorieth, let him glory in the Lord', 2 Corinthians 10: 17.
142. *Secunde ... Corinthios*: 'of the second (epistle) to the Corinthians'.
144. *Autoritees*: authoritative statements.
145. *hundrith*: hundred.   *lete ... a-gree*: may they be taken favourably.
146. *lerned*: taught.
147. *worshipid*: honoured.

Glose

Cesar Augustus was emperour of the Romaynes and of alle
the worlde. And because that in the tyme of his reigne pes was   150
in alle the worlde and that he regned pesibilly, lewde peopil
and mysbelevers thought that the pes was because of his
goodnes, but it was not. For it was Crist Jhesu, the which was
borne of the Virgine Marie and was that tyme on the erthe,
and as longe as he was on erthe, it was pes over all the worlde.   155
So thei wolde have worshipid Cesar as God. But than Sibille
bad him to be well ware, that he made him not to be
worshipid, and that ther was no God but oone aloone, the
which had made all thinge, and thanne she ledde him to an
high mountaigne withoute the cite, and in the sonne, by the   160
wil of Oure Lorde, aperid a virgine holding a childe. Sibille
shewid it to him and seide to him that there was verry God,
the which shoulde be worshipid; and thanne Cesar worshipid
him. And because that Cesar Augustus, the which was prince
of all the worlde, lerned to knowe God and the beleve of a   165
womman, to the purpos may be seide the auctorite that
Hermes seith: 'Be not ashamed to here trouthe and good
teching, of whom that ever seith it. For trouthe noblith him
that pronounceth it.'

149–64. Cesar . . . him: this story comes from *The Golden Legend*, a
compilation of saints' lives and other material made by Jacobus de Voragine
(*c.* 1230–98), which was enormously popular in the Middle Ages (*Legenda
Aurea*, p. 44).
150. pes: peace.
151. pesibilly: peaceably.   *lewde*: foolish, uneducated.
152. mysbelevers: infidels, non-believers.
156. Sibille: the Sibyll. There were traditionally ten sibylls, or ecstatic
prophetesses, in the Ancient World; they were thought to have prophesied
the coming of Christ and the Last Judgement.
157–8. bad . . . worshipid: told him to be very careful that he should not
have himself worshipped.
158. oone aloone: only one.
160. withoute: outside.   *sonne*: sun.
161. aperid: appeared.
162. verry: true.
165. beleve of: faith in.
167. Hermes: Hermes Trismegistus (see above, n. to l. 55), thought by the
Middle Ages to have been an Egyptian sage who instructed Moses, was,
like the Sybill, a symbol of continuity with the world of pagan wisdom.
168. of . . . it: from whomever says it.   *noblith*: ennobles.

Allegorie 170

There where Othea seith that she hath writen to him an hundrith auctorites and that Augustus lerned of a womman, is to undirstand that good wordis and good techingis is to preise, of what persoone that seith it. Hewe de Seint Victor spekith here-of in a book callid Didascolicon, that a wise man gladly 175 herith al manere of techingis. He dispisith not the scripture; he dispiceth not the persone; he dispiceth not the doctrine; he seekith indifferently over all, and al that evere he seeth of the which he hath defaute, he considerith not what he is that spekith, but what that is the which he seith; he takith noon 180 hede how myche he can himself, but how myche he can not. To this purpos the wise man seith: *Auris bona audiet cum omni concupiscencia sapienciam. Ecclesiastici sexto capitulo.*

From *The Body of Policy*

d) *The Value of Higher Education*
(CUL MS Kk. 1. 5, ff. 69–71ᵛ)

Here we begynne to speke of thre estatis of the people; and first of the clergie, studyyng in science. 185

172. of: from.
173. preise: be praised.
174. what: whatever.
174–5. Hewe . . . Didascolicon: Hugh of St Victor (d. 1142), *Didascalion* III, xiv (*PL* 176: 774). Hugh was an Augustinian canon who wrote prolifically on theological subjects.
176. scripture: writing.
177. dispiceth: despises.   *doctrine*: teaching.
178. indifferently: impartially.   *over all*: everywhere.
178–9. al. . . defaute: all that he ever sees in which he is deficient.
179–80. he(2) *. . . seith*: elsewhere Christine attributes this maxim to Seneca (see ll. 412–13); it was clearly important to her as it justified her adoption of a didactic role, even though she was a woman.
181. can: knows.
182–3. Auris . . . . sapienciam: 'a good ear will hear wisdom with all desire', Ecclesiasticus 3:31.
183. Ecclesiastici . . . capitulo: 'in the sixth chapter of Ecclesiasticus'.
184. thre . . . people: Christine follows the standard medieval division of society into three 'estates' (social classes): the prince; the knights and nobles; and 'the people', a group further subdivided into three.
185. clergie: clerics.   *science*: knowledge, learning.

Into the comonte of the people be comprysed three estates, that is to knowe in the cittee of Parys and also in othre citees. Firste the clergie; the bourgeyses and the marchauntes; and than the comon people, like as we may sey, men of crafte and labourers. Nowe we muste advyse us what thyngis we may   190 seye that be profytable in gevyng examples to everychone of theis estates to lyve well and truely aftir his ordre. And for bycause that the state of the clergie is among all othre highe, noble and worthy in honour, I caste to dresse my matere and speke firste of theim, that is to seye of the studyantes, as in the   195 Universite of Parys or in othre parties.

People well councelled or people that be ewrous, I sey to you, the disciples of studye and of wysedom, whiche by the grace of God and of good fortune or of good nature ben applied to serge out the highnesse of the clere rejoyssyng   200 sterre, that is to knowe the sterre of science, takyng diligently the good tresour of that clere and helthefull fountayne: fulfille youreselfe of that plesaunt refeccion that may so moche avayle you and bryng you to worchipp. For what thyng is more worthy to a man than sciens and highnesse of cunnyng?   205 Certaynly thou that desierest it and emplyest thyselfe thereto haste chosen a gloryous lyfe.

For by that thou maiste comprehende the eleccion of vertue

---

186. *Into . . . . comprysed*: in the general mass of the people are included.
187. *that . . . knowe*: that is.
188. *bourgeyses*: citizens.
189. *than*: then.   *men . . . crafte*: craftsmen.
190. *advyse us*: think.
191. *gevyng*: giving.   *everychone*: each one.
192. *aftir . . .ordre*: according to his rank.
192–3. *for . . . that*: i.e. since (F. *por ce que*).
193. *state*: estate, class.
194. *caste . . . matere*: intend to arrange my material.
195. *studyantes*: (university) students.
196. *parties*: parts.
197. *councelled*: advised.   *ewrous*: fortunate, prosperous (F. *heureux*).
199. *nature*: natural ability.
199–200. *ben . . . serge*: apply yourselves to search.
200–1. *highnesse . . . sterre*: height of the bright joyful star.
202. *tresour*: treasure.   *fulfille*: fill.
203. *of*: with.   *refeccion*: refreshment.   *avayle*: profit.
204. *worchipp*: honour.
205. *sciens*: knowledge.   *cunnyng*: learning.
206. *emplyest*: devote, apply.
208. *eleccion*: choice.

and the eschewing of vice, like as it stereth the to the ton and
defendeth the from that othre. For there is nothyng more 210
parfyte than the trouthe and clerenesse forto undirstonde and
knowe the parfytenesse of thyngis, whiche cannot be
undirstonde withoute connyng of science. For a wyse man
wolde take peyne to gete the leste savour of the reliques of
wysedom. And certaynly I dare well saye, whatsoever any man 215
seith, that ther nys joye ne tresour semelable to the tresour of
undirstondyng. Wherefore ye champions of science and
sapience, if ye will do any labour or payne, I councelle you
that ye labour to gete science. For and ye have it and use it
well, ye be noble, ye be ryche, ye be all parfyte. 220

And this is playnly shewed in the doctrine of philosophirs
whiche shewe and teche the wey to com by wysedome to the
tresour of pure and parfyte suffisauns. A prudent philosophyr
that was called Clentes had suche a desiere to taste of the
grete goodnesse of sapience and loved it so well, notwith- 225
stondyng that he was so poore that he coude not fynde the
meanes to com thereto but by gret labour that he had in the
nyght, and that was this: he drowe watyr all the nyght whiche
was necessarie to the use of the scolers. And so by that meane
he gat his lyvyng. And in the day he entendid to the studye 230

209. eschewing: rejection.
209–10. like . . . othre: in that it directs you towards the one and forbids
you the other.
211. parfyte: perfect.   *clerenesse*: perspicacity.
214. peyne: pains.   *gete*: get, obtain.
   leste savour: least touch, vestige (F. *goute*, 'drop').
   reliques: leavings, remnants.
216. nys: is not.   *semelable*: similar.
218. payne: effort.
219. and: if.
220. all: completely.
221. doctrine: teaching.
223. suffisauns: sufficiency.
224. Clentes: i.e. Cleanthes (331–232 BC), a Greek Stoic philosopher.
This story, like other anecdotes in this passage, comes from Valerius
Maximus, *Factorum et dictorum memorabilium libri novem*, Bk VIII, Ch. VII,
pp. 392/6–15 (see above, p. 137).
225. sapience: wisdom.
227. but: except.
228. drowe: drew, pumped.
229. scolers: scholars.   *meane*: means.
230. gat: got, gained.   *entendid*: devoted his attention.
   the studye: studying.

and to the lessons of Crysypus, whiche was a solempne
philosophre, to that intent that he myght be fulfilled of the
connyng of this wyse man. And by that techeingis and long
continuans, he becam a soverayne man. Wherefore me semeth
truly that this man was worthy to have a grete laude as well for   235
the constaunce of his labour as for the grete science that he
gat. Wherefore Senec seith in a epistell that Clentes by his
grete labour hylpe himselfe to come to the perfeccion of
science.

Yett to the purpos to love science and be diligent to lerne it,   240
for the grete goodnesse that may falle to him that liste to
labour there-fore, we will speke a lytle of othre philosophirs
forto sharpe the appetite of theim that stody forto lerne. The
philosophre Plato loved science so moche that thoroughe the
diligence that he made forto gete it, he filled himself with   245
wysedome of doctrine. This Plato was mastir to Aristotill and
was in the tyme of Socrates the philosophre. And he proffited
so moche in doctrine that for the noblesse of his witt was
counted the wysest man levyng. And that he loved science he
shewed it wele. For he went all aboute forto serche out all the   250
doctrine of bokes, namely in Ytalye.

Wherefore Valere speketh of his gret diligence and desiere

---

231. Crysypus: Chrysippus (*c.* 280–207 BC), another Stoic philosopher.
   solempne: famous, renowned.
232. to ... intent: in order.   *fulfilled*: filled.
233. connyng: wisdom.
233–4. long continuans: lengthy perseverance.
234. soverayne: outstanding.   *me semeth*: it seems to me.
235. laude: praise.
235–6. as well ... as: both ... and.
236. constaunce: constancy, persistence.
237. Senec ... epistell: Lucius Annaeus Seneca (*c.* 4 BC–AD 65), the
Roman Stoic philosopher, better known in the Middle Ages for his *Moral
Epistles* than for his tragedies.
238. hylpe: helped.
240. to(1) ... *love*: on the subject of loving; this clause is dependent on 'we
will speke ...' (l. 242).
241. liste: desires.
243. sharpe: sharpen, whet.
244. Plato: the story comes from Valerius Maximus, Bk VIII, Ch. VII, pp.
388/12–389/8.
247. proffited: progressed.
248. doctrine: learning, teaching.   *noblesse*: nobility.   *witt*: intelligence.
249. levyng: living.   *that*: (the fact) that.
251. namely: especially.
252. Valere: i.e. Valerius Maximus.

that he had forto knowe and undirstonde that the grete
thought that he toke forto gete bookes togedir, was for
nothyng ells but that science and connyng myght be caste 255
abrode by him thoroughe all the worlde. This solempne
philosophre died in the age of eighty eight yere. And happed
well at his dethe the gret love that he had to all maner of
bokes, for they founde lyyng by him the bookes of a woman
that was a poete, whiche was named Saphoo and wroote of 260
love in plesaunt and goodly verses, as Orace seith. And
paraventure he loked upon theim for takyng of his pleasour in
his plesaunt sayingis.

And yett there is conteyned in the boke of Valere of the
philosophir Democratus, whiche was a famous man in naturall 265
philosophye. And as Aristotill telleth in the firste boke of
Generacion and of Corupcion and chargeth of all thyngis, that
is to sey he wolde geve comendacion to the saying of
Democratus. And therefore Aristotill comendith him gretly in
dyvers places for his naturell philosophie and alowed gretly his 270
opynions. Also Valere recomendith moche the said philosophre

253. he: i.e. Plato.
255–6. caste abrode: spread abroad.
256. thoroughe: throughout.
257. eighty eight: emended on the basis of the F. here. *yere:* years.
257–8. happed well: (it) was very clear (F. *Si parut bien*).
260. Saphoo: Sappho of Lesbos, the Greek woman poet who wrote of her love for other women; probably the earliest references to her in English. Valerius Maximus says Plato died reading a copy of the mimes of 'Sophron' (a fifth-century Greek writer) but the French paraphrase and translation of Simon of Hesdin and Nicholas Gonesse which Christine used (see Lucas 1970) changes 'Sophron' to 'Sappho'. The Middle Ages knew of Sappho through Ovid's poem *Heroides* XV, which purports to be a farewell letter to her (male) lover immediately before she committed suicide.
261. Orace: the manuscript has *Orose*, i.e. Orosius, the first Christian historian, whose work contains no reference to Sappho. The F. has *Orace*, i.e. Horace, whose poetry contains two approving references to Sappho.
262. paraventure: perhaps.
263. his: a mistranslation of *ses*, 'her'.
264. yett: further. *of*(2): (a story) about.
265. Democratus: i.e. Democritus (*c.* 460 BC), the Greek philosopher who first proposed the atomic theory; see Valerius Maximus, Bk VIII, Ch. VII, p. 389/9–18.
265–6. naturall philosophye: science.
266–7. Aristotill . . . Corupcion: i.e. Aristotle, *De Generatione et Corruptione*; Bk I contains several references to Democritus and his theories.
267. chargeth . . . thyngis: a misunderstanding of F. which says here that he, i.e. Democritus, was interested in the causes of all things.
268. geve comendacion: commend.
270. dyvers: various. *alowed:* praised.

for because he dispreysed richesse gretly, whiche oftyn tymes
hath done many a man moche hurte and lettyng in getyng of
philosophie, and seith that this Democratus myght have gretly
haboundid in rychesse if he had wolde. For his fadir was so   275
passyngly ryche that he fedde all the hoste of Kyng Zerses.
Yett notwithstondyng all that rychesse, he drewe him to
stodye. But whan the goodes felle unto him, he distribued
theim to his frendes and to the people and unnethe lefte him
anythyng to leve upon.   280
    Secondly, Valere recomendeth him in as moche as he never
desiered worldly honours, whiche empeched gretly to conquere
sapience. And as he dwelled long in Athenes, he employed all
his tyme in exercise of doctrine and leved there long tyme
unknowen in the said citee, like as himselfe wittnesseth in on 285
of his volumes, for he chase to lyfe solitaryly forto be out of
noyse and stryffe whiche letteth gret speculacion. Than it
appered well that he had grete desiere of connyng, for he
eschewed to his powr all maner thyngis that myght lett him fro
the getyng of science.   290
    Yett to the same purpos that men shulde love science and
stodye, Valere speketh of the philosophre Carnyades, seying
that he was the werrey knyght that laboured sciences; for
eighty yere he leved in philosophie. And he was mervellously
conjoyned to the werkes of doctrine, that it semed ofte tymes   295

272. *dispreysed*: condemned, disparaged.   *richesse*: riches.
273. *lettyng*: hindrance.
275. *haboundid*: abounded.   *wolde*: wanted.
276. *passyngly*: surpassingly.   *fedde*: fed.   *hoste*: army.
       Zerses: i.e. Xerxes, king of Persia 486–465 BC.
277. *drewe him*: betook himself.
278. *goodes . . . unto*: property descended to.
       distribued: distributed.
279. *unnethe*: scarcely.   *him*: himself.
280. *leve*: live.
282. *empeched . . . conquere*: greatly prevented obtaining.
284. *exercise of doctrine*: pursuit of learning.
285. *like*: just.   *on*: one.
286. *chase*: chose.
287. *stryffe*: strife.   *letteth*: hinders, prevents.
       speculacion: speculative thought.
289. *eschewed . . . powr*: avoided to (the best of) his ability.
291. *Yett . . . purpos*: still with the same intention.
292. *Carnyades*: i.e. Carneades (214–129 BC), a follower of Aristotle; see
Valerius Maximus, Bk VIII, Ch VII, pp. 389/19–390/6.
293. *werrey*: true.   *laboured*: worked at.
294–5. *mervellously conjoyned*: marvellously wedded.
295. *werkes of doctrine*: the tasks of learning.

as he satte at his mete that he toke his refeccion in stodying of
doctrine, so that Meleysa his servant was fayn oftyn tymes to
take him by the honde and put it to his mete, seing the gret
stodye whiche he was ynne. This said philosophre sette by
nothyng in the worlde but only by vertu.   300

Of many othre philosophirs and sewers of wysedom a man
myght speke of, but for abryggeing of this matier I will passe
over. And theis matiers here-before I have brought to mynde
to that intent that I may reduce and bryng to knoleche of the
good stodyentes, suche as desiere to lerne science and vertue.   305
For it is no doubte but the sciences maken a man to be
gracious and well-governed, but if it be suche on as is
undiscrete and weneth himself that he knowe all sciences, but
in hemselfe they shewe it not but teche it to othre. And suche
maner men as techen sapience and do nothing theimselfe of   310
the same, ben likened to suche as dye for hungyr and theire
good lyyng by theim. And othre men helpe theimselfe with
that good and suche men ben more blameworthy whan they
doo amysse than othre.

Yitt the same   315
For bycause that this fayre matere is right covenable to be
knowen, and also that every man hathe not the boke of Valere
forto gadre oute to theire plesaunce all the matiers that he
speketh of, it liketh me yett to speke of the good purpos that
longithe to studye for bycause I have said here before that the   320

---

296. mete: food.   *refeccion*: refreshment.
297. Meleysa: i.e. Melissa.   *fayn*: obliged.
299. sette: set store.
301. sewers: pursuers.
302. abryggeing: abbreviating, abridging.   *matier*: subject matter.
304. reduce: recall.   *bryng . . . of*: make known to.
306. it . . . but: there is no doubt that.
307. gracious: virtuous.   *well-governed*: well regulated.
307–8. but . . . undiscrete: unless he is the sort of person that is foolish.
308. weneth: thinks.
309–11. suche . . . same: the sort of men who teach wisdom and do not act
according to it.
311–12. and . . . theim: while their money lies beside them.
314. doo amysse: act wrongly.
316. For . . . that: i.e. since (F. *por ce que*).   *fayre matere*: splendid subject.
     right covenable: entirely worthy.
318. gadre oute: extract.   *to . . . pleasaunce*: for their enjoyment.
319. it . . . me: I would like.
319–20. purpos . . . to: intention that belongs to; a mistranslation of F. *à
propos d'estude*, 'in connection with study'.

studyantes ought to do gret diligence in the getyng of science, as Valere reciteth and sheweth houghe that diligens well-modered without the gret excesse shall bryng a man in gret exercise of connyng. And he assigneth the causes why he seith so.　　　　　　　　　　　　　　　　　　　　　　　　　　325

　　Scevola, whiche was an excellent legistre at Rome, composed certain lawes whiche othre legistirs usen yett. And aftir his gret occupacion and stodye, wolde take recreacion of dyverse playes. And that a man shulde do soo, Valere sheweth that it is reason and seith that the nature of thyngis will not　330 suffre a man continually to be in labour. That is to sey, he muste nedes at som tyme have reste in ydelnesse. But this ydilnesse shulde not be that a man shulde cesse from all bodely labours. But it is to undirstonde that a man shulde be occupied in som joyfull disporte by the whiche his undir-　335 stondyng may be the more freshe. For by long studying all the sensytyfe vertues of a man be made wery and dulle. And also they be not brought agayn to theire reste and tranquillyte by cessyng of all maner werkes. For they that be travailled in studye, if they be not occupied with som gladnesse, they shall　340 be full of malyncoly for the spryt that hathe be in so gret labour of stodye before. And if they goo to bedde so, they shall suffre payne in theire slepe, as in dremyng and othirwyse. And therefore the remedie of that travaylle is forto

---

321. do . . . diligence: take great care.
322. reciteth: recounts.　　　　*houghe*: how.
322–3. well-modered: well-moderated (F. *modérée*).
323–4. in . . . connyng: to considerable practice of wisdom.
324. assigneth: specifies.
326. Scevola: P. Mucius Scaevola, a Roman lawyer; see Valerius Maximus, Bk VIII, Ch. VIII, p. 394/16–24.
326. legistre: lawyer.
327. composed: drafted.　　　*usen yett*: still use.
329. dyverse playes: various diversions.
331. suffre: allow, permit.
334. it . . . undirstonde: it should be understood.
335. joyfull disporte: pleasant recreation.
337. sensytyfe vertues: the sensitive powers, i.e. the faculties such as the five senses that inform the soul about the external world.
337. wery: weary, tired.
338. brought agayn: restored.
339. cessyng . . . werkes: cessation of all kinds of activity.
　　　travailled: overworked.
340. gladnesse: enjoyable activity.
341. malyncoly: melancholy, depression.　　　*spryt*: spirit, mind.

rejoyse his spryte with som goodly pley and disporte. And in 345
like wyse as the plesaunte metes pleaseth more at som tyme
whan they be entirmedled with groos metes, in like wyse the
werke of studye is the bettir noryshed whan a man at som
tyme applyeth himselfe to pleye and disporte.

And therefore Caton seith, 'Entirmedle thy werkes among 350
with disportes.' Also Aristotill seith, in the thredde booke of
Etiques, 'A man in his labour shulde use vertuously as well
pley as labour.' To the whiche thyng Seneca accordeth in his
booke of Tranquyllyte of Courage and seith that the lusty and
well-beryng fyldees be sone hurte by continuell fertilite 355
withoute they be othrewyse refreshed. In lyke wyse continuall
labour in any science hurteth the courage of any persone and
ingendrethe fransye. And therefore Nature geveth men
inclinacions of disporte and pleye othirwhile. And for that
cause also they that stablysshed the lawes in olde tyme 360
ordeyned festes to that entent that all maner of people shulde
assemble forto disporte and pley and leve theire laboure. To
this purpos it is said of Socrates, whiche no parte of scieence
was hid froo, that he was not ashamed whan he was mokked

345. rejoyse: gladden.   *goodly pley*: virtuous recreation.
346. plesaunte metes: delicacies.
347. entirmedled: mingled.   *groos metes*: plain, simple food.
350. Caton: Cato. Cato's *Distichs*, a collection of proverbial sayings written
in Latin couplets, was a popular school text in the Middle Ages; composed
in the late third or early fourth century, its true author is unknown. The
reference here is to *Distichs* III, 6.
351–2. thredde ... Etiques: third book of the *Ethics* (probably *Nicomachean
Ethics* X, iv, 9).
352–3. as ... labour: both play and work.
353–4. Seneca ... Courage: Seneca, *Ad Serenum de Tranquillitate Animi*,
XVII, 5, in *Seneca: Moral Essays*, II, p. 281.
353. accordeth: agrees.
354. lusty: vigorous.
355. well-beryng: fruitful.   *fyldees*: fields.
356. withoute ... refreshed: unless they are reinvigorated in some other way.
357. hurteth ... courage: damages the mind.
358. ingendrethe fransye: engenders madness.
359. inclinacions ... pleye: inclinations for relaxation and enjoyment.
      othirwhile: sometimes.
360. stablysshed: established.
361. ordeyned: decreed.   *festes*: feasts, holidays.
362. assemble: gather together.   *leve*: leave.
363–4. whiche ... froo: from whom no aspect of wisdom was hidden.
364–5. mokked of: mocked by.

of Achipiades bycause he founde him playing with litle   365
childyrn. But he did it for bycause that the recreacion whiche
he had among theim shulde sharpe and refreshe his witte and
make it more quycke to the stodye. And for that cause, as olde
as he was, he lerned to pleye on the harpe.

From *The Book of Faits* of Arms and of Chivalry*

e) *The Prologue*
(sigs Ai–ii)

Bycause that hardynes is so moche necessarye to entrepryse   370
hye thynges, whiche without that shold never be enprysed,
that same is covenable to me at this present werke to put it
forth without other thyng, seen the lytylhed of my persone,
whiche I knowe not digne ne worthy to treate of so hye
matere, ne durst not only thynke what blame hardynes causeth   375
whan she is folyssh. I thenne, nothyng moeved by arrogaunce
in folyssh presumpcion, but admonested of veray affeccion
and good desyre of noble men in th'offyce of armes, am
exorted after myne other escriptures passed (lyke as he, that

---

365. Achipiades: Alcibiades (*c.* 450–404 BC), Athenian general and
statesman, intimate friend and pupil of Socrates.
366. he: i.e. Socrates; see Valerius Maximus, Bk VIII, Ch. VII, p. 395/1–4,
and Seneca, *Ad Serenum de Tranquillitate Animi*, XVII, 4.
*. Faits: deeds.
370. hardynes: courage, valour.   *entrepryse*: undertake.
371. hye: high, i.e. serious, important.   *enprysed*: undertaken.
372. covenable: fitting, necessary.
372–3. put it forth: make it public.
373. without other thyng: i.e. with no other justification (than that of
courage, or perhaps rashness).
373. seen . . . persone: my personal insignificance being seen.
374. digne: worthy.   *treate of*: discuss.
375. matere: subject.
375–6. ne . . . folyssh: the rest of this sentence does not make complete
sense because the translation omits several lines of French after 'thynke'.
376. nothyng moeved: not at all moved, motivated.
377. admonested of: encouraged, prompted by.   *veray affeccion*: true love.
378. th'offyce: the service.
379. exorted: urged.   *escriptures passed*: past writings.

hath toforn beten doun many stronge edyfices, is more hardy   380
to charge hymself defye or to bete doun a castell or forteresse,
whan he feleth hymself garnysshed of covenable stuffe therto
necessarye) thenne to entrepryse to speke in this present book
of the right honorable offyce of armes and of chyvalrye, as wel
in thynges whiche therto ben convenyent as in droytes whyche   385
therto be appertenaunt, lyke as the lawes and dyverse auctours
declaren it.

To the purpoos I have assembled the maters and gadred in
dyverse bokes forto produce myne entencion in this present
volume. But as it apperteyneth this matere to be more   390
executed by fayt of dyligence and witte, than by subtyltees of
wordes polisshed, and also considered that they that ben
excersyng and experte in th'arte of chyvalrye be not comunely
clerkys ne instructe in science of langage, I entende not to
treate but to the most playn and entendible langage that I shal   395
mowe; to that ende that the doctryne gyven by many auctors,
whiche by the helpe of God I purpose to declare in this
present boke, may be to alle men clere and entendible.

And bycause that this is thyng not accustomed and out of
usage to wymen, whiche comynly do not entremete but to   400
spynne on the distaf and ocupie theim in thynges of houshold,
I supplye humbly to the said right hie offyce and noble state of
chyvalrye, that in contemplacion of theyr lady Mynerve, born
of the contre of Grece, whome the auncyents for hir grete
connyng reputeden a goddesse, the whiche fonde, lyke as olde   405

380. *toforn*: formerly.   *beten*: beaten.
381. *charge hymself*: take upon himself.
382. *garnysshed of*: equipped with.   *covenable*: suitable.
384–5. *as wel . . . as*: both . . . and.
385. *convenyent*: appropriate.
385–6. *droytes . . . appertenaunt*: customs that appertain to it.
388. *gadred*: collected.
389. *produce . . . entencion*: bring forth my design.
391. *fayt . . . witte*: by the workings of care and intelligence.
392. *wordes polisshed*: polished words.
393. *excersyng*: practised.
394. *clerkys*: learned men.   *instructe*: instructed.   *science*: knowledge.
394–6. *I . . . mowe*: I intend to use only the most unadorned and
comprehensible language of which I am capable.
396. *doctryne*: instruction.
399–400. *out of usage*: unusual.
400–1. *entremete . . . spynne*: engage in any activity other than spinning.
401. *ocupie theim*: busy themselves.
402. *supplye*: supplicate.   *state*: estate.
405. *connyng*: wisdom, skill.   *reputeden*: considered.   *fonde*: invented.

wrytyngis sayen and as I have other tymes sayd – and also the
poete Boece recyteth in his Boke of Clere and Noble
Wimmen, and semblably recyten many other – the arte and
manere to make harnoys of yron and steel; whiche wyl not
have ne take it for none evyl yf I, a woman, charge myself to   410
treate of so lyke a matere, but wyl ensewe th'enseignement
and techyng of Seneke whiche saith, 'Retche the not what
they saye, soo that the wordes be good.'
    And therfore and to purpos, in manere poetyke it plaiseth
me t'adresse suche a prayer to the foresayd lady: 'O Mynerve,   415
goddesse of armes and of chyvalrye, whiche by vertue of hye
entendement above alle other wymen fondest and institutest,
emonge th'other noble artes and sciences whiche of the toke
their begynnyng, th'usage to forge of yron and steel armours
and harnois propice and covenable to couvre and targe the   420
body of man agaynst the strokes of dartes, noyous shotte and
speres in batayle; in fayttes of armes, helmes, sheldes, targes
and other harnoys defensable fro the first comen, institutest
and gavest manere and ordre to arenge batailles and t'assaille

406. I . . . sayd: compare ll. 7–10 above.
407. Boece: an error for *Bocace*, i.e. Boccaccio (1313–75), humanist writer
of prose and verse in Italian and Latin.
407. recyteth: rehearses.
407–8. Boke . . . Wimmen: *De Claris Mulieribus*, which Christine uses
extensively in *Othea* and *The Book of the City of Ladies*.
408. semblably: similarly.
409. harnoys: armour.   *whiche*: i.e. 'the lofty profession of arms'.
410. have . . . evyl: hold or take it amiss.
411. lyke: similar.   *ensewe*: follow.   *enseignement*: instruction.
412. Seneke: Seneca; the quotation is possibly from *Ad Serenum de
Tranquillitate Animi* (which Christine also used in *The Body of Policy* – see
above, notes to ll. 353–4 and 366), XI, 8: 'I shall never be ashamed to
quote a bad author if what he says is good' (*Seneca: Moral Essays*, II, p. 259).
412. Retche the not: do not mind.
413. soo that: as long as.
414. manere poetyke: poetic fashion.
416–17. hye entendement: lofty thought.
417. institutest: established.
418. emonge: among.   *of the*: from thee.
419. th'usage . . . forge: the practice of forging.
420. propice: advantageous.   *covenable*: suitable.   *couvre*: cover.
    targe: shield.
421. noyous shotte: harmful bullets.
422. fayttes: deeds.   *targes*: shields.
423. harnoys defensable: protective armour.
424. arenge: draw up.   *batailles*: battles.

and fight in manere: adoured Lady and hie Goddesse, be thou 425
not displeased that I, symple and lytyl woman, lyke as nothyng
unto the gretenes of thy renommee in cunnyng, dare presently
compryse to speke of so magnyfike an offyce as is th'office of
armes, of whiche fyrst in the said renomed contree of Grece
thou gavest th'usage. And in so moche it may plaise the to be 430
to me favorable that I may be somwhat consonaunt in the
nacyon where thou was born, whiche as thenne was named
the Grete Grece, the contree beyonde the alpes or montaygnes,
whiche now is sayd Puylle and Calabre in Ytalye, where thou
were born; and I am, as thou were, a woman Ytalien.' 435

Textual notes

27. *Wherefore*] Where.
106. *vita*] vitam.
141. *apostle*] a apostle.
186. *be*] he.
189. *men of crafte*] men crafte.
209. *stereth the*] stereth.
214. *savour*] favour.
225. *it*] id.
255. *myght*] mght.
257. *eighty*] x iiij.
261. *Orace*] Orose.
280. *leve*] love.
291. *shulde love*] love.
294. *eighty*] xx (F. iiii xx).
301. *sewers*] shewers.
309. *hemselfe*] himselfe.
323. *bryng a man*] bryng.

425. *adoured*: adored, worshipped.
427. *unto*: (compared) with.   *renommee*: renown.
     presently: at this moment.
428. *compryse*: contrive.   *magnyfike*: magnificent, splendid.
429. *renomed*: renowned.
430. *usage*: practice.
431. *consonaunt in*: in harmony with, compatible with.
432. *nacyon*: country, people.   *as thenne*: at that time.
433. *Grete Grece*: i.e. Magna Graecia, which included part of Italy.
     montaygnes: mountains.
434. *sayd*: called.   *Puylle*: Apulia.   *Calabre*: Calabria.
435. *woman Ytalien*: Italian woman.

337. *sensytyfe*] sentyfe.
340. *they*(2)] the.
371. *enprysed*] enpryses.
386. *therto*] thrto.
422. *in fayttes*] fayttes.

10 A Revelation of Purgatory

The anonymous writer of *A Revelation Showed to a Holy Woman* was a woman leading a secluded, devout life, probably in Winchester in the early fifteenth century (see Ogilvie-Thomson 1980). She was clearly not a nun, as she lived with only a maidservant for company; nor was she a strictly enclosed solitary (like Julian of Norwich), for she was free to visit local priests and to make a pilgrimage to a local shrine. She was presumably a widow who had taken vows, or a non-institutionalised devout woman like Margery Kempe.

The text takes the form of a letter (compare the opening and closing formulas with those of the Paston Letters, below, pp. 240–61) to the woman's confessor, John Forest, archdeacon of Surrey, who died in 1446. It records a series of dreams which took place in August 1422, in which the soul of her friend, the nun Margaret, appears, shows the dreamer her own sufferings in Purgatory and those of others, and asks for her friends' prayers and for masses to be said by various priests. After the dreamer has arranged all this, she witnesses Margaret's vindication by the Virgin and triumphant entry into heaven. Certain individuals mentioned by name have been convincingly identified by recent research, suggesting that this is an actual letter rather than a literary text making use of epistolary conventions and the letter form.

Comment: The literary account of a visionary journey to the other world is of course a well-established genre, of which the most notable medieval example is Dante's *Divine Comedy*. The content, however, of these dreams is entirely derived from popular piety and exemplifies the late medieval obsession with Purgatory. Fifteenth-century wills often make lavish provision for the kind of prayers and masses which Margaret requests, to ensure the testator's quick passage through Purgatory into Heaven (see Carpenter 1987; Keiser 1987a). Eleanor Hull (see below, p. 219) left instructions that a thousand masses should be said for the repose of her soul.

The text also makes clear the dependence of medieval women on the services of men, for it is priests who must say the masses to release Margaret from her sufferings. Paradoxically, though, only the woman dreamer is in touch with the dead and can act as intermediary, and finally it is the Virgin who routs the Devil, vindicates Margaret and presents her as a newly born soul to the Great High Priest, her son.

The writer's style is vigorous and unselfconscious. She tells her rather lurid story effectively, though the repetitious nature of her sentence structures – typically a succession of simple sentences introduced by 'and then me thought' and strung together with 'and' – suggests that she was an unpractised writer. Her imagination is vivid though crude; in her lively description of the pains inflicted on the unfortunate Margaret there is a horrifying undercurrent of grotesque, almost pornographic violence. This may result as much from the dreamer's internalisation of her society's hostile attitudes towards women as from the more general late medieval preoccupations with death and suffering.

Manuscripts: Extant in three fifteenth-century manuscripts: Lincoln Cathedral MS 91 (the Thornton Manuscript), ff. 251ᵛ–258; Longleat Hall MS 29, ff. 155ʳ–65ᵛ; Oxford Bodley MS Eng. theol. c. 58, ff. 10–12ᵛ. The three versions are not closely related. The extracts here are edited from the facsimile of the Thornton Manuscript.

Further reading (for full details see Bibliography): On the development of the concept of Purgatory, see Le Goff 1984; on fifteenth-century attitudes towards it, see Carpenter 1987: 53–74; on the text itself, see Keiser 1987a: 143–52.

A Revelation Showed to a Holy Woman

a) *The Haunting of a Holy Woman*
(Lincoln Cathedral MS 91, ff. 250ᵛ–251ᵛ)

Fadir, I do yow to wiete how grete trybulacyon I had in my slepe appone Saynt Lowrence Day at nyghte, the yere of Oure Lorde a thowsande fowre hundrethe twenty and two.

I wente to my bede at eghte of the cloke, and so I felle appon slepe; and so bytwyx nyne and ten me thoghte I was   5
raveschede into purgatorye and sodanly I sawe all the paynes whilke was schewed me many tyms byfore, als ye, fadir, knowe wele be my confessyone and tellynge. Bot, dere syre, I was noghte schewede by no spyrite the syghte of tham on this nyghte of Saynt Lowrence, bot so sodanely, dere fadir, me   10

1. *I . . . wiete*: I am letting you know.   *how*: what.
2. *appone*: upon.   *Saynt Lowrence Day*: the feast of St Lawrence, 10 August.
2–3. *the . . . two*: AD 1422.
4. *eghte . . . cloke*: eight o'clock.
4–5. *felle . . . slepe*: fell asleep.
5. *bytwyx*: between.   *me thoghte*: it seemed to me.
6. *raveschede into*: transported to.
   purgatorye: Purgatory, a place of purification for those souls which will ultimately be saved because they died in a state of grace but still need to be punished for their sins.
6. *sodanly*: suddenly.   *paynes*: pains, torments.
7. *whilke was*: which were.   *als*: as.
8. *confessyone*: confession.
9. *noghte*: not.
   by . . . spyrite: by any spirit; apparently on previous occasions the holy woman had had a spiritual guide (presumably an angel).
9. *syghte*: sight, vision.   *tham*: them.

thoghte I sawe tham; and forsothe, dere fadir, I was never so evylle afferde when I woke for scheweynge of the paynes als I was than, and the cause was that I was noghte ledde by no spyrite that I knewe before, that myghte hafe comforthed me, and in this sighte of purgatorye me thoghte I sawe thre grete   15
fyres, and me thoghte ylk a fyre was at other ende. Bot, sir, there was no depertynge bytwene tham, bot ylkane was eked to othir.

And thies thre fyres was wondirfull and horrybill, and specyally the moste of alle was in the myddis. For that fyre   20
was so horribill and so stynkande that all the creaturs in the werlde myghte never telle the wykkede smellynge thereof; for thare was pykke and tarre, ledde and bromestane and oyle, and alle manere of thynge that myghte brynne, and alle manere of paynes that man couthe thynke, and alle manere of   25
crysten men and women that hade lyffede here in this werlde, of whate degre thay were.

Bot amange alle the paynes that I sawe of alle men and wymmen, me thoghte that prestes that hade bene lechours in thaire lyves, and thaire wymen with tham, whether thay were   30
relegyous men and wymen, or seculer men and wymen of ordire, me thoghte in that syghte that thay hade moste payne.

And in that grete fyre me thoghte I sawe the spiryte of a

11. *forsothe*: truly.
12. *evylle afferde*: badly frightened.
13. *than*: then.   *ledde*: conducted, guided.
14. *hafe*: have.   *comforthed*: comforted, strengthened.
16. *ylk a*: every, each.   *other*: the other, opposite.
17. *depertynge*: separation.   *ylkane*: each one.   *eked*: added.
19. *thies*: these.
20. *moste*: largest.   *myddis*: midst, middle.
21. *stynkande*: stinking.
22. *werlde*: world.   *myghte*: could.   *wykkede smellynge*: evil smell, stench.
    thereof: of it.
23. *thare*: there.   *pykke*: pitch.   *ledde*: (molten) lead.
    bromestane: brimstone, burning sulphur.   *oyle*: oil.
24. *brynne*: burn.
25. *couthe*: knows how to.
26. *lyffede*: lived.
27. *whate degre*: whatever status, position in society.
28. *amange*: among.
29. *prestes*: priests.   *lechours*: lechers.
30. *thaire*: their.
31. *relegyous*: religious, i.e. bound by religious vows.
31–2. *seculer … ordire*: seculars (priests who did not belong to a religious order but were still vowed to continence) and nuns.

woman that I knewe, the whilke woman was in hir lyfe a syster
of ane house of relygyone, the whilke woman the while scho   35
lyffede was callede Margarete; whilke me thoghte I sawe in
this horrible fyre, and had so grete paynes that for drede I
myghte nott dyscryve tham at that tym. And in a dredfull fere
I wokke, and by-tyme smote the houre of ten byfore
mydnyghte. And for drede and for fere to slepe agayne I rose   40
upe, and a littill mayden childe with me, and we two sayde the
Seven Psalmes and the Letanye. And by we hade saide owte
the Agnus Dei, I was so hevy of slepe I myghte noghte make
ane ende, bot made my childe go to bedde and so did I. And
by that tyme it smate elleven of the clokke, and by I had tolde   45
the laste stroke, I bygan to slepe.

And onone me thoghte come to me the speryte of this
woman Mergarete, the whilke I sawe byfore in paynes, and me
thoghte scho was full of stronge wondes als scho hade bene
drawen with kames, and so me thoghte scho was wondede and   50
rent; bot specyaly at hir herte me thoghte I sawe a grevous
and ane orybille wounde, and owte of that wonde come

34–5. syster . . . relygyone: i.e. a nun; the 'house of religion' was most likely
the Benedictine nunnery of Nunnaminster, in Winchester.
35. scho: she.
37. drede: terror.
38. myghte . . . dyscryve: could not look at, discern.   *fere:* fear.
39. wokke: woke.   *by-tyme:* promptly.   *smote:* struck.
40. for: because of.
40–1. rose upe: got up.
41. mayden childe: girl.
42. Seven Psalmes: i.e. the Penitential Psalms, often used as a private
devotion (see Eleanor Hull, below, p. 219).
42. Letanye: Litany, a long series of invocations of various aspects of God
and the saints.
42. by: by the time that.   *saide owte:* recited completely.
43. Agnus Dei: the liturgical formula 'O Lamb of God, that takest away the
sins of the world'.
43. hevy of: heavy with.   *myghte noghte:* could not.
45. by . . . tyme: by the time that.   *smate:* struck.   *tolde:* counted.
46. bygan: began.
47. onone: immediately.   *come:* came.   *speryte:* spirit, ghost.
49. stronge: deep.   *wondes:* wounds.   *als:* as if.
50. drawen . . . kames: maltreated with combs, i.e. toothed implements of
torture.
50. wondede: wounded.
51. rent: torn.
52. orybille: horrible.

flawme of fyre. And scho said, 'Cursede mote thou be and wo worthe the, bot if thou haste the to be my helpe.' And me thoghte by scho hade saide that worde, I was so ferde I myghte noghte speke, bot ever I thoghte in myn herte, 'Jhesus passioun be my helpe', and with that I was comforthede in my spiryte.

And than me thoghte scho wolde hafe casten fyre appon me, and styrte to me to hafe slayne me, bot me thoghte scho hade no powere, for the passyone of God comforthed me; bot the grysely syghte of hir afferdede me. And me thoghte scho had a littill hounde and a littill catte folowyng hir, alle one fyre brynnynge. And than me thoghte I said to hir, 'What arte thou, in Goddes name, that thus sore travells me? And I conjure the in the Fadirs name and the Sone and the Haly Gaste, thre persouns and o Godd in trynyte, that thou telle me whate thou arte that thus travells me and whethir thou be a sperit of purgatorye to hafe helpe of me or a sperit of helle to overcome me and to trobble me?'

And than scho said, 'Naye, I am a spirit of purgatorye that walde hafe helpe of the, and noghte a spirit of helle to dryche the; and if thou will wiete whate spirit I am that suffirs grete paynes in purgatorye for my synnes, I ame the spirit of Margarete, the whilke was syster in a systers house of relegyon, as thou knewe wele, and also thou knewe me when I duellede therin. And in the name of God I aske helpe of the.'

55

60

65

70

75

---

53. *flawme*: flame. *mote*: may.

53–4. *wo worthe the*: woe betide you.

54. *bot if*: unless. *haste the*: hasten, hurry (reflexive).

55. *by*: when. *ferde*: afraid.

56. *ever*: constantly.

56–7. *Jhesus ... helpe*: may the Passion of Jesus be my help.

57. *comforthede*: strengthened.

59. *wolde hafe*: would have. *casten*: thrown.

60. *styrte ... me*(2): rushed at me to kill me.

62. *grysely*: grisly, grim. *afferdede*: terrified.

63. *hounde*: dog. *catte*: cat. *one*: on.

65. *sore travells*: bitterly troubles.

66. *conjure*: solemnly charge.

66–7. *in ... Gaste*: in the name of the Father, Son and Holy Ghost.

67. *o*: one.

69. *to hafe*: (wanting) to have.

72. *walde*: would. *of*: from. *dryche*: hurt, destroy.

73. *will wiete*: wish to know.

77. *duellede*: dwelt, lived. *therin*: in it.

b) *Margaret's Sufferings in Purgatory*
(f. 253^{r-v})

Now, fadir, the nexte nyghte appon that folowyng, I went to
bede and felle one slepe, and so sodaynely was schewede to
me hir paynes in purgatorye and other many one. Bot, fadir,   80
nowthir scho nor none other spiryte led me therto bot, fadir,
when I was one slepe me thoghte I sawe tham onone
withowtten any ledyng. And onone me thoghte I sawe
Margarete in hir werste clothes as scho wente one erthe, and
in the gretteste fyre of thir the whilke I sawe byfore in   85
purgatorye; and me thoghte I sawe abowte hir seven devylles,
and one of tham clede hir with a longe gown and a longe
trayle folowyng hir, and it was full of scharpe hukes withinn,
and the gowne and the hukes me thoghte were alle rede fyre.
And than the same devell tok wormes and pykk and tarre and   90
made lokkes and sete tham appon hir hede, and he toke a
grete longe neddir and putt all abowte hir hede and that, me
thoghte, hissed in hir hede, as it had bene hote brynnyng iryn
in the colde water; and me thoghte scho cryed when scho was
so arrayede, als me thoghte that alle the werlde myghte hafe   95
herde hir. And the littill hounde and the catt forfrette in
sondir hir legges and hir armes.
And than sayd that devele that arayed hir thus, 'This sall

78. *appon . . . folowyng*: following on that.
79. *one slepe*: asleep.
80. *hir*: her.   *other . . . one*: many others.
81. *nowthir*: neither.
83. *withowtten . . . ledyng*: without any guidance.
84. *werste*: worst, i.e. shabbiest.   *wente one erthe*: walked about on earth.
85. *gretteste*: greatest.   *thir*: those.   *the whilke*: which.
86. *abowte*: about, around.
87. *tham*: them.   *clede*: clad, clothed.
88. *trayle*: train.   *hukes*: hooks.   *withinn*: inside.
89. *rede fyre*: fiery red.
90. *wormes*: snakes.   *pykk*: pitch.
91. *lokkes*: locks (of hair).   *sete*: set, placed.
92. *neddir*: adder (a venomous snake).   *putt . . . abowte*: twined it round.
93. *in*: on.
93–4. *as . . . water*: as if it had been red-hot iron in cold water.
94. *cryed*: cried out, shrieked.
95. *arrayede*: dressed.   *als*: as.
96. *herde*: heard.
96–7. *forfrette in sondir*: chewed to pieces.
98. *sall*: shall, must.

thou hafe for thi foule stynkkyng pryde and boste that thou
usede in the werlde agayne mekenes; and this hounde and this   100
catt sall ever frete appon the the while thou erte here, for
thyne unresonabille lufe that thou luffede tham in erthe. For I
am the develle of Pryde, [. . .] I sall do myn ofyce in this payne
and qwyte the thi mede for the servyce that thou servede me.'
And me thoghte many develles were with hir.   105

    And than onone me thoghte that thare come owte other
seven devels. And one pullede owte hir tunge and ane other
pullede owte hir herte, and me thoghte thay raked it wyth iryn
rakes. 'And this,' thay sayd, 'thou sall hafe for thi wrethe and
thyne envy and for false forswerynge and for bakbyttyng and   110
sclandirynge, for all thies thou usyde in thi lyfe; and we are
the devels of Wrethe and of Envye, and all thies neddirs and
snakes that thou seese with us, that sall tourment the for thi
wykkede vyces that thou usede in erthe, and dyde noghte thi
penance or thou come here.'   115

    And than me thoghte that there come owte other two
develis, of the whilke one had scharpe rasours and he ferde
als he wolde forcute hir flesche, and so he did to my syghte,
and me thoghte he paride awaye all hir lyppes and he tuke a

---

99. *foule . . . boste*: foul stinking pride and boasting.
100. *usede*: practised.   *werlde*: world, i.e. on earth.
    agayne mekenes: contrary to humility.
101. *frete*: bite.   *the*(2) . . . *erte*: while thou art.
102. *unresonabille lufe*: unreasonable (excessive) love.   *that*: with which.
    luffede: loved.
103. *do . . . ofyce*: carry out my duty.
104. *qwyte . . . mede*: give you your reward.
    for . . . me: for the service you rendered me.
108. *iryn*: iron.
109. *wrethe*: wrath, anger.
110. *false forswerynge*: perjury.
110–11. *bakbyttyng and sclandirynge*: backbiting and slandering. It is
interesting to note the preoccupation with this sin among women; compare
the praise of the Virgin's silence in *Meditations upon the Seven Days of the
Week*, ll. 186–8.
111. *thies*: these.
113. *seese*: seest.   *sall*: shall.
114–15. *dyde . . . penance*: did not do penance for.
115. *or*: before.   *come*: came.
116. *other two*: another two, two more.
117. *rasours*: razors.   *ferde*: acted.
118. *als*: as if.   *wolde forcute*: was about to cut off.
    to my syghte: in full sight of me.
119. *paride*: pared, sliced.   *lyppes*: lips.   *tuke*: took.

grete huke of yryn and smote thorowe-oute hir herte; and that   120
other devele melted lede and bromstane and alle manere of
stynkynge venym that man myghte thynke, and also he
ordeyned hir alle manere of lykenes of metis and drynkes that
was delycate in this werlde, the whilke that scho usede to styre
hir more to syn than to vertu; and those metis me thoghte was   125
alle neddyrs and snakkes, and those thay made hir to ete
agayne hir will, and also thay made hir forto drynke alle maner
of cursede venym, and said, 'Ete and drynke this for thi
cursede glotonye and myspendynge, wastyng and takyng over-
mekyll the while thou was one lyve.'   130

And than me thoghte this devele and that other devele cutt
awaye hir flesche and hir lyppes, and thriste the huke into hir
herte. And than thay drewe hir into a grete blake water and
that semyd als colde als any ise, and mekyll therof was freside
to my syghte; and therin thay keste hir and possede hir up and   135
down and sayd, 'Take the this bathe for thi slewthe and thi
glotonye.' And anone thay tuke hir owte of the water and
threwe hir into a grete fyre, and thare thay lefte hir styll and
that, thay saide, solde be hir bedde for the slewthe that scho
lufed so wele here in erthe and wolde noghte come to Goddis   140
servyce when scho myghte. And ther thay lefte hir styll with
many wormes aboute hir.

120. *huke*: hook.   *smote thorowe-oute*: struck through.
121. *lede*: lead.
122. *venym*: venom, poison.   *man ... thynke*: one could imagine.
123. *ordeyned hir*: provided for her.
     alle ... drynkes: all kinds of imitations of food and drink.
124. *was delycate*: were delicacies.   *styre*: stir, provoke.
126. *snakkes*: snakes.
129. *glotonye*: gluttony, greediness.   *myspendynge*: excessive expenditure.
129–30. *over-mekyll*: over-much, excess.
130. *one lyve*: alive.
132. *thriste*: thrust.
133. *drewe*: dragged.   *blake water*: black lake.
134. *ise*: ice.
134–5. *mekyll ... syghte*: much of it was frozen as far as I could see.
135. *keste*: cast, threw.   *possede*: pushed.
136. *Take the*: take to yourself.   *slewthe*: sloth, laziness.
139. *solde*: should, ought to be.   *bedde*: bed.
140. *lufed*: loved, liked.   *wolde noghte*: refused to.
140–1. *Goddis servyce*: i.e. the round of liturgical offices nuns had to sing.
141. *myghte*: was able to.
142. *wormes*: snakes.

c) *Margaret Explains her Sufferings to her Friend* (ff. 254ᵛ–255ᵛ)

And sone after scho come agayne to me, and than scho said to
me, 'Now hase thou sene my bytter paynes that I suffirde in
thiese grete fyres of purgatorye.' And than, fadir, me thoghte   145
onone that scho come owte of the grete fatte and come to me;
and than scho sayd, 'Thou may knawe by the devels that were
my tourmentours and by the tourmentes that thay did me,
what syn that I hafe done; and therefore thay sall never
tourment me more, God it the foryelde and all my helpers   150
that hase sped me owt of my paynes.'

And than I askede hir whi scho cryed so petousely, 'Swete
Lady, be myn helpe', and whi scho cryed more one Oure
Lady than scho did one God Almyghty or one any other
sayntes. And than scho said, 'Yis, for scho es hede of all other   155
sayntes except God allane, and for scho es welle of mercy, I
cryede one hir in my grete woo, and also for I solde the
rathere be delyverde thurgh hir bone and prayere, and also
the whils I was one lyfe, I fastede hir faste.' And the sperit
sayd me agayne there sulde never none fayle of Oure Ladys   160

144. *hase*: hast.   *sene*: seen.
146. *fatte*: vat, vessel (in which Margaret was tormented).
147. *knawe*: know.
149. *therefore*: for that.   *sall*: shall.
150. *God ... foryelde*: may God reward you.
151. *hase sped*: have speeded (Margaret had asked her friend to have masses said for her).
152. *petousely*: piteously, pitifully.
153–5. *whi ... sayntes*: with the Virgin as 'Well of Mercy' who releases souls from Purgatory, compare Eleanor Hull's invocation of her as 'Mother of Mercy' (below, p. 226).
153. *one*: on.
155. *Yis*: Yes.   *for*: because.   *es*: is.   *hede*: head, principal.
156. *allane*: only, alone.   *welle*: well, fount.
157. *woo*: woe, sorrow.   *solde*: should.
157–8. *the rathere*: the more quickly.
158. *bone*: request, petition.
159. *the whils*: while.

   fastede hir faste: kept her fast. 'Our Lady's Fast' was kept on
Saturdays, regarded as sacred to the Virgin because on Holy Saturday (the
day between the Crucifixion on Good Friday and the Resurrection on
Easter Sunday) she alone had kept faith with her Son.
159. *sperit*: spirit.
160–1. *there ... helpe*: no one would ever lack Our Lady's help.

helpe that comes into purgatorye, that hase fastede hir faste
byfore.

And than I askede hir whi scho cryede so dullefully in that
grete fatte that scho was in, and why I myghte noghte see hir.
And than scho said, 'If thou had sene my paynes, thou sulde   165
hafe bene so ferde that thi body solde noghte wele hafe borne
thi sperit withowtten grete trybulacione of thi wittes, or ells
strange seknes, for my paynes were so strange; and therfor I
cryede so horribily.'

And than I askede hir whi that flawme of fyre come owte of   170
hir mouthe, and why at hir herte come owte so many sparkes
of fyre, and why hir herte was so woundide, and whi the littill
honde and the cate folowed hir, and what gude did thase
messes hir and thase prayers hir that scho bade saye for hir?
And than scho sayde, als towchynge the flawme of fyre at hir   175
mouthe, that was for hir grete athes that scho usede in hir
lyfe; and also towchynge the wonde at hir herte and the
sparkelynge fyre thareof, it was for hir athes was mekyll by
Oure Lordes hert, and that was the cause that the sparkes of
fyre come owte at hir herte; and that was one, scho sayde, of   180
the gretteste paynnes that scho hade. And as touchynge the
lyttill hounde and the cate, thay were hir mawemetts the whils
scho was one lyfe, and scho sett hir herte to mekill one swylke
foulle wormes.

'And thare thay folowe me to encrese my paynes, ay till the   185

---

163. dullefully: dolefully, wretchedly.

166. ferde: afraid.

166–7. solde . . . sperit: would not have been able well to sustain your spirit.

167. trybulacione . . . wittes: troubling of your sanity.

168. strange seknes: strong, i.e. violent, sickness.

170. flawme: flame.

173. gude: good, profit.   *thase*: those.

174. messes: masses.   *hir*: her.

175. als towchynge: as regards.

176. athes: oaths.

178. for: because.   *was mekyll*: were greatly.

179. Oure . . . hert: devotion to the Heart of Jesus increased during the
Middle Ages (see Mechtild of Hackeborn, above, p. 51); clearly Margaret
had come to treat it too casually.

182. mawemetts: idols, false gods. It is interesting that the nun Margaret is
specifically punished for her devotion to her pets, earlier described as an
'unreasonable love': cf. Chaucer's Prioress and her love of her little dogs
(General Prologue, *CT* A (I): 146–9).

183–4. sett . . . wormes: set her heart too much on such disgusting vermin.

185. thare: therefore.   *encrese*: increase.   *ay*: constantly.

bandes of syn be worne in sondir. And towching the messis-
saying and the prayers that was done for me, thay hafe hasted
me the tytter owt of my paynes, and also fro hethen-forwarde
I sall never be tourment more with devels safe with one, and
that es with my wykkede angelle, and he sall brynge me   190
thurgh thise two fyrs of purgatorye, and if thar be any drosse
of syn, there sall I be clensed; and this honde ne this cate sall
never folow me more.' And than scho saide, 'Fare wele', and
nenned my name, and said scho suld never travelle me more
in the syghte of paynes bot ane other nyghte. And than me   195
thoghte scho went fro me, bot scho cryed noghte als scho dyd
byfore. And than, fadir, I woke of my slepe; and than me
thoght I was full wery and full evylle afferde. And, fadir, thus
mekill me thoghte I sawe on that nyghte.

d) *Margaret is Released into Heaven* (ff. 257)

And than scho said, 'Now hafe I tolde the all thynges als God   200
will and made ane end of purgatorye. And now take gud hede
what thou sees me doo nowe; and if thou had noghte gone to
Sowthwyke one pilgremage for me in the wyrchipe of God
and of Oure Lady, for I had vowede it and myght noghte do it
and thou hase done it for me, and ells I sulde full foule hafe   205
bene lettide of my passage when I solde hafe bene weyhede
oute of thise paynes, and that sall thou sone see.' And me

186. *bandes*: bonds, chains.   *worne in sondir*: worn through.
186–7. *messis-saying*: saying of masses.
187. *done*: i.e. carried out.   *hasted*: hastened.
188. *tytter*: quicker.   *fro ... forwarde*: from now onwards.
189. *tourment*: tormented.   *safe with*: except by.
191. *drosse*: dross, impurity.
194. *nenned*: named.   *travelle*: disturb.
195. *syghte*: vision.   *bot ane other*: except for one more.
196. *went fro*: left.   *cryed*: cried, shrieked.
197. *of*: out of.
198. *evylle afferde*: badly frightened.
198–9. *thus mekill*: this much.
201. *made ... of*: finished with.   *take ... hede*: pay particular attention to.
203. *Sowthwyke*: Southwick in Hampshire, where there was a shrine of the
Virgin at the priory of Augustinian canons.
203. *wyrchipe*: honour.
205. *and ells*: otherwise.
205–6. *sulde ... of*: should have been very badly hindered from.
206. *when ... weyhede*: when I had to be weighed in the balance.

thoghte sone after that thare come a fayre lady and a fayre
yonge man with hir, of the age of twenty wynter, and he
broghte weyhes in his hand, and he was clede alle in whitte   210
clothes; and me thoghte this lady was cled in white clothe of
golde, and sternes of golde was in hir garment, and a royale
crowne scho had one hir hede of gold, and a septre in hir
hande, and on the ende of the septre was a lyttill crose.

And than scho spake to the man in white, 'Sone', scho said,   215
'take this woman and late hir be weyhed.' And anone sodanly
scho was in the weyhes; and onone the devele weyhed agayne
hir, and a grete lange worme with hym. And twyse scho felle
down to the develle and the devele rehersed all hir synnes
whilke scho hade bene in paynes fore. And than sayd the man   220
in white, 'Hir synnes ere forgeffen, for scho hase done hir
penance therfore, and scho es gyffen to the Welle of Mercy
that es present, the Qwene of heven and of erthe, Empryce of
helle and of purgatorye, and the blyssed Modir of God, and
scho es gyffen to hir. Whate cane thou saye to this woman?'   225

And than me thoghte the devele tuke owte that grete worme
and saide, 'Here es the worme of conscyence, that yit sall
travelle hir for a thynge that es byhynde, and that es scho
made a vowe to a pilgremage and fulfilled it noghte.' And than
me thoghte that that faire lady said, 'Here es one that hase   230
done it for hir, and my sone and I hase gyffen this woman

210. weyhes: balances, pair of scales.   *clede*: clad, dressed.
212. sternes: stars.   *in*: on.
212–13. a . . . gold: she had a regal crown of gold on her head.
213. septre: sceptre.
214. crose: cross.
216. late: let.
217. agayne: against, opposite.
218. lange: long.   *twyse*: twice.   *felle*: dipped.
219. rehersed: repeated, enumerated.
221. ere forgeffen: are forgiven.
222. therfore: for them.   *gyffen*: given.
223. Empryce: empress.
226. tuke owte: took out, i.e. produced.
227. worme of conscyence: the 'worm (i.e. snake) of conscience', a symbol of
remorse, is usually metaphorical rather than literal, as here.
227. yit: yet, still.
228. travelle: torment.   *byhynde*: still to come.
228–9. scho . . . noghte: medieval writers often warned the devout against
making rash or unnecessary vows – cf. *The Faits and the Passion of Our Lord
Jesu Christ* (below, p. 217) – precisely because of the spiritual dangers if
they were not fulfilled.
229. to: of.

mercy. And fy one the, foule Sathanas! Thou and the worme
of conscience sall never dere hir more.' And with that worde,
me thoghte scho weyhede even down to the faire lady. And
me thoghte the devele and the worme made a grete crye, and   235
anone thay voydede awaye.

And than that faire lady tuke a white clothe and wrapped all
aboute hir and than this lady saide, 'Come one, dogheter, with
me and thou sall ressayve the oyle of mercy and thi conscience
sall be made clene. And full grete mede sall thay all hafe that   240
hase helpede the so sone out of thi paynes, and when thay sall
come to purgatorye thay sall sone fynd the grete mercy of
Almyghty God and the sonere be spede owte of thaire paynes
for thi sake.'

And than onone this fayre lady ledd hir ovre a strong   245
brygge and at the brygges ende was a faire white chapelle, and
me thoghte thare come owte mekill multitude of pepill that
come agaynes hir with faire processione and mery sange. And
than this faire lady and this procession broghte hir to a fayre
welle and thare all hir body was weschen. And sodanly besyde   250
the welle was a white chapelle and this lady and this
procession broghte Margarete therin. And anone come in
thirtene men and one of tham sange a messe, and me thoghte
this faire lady offirde Margarete to hym, and sodanely me
thoghte ther was a crown sett one hir hede and a septre in hir   255
hande. And than said the man that sange the messe,
'Dogheter, take here the crown of grace and mercy and this
septre of victorye, for thou erte passed all thyn enemys.' And

232. *fy*: shame.   *Sathanas*: Satan.
233. *dere*: hurt, hinder.
234. *weyhede . . . to*: balanced evenly and then sank down towards.
236. *voydede*: vanished.
237. *tuke*: took.
237–8. *wrapped . . . aboute*: wrapped (it) all around.
239. *ressayve*: receive.
　　　oyle: oil (used for cleansing, soothing and also sacramentally in baptism, etc.).
240. *mede*: reward.
245. *ledd*: led.   *ovre*: over.
246. *brygge*: bridge.
248. *agaynes*: towards.   *faire processione*: a beautiful procession.
　　　mery sange: joyful song.
250. *weschen*: washed.
254. *offirde*: offered, presented.
255. *crown*: in 'Pearl', too, the souls of the blessed are dressed as queens (ll. 205–6, 447–52).
258. *erte passed*: have surpassed, overcome.

me thoghte this man sange owte the messe, and when the
messe was saide, thay wente owte of the chapelle ylkane, and 260
this man that sange the messe toke Margarete with hym and
broghte hir tyl a goldyn yate, and the procession with hym.
And he saide to Margarete, 'Dogheter, go in at this yate and
ressayve the blysse of paradyse and of heven, whilke that es thi
kynde heritage, and that Adam was in.' And anone, fadir, I 265
woke and all thynge was vaneschede.

No more, fadir, at this tyme, bot God bryng us to his
kyngdome. Amen.

Textual notes

8. *Bot*] Bod.
31. *seculer*] seculers.
91. *lokkes*] lokedes.
103. [. . .] not legible in MS: Horstmann reads 'and thare [fore]'.
128. *thi*] this.

259. *owte*: i.e. to the end.
260. *ylkane*: each one.
262. *tyl*: to.   *yate*: gate.
264. *blysse*: bliss, glory.   *whilke that es*: which is.
265. *kynde heritage*: natural inheritance.
267. *No . . . tyme*: no more for now, father.   *God bryng*: may God bring.

11 Margery Kempe

Margery Kempe, born at Lynn, Norfolk, c. 1373, was the daughter of John Burnham, five times Mayor of Lynn, holder of other civic offices and local Member of Parliament. She married John Kempe c. 1393 and bore him thirteen children, of which at least one survived to adulthood. Margery's career as brewer, miller, pilgrim and holy woman was varied; she travelled widely in England, made pilgrimages to Jerusalem and the Holy Land, Rome and Santiago, and also accompanied her widowed daughter-in-law to Danzig. Her husband and her eldest son died c. 1431; she was still alive in 1439 (see Atkinson 1983).

Most of what we know about Margery comes from *The Book of Margery Kempe*, which was written, or written down at her dictation (she could not read or write), first by an Englishman who had lived for many years in Germany and who died after he had done very little, and then by a priest at Lynn who after many doubts and practical difficulties undertook the task, completing Book I in 1436 and beginning to write Book II in 1438. It is virtually impossible to say how much influence the latter had on the final form of the text; on this problem see Hirsh 1975.

Margery's spirituality is very much in the tradition of the Continental women visionaries (see Hirsh 1989). She was particularly influenced by Bridget of Sweden, whose revelations her confessor read to her. Bridget was, like Margery, a married woman, mother of many children, who had not withdrawn into a convent. Another influence seems to have been *The Revelations of Saint Elizabeth* (see above, p. 71; Ellis 1990: 164–8). Margery's own visionary experiences often sound like pale imitations of their more vivid originals. But her *Book* is extraordinarily revealing of her personality, far more so than the writings of any other medieval visionary. In misunderstanding her models she inadvertently produced the first example in English of the genre of confessional autobiography.

Comment: The first extract (Book I, Chapters 4–6) concerns an early stage of Margery's spiritual life. After the difficult birth of her first child and a traumatic experience with an unsympathetic and tactless confessor when she thought she was about to die, she developed a post-puerperal psychosis ('this creature went out of her mind'). She experienced hallucinations, heard voices, abused her family and friends, mutilated herself and became suicidal. She was healed by a vision of Christ but in spite of this religious experience she was not converted to the devout life until her mid thirties. Then after two years of apparently effortless spiritual progress she encountered three years of intense sexual temptations. These chapters tell the story of these years of struggle, of their resolution, and of her transition to contemplative prayer.

The second extract (Book I, Chapter 15) recounts Margery's first brush with ecclesiastical authority, probably in 1413. In preparation for her pilgrimage to the Holy Land, Margery wanted to take a public vow of chastity before a bishop, although her husband was still alive, and to be clothed formally in white as an outward sign of her new life of continence.

Throughout her life Margery had a series of increasingly acrimonious encounters with authorities of Church and State and some recurrent themes, such as her willingness to adopt a prophetic role by rebuking even the most exalted ecclesiastics, are foreshadowed here.

The third extract (Book I, Chapter 18) concerns Margery's visit to Julian of Norwich. It provides invaluable evidence of Julian's reputation as a skilled spiritual director, shows Margery seeking advice and validation from another woman for once, rather than from an authoritative man, and also indicates Margery's own recurrent anxieties (shared by even her most sympathetic advisers) about some of the more idiosyncratic aspects of her spiritual life.

The final extract (Book I, Chapters 75 and 76) gives us a glimpse of Margery in later life, living the 'mixed life' in the world, of prayer and contemplation on the one hand and of good works on the other. This includes caring for her incapacitated elderly husband; Christ's approval validates and sanctifies women's domestic labour in a way that develops out of Margery's earlier fantasies of working as a domestic servant of the Virgin, St Anne and St Elizabeth. Her activities suggest that she had achieved a certain standing in her community, even though her difficult vocation as a married person who had renounced sexual activity during the lifetime of her spouse always left her vulnerable to criticism.

Manuscript: British Library Add. MS 61823 (the Butler-Bowden Manuscript), the unique manuscript; in the fifteenth century it belonged to the Carthusian monastery of Mount Grace in Yorkshire.

Further reading (for full details see Bibliography): Much has been written on Margery; for bibliographies, see Lagorio and Bradley 1981: 127–32; Petroff 1986: 306, n. 7. The best general study is Atkinson 1983; see also Hirsh 1989.

The Book of Margery Kempe

a) *Margery Moves from Conversion through Temptation to Contemplation*
(BL MS Add. 61823, ff. 7^v–10)

The fyrst too yere whan this creature was thus drawyn to Owyr Lord, sche had gret quiete of spyryt as for ony temptacyons. Sche mygth wel dure to fastyn, it grevyd hire

1. too yere: two years.
   this creature: i.e. Margery Kempe, who almost invariably refers to herself in the third person.
1. drawyn: attracted.
2. quiete of spyryt: spiritual peace.
2–3. as . . . temptacyons: with respect to any temptations.
3. mygth: might, i.e. was able to.   *dure*: endure, bear.
   grevyd: troubled, distressed.   *hire*: her.

not. Sche hatyd the joys of the world. Sche felt no rebellyon
in hyr flesch. Sche was strong, as hire thowt, that sche dred 5
no devylle in helle, for sche dede so gret bodyly penawnce.
Sche thowt that sche lovyd God more than he hire. Sche was
smet wyth the dedly wownd of veynglory and felt it not. For
sche desyryd many tymes that the crucifix xuld losyn hys
handys fro the crosse and halsyn hire, in tokyn of lofe. 10
   Ower mercyful lord Crist Jhesu, seyng this creaturys
presumpcyon, sent hire, as is wrete before, thre yere of greet
temptacyon. Of the whech on of the hardest I purpos to
wrytyn for exampyl of hem that com aftyr, that thei schuld not
trostyn on here owyn self, ne have no joy in hemself as this 15
creature had. Fore no drede, owyr gostly enmy slepyth not,
but he ful besyly sergyth our complexions and owyre
dysposycionys, and where that he fyndyth us most freel, ther
be Owyr Lordys sufferawns he leyth hys snare, whech may no
man skape be hys owyn powere. 20
   And so he leyd beforn this creature the snare of letchery,
whan sche wend that alle fleschly lust had al hol ben
qwenchyd in hire. And so long sche was temptyd wyth the syn
of letchory, for owt that sche cowd do; and yet sche was oftyn

---

5. *flesch*: flesh, body.   *hire thowt*: it seemed to her.
   that . . . dred: so that she dreaded.
6. *dede*: did, performed.
   bodyly penawnce: physical penance (i.e. fasting, wearing a hair shirt, etc.).
7. *thowt*: thought.
8. *smet*: smitten, struck.   *dedly wownd*: mortal wound.   *veynglory*: vanity.
9. *crucifix*: figure of Christ crucified.   *xuld*: should.   *losyn*: loose, release.
10. *halsyn*: embrace; this was in fact an experience commonly reported by
medieval visionaries.
10. *in . . . lofe*: as a sign of love.
11. *seying*: seeing.
12. *presumpcyon*: presumption, arrogance.   *wrete*: written.
13. *Of . . . hardest*: one of the hardest of which.
13–14. *purpos to wrytyn*: intend to write down.
14. *for . . . hem*: as an example for them.
15. *trostyn on*: trust in.   *here*: their.   *hemself*: themselves.
16. *no drede*: doubtless.
   owyr . . . enmy: our spiritual enemy (i.e. the Devil).
17. *ful besyly*: very industriously.   *sergyth*: searches, investigates.
   complexions: temperaments.
18. *dysposycionys*: characters.   *freel*: frail, vulnerable.
19. *be . . . sufferawns*: by Our Lord's permission.   *leyth*: lays, spreads.
20. *skape*: escape.   *be*: by.
21. *beforn*: before, in front of.   *letchery*: lechery, lust.
22. *wend*: thought.   *al hol*: completely.
23. *qwenchyd*: quenched, extinguished.
24. *owt*: aught, anything.   *cowd*: could, i.e. knew how to.

schrevyn, sche weryd the hayr and dede gret bodyly penawns   25
and wept many a bytter teere and preyd ful oftyn to Owyre
Lord that he schuld preserve hire and kepe hire that sche
schuld not fallyn into temptacyon. For sche thowt sche had
lever ben deed than consentyn therto. And in al this tyme sche
had no lust to comown wyth hire husbond, but it was very   30
peynful and horrybyl unto hire.

In the secunde yere of hire temptacyons, yt fel so that a
man whech sche lovyd wel seyd onto hire on Seynt
Margaretys Evyn before evynsong that for anythyng he wold ly
be hire and have hys lust of hys body, and sche xuld not   35
wythstond hym. For yf he mygth not have hys wyl that tyme,
he seyd, he xuld ellys have it another tyme; sche xuld not
chese. And he dede it forto preve hire, what sche wold do, but
sche wend that he had ment ful ernest as that tyme, and seyd
but lytyl therto. So they partyd asondyr as than, and wentyn   40
bothen forto here evensong, for here cherch was of Seynt
Margaret.

This woman was so labowrd wyth the mannys wordys that
sche mygth not heryn hire evynsong, ne sey hire Pater Noster,
er thynkyn ony other good thowt, but was more labowrd than   45
ever sche was before. The devyl put in hire mende that God

---

25. *schrevyn*: confessed and absolved.   *weryd the hayr*: wore a hair shirt.
26. *teere*: tear.
29. *lever*: rather.   *deed*: dead.   *therto*: to it.
30. *lust*: desire.   *comown*: have intercourse.
31. *peynful*: painful.
32. *yt . . . so*: it so happened.
33. *whech*: whom.   *seyd*: said.
33–4. *Seynt Margaretys Evyn*: the Vigil of the Feast of St Margaret (i.e. 19 July).
34. *evynsong*: evensong, vespers.   *for anythyng*: come what may, regardless.
34–5. *ly be hire*: lie by (i.e. with) her.
36. *wythstond*: resist.   *mygth*: might, i.e. could.   *wyl*: desire.
37. *ellys*: else, otherwise.
38. *chese*: choose.   *forto preve*: to test.
39. *ment . . . ernest*: meant it really seriously.
40. *but lytyl*: only a little.   *partyd asondyr*: separated.
    as than: i.e. for the time being.
41. *bothen*: both.   *here*(1): hear, i.e. attend.
41–2. *for . . . Margaret*: the parish church at Lynn was, and is, dedicated to St Margaret, Virgin and Martyr, immensely popular in the Middle Ages.
43. *labowrd*: tormented, troubled.
44. *heryn*: hear.   *ne sey hire Pater Noster*: nor recite the Lord's Prayer.
45. *er*: or.
46. *mende*: mind.

had forsakyn hire, and ellys xuld sche not so ben temptyd. She
levyd the develes suasyons and gan to consentyn for because
sche cowde thynkyn no good thowt. Therfore wend sche that
God had forsake hire.   50

And whan evensong was do, sche went to the man
beforeseyd that he xuld have hys lust, as sche wend that he
had desyryed, but he made swech symulacyon that sche cowd
not knowe hys entent, and so thei partyd asondyr for that
nygth. This creature was so labowrd and vexyd al that nygth   55
that sche wyst never what sche mygth do. Sche lay be hire
husbond, and forto comown wyth hym it was so abhomynabyl
onto hire that sche mygth not duren it, and yet was it leful
onto hire in leful tyme, yf sche had wold. But ever sche was
labowrd wyth the other man forto syn wyth hym, inasmech as   60
he had spoke to hire.

At the last, thorw inoportunyte of temptacyon and lakkyng
of dyscrecyon, sche was overcomyn and consentyd in hire
mend, and went to the man to wetyn yf he wold than
consentyn to hire. And he seyd he ne wold for al the good in   65
this world. He had lever ben hewyn as smal as flesch to the
pott. Sche went away al schamyd and confusyd in hireself,
seyng hys stabylnes and hire owyn unstabylnes. Than thowt
sche of the grace that God had yovyn hire before-tyme, how
sche had too yere of gret qwyet in sowle, repentawns of hire   70

---

48. *levyd*: believed.   *suasyons*: persuasions.   *gan*: began.
50. *forsake*: forsaken, abandoned.
51. *do*: done.
53. *swech symulacyon*: such excuses.
54. *entent*: intention.
55. *nygth*: night.
56. *wyst*: knew.
58. *duren*: endure, bear.
59. *in leful tyme*: at a permissible time; in the Middle Ages sexual
relations between husband and wife were discouraged at certain times of
the year, such as during Lent and Advent.
59. *yf . . . wold*: if she had wanted.
60. *inasmech*: in that.
62. *thorw*: through.   *inoportunyte*: importunity, persistence.
62–3. *lakkyng of dyscrecyon*: failure of judgement.
64. *wetyn*: know.
65. *ne wold*: would not.   *good*: money, wealth.
66. *hewyn*: chopped up.   *flesch*: meat.
68. *stabylnes*: firmness.   *unstabylnes*: weakness.
69. *yovyn*: given.

synne, wyth many bytter teerys of compunccyon, and parfyt
wyl never to turne ageyn to hire synne but rather to be deed –
hire thowt.

And now sche saw how sche had consentyd in hire wyl forto
don synne, than fel sche half in dyspeyr. Sche thowt sche   75
wold a ben in helle for the sorw that sche had. Sche thowt
sche was worthy no mercy, for hire consentyng was so wylfully
do, ne never worthy to don hym servyse, for sche was so fals
unto hym. Neverthelesse sche was schrevyn many tymes and
oftyn, and dede hire penawns whatsoever hire confessour   80
wold injoyne hire to do, and was governd after the rewelys of
the Chirch. That grace God yafe this creature, blyssyd mot he
be, but he wythdrowe not hire temptacyon but rather incresyd
it, as hire thowt. And therfore wend sche that he had forsakyn
hire, and durst not trostyn to hys mercy but was labowrd wyth   85
horrybyl temptacyons of letcherye and of dyspeyre ny al the
next yere folwyng; save Owyr Lord of hys mercy, as sche seyd
hireself, yaf hire ech day for the most party too owerys of
compunccyon for hire synnys wyth many bytter teerys and
sythen sche was labowrd wyth temptacyons of dyspeyre, as   90

71. compunccyon: compunction, i.e. the pain caused by remembrance of
one's sins, associated with the gift of tears (see further below).
71–2. parfyt wyl: perfect will, intention.
74. consentyd . . . wyl: the essential element in mortal sin is the consent of
the will, whether or not the sinful intention is actually carried out.
75. fel: fell.   *dyspeyr*: despair.
76. wold a ben: would have been.
77. worthy: worth.
77–8. hire . . . do: her consent was so willingly given.
78. don . . . servyse: serve him.   *fals*: unfaithful.
79. schrevyn: shriven, i.e. confessed and absolved.
81. injoyne: enjoin.   *governd after*: regulated according to.   *rewelys*: rules.
82. yafe: gave.
82–3. blyssyd . . . be: may he be blessed.
83. wythdrowe: withdrew.   *incresyd*: increased.
85. durst . . . to: dared not trust in.
86–7. ny . . . folwyng: nearly all the subsequent year.
87. save: except that.
88. yaf: gave.   *for . . . party*: for the most part, in general.
     too owerys: two hours.
89. compunccyon . . . teerys: Margery's tears of compunction, a common
phenomenon among Continental women visionaries, caused her much
trouble and anxiety. They were not under her conscious control and evoked
much hostility from others, though considered a grace by the theologically
well informed. They were distinct from her 'cries', which first occurred in
Jerusalem and were noisier and more violent.
90. sythen: then.

sche was before and was as for fro felyng of grace as thei that
never felt noon. And that mygth sche not beryn and therfore
alwey sche dyspeyrd, safe for the tyme that sche felt grace,
hire labowrs were so wondyrful that sche cowd evel fare wyth
hem, but ever mornyn and sorwyn as thow God had forsakyn 95
hire.

Than on a Fryday beforn Crystmes Day, as this creature,
knelyng in a chapel of Seynt John wythinne a cherch of Seynt
Margrete in N., wept wondir sore, askyng mercy and foryyfnes
of hire synnes and hire trespas, owyr mercyful lord Cryst 100
Jhesu, blyssyd mot he be, ravysched hire spyryt and seyd onto
hire, 'Dowtyr, why wepyst thow so sore? I am comyn to the,
Jhesu Cryst that deyd on the crosse sufferyng bytter peynes
and passyons for the. I, the same God, foryefe the thi synnes
to the utterest poynt. And thow schalt never com in helle ne in 105
purgatorye but, whan thow schalt passyn owt of this world,
wythin the twynkelyng of an eye thow schalt have the blysse of
hevyn. For I am the same God that have browt thi synnes to
thi mend and mad the to be schreve therof. And I grawnt the
contrysyon into thi lyves ende.' 110

91. for fro: far from.
92. never . . . noon: never experienced any.
93. alwey: more and more.   *safe*: except.
94. labowrs: sufferings.   *wondyrful*: astonishing.
94–5. cowd . . . hem: could with difficulty cope with them.
95. mornyn and sorwyn: mourn and sorrow (the verbs are infinitive in form
and dependent on *cowd*).
95. thow: though.
98. cherch: church.
99. N.: i.e. Lynn.   *wondir sore*: astonishingly bitterly.
     foryyfnes: forgiveness.
100. trespas: transgression, offence.
101. ravysched hire spyryt: caught up her spirit into ecstasy.
102. Dowtyr: Daughter (Christ's usual way of addressing Margery
throughout).
102. thow: thou (the intimate form of address used to equals or inferiors).
     am comyn: have come.
103. deyd: died.
104. passyons: sufferings.   *foryefe*: forgive.
105. utterest poynt: furthest extent.
106. passyn owt: pass from, i.e. die.
107. blysse: bliss, glory.
108. browt: brought.
109. mad: made.
109–10. grawnt the contrysyon: grant thee contrition, i.e. true sorrow for and
detestation of sin, combined with purpose of amendment.

'Therfore I bydde the and comawnd the, boldly clepe me
Jhesus, thi love, for I am thi love and schal be thi love
wythowtyn ende. And dowter, thou hast an hayre upon thi
bakke. I wyl thou do it away, and I schal yive the an hayre in
thin hert that schal lyke me mych better than alle the hayres in   115
the world. Also, my derworthy dowter, thou must forsake that
thow lovyst best in this world, and that is etyng of flesch. And
instede of that flesch thow schalt etyn my flesch and my blod,
that is the very body of Crist in the sacrament of the awtere.
Thys is my wyl, dowter, that thow receyve my body every   120
Sonday. And I schal flowe so mych grace in the that alle the
world xal mervelyn therof.'

'Thow xalt ben etyn and knawyn of the pepul of the world
as any raton knawyth the stokfysch. Drede the nowt, dowter,
for thow schalt have the vyctory of al thin enmys. I schal yeve   125
the grace inow to answere every clerke in the love of God. I
swere to the be my mageste that I schal never forsakyn the in
wel ne in wo. I schal helpyn the and kepyn the that ther schal

111. bydde: bid.   *comawnd*: command.   *clepe*: call.
113. wythowtyn: without.
114. bakke: back, i.e. body.   *do . . . away*: get rid of it.
115. lyke: please.   *mych*: much.
116. derworthy: dear, precious.
117. etyng: eating.
119. very: true.   *awtere*: altar.
120. receyve my body: i.e. take communion. In the Middle Ages weekly
communion was very unusual, even among religious (monks and nuns). Lay
people were required to communicate at least once a year; religious might
communicate about once a month (the author of *Ancrene Wisse* expected his
anchoresses to communicate fifteen times a year). Strictly speaking
Margery needed episcopal permission for such frequent communion, which
she later obtained from the Archbishop of Canterbury himself. Her
eucharistic devotion is characteristic of medieval women visionaries (see
Bynum 1987).
121. flowe: (cause to) flow, i.e. infuse.
122. therof: at it.
123. xalt: shalt.   *etyn . . . knawyn*: eaten and gnawed at.
     of(1) *. . . world*: by worldly people.
124. raton: rat.
     stokfysch: salt cod (Lynn was an important fishing port in the Middle
Ages).
124. Drede . . . nowt: Fear not.
125. of: over.   *yeve*: give.
126. inow: enough.   *clerke*: cleric, learned man.
127. mageste: majesty.
127–8. in . . . wo: in good times or bad.
128. kepyn: keep, preserve.

never devyl in helle parte the fro me, ne awngel in hevyn, ne
man in erthe. For develys in helle mow not, ne awngelys in   130
hevyn wyl not, ne man on erthe schal not.'

'And, dowter, I wyl thow leve thi byddyng of many bedys
and thynk swych thowtys as I wyl putt in thi mend. I schal
yevyn the leve to byddyn tyl sex of the cloke, to sey what thow
wyld. Than schalt thow ly stylle and speke to me be thowt and   135
I schal yefe to the hey medytacyon and very contemplacyon
and I byd the gon to the ankyre at the Frere Prechowrys and
schew hym my prevyteys and my cownselys whech I schewe to
the, and werk after hys cownsel, for my spyrit xal speke in
hym to the.'   140

Than this creature went forth to the ankyre as sche was
comawndyd and schewyd hym the revelacyons swech as were
schewyd to hire. Than the ankyr wyth gret reverens and
wepyng, thankyng God, seyd, 'Dowter, ye sowkyn evyn on

129. *awngel*: angel.
130. *mow not*: are unable to.
131. *schal not*: are not allowed to.
132. *leve*: leave, give up.   *byddyng ... bedys*: recitation of many prayers.
133. *thowtys*: thoughts. Christ is instructing her to give up vocal (i.e. verbal)
prayer in favour of meditation, which is wordless and uses the reason, the
intellect and the will.
134. *yevyn the leve*: give thee permission.   *byddyn*: pray (vocally).
   sex of the cloke: six o'clock (in the evening).
135. *wyld*: wilt, i.e. want.   *stylle*: quietly.
   be thowt: by thought, i.e. mentally.
136. *hey*: high, exalted.   *very*: true.
137. *gon*: go.   *ankyre*: anchorite.
   Frere Prechowrys: the Friars Preachers, i.e. the Dominicans, who had a
reputation as learned and subtle theologians and on the Continent were
prominent as spiritual directors of women mystics.
138. *schew*: show.   *prevyteys*: mysteries.   *cownselys*: secrets.
139. *werk ... cownsel*: act according to his advice.
142. *swech*: such.
143–50. *Than ... devyl*: it is interesting to compare the Dominican
anchorite's style of spiritual direction with that of Julian of Norwich (see
below, ll. 362–92); he is both less cautious and places more stress on his
personal authority.
144–5. *sowkyn ... brest*: you are sucking even at Christ's breast; a startling
but not unprecedented image of Christ feeding the faithful with his body
and blood, just as a mother feeds her child with the milk which is created
from her blood. In many medieval mystics, Christ's wounded side is
equated with the maternal breast. Julian of Norwich develops a whole
theology of the Second Person of the Trinity as Mother (see above, p. 109),
but Margery herself does not elsewhere speak of Jesus as Mother; for her,
he is either Father or Spouse.

Crystys brest, and ye han an ernest-peny of hevyn. I charge   145
yow, receyveth swech thowtys, whan God wyl yeve hem, as
mekely and as devowtly as ye kan and comyth to me and
tellyth me what thei be, and I schal, wyth the leve of Owere
Lord Jhesu Cryst, telle yow whether thei ben of the Holy Gost
or elles of your enmy the devyl.'   150

Another day this creature schuld yeve hire to medytacyon as
sche was bodyn before, and sche lay stylle, nowt knowyng
what sche mygth best thynke. Than sche seyd to Owere Lord
Jhesu Crist, 'Jhesu, what schal I thynke?' Owere Lord Jhesu
answeryd to hire mende, 'Dowter, thynke on my modyr, for   155
sche is cause of alle the grace that thow hast.'

And than anoon sche saw Seynt Anne, gret wyth chylde.
And than sche preyd Seynt Anne to be hire mayden and hire
servawnt. And anon Owere Lady was born, and than sche
besyde hire to take the chyld to hire and kepe it tyl it were 160
twelve yere of age, wyth good mete and drynke, wyth fayr
whyte clothys and whyte kerchys. And than sche seyd to the
blyssed chyld, 'Lady, ye schal be the modyr of God.' The
blyssed chyld answeryd and seyd, 'I wold I were worthy to be
the handmayden of hire that xuld conseive the Sone of God.'   165
The creature seyd, 'I pray yow, Lady, yyf that grace falle yow,
forsake not my servyse.'

The blysful chyld passyd awey for a certeyn tyme, the
creature being stylle in contemplacyon, and sythen cam ageyn
and seyd, 'Dowter, now am I bekome the modyr of God.' And   170

145. *han*: have.   *ernest-peny*: pledge.   *charge*: instruct.
146. *receyveth*: receive, accept.
147. *kan*: can, i.e. know how to.
149–50. *telle . . . devyl*: the ability to make this distinction, known as the
discretion or discernment of spirits, was vitally important for medieval
mystics and is the subject of much of Julian's advice to Margery.
151. *schuld*: was about to.   *yeve hire*: devote herself, give herself over to.
152. *bodyn*: bid, instructed.   *nowt*: not.
157. *anoon*: at once.   *gret . . . chylde*: heavily pregnant.
158. *mayden*: handmaid.
159. *sche*: i.e. Margery.
160. *kepe*: look after.
162. *kerchys*: kerchiefs, head coverings.
163. *modyr*: mother.
166. *yyf*: if.   *falle*: befalls, happens to.
167. *forsake . . . servyse*: do not reject my service.
168. *passyd awey*: was absent.
169. *stylle*: i.e. transfixed, immobile.   *sythen*: then.
     cam ageyn: (the Virgin) came back.
170. *am I bekome*: I have become.

than the creature fel down on hire kneys wyth gret reverens
and gret wepyng and seyd, 'I am not worthy, lady, to do yow
servyse.' 'Yys, dowtyre,' sche seyde, 'folwe thow me, thi
servyse lykyth me wel.'

Than went sche forth wyth Owyre Lady and wyth Josep,   175
beryng wyth hire a potel of pyment and spycys therto. Than
went thei forth to Elysabeth, Seynt John Baptystys modire,
and whan thei mettyn togydere, eyther of hem worshepyd
other, and so thei wonyd togedyre wyth gret grace and
gladnesse twelve wokys. And than Seynt John was bore, and   180
Owyre Lady toke hym up fro the erthe wyth al maner reverens
and yaf hym to hys modyre, seyng of hym that he schuld be an
holy man, and blyssed hym. Sythen thei toke here leve eyther
of other wyth compassyf terys. And than the creature fel down
on kneys to Seynt Elyzabeth and preyd hire sche wold prey for   185
hire to Owyr Lady, that sche mygth do hire servyse and
plesawns. 'Dowter, me semyth,' seyd Elysabeth, 'thou dost
ryght wel thi dever.'

And than went the creature forth wyth Owyr Lady to
Bedlem and purchasyd hire herborwe every nyght wyth gret   190
reverens, and Owyr Lady was receyved wyth glad chere. Also
sche beggyd Owyr Lady fayr whyte clothys and kerchys forto
swathyn in hire sone whan he were born. And whan Jhesu was
born, sche ordeyned beddyng for Owyre Lady to lyg in wyth

171. kneys: knees.
173. Yys: Yes.
174. lykyth: pleases.
175. Josep: Joseph.
176. beryng: carrying.   *potel*: large flask.   *pyment*: spiced wine.
spycys therto: spices as well.
177. Elysabeth: Elizabeth, wife of Zacharias and cousin of Mary.
modire: mother.
178. mettyn togydere: met together.   *eyther of hem*: each of them.
worshepyd: honoured.
179. wonyd: dwelt.
180. wokys: weeks.   *bore*: born.
181. toke . . . erthe: lifted him up from the ground.
al maner reverens: all kinds of respect.
183. blyssed: blessed, made the sign of the cross over.
toke here leve: took their departure.
184. compassyf: compassionate.
186–7. do . . . plesawns: serve her and please her.
187–8. thou . . . dever: you do your duty very well.
190. Bedlem: Bethlehem.   *purchasyd hire herborwe*: obtained her lodgings.
191. wyth glad chere: warmly.
192. beggyd Owyr Lady: begged for Our Lady.
192–3. forto . . . sone: to swaddle her son in.
194. ordeyned: provided.   *lyg in*: lie on.

hire blyssed sone. And sythen sche beggyd mete for Owyre   195
Lady and hire blyssyd chyld. Afterward sche swathyd hym
wyth bytter teerys of compassyon, havyng mend of the scharp
deth that he schuld suffyre for the lofe of synful men, seyng to
hym, 'Lord, I schal fare fayr wyth yow; I schal not byndyn yow
soore. I pray yow beth not dysplesyd wyth me.'   200

b) *Preparing for Pilgrimage:*
Margery Meets the Bishop of Lincoln
(ff. 16–18)

Thys creature, whan Owyr Lord had foryovyn hire hire synne,
as is wrete beforn, had a desyre to se tho placys where he was
born and where he sufferyd hys passyon and where he deyd,
wyth other holy placys wher he was in hys lyve and also after
hys resurrexyon. As sche was in these desyres, Owyr Lord bad   205
hire in hire mend, too yere er than sche went, that sche
schuld gon to Rome, to Jherusalem, and to Seynt Jamys. For
sche wold fayn a gon but sche had no good to go wyth. And
than sche seyd to Owyr Lord, 'Wher schal I han good to go
wyth to thes holy placys?'   210
    Ower Lord seyd ayen to hire, 'I schal send the frendys

195. *mete*: food.
196. *swathyd*: swaddled.
197. *havyng mend*: being mindful.   *scharp*: sharp, bitter.
198. *lofe*: love.
199. *fare . . . yow*: treat you gently (swaddling was presumably an uncomfortable experience for the medieval baby).
199. *byndyn*: bind, constrict.
200. *soore*: tightly.   *beth . . . dysplesyd*: do not be displeased.
201–7. *Thys . . . Jamys*: St Bridget, Margery's principal role model, also went to the Holy Land (where she received her visions of the Nativity – see pp. 86–9 – and Crucifixion), Rome and Spain.
201. *foryovyn*: forgiven.
202. *wrete*: written.   *se*: see.   *tho placys*: those places.
203. *deyd*: died.
204. *lyve*: life.
205. *resurrexyon*: resurrection.   *in . . . desyres*: i.e wishing this.
        bad: bade, commanded.
206. *too . . . er*: two years before.
207. *Seynt Jamys*: i.e. the shrine of Saint James at Compostella in Spain.
208. *wold . . . gon*: would gladly have gone.
        good . . . wyth: money with which to go.
209. *Wher*: whence.   *han*: have.
211. *seyd ayen*: replied.
211–12. *frendys anowe*: enough friends.

anowe in dyvers contreys of Ynglond to help the. And, dowter,
I xal go wyth the in every contre and ordeyn for the; I xal
ledyn the thyder and brynge the ageyn in safte, and noon
Englyschman schal deyn in the schyp that thow art in. I xal 215
kepe the fro alle wykked mennys powere. And dowter, I sey to
the I wyl that thou were clothys of whyte and non other
colour, for thou xal ben arayd after my wyl.'
'A, dere Lord, yf I go arayd on other maner than other
chast women don, I drede that the pepyl wyl slawndyr me. 220
Thei wyl sey I am an ypocryt and wondryn upon me.' 'Ya,
dowter, the more wondryng that thow hast for my lofe, the
more thou plesyst me.'
Than this creature durst non otherwyse do than sche was
comawndyd in hire sowle. And so sche went forth wyth hire 225
husbond into the cuntre, for he was ever a good man and an
esy man to hire, thow that he sumtyme for veyn dred lete hire
alone for a tyme. Yet he resortyd evermore ageyn to hire, and
had compassyon of hire, and spak for hire as he durst for dred
of the pepyl. But alle other that went wyth hire forsokyn hire 230
and ful falsly thei accusyd hire, thorw temptacyon of the devyl,
of thyngys that sche was never gylty in. And so dede o man
whech sche trostyd gretly on, and proferyd hymself to gon

212. *dyvers ... Ynglond*: various parts of England.
213. *ordeyn*: provide.
214. *ledyn*: lead, conduct.   *thyder*: thither.   *ageyn*: back.
   safte: safety.   *noon*: no.
215. *deyn*: die.   *schyp*: ship.
216. *kepe*: preserve.
217. *were*: wear.   *clothys*: clothes.
218. *arayed*: dressed.   *after*: according to.
219. *on ... maner*: in another manner.
220. *chast*: chaste.   *drede*: am afraid.   *pepyl*: people.
   slawndyr: slander, defame.
221. *ypocryt*: hypocrite.
   wondryn upon: gawp at (because white clothing traditionally symbolised virginity and Margery's neighbours all knew that she was married and had born many children).
221. *Ya*: Yes.
224. *durst ... do*: dared not do otherwise.
226. *cuntre*: country.
227. *esy*: kind, indulgent.   *thow that*: although.   *veyn dred*: foolish fear.
227–8. *lete ... alone*: forsook her.
228. *resortyd ... hire*: always came back to her.
229. *spak for*: spoke up for.   *as he durst*: as far as he dared.
230. *forsokyn*: forsook, abandoned.
232. *gylty in*: guilty of.   *dede*: did.   *o*: one.
233. *whech*: whom.   *trostyd*: trusted.
   proferyd hymself: (he) volunteered himself.

wyth hire into the contre, wherthorw sche was rygth glad, trostyng he wold wel supportyn hire and helpyn hire whan sche had nede. For he had ben dwellyng long tyme wyth an ankyre, commensowre in dyvinyte and an holy man, and that ankyr was this womans confessour. 235

And so hys servawnt toke leve be hys owyn steryng to gon wyth this creature into the contre, and hire owyn mayden went wyth hire, also long as thei ferd wel and no man seyd nothyng ageyns hem. But as sone as the pepyl thorw entysyng of owyr gostly enmy and be the sufferawns of Owyr Lord spak ageyn this creature for sche wept so sore, and seyd sche was a fals ypocryte and falsly deceyved the pepyl, and thretyd hire to be brent, than the forseyd man, that was holdyn so holy a man and that sche trustyd so mech upon, utterly reprevyd hire, and fowely despysed hire, and wold no forther gon wyth hire. 240 / 245

Hire mayden, seyng dysese on every syde, wex boystows ayens hire maystres. Sche wold not obeyn ne folwyn hire cownsel. Sche let hire gon alone in many good townys and wold not gon wyth hire. And ever hire husbond was redy whan alle other fayled and went wyth hire where Owyr Lord wold sende hire, alwey trostyng that al was for the best and xuld comyn to good ende whan God wold. 250 / 255

---

234. wherthorw: because of which.
235. supportyn: support, help.
236. had nede: needed.
237. commensowre in dyvinyte: Doctor of Divinity, i.e. theology.
237–8. that ankyr: i.e. the anchorite mentioned in l. 137.
239. toke leve: left.   *be . . . steryng*: at his own desire.
240. mayden: maidservant.
241. also: as.   *ferd*: fared.
242. entysyng: enticing, temptation.
243. sufferawns: sufferance, permission.   *ageyn*: against.
244. for: because.
245. deceyved: deceived.
245–6. thretyd . . . brent: threatened to burn her (the usual punishment for witches and heretics, also the usual method of capital punishment for women in the Middle Ages: see Shahar 1983: 20–1).
246. than: then.   *forseyd*: aforesaid.   *holdyn*: held, considered.
247. reprevyd: reproached, rebuked.
248. fowely: foully.   *despysed*: treated with contempt.   *forther*: further.
249. dysese: trouble.   *wex boystows*: grew disobedient.
250. maystres: mistress.
250–1. folwyn . . . cownsel: follow her instructions.
251. townys: towns.
252. redy: ready, available.
255. xuld . . . ende: should end successfully.

And at this tyme He led hire to spekyn wyth the Bysshop of Lynkoln, whech hygth Philyp, and abod thre wekys er thei mygth speke wyth hym. For he was not at hom at hys paleys. Whan the bysshop was comyn hom and herd seyn how swech a woman had abedyn hym so long to speke wyth hym, anon he 260 sent for hire in gret hast to wetyn hire wylle. And than sche cam to hys presens and salutyd hym, and he derly wolcomyd hire and seyd he had long desyred to speke wyth hire and he was rygth glad of hire comyng. And so sche prayd hym that sche mygth speke wyth hym in cownsel and schewyn hym the 265 secretys of hire sowle, and he lymyt hire a tyme convenyent therto.

Whan the tyme cam, sche schewyd hym hyr meditacyons and hy contemplacyons and other secret thyngys, bothe of

256. *spekyn*: speak.

256–7. *the ... Lynkoln*: Philip Repingdon, Bishop of Lincoln 1405–19. An Augustinian canon from the Abbey of St Mary de Pré, Leicester, while at the University of Oxford he had supported Wycliffe and was excommunicated by the Archbishop of Canterbury in 1382. After a few months, however, he was reconciled and abjured his heretical opinions. He became Abbot of St Mary de Pré, several times Chancellor of the University of Oxford, close friend, chaplain and confessor to Henry IV, and was consecrated Bishop of Lincoln (in the Middle Ages a vast diocese which included Oxford) in 1404. He was a relentless persecutor of the Lollards and when Margery arrived may have been away holding a visitation (an official inspection) of the University of Oxford because of the prevalence there of heresy. He resigned as bishop in 1419 and died in 1424. Roger Huswyff, the spiritual and legal advisor of Eleanor Hull (see p. 219), was in his service at one time. Margery probably went to see him, though her home town of Lynn was in the diocese of Norwich, because that see was, for all practical purposes, vacant between 1413 and 1415.

257. *whech hygth*: who was called.   *abod*: waited.   *wekys*: weeks.

257–8. *er ... mygth*: before they could.

258. *hom*: home.   *paleys*: palace.

259. *was comyn*: had come.   *herd seyn*: heard it said.
     swech: such and such, a certain.

260. *abedyn hym*: waited for him.   *anon*: at once.

261. *gret hast*: great haste.   *wetyn ... wylle*: know what she wanted.

262. *to ... presens*: into his presence.   *salutyd*: greeted.
     derly wolcomyd: kindly welcomed.

264. *rygth*: truly.

265. *in cownsel*: confidentially.   *schewyn*: show, reveal.

266. *lymyt*: assigned.   *convenyent*: suitable.

269. *hy*: high.

269–70. *bothe ... ded*: concerning both the living and the dead; visionaries such as St Bridget would often claim to know if the recently dead were still in Purgatory and in need of prayers and masses (see also *A Revelation Showed to a Holy Woman*, above, p. 163).

qwyk and of ded, as Owyr Lord schewyd to hire sowle. He 270
was rygth glad to heryn hem, and suffryd hire benyngly to sey
what hire lysted, and commendyd gretly hire felyngys and hire
contemplacyons, seyyng thei wer hy maters and ful devowt
maters and enspyred of the Holy Gost, cownselyng hire sadly
that hire felyngys schuld be wretyn; and sche seyd that it was 275
not Goddys wyl that thei schuld be wretyn so soon, ne thei
wer wretyn twenty yere after and more.

And than sche seyd ferthermore, 'My lord, yf it lyke yow, I
am comawndyd in my sowle that ye schal yyve me the mantyl
and the ryng and clothyn me al in whygth clothys. And yf ye 280
clothyn me in erth, Owyr Lord Jhesu Cryst xal clothyn yow in
hevyn, as I undyrstond be revelacyon.' Than the bysshop seyd
to hire, 'I wyl fulffyllen your desyre yyf your husbond wyl

271. *heryn*: hear.   *suffryd*: allowed, permitted.   *benyngly*: kindly.
272. *what . . . lysted*: what she liked.   *commendyd*: recommended, praised.
    felyngys: thoughts.
273. *seyyng*: saying.
274. *enspyred of*: inspired by.   *cownselyng*: advising.   *sadly*: seriously.
276. *that . . . wretyn*: Margery says in the Proem that, long before God
commanded her to do so, many people suggested she should have her
experiences written down. The first person to do so seems to have been
Repingdon; presumably he knew of the writings in the vernaculars and in
Latin of Continental women mystics such as Bridget of Sweden and
Catherine of Siena (see above, pp. 84 and 95), which were available in
Middle English translations by the early fifteenth century. The only native
English precedent, apart from *A Revelation Showed to a Holy Woman*, dated
1422, could be Julian of Norwich, who wrote the Short Version of *A
Revelation of Love c.* 1373, but it is not known how widely it circulated, if at
all. It has not perhaps previously been noted just how extraordinary
Repingdon's suggestion must have seemed to Margery at the time.
277. *twenty . . . more*: for more than twenty years afterwards.
278. *yf . . . yow*: if it please you.
279. *yyve*: give.
279–80. *mantyl . . . ryng*: the cloak and the professional ring, outward signs
of a woman (usually a widow) who had taken a vow of chastity before a
bishop; the practice, common in the fifteenth century, was often
encouraged by husbands in their wills. Lady Margaret Beaufort took a
formal vow of widowhood, and Eleanor Hull may well have done so.
280. *clothyn*: (ceremonially) clothe.
    al . . . clothys: completely in white clothing.
281. *in erth*: on earth.
282. *be revelacyon*: by revelation.
283. *fulffyllen . . . desyre*: carry out your wishes.
283–4. *yyf . . . therto*: Margery's vow of chastity necessarily entailed
permanent continence for John Kempe too, for he would not be free to
remarry.

consentyn therto.' Than sche seyd to the bysshop, 'I prey yow, late myn husbond come to your presens, and ye xal heryn 285 what he wyl sey.'

And so hyr husbond cam before the bysshop, and the bysshop askyd hym, 'John, is it your wyl that your wyf xal take the mantyl and the ryng and levyn chast, and ye bothen?' 'Ya, my lord,' he seyd, 'and in tokyn that we bothen vowyn to leve 290 chast, here I offyr myn handys into yowyr.' And he put hys handys betwen the bysshopys handys and the bysshop dede no more to us at that day, save he mad us rygth good chere and seyd we were rygth wolcome.

Another day this creature cam to mete at the request of the 295 bysshop. And sche saw hym yevyn wyth hys handys, er he set hym to mete, to thriteen powyre men thriteen pens and thriteen lovys wyth other mete, and so he dede every day. This creature was steryd to hy devocyon wyth this sygth, and yaf God preysyng and worshepyng that He yaf the bysshop 300 grace to don thes good dedys wyth plentyvows wepyng, in so

284. *therto*: to it.
285. *late*: let.   *xal heryn*: shall hear.
288. *take*: adopt.
289. *levyn chast*: live chastely, i.e. without marital relations.
    ye bothen: both of you.
290. *in tokyn*: as a sign.   *vowyn*: vow.
291. *into yowyr*: into your (hands).
291-2. *he . . . handys*(2): this was a common gesture of submission in the Middle Ages in swearing loyalty and obedience to institutions such as colleges or to individuals such as feudal lords, abbots and bishops; cf. Elizabeth of Hungary, above, p. 73, where she vows herself to the Virgin's service in a similar way.
292. *dede*: did.
293-4. *us . . . us . . . we*: one of the rare occasions on which Margery uses the first person plural pronoun to refer to herself and her husband.
293. *mad . . . chere*: treated us very well.
294. *rygth wolcome*: very welcome.
295. *cam to mete*: came to dinner.
296. *yevyn*: give.
296-7. *er . . . mete*: before he sat down to his meal.
297. *thriteen*: probably because thirteen was the number of Christ plus the twelve Apostles.
297. *powyre*: poor.   *pens*: pennies.
298. *lovys*: loaves.   *mete*: food.
299. *steryd*: stirred, moved.   *wyth . . . sygth*: by the sight of this.
300. *yaf . . . worshepyng*: gave God praise and honour.
301. *plentyvows*: plenteous, abundant.
301-2. *in so mych*: so much so.

mych that alle the bysshopys meny wer gretly merveylyng what
hyre eyled. And sythen sche was set to mete wyth many
worthy clerkys and prestys and swyers of the bysshoppys. And
the bysshop hymself sent hire ful gentylly of hys owyn mees.   305
The clerkys askyd this creature many hard qwestyons, the
wych sche be the grace of Jhesu resolvyd, so that hire
answerys lykyd the bysshop rygth wel and the clerkys had ful
gret mervayl of hire, that sche answeryd so redyly and
pregnawntly.   310
    Whan the bysshop had etyn, he sent for this creature into
hys chawmbyre, seying to hire, 'Margery, ye and your
husbond spak to me forto yyfe yow the mantyl and the ryng,
for whech cause I have take my cownsel, and my cownsel wyl
not yyf me to professe yow in so synguler a clothyng   315
wythowtyn better avysement. And ye sey, be the grace of God
ye wyl go to Jerusalem. Therfore prayth to God that it may
abyden tyl ye come fro Jerusalem, that ye be better prevyd and
knowyn.'
    On the next day this creature went to chirch and prayd   320
to God wyth alle hyr spyritys that sche mygth han knowlach
how sche xuld be governd in this mater and what answere
sche mygth gife to the bysshop. Owyr Lord Jhesu Crist

---

302. *meny*: household.
302–3. *what . . . eyled*: what was wrong with her.
303. *sythen*: then.
304. *prestys*: priests.   *swyers*: squires, i.e. attendant gentlemen.
305. *sent . . . mees*: very courteously sent her some of his own meal. The
bishop would sit at the high table with his more distinguished guests and
would be served a different menu from most of those eating in hall; it was a
mark of favour if he sent some of his superior meal to a person sitting at
one of the tables in the body of the hall.
307. *resolvyd*: answered.
308. *lykyd . . . wel*: pleased the bishop very much.
308–9. *had . . . hire*: were extremely astonished at her.
309. *redyly*: readily, promptly.
310. *pregnawntly*: cogently.
312. *chawmbyre*: room, apartment.
313. *spak . . . yyfe*: asked me to give.
314. *take my cownsel*: taken advice.   *cownsel(2)*: advisers.
315. *yyf me*: allow me.   *professe*: accept your profession (public vows).
    synguler: unusual.
316. *wythowtyn . . . avysement*: without more careful consideration.   *be*: by.
318. *abyden*: wait.   *fro*: (back) from.   *that*: (so) that.
    prevyd: proved, tested.
321. *wyth . . . spyritys*: with all her heart and soul.   *han knowlach*: i.e. know.
322. *be governd*: conduct herself.

answeryd to hire mend in this maner: 'Dowter, sey the
bysshop that he dredyth more the schamys of the world than   325
the parfyt lofe of God. Sey hym, I xuld as wel han excusyd
hym yyf he had fulfyllyd thi wyl, as I dede the chyldren of
Israel whan I bad hem borwe the goodys of the pepyl of Egypt
and gon awey therwyth. Therfore, dowter, sey hym, thow he
wyl not don it now, it xal be don another tyme whan God wyl.'   330
    And so sche dede hire massage to the Bysshop of Lyncolne
as sche had in comawndment. Than he preyd hyre to gon to
the Archbusshop of Cawnterbery, Arundel, 'and preyn hym to
grawntyn leve to me, Bysshop of Lyncoln', forto yevyn hire the
mentyl and the ryng, inasmech as sche was not of hys dyocyse.   335
This cawse he feyned thorw cownsel of hys clerkys, for thei
lovyd not this creature.
    Sche seyd, 'Sere, I wyl go to my lord of Cawnterbery wyth
rygth good wyl for other cawsys and materys whech I have to
schewe to Hys Reverens. As for this cawse I xal not gon, for   340
God wyl not I aske hym theraftyr.' Than sche toke hire leve of

324. sey: tell.
325. dredyth: fears.   *schamys*: embarrassments.
326. parfyt lofe: perfect love.
326–7. xuld ... han ... hym: should have exonerated him.
327–9. as ... therwyth: a reference to the Spoiling of the Egyptians
immediately before the flight of the Jews from Egypt (see Exodus 12:36), an
event more usually used to justify the Christian use of pagan classical
culture.
328. borwe: borrow, i.e. steal.   *goodys*: goods, property.
329. therwyth: with them.   *thow*: although.
331. dede ... massage: gave her message.
332. preyd: prayed, requested.
333. Archbusshop ... Arundel: Thomas Arundel (1353–1414), consecrated
Archbishop of Canterbury in 1397, a strong supporter of the Lancastrian
monarchs and persecutor of the Lollards; he was responsible for the 1408
Constitutions of Oxford which forbade the reading of unauthorised Bible
translations.
333. preyn: pray, ask.
334. grawntyn leve: give permission.
335. inasmech: in that.
335. sche ... dyocyse: Repingdon was acting punctiliously as Margery came
from Lynn in the diocese of Norwich.
336. cawse: cause, reason.   *feyned*: invented.
338. Sere: Sir.
340. As ... cawse: as far as this reason is concerned.
341. God ... not: God does not will.   *theraftyr*: for it.

the Bysshop of Lyncolne, and he yaf hire twenty-six
schelyngys and eight pens, to byen hyre clothyng wyth and
forto prey for hym.

c) *Julian of Norwich Counsels Margery*
(f. 21ʳ⁻ᵛ)

And than sche was bodyn be Owyr Lord forto gon to an   345
ankres in the same cyte, whych hyte Dame Jelyan. And so
sche dede and schewyd hire the grace that God put in hire
sowle of compunccyon, contricyon, swetnesse and devocyon,
compassyon wyth holy meditacyon and hy contemplacyon, and
ful many holy spechys and dalyawns that Owyr Lord spak to   350
hire sowle, and many wondirful revelacyons, whech sche
schewyd to the ankres to wetyn yf ther were any deceyte in
hem. For the ankres was expert in swech thyngys and good
cownsel cowd yevyn.

The ankres, heryng the mervelyows goodnes of Owyre   355
Lord, hyly thankyd God wyth al hire hert for hys visitacyon,
cownselyng this creature to be obedyent to the wyl of Owyr
Lord God, and fulfyllyn wyth al hire mygthys whatever he put
in hire sowle, yf it were not ageyn the worshep of God and

342–3. twenty-six . . . pens: a considerable sum of money, made up of one
pound (twenty shillings) and half a mark (a mark was thirteen shillings and
fourpence). Repingdon was acting with prudence; he would not publicly
accept a vow of chastity from a married woman from another diocese
(though he had privately accepted her husband's vow) but he did not wish
to alienate someone who might well have considerable influence at the
Court of Heaven.

343. to . . . wyth: to buy herself clothes with.

345. And than: After returning to Lynn from London, Margery next visited
Norwich where she first consulted a Carmelite friar.

345. bodyn: bidden, commanded.

346. ankres: anchoress.   *whych hyte:* who was called.   *Jelyan:* i.e. Julian.

348. compunccyon: compunction.   *contricyon:* contrition.

350. dalyawns: conversations.

352. wetyn: know.

      deceyte: deception. Margery consults Julian as to whether she is the
victim of diabolical delusions.

353. expert . . . thyngys: i.e. Julian had a reputation for having the gift of
discretion of spirits (see above).

353–4. good . . . yevyn: knew how to give good advice.

356. hyly: highly, greatly.   *visitacyon:* visitation (of Margery by God).

358. mygthys: powers.

359. ageyn: against, contrary to.   *worshep:* honour.

profyte of hire evyn-christen; for yf it were, than it were nowt   360
the mevyng of a good spyryte but rather of an evyl spyrit.

'The Holy Gost mevyth never a thing ageyn charite, and yf
he dede, he were contraryows to hys owyn self, for he is al
charite. Also he mevyth a sowle to al chastnesse, for chast
levars be clepyd the temple of the Holy Gost, and the Holy   365
Gost makyth a sowle stabyl and stedfast in the rygth feyth and
the rygth beleve. And a dubbyl man in sowle is ever unstabyl
and unstedfast in al hys weys. He that is evermore dowtyng is
lyke to the flood of the see, the whech is mevyd and born
abowte wyth the wynd, and that man is not lyche to receyven   370
the yyftys of God. What creature that hath thes tokenys he
muste stedfastlych belevyn that the Holy Gost dwellyth in hys
sowle.'

'And mech more, whan God visyteth a creature wyth terys
of contrisyon, devosyon er compassyon, he may and owyth to   375
levyn that the Holy Gost is in hys sowle. Seynt Powyl seyth
that the Holy Gost askyth for us wyth mornynggys and

360. profyte . . . evyn-christen: benefit of her fellow Christians.   *than*: then.
361. mevyng: prompting.
362–73. The . . . sowle: Julian's words as reported by Margery sound
authentic and are entirely consonant with her teachings in *A Revelation of
Love*. Margery, who could not read or write, clearly had the kind of accurate
verbal memory which is often associated with an oral rather than literate
culture.
362. mevyth: prompts, inspires.   *charite*: charity, love.
363. dede: did.   *contraryows*: contrary.
364. chastnesse: chastity.
364–5. chaste levars: those who live chastely.
365. clepyd: called.   *temple . . . Gost*: by St Paul; 1 Corinthians 6:19.
366. stabyl: stable, firm.   *rygth feyth*: right, true faith.
367. beleve: belief.   *dubbyl*: duplicitous.   *unstabyl*: unstable.
368. dowtyng: doubting.
369. see: sea.   *mevyd*: moved, shifted.
369–70. born abowte: carried around.
370. lyche: likely, suitable.
371. yyftys: gifts.
        thes tokenys: these signs, i.e. stability and steadfastness in the true
faith.
372. stedfastlych: steadfastly.   *belevyn*: believe.
374. mech: much.   *terys*: tears.
375. devosyon: devotion.   *er*: or.
375–6. may . . . levyn: can and ought to believe.
376. Powyl: Paul.
377. askyth: prays.
377–8. mornynggys . . . unspekable: lamentations and unspeakable weeping
(Romans 8:26).

wepyngys unspekable, that is to seyn, he makyth us to askyn
and preyn wyth mornynggys and wepyngys so plentyvowsly
that the terys may not be nowmeryd. Ther may non evyl spyrit   380
yevyn thes tokenys, for Jerom seyth that terys turmentyn more
the devylle than don the peynes of Helle. God and the devyl
ben evermore contraryows, and thei xal never dwellyn
togedyre in on place, and the devyl hath no powyr in a mannys
sowle.'   385
'Holy Wryt seyth that the sowle of a rytful man is the sete of
God, and so I trust, syster, that ye ben. I prey God grawnt
yow perseverawns. Settyth al your trust in God and feryth not
the langage of the world. For the more despyte, schame and
repref that ye have in the world, the more is your meryte in   390
the sygth of God. Pacyens is necessary unto yow, for in that
schal ye kepyn your sowle.'
Mych was the holy dalyawns that the ankres and this
creature haddyn be comownyng in the lofe of Owyr Lord
Jhesu Crist many days that thei were togedyre.   395

379. *plentyvowsly*: plenteously.
380. *nowmeryd*: numbered, counted.
381. *yevyn*: give.
     Jerom seyth: St Jerome (*c.* 342–420), one of the four Fathers of the
Church; elsewhere this saying is attributed to St Bernard.
381. *turmentyn*: torment.
383–4. *dwellyn . . . place*: live together in one place, coexist.
384. *mannys*: person's.
386. *Holy Wryt seyth*: e.g. 2 Corinthians 6:16. Compare also Julian of
Norwich, above, p. 132.
386. *rytful*: righteous, virtuous.   *sete*: seat.
387. *ye*: Julian uses the formal, respectful form of the pronoun to address
Margery.
388. *perseverawns*: perseverance, i.e. steadfast purpose until death.
     Settyth: set, place.   *feryth*: fear.
389. *langage . . . world*: what the world says.   *despyte*: contempt.
     schame: shame, disgrace.
390. *repref*: criticism, reproof.
391. *sygth*: sight.   *Pacyens*: patience.
392. *kepyn*: keep, preserve.
393. *Mych*: much.
394. *be comownyng*: in talking about.

d) *The Scope of Margery's Active Mature Ministry* (ff. 86ᵛ–88ʳ)

As the sayd creature was in a chirch of Seynt Margaret to sey
hire devocyons, ther cam a man knelyng at hire bak, wryngyng
hys handys and schewyng tokenys of gret hevynes. Sche,
parceyvyng hys hevynes, askyd what hym eylyd. He seyd it
stod ryth hard wyth hym, for hys wyfe was newly delyveryd of   400
a childe and sche was owt hire mende. 'And, dame,' he seyth,
'sche knowyth not me ne non of hire neyborwys. Sche roryth
and cryith so that sche makith folk evyl afeerd. Sche wyl bothe
smytyn and bityn, and therfore is sche manakyld on hire
wristys.' Than askyd sche the man yyf he wolde that sche went   405
wyth hym and sawe hire, and he seyd, 'Ya, dame, for Goddys
lofe.'

So sche went forth wyth hym to se the woman. And whan
sche cam into the hows, as sone as the seke woman that was
alienyd of hire witte saw hire, sche spak to hire sadly and   410
goodly and seyd sche was ryth wolcome to hire. And sche was
ryth glad of hire comyng and gretly comfortyd be hire presens.

---

397. at . . . bak: behind her.   *wryngyng*: wringing.
398. schewyng tokenys: showing signs.   *hevynes*: unhappiness.
399. parceyvyng: perceiving.   *hym eylyd*: ailed him.
399–400. it . . . hym: he was in a very difficult situation.
400–1. newly . . . childe: had just borne a child.
401. owt . . . mende: out of her mind. His wife's post-puerperal psychosis
sounds very similar to that suffered by Margery after the birth of her first
child (see above, p. 177), just as the younger woman's expulsion from the
town mirrors the rejection Margery repeatedly suffered because of her own
noisy 'cries'.
401. dame: madame.
402. knowyth not: does not recognise.
    ne . . . neyborwys: nor any of her neighbours.   *roryth*: roars, screams.
403. evyl afeerd: badly frightened.
404. smytyn: strike.   *bityn*: bite.
404–5. manakyld . . . wristys: her wrists are manacled.
405. wolde . . . went: wanted her to go.
406. Ya: Yes.
407. lofe: love.
409. hows: house.
410. alienyd . . . witte: out of her mind.   *sadly*: soberly.
411. goodly: kindly.   *ryth wolcome*: truly welcome.
412. be: by.

'For ye arn,' sche seyd, 'a ryth good woman, and I behelde
many fayr awngelys abowte yow and therfore I pray yow, goth
not fro me, for I am gretly comfortyd be yow.' And whan　　415
other folke cam to hire, sche cryid and gapyd as sche wolde an
etyn hem, and seyd that sche saw many develes abowtyn hem.
Sche wolde not suffyrn hem to towchyn hire be hyre good wyl.
Sche roryd and cryid so bothe nyth and day for the most part,
that men wolde not suffyr hire to dwellyn amongys hem, sche　　420
was so tediows to hem.

Than was sche had to the forthest ende of the town, into a
chambyr, that the pepil xulde not heryn hire cryin. And ther
was sche bowndyn handys and feet wyth chenys of yron, that
sche xulde smytyn nobody. And the sayd creature went to hire　　425
iche day onys er twyis at the lest wey. And whyl sche was wyth
hire, sche was meke anow, and herd hire spekyn and dalyin
wyth good wil wythowtyn any roryng er crying. And the sayd
creature preyid for this woman every day that God xulde, yyf
it were hys wille, restoryn hire to hire wittys ageyn. And Owre　　430
Lord answeryd in hire sowle and seyd, 'Sche xulde faryn ryth
wel.'

Than was sche more bolde to preyin for hire recuryng than
sche was beforn, and iche day, wepyng and sorwyng, preyid
for hire recure tyl God yaf hire hire witte and hire mende　　435
ayen. And than was sche browt to chirche and purifiid as

413. *ye arn*: you are (the young woman uses the respectful formal plural
pronoun to Margery).
414. *abowte*: around.
416. *gapyd*: gaped, opened her mouth.
416–17. *as ... hem*(1): as if she wanted to eat them.
417. *abowtyn*: around.
418. *suffyrn*: suffer, allow.　　*towchyn*: touch.　　*be ... wyl*: with her consent.
419. *roryd*: roared, screamed.
　　bothe ... part: for most of the day and night.
421. *tediows*: troublesome, disagreeable.
422. *was ... had*: she was taken.　　*forthest*: furthest, most distant.
423. *xulde ... cryin*: should not hear her cry.
424. *bowndyn*: bound.　　*chenys of yron*: iron chains.
426. *iche*: each.　　*onys ... wey*: once or twice at the very minimum.
427. *meke anow*: tractable enough.　　*dalyin*: converse.
428. *wyth ... wil*: gladly, willingly.
430. *restoryn ... ageyn*: bring her back to her senses.
431–2. *xulde ... wel*: should get better.
433. *recuryng*: recovering.
435. *recure*: recovery.
436. *browt*: brought.
436–7. *purifiid ... be*: purified ('churched') as other women are. Childbirth

other women be. Blyssed mote God ben! It was, as hem thowt
that knewyn it, a ryth gret myrakyl, for he that wrot this boke
had never before that tyme sey man ne woman, as hym thowt,
so fer owt of hireself as this woman was, ne so evyl to rewlyn   440
ne to governyn, and sithyn he sey hire sad and sobyr anow.
Worschip and preysyng be to Owre Lord wythowtyn ende for
hys hy mercy and hys goodnes that ever helpith at nede.

It happyd on a tyme that the husbonde of the sayd creature,
a man in gret age, passyng thre score yere, as he wolde a   445
comyn down of hys chambyr barefoot and barelegge, he
slederyd er ellys faylyd of hys fotyng and fel down to the
grownd fro the gresys and hys hevyd undyr hym grevowsly
brokyn and bresyd, in so meche that he had in hys hevyd fif
teyntys many days whil hys hevyd was in holyng. And as God   450
wold, it was knowyn to summe of hys neybowrys how he was
fallyn downe of the gresys, peraventure thorw the dene and
the luschyng of hys fallyng. And so thei comyn to hym and
fowndyn hym lying wyth hys hevyd undir hym, half on lyfe, al
rowyd wyth blood, never lyke to a spokyn wyth preyst ne wyth   455
clerk but thorw hy grace and myracle.

was considered a ritually defiling experience, but the churching of women,
based on the Jewish rite of purification after childbirth, was also a form of
thanksgiving.

437. *hem thowt*: it seemed to those.
439. *sey*: seen.
440. *fer . . . hireself*: deranged.
440–1. *evyl . . . governyn*: difficult to control or govern.
441. *sithyn*: since.   *sey*: saw.   *anow*: enough.
443. *at nede*: in time of necessity.
445. *in . . . age*: very old.   *passyng . . . yere*: more than sixty.
445–6. *wolde a comyn*: would have, was trying to, come.
446. *of*: out of.   *barelegge*: bare-legged.
447. *slederyd*: slipped.   *faylyd . . . fotyng*: missed his footing.
448. *fro the gresys*: from the steps.   *hevyd*: head.
448–9. *grevowsly . . . bresyd*: badly cut and bruised.
449. *in so meche*: so much so.
449–50. *fif teyntys*: five linen plugs (to drain the wound).
450. *whil . . . holyng*: while his head was healing.
451. *wold*: willed.
452. *peraventure*: perhaps.   *dene*: din.
453. *luschyng*: crashing noise.
454. *fowndyn*: found.   *on lyfe*: alive.
455. *rowyd*: streaked, smeared.
    never . . . preyst: never likely to have been able to speak to a priest.
456. *but*: except.   *hy*: high.

Than the sayd creature, hys wife, was sent fore and so sche
cam to hym. Than was he takyn up and hys hevyd was sowyd
and he was seke a long tyme aftyr, that men wend that he
xulde a be deed. And than the pepil seyd, yyf he deyd, hys   460
wyfe was worthy to ben hangyn for hys deth, for asmeche as
sche myth a kept hym and dede not. They dwellyd not togedyr
ne thei lay not togedyr for, as is wretyn beforn, thei bothyn
wyth on assent and wyth fre wil of her either haddyn mad a
vow to levyn chast. And therfore to enchewyn alle perellys thei   465
dwellyd and sojowryd in divers placys wher no suspicyon
xulde ben had of here incontinens. For first thei dwellyd
togedir aftyr that thei had mad here vow, and than the pepil
slawndryd hem and seyd thei usyd her lust and here likyng as
thei dedyn beforn her vow-makyng. And whan thei wentyn   470
owt on pilgrimage er to se and spekyn wyth other gostly
creaturys, many evyl folke whos tongys were her owyn hurt,
faylyng the dreed and lofe of Owre Lord Jhesu Crist, demtyn
and seydyn that thei went rather to woodys, grovys er valeys to
usyn the lust of her bodiis, that the pepil xuld not aspyin it ne   475
wetyn it.

They, havyng knowlach how prone the pepil was to demyn
evyl of hem, desiryng to avoydyn al occasyon, inasmech as thei

458. *takyn*: lifted.   *sowyd*: sewed, stitched.
459. *seke*: sick.   *wend*: thought.
460. *xulde . . . deed*: would have died.   *deyd*: died.
461. *hangyn*: hanged.   *for asmeche*: for as much, in that.
462. *myth a kept*: could have looked after.
462–3. *dwellyd . . . togedyr*: did not live together or sleep together.
463. *bothyn*: both.
464. *wyth . . . assent*: with one accord.
     wyth . . . either: voluntarily on both their parts.   *mad*: made.
465. *levyn*: live.   *enchewyn*: avoid.   *perellys*: perils, dangers.
466. *sojowryd*: stayed, lodged.   *divers*: separate.
467. *here incontinens*: their unchastity.
469. *slawndryd*: slandered.
     usyd . . . likyng: carried out their lusts and pleasures.
471. *er*: or.
471–2. *gostly creaturys*: spiritually-minded people.
472. *tongys*: tongues.
473. *faylyng*: lacking.   *demtyn*: thought.
475. *usyn . . . bodiis*: indulge in physical lust.   *that*: so that.
     aspyin: observe.
476. *wetyn*: know.
477. *havyng knowlach*: knowing.
478. *occasyon*: opportunity.

myth goodly, be here good wil and here bothins consentyng, thei partyd asundyr, as towchyng to her boord and to her 480 chambrys, and wentyn to boord in divers placys. And this was the cawse that sche was not wyth hym, and also that sche xulde not be lettyd fro hire contemplacyon. And therfore whan he had fallyn and grevowsly was hurt, as is seyd beforn, the pepil seyd yyf he deyid, it was worthy that sche xulde 485 answeryn for hys deth.

Than sche preyid to Owre Lord that hire husbond myth levyn a yere and sche be deliveryd owt slawndyr, yyf it were hys plesawns. Owre Lord seyd to hire mende, 'Dowter, thou xalt have thi bone, for he xal levyn and I have wrowt a gret 490 myrakyl for the that he was not ded. And I bydde the take hym hom and kepe hym, for my lofe.' Sche seyd, 'Nay, good lord, for I xal than not tendyn to the as I do now.'

'Yys, dowter,' seyd Owre Lord, 'thou xalt have as meche mede forto kepyn hym and helpyn hym in hys nede at hom as 495 yyf thou were in chirche to makyn thi preyerys. And thou hast seyd many tymys that thou woldist fawyn kepyn me. I prey the now kepe hym for the lofe of me, for he hath sumtyme fulfillyd thi wil and my wil bothe. And he hath mad thi body fre to me that thou xuldist servyn me and levyn chast and 500 clene. And therfore I wil that thou be fre to helpyn hym at hys nede in my name.'

'A, lord,' seyd sche, 'for thi mercy grawnt me grace to obeyn thi wil and fulfille thi wil and late never my gostly

479. *be . . . consentyng*: voluntarily and with the consent of both of them.
480. *partyd asundyr*: separated.
480–1. *as . . . chambrys*: with respect to their eating and sleeping.
481. *wentyn to boord*: i.e. took their meals.
482. *cawse*: cause, reason.
483. *lettyd fro*: hindered from.
486. *answeryn*: be held responsible.
487–8. *myth levyn*: might live.
488. *deliveryd . . . slawndyr*: delivered from slander.
489. *plesawns*: pleasure.
490. *bone*: boon, request.   *wrowt*: wrought.
492. *kepe*: care for.
493. *tendyn*: attend.
495. *mede*: reward.
496. *makyn thi preyerys*: say thy prayers.
497. *fawyn*: gladly, eagerly.
498. *sumtyme*: in the past.
499–500. *mad . . . fre*: released your body.
504. *late*: let.

enmys han no powyr to lett me fro fulfillyng of thi wil.'   505
  Than sche toke hom hire husbond to hire and kept hym
yerys after, as long as he levyd, and had ful mech labowre
wyth hym, for in hys last days he turnyd childisch ayen and
lakkyd reson, that he cowd not don hys owyn esement, to go
to a sege – er ellys he wolde not – but as a childe voydyd his   510
natural digestyon in hys lynyn clothys ther he sat be the fyre er
at the tabil, whether it were, he wolde sparyn no place. And
therfore was hire labowre meche the more in waschyng and
wryngyng, and hire costage in fyryng, and lettyd hire ful
meche fro hire contemplacyon, that many tymys sche xuld an   515
yrkyd hire labowre, saf sche bethowt hire how sche in hire
yong age had ful many delectabyl thowtys, fleschly lustys and
inordinat lovys to hys persone. And therfore sche was glad to
be ponischyd wyth the same persone, and toke it mech the
more esily and servyd hym and helpyd hym, as hire thowt, as   520
sche wolde a don Crist hymself.

Textual notes

151. schuld] schul.
220. slawndyr] slawdyr.
372. muste] m (bottom corner of page torn away).

505. lett: hinder.
507. levyd: lived.
508. turnyd ... ayen: reverted to childishness.
509. lakkyd reson: lost his ability to reason.
    don ... esement: see to his own toileting.
509–10. go ... sege: use a seat, commode.
510–11. voydyd ... digestyon: emptied his bowels.
511. lynyn clothys: linen clothes, i.e. underwear.   *ther*: where.
512. whether it were: wherever it was.   *sparyn*: spare.
514. costage: expense.   *fyryng*: heating (of water for washing).
515–16. xuld ... labowre: would have resented her toil.
516. saf: except that.   *bethowt hire*: thought, remembered.
517. yong age: youth.   *delectabyl*: delightful, pleasurable.
518. inordinat lovys: excessive love.   *to hys persone*: towards his body.
519. ponischyd wyth: punished by.
521. wolde a don: would have done.

12 A Collection of Prayers

The Feitis and the Passion of Our Lord Jhesu Crist is a collection of meditative prayers composed by an anonymous woman at the request of her 'religious sister'. She writes:

> O myn sustir, preie my lord God the Trinite that for his gret bounte and for his endeles mercy, have mercy and pite on me, sinful, and make me a good woman.

The author was probably herself a nun: she has a strongly clerical point of view and seems to identify with priests, monks and nuns as a distinct group in medieval society. She may have been a Bridgettine, a member of the austere and fervent double order for men and women founded by St Bridget of Sweden (see above, p. 84). The only house of the Order in England was Syon Abbey which had been founded by Henry V in 1415 and was distinguished by its respect for learning. Syon had close links with the monarchy and it is noticeable that the prayers include special supplications for the welfare of the King.

Comment: Collections of prayers that encourage meditation on the life of Christ are very common in the later Middle Ages. They usually dwell on the human aspects of Jesus's life (cf. above, p. 50) and try to arouse compassion through an intense imaginative recreation of the events recounted in the Gospels. The writer of this collection mainly treats her meditative subjects with restraint and in her address to Christ keeps a respectful distance, very different from the intimate conversation or 'daliance' of Margery Kempe. Her compilation is modest and unpretentious in scope; it should be compared with the much more ambitious and elaborate set of *Meditations upon the Seven Days of the Week* translated by Eleanor Hull (see below, p. 220).

The author explains the principle upon which she has constructed her text as follows:

> at every preiere I sette a *Pater Noster*, as for the most principal preire of alle other preieris, whiche is an ABCe and former of alle other orisons . . . . Oure Lord that made that preier, makith alle othere preieris, for be his grace it is doon (p. 2).

She explains that the Lord's Prayer follows each of her own prayers because it provides a pattern, or paradigm, for all Christian prayer; the metaphor of the alphabet suggests that it contains in embryo all possible prayers. Paradoxically, she makes the highest and most daring claim for her writing – that in a sense Christ himself is the author – while at the same time minimising her own role in the process of textual production. She is simply 'spelling out' by God's grace what is already there.

The first selection concentrates on various women who play a part in Jesus's earthly ministry. This is unusual as collections of meditations (like the religious lyrics to which they are so closely related) tend to concentrate on the events surrounding the Nativity and the Passion. A third of this text is indeed devoted to the latter topic, but in these passages the author is apparently encouraging her audience to identify with these New Testament women who are all, in some way, even more marginalised than is usual for women. The Samaritan Woman, like the Woman Taken in Adultery, is an outcast because she has offended against chastity and is also, like the Canaanite Woman, non-Jewish, while Mary Magdalene is potentially a comprehensive symbol of female deviance (see Notes). In all these stories Christ accepts the women as full human beings in defiance of conventional attitudes. The author, however, does not draw out all the implications of her material. For instance, out of all the possible emphases she focuses on Mary Magdalene as a model for contemplatives, which again betrays her professionally religious outlook on life.

In the second passage the author, adopting a teaching role, demonstrates further a tolerance of others that was already evident. She is well aware of the dangers of complacency and of phariseeism or hypocrisy, the occupational hazards of those who, like medieval nuns or anchoresses, have consciously decided to live differently from most people. From her remarks on the need for humility we may deduce that not all medieval nuns readily absorbed the steady diet of self-abasement on which they were fed. Their awareness of their status as professional religious may well have led them to resist the prevailing view of women as merely weak and sinful, and to assert a certain (limited) equality with men in their capacity for the religious life. Indeed, the author's adoption of a role as teacher and guide, if only in relation to other religious women, expresses that sense of status.

Manuscript: Oxford Bodley MS Holkham Misc. 41, pp. 1–98, *c.* 1450, the unique manuscript; unpublished.

Further reading (for full details see Bibliography): The only discussion of this text is Pollard 1987.

From *The Faits and the Passion of Our Lord Jesu Christ*

a) *Women of the New Testament*
(Oxford Bodley MS Holkham Misc. 41)

(i) *The Woman of Samaria*
(pp. 31–3)

O Jhesu ful of benignite, I yelde yow thankynges that ye so
meke and mildeli spak a good while with the woman
Samaritan, that come to the welle ther ye sat to fetche watyr.
And ye, benigne Jhesu, bad here yeve yow drinke and seide to
here, who that drank of the water of lif that ye yevin, that thei   5
schulde not thurstyn perpetueli. For that watir, ye seiden, is
the wele that hem schal lede to everlastyng lif. And thus ful
homli ye spak with here a good while and told here her prive
secrees. O goode Lord, come into my soule, tel and schew me
the derkhed and defaute that priveli lurkyn withinne me.   10
Suffre me not to make of vertu vice, ne of vice vertu. Voide
fro me alle evil custumes and yeve me cler syht of trewe
vndirstonding and sothfast knowinge so that I may fully
amende me of alle myne defautes. A, gracious Jhesu, graunte
me also the water of lif that I thurste not endelesli and make   15
me drunke in youre swete love, wherthorw I may at the laste
come to everlesting lif. Amen. *Pater noster. Ave.*

---

1. benignite: kindness.   *yelde*: yield, render.
2–3. woman Samaritan: the story of Christ's encounter with the Samaritan
Woman, who had had five husbands and was currently living with a man
who was not her husband, comes from John 4: 4–29.
3. ther: where.
4. bad: asked.   *yeve*: to give.
5. here: her.   *who that*: whoever.   *yevin*: give.   *thei*: they.
6. schulde: should.   *thurstyn*: thirst.   *perpetueli*: eternally.
7. wele: well.   *hem*: them.
8. homli: intimately.
8–9. prive secrees: intimate secrets.
10. derkhed: darkness.   *defaute*: failure, inadequacy.   *priveli*: secretly.
   lurkyn: lie hidden.
11. Voide: expel.
12. custumes: habits.   *cler syht*: clear vision.
13. sothfast: truthful.
15. endelesli: eternally, perpetually.
15–16. make . . . love: drunkenness is often used as a symbol of ecstasy in
medieval mystical writings.
16. wherthorw: through which.
17. everlesting: everlasting, eternal.

(ii) *Mary Magdalene*
(pp. 35–41)

Jhesu ful of debonerte, I thanke and magnifie yow that ye clepid and receyvid the seventi and two disciples and for ye healede the pepile of ydropesies and palsies and of rennyng   20 blod. And speciali I yeld yow thankinges that ye, benigne Jhesu, suffrede Marie Maudeleyne, whan sche was holde so sinful that sche hadde sevene fendis withinne here, to aproche to youre holy feet in the hous of the phariseye and ther sche wepte for here misdedis and wessch youre feet with here terys   25 and wipid hem with here heer. Also I thanke yow, gode Lord, that ye mercyfulli foryaf here alle her sinnes.

O dereworthi Jhesu, suffre me thowgh I be wikkid, werst of alle othire, to aprochin to youre holy feet and yeve me grace there to abide and wepe for my grete misdedis, til youre   30 merciful herte foryeve me alle min sennes. *Pater noster. Ave Maria.*

I thanke and magnifie yow, Jhesu ful of grace, that ye have

18. debonerte: kindness.
19. clepid: called.
20. ydropesies: dropsies.
20–1. rennyng blod: haemorrhages (a reference to the story of the woman 'having an issue of blood twelve years' in Luke 8: 43–8).
22. suffrede: permitted.
Marie Maudeleyne: in Western tradition Mary of Magdala, from whom Christ had cast out seven devils (Luke 8: 1–2), was identified with 'the woman who was a sinner', i.e. a prostitute, who broke the box of precious ointment in the house of Simon the Pharisee to anoint Christ's head and washed his feet with her tears (Luke 7: 37–50) and also with Mary the sister of Martha and Lazarus (Luke 10: 38–42) who preferred listening to Christ to helping with the cooking; she thus became a powerful symbol of the many manifestations of female deviance.
22. holde: held, considered.
23. fendis: fiends, devils.   *aproche*: approach.
24. phariseye: pharisee.
25. misdedis: misdeeds, sins.   *wessch*: washed.
26. heer: hair.
27. foryaf: forgave.
28. thowgh: although.   *werst*: worst.
29. othire: others.
30. wepe . . . misdedis: this is a prayer for tears of compunction, which were highly prized by some mystics. Margery Kempe had this grace in abundance but for her, living outside the convent, it was a source of embarrassment, conflict and controversy (see above, p. 182).

no despit ne indignacion of the sinful that wele forsake here
sinnes, but in gret charete ye receyve hem to youre grace. O   35
lord of purete and of clennesse, ye arn not skeymous of hem,
thowgh thei have been fowle and al defacid thorw sinnes, but
anoon as thei been contrit, ye make hem fair and brith and
famuliarli in hem ye make youre habitacion. O Lord, gret is
youre bounte, blissid and preisid, thankid and heried, glorified   40
and magnified be ye evere therfore.

Also, swete Jhesu, I yelde yow thankinges that ye so
debonerli excusid Marie Maudeleyne thries there to the
phariseies, whan sche wepte at youre feet. Anothir time ye,
meke Jhesu, excusid here, what tyme here sustir Martha   45
compleinid to yow that sche wolden not helpyn here. Ful
graciousli ye seiden thanne to Martha that Marie hadde
chosin the betir partye which schulde nevere be benomyn
here. The thridde tyme, benigne Jhesu, ye excusid here whan
Judas grucchid the precious oynement that sche spendid on   50
yow. O gode Lord, yeve me grace to have perfith charite to
alle myn evencristen and schilde me that I nevere have despit
ne disdein of hem for senne, but love the persones and hate
the sinne.

O charitable God, make me to folwe youre purete and   55
youre vertues. Jhesu myn joye and myn comfort, myn hope
and al myn hele, fulfille me with youre goodnesse and sadli
stable me therinne. Jhesu myn strengthe and myn socour,
schilde me from alle bodili and gostli periles and, gracious

34. *despit*: contempt, scorn.   *wele*: want to.
35. *charete*: charity, love.
36. *arn*: are.   *skeymous of*: squeamish, fastidious about.
37. *fowle*: foul, disgusting.   *defacid*: disfigured.
38. *anoon*: as soon.   *brith*: bright, shining.
39. *famuliarli*: intimately.   *habitacion*: dwelling.
40. *heried*: praised.
43. *debonerli*: graciously.   *excused*: defended.   *thries*: three times.
45. *what tyme*: the time that.
46. *helpyn*: help.
48. *partye*: part.   *benomyn*: taken away from.
49. *thridde*: third.
50. *grucchid*: begrudged.   *oynement*: ointment.
     spendid: expended, lavished.
51. *perfith*: perfect.
52. *evencristen*: fellow Christians.   *schilde*: shield, guard.
53. *disdein*: contempt.   *for senne*: because of sin.
55. *folwe*: follow.
57. *hele*: health, salvation.
57–8. *sadli stable*: solemnly establish.

Lord, for the gret pite and mercy that ye hadde of Marie   60
Maudeleyne, and also for the gret love that sche hadde to yow
here in erthe and hath now in hevene, blissid Trinite, beholde
me with youre pitable yen and graunte me yowre love.

O allas, I sinful, how dar I thus homli spekin with my lord
God, that with his myht hevene and erthe made and alle thing   65
of nowht. Certeinli I, sinful wreche, am not worthi to speke to
hym ne to hevyn up myn eyn to hevene, but as a sinful worm
doun to the erthe, as sche that is not worthi to preise God ne
to nemme his name. For the profith seith, 'The preising of
God is not fair in a sinful mouth.'   70

O merciful Lord, Holi Trinite, mercy, mercy; my sinnes
putten me often tymes abake so that I dar not spekyn ne come
into youre presence. But youre mercy which hath noon ende
ne noumbre drawith me alwey forth and makith me to been
homli and familier with yow. Wherfore, benigne God, I yelde   75
yow thankinges and thankid be ye as often as alle hertis can or
may devise. And, myhtful Lord, I beseche yow sithin I am not
worthi to preise yow, make me worthi and able therto; and
youre owyn goodnesse preise, blisse and magnifie yow in me,
so that whatevere I write, thinke or speke of yow and for yow,   80
be it youre werk and not myn. And seie to me and to alle that
have forsake the world for yow, as ye seide to Martha of
Maudeleyne, that we have chose the betir partye that nevere
schal be benomyn us. *Pater noster. Ave Maria.*

62. *erthe*: earth.
63. *pitable yen*: merciful eyes.
64. *homli spekin*: speak familiarly.
66. *of nowht*: from nothing.
67. *hevyn . . . eyn*: lift up my eyes.
69. *nemme*: name.
    profith: prophet; the reference is to Ecclesiasticus 15:9, 'Praise is not
seemly in the mouth of a sinner.'
72. *putten . . . abake*: often drive me back.   *spekyn*: speak.
74. *noumbre*: measure, limit.   *drawith . . . forth*: always attracts me.
76. *hertis*: hearts, minds.
76–7. *can . . . devise*: know how, or are able, to imagine.
77. *myhtful*: mighty.   *sithin*: since.
78. *able therto*: capable of that.
79. *blisse*: bless.
80. *whatevere . . . yow*(2): as the writer of these meditations is very
conscious that they are to be used by another woman (see final passage) this
suggests that she envisaged her recipient perhaps writing similar texts,
possibly devotional poetry.
81. *werk*: work, composition.
82. *forsake*: given up.

The Woman Taken in Adultery and
the Canaanite Woman
(pp. 48–55)

Blisful Jhesu, I thanke and magnifie yow for the myht and   85
mercy that ye schewed into the woman that was foundin in
avowtrie. Whan the maistiris of the phariseyes browten here to
yow and askid what thei schulden doon with here – for thei
seiden that Moises hadde comoundid that swichche schulde
been stonid – and this thei dede for yef ye hadde seide, 'Stone   90
here', thei schulde have askried yow for cruel. For the pepil
that helde yow so pitous schulde have loved yow the lesse.
And yef ye hadde seide, 'Let here go quyt', thei schulde have
take yow as him that hadde doon ayens Moyses lawis. But ye,
meke Jhesu, that knewe al here malice, wrowhte al anothir.   95
And whanne ye saw the woman come, ye enclinid and lokid
doun and wrot in the erthe, for the woman schulde not be
aschamid. Ye savid here also that day fro deth.

A, gentil Lord ful of curtesie, I yelde yow thankinges for
this dede that ye, meke Jhesu, of youre gret benignite deede;   100
and thei than fersli askid you what thei schulde doo with the
woman and ye fersli lokid on hem and bad which of hem that

86. schewed: showed.
86–7. woman . . . avowtrie: the story of the Woman Taken in Adultery,
whom Christ saved from the death by stoning decreed by the Mosaic Law
with his words, 'He that is without sin among you, let him first cast a stone
at her', comes from John 8:3–11. It was a popular subject in the mystery
cycles.
87. maistiris: masters, leaders.   *browten*: brought.
89. comoundid: commanded.   *swichche*: such (a one).
90. stonid: stoned.   *dede*: did.   *yef*: if.
91. askried yow: cried out on you.
92. pitous: compassionate.
93. quyt: scot-free.
94. take: caught, arrested.   *as him*: as someone.
94. doon ayens: acted contrary to.
95. wrowhte al anothir: acted completely differently.
96. enclinid: bent down.
97. for: so that. Significantly, this explanation of Christ's action assumes
that the woman could read without speaking the words aloud.
98. aschamid: embarrassed.
99. gentil: noble.
100. deede: did.
101. than: then.   *fersli*: fiercely, aggressively.
102. bad: commanded.

was withoutyn sinne schulde castin on here the first ston. And
forthriht ye enclinid to the erthe anothir tyme and wrot in the
erthe and everich of hem saw there here owin sinnes and for   105
schame anoon thei stal awei be on and on til ther was never
on in that place but ye and the woman. And thanne ful
debonerli ye seide to here, 'Woman, where been thei that
accusid thee? Dampnid thee no man?' 'Noo, Lord,' quod
sche, 'no man.' And than ye, mercyable God, seide to here   110
that ye wolde not dampne here and bad here go and welne to
sinne no more.

O goode Lord, I preye yow that alle thoo that hatin and
despisen folkis of Holi Chirche and beth glad to finde hem
with defautes, writ in the ground of here hertis and opne the   115
eye of here soules that thei may se here owyn sinnes and
defautes, that thei may be aschamid of here pride. And, goode
Lord, yeve hem grace to have verray contricion of alle here
sinnes and to amende hem of here misdedis. *Pater noster. Ave
Maria gratia.*   120

I thanke and magnifie yow, Jhesu ful of grace, that ye
chasid the fendis awey, and legions of fendes fro men and
women. And speciali I yelde yow thankinges for the womanes
doughter of Cananee, that ye chasid the fend from here at the
preying of here modir. O Lord, mercyable Jhesu, but first ye   125

---

103. castin: throw.
104. forthriht: immediately.
105. everich of hem: each one of them.   *owin*: own.
106. stal: stole, crept.   *be on and on*: one by one.
107. on: (a single) one.   *but*: except.
108. debonerli: graciously.
109. Dampnid. . . man: has no man condemned you.   *Noo*: No.
110. mercyable: merciful.
111. welne: will, have the intention.
113–15. alle . . . defautes: a reference to the numerous critics, both
orthodox and heretical, of clerics in the late medieval Church; anti-clerical
satire is pervasive in the writings of Chaucer and Langland as well as of the
Wycliffites.
113. thoo: those.
114–15. finde . . . defautes: find fault with them.
115. opne: open.
118. verray contricion: true contrition.
119. misdedis: misdeeds, sins.
122. chasid . . . awey: expelled the devils.
123–4. womanes . . . Cananee: the daughter of the Woman of Canaan; the
story of the Canaanite (i.e. Palestinian) Woman is from Matthew 15:
22–28.
125. preying: prayer, request.   *modir*: mother.

made daunger whan ye seide to here that it was not leful to
take the bred that was ordeynyd to the children and yeven it to
the houndes, and sche answerde, 'Lord, noo. But houndes
may ete the crummes that fallin doun from the lordis bord out
of children handes.' A, benigne Jhesu, it plesid yow ful mechil   130
the meke answere of this woman, which made yow ful myldeli
to saye, 'O woman, mochil is thi feith; be it as thow wilt.' A,
dere Jhesu, therfore ye made so straunge atte beginnyng of
here preiere for sche schulde gete here the more mede and
thanke of yow and also to yeve us ensaumple that we schulde   135
mekli abide in preiere though firste we finde straungenesse
and have not oure preieres anoon whan we wolde. For youre
bounte wele not werne us oure preieres and if it be skilfulli
askid, yef we abide mekeli ther-upon.

O mercyful Trinite, thowgh I be most unworthi and am an   140
hound thorw bestli condicions and werse than an hound as in
that that I have wrethed yow, yet, goode Lord, I preie yow
yeve me crummes of youre mercy and grace and the bred of
evirlasting life and make me with al feith and mekenesse
continualli to abide in preiere that myne preieres mowyn been   145
herd and grauntid of yow as was the womanes of Cananee.
Pater noster.

126. daunger: difficulties.   *leful*: lawful.
127. bred: bread.   *ordeynyd to*: provided for.   *yeven*: give.
129. crummes: crumbs.   *lordis bord*: lord's table.
130. children handes: the hands of children (a realistic detail not in the
Bible).
130. ful mechil: very greatly.
131. the meke answere: in contrast, modern commentators like to stress the
Canaanite Woman's lively wit.
132. mochil: great.
133. made so straunge: were so uncooperative.
134. gete here: get for herself.   *mede*: reward.
135. ensaumple: an example, model.
136. abide: persevere.   *straungenesse*: aloofness.
137. anoon: at once.
138. bounte: goodness.   *werne*: refuse.   *and if*: if.   *skilfulli*: reasonably.
139. yef ... upon: if we wait for it humbly.
140. thowgh: although.
141. bestli condicions: bestial nature, character.   *werse*: worse.
141–2. as in that that: in that.
142. wrethed: angered.
143–4. bred ... life: i.e. the Sacrament.
145. mowyn: may.

b) *The Author's Conclusion*
(pp. 89–98)

Ithankid be Oure Lord, good sustir, now have I ende that ye
desired. I have write alwey at the beginninges of these
preyeres and meditacions thankynges and hereynges to God,   150
for we owyn ever to thanke God for alle the grete werkis that
he hath doon for man and for alle yeftes and graces that he of
his benigne goodnesse to us yevith and sendith, and for alle
gostli and bodili victories, for be his helpe and grace it is
doon. And but yef we yelde thankinges to God for alle these   155
beforeseide, we been unkende, wherthorw we gretli displese
him, as ye may pleinli se be ensample of King Ezechie, that
after a gret victorie that he hadde, he made no canticle
thanking God of his victorie and therfore was God displesid
and sente him to sein, be his prophete, that he schulde dien.   160
Wherfore I counseile alwey that ye in al mekenesse and
reverence thanke and herie God at alle tymes for his
beenfetis.

Ferthermore, myn sustir, mo peynes I have wretin than I

---

148. Ithankid: thanked.   *sustir*: sister.   *ende*: completed.
149. write: written.
150. hereynges: praisings.
151. owyn: ought.
152. doon: done.   *yeftes*: gifts.
155. but yef: unless.
156. unkende: unnatural.   *wherthorw*: through which.
157. pleinli: plainly.   *be ensample*: by the example.
    King Ezechie: see Isaiah 36, 37. The Bible does not explicitly say that
the king's sickness was a consequence of his failure to thank God after He
had destroyed the Assyrians; this however was the interpretation given by
the *Glossa Ordinaria*, the standard medieval commentary on the Bible,
which says of Isaiah 38:1 ('In those days Ezechias was sick even to death,
and Isaias the son of Amos the prophet came unto him, and said to him:
Thus saith the Lord: Take order with thy house, for thou shalt die, and not
live'), '*In those days he was sick* because he did not render God proper thanks
for the victory but was carried away with pride, as the books of Kings and
Chronicles make clear' (*PL* 113: 1279). It is interesting that a nun should
have been familiar with this Latin gloss.
158. canticle: song of praise.
160. sein . . . prophete: be told by His prophet.   *schulde dien*: was to die.
161. counseile: advise.
162. herie: praise.
163. beenfetis: blessings.
164. Ferthermore: furthermore.   *mo peynes*: more sufferings.

finde in the passion of the Gospel, the whiche was be 165
revelacion of God schewid to a religious persone. Alle the
evangelistes witnessin weel in here writing that ther was more
of oure Lord Crist Jhesu than thei wretin of him and therfore
it may leeffuli been seide or wretin, thing that hath be schewid
be Godes goodnesse, although it be not in the Gospel. 170

Also I write in divers places 'us' and 'we' for ye schulde at
swich places take youre evenchristen with yow in youre
preieres. For whan we preie for us-self, it plesith God gretli
that we take oure evencristen with us. And treuli, sustir, yef
we do so, he of his gret goodnesse wole thanne here oure 175
preiere the sonere.

I have set yow in this writing of lesse pris than I hope ye
been in the syght of God, for this cause: for though a man or
woman be never so good a lever and though thei have never
so mochil grace of God, gostli and bodili, thei schulde alwey 180
sette lest of hemself and holde hemself most sinful and lest
worthe of alle othire. But summe ther beth that seyn that thei
cannot holden hemself most sinful of alle othire. For thei seye
that othir han doon grete dedli sinnes that thei dede nevere.
And to hem that sein so I answere, yef thei wolde opin the eye 185
of sothfastnesse, it were ful litil maystrie to holden hemself
most sinful of alle othire. For yef the most perfith liver that is
this day on lyve and lest sinne hath doon, and he hadde

165. *passion*: (account of Christ's) Passion.
166. *religious persone*: i.e. monk or nun.
167. *witnessin weel*: give firm witness.
167–70. *ther . . . Gospel*: this is the usual medieval defence for the use of apocryphal material or details taken from private revelations, such as those of Bridget of Sweden or Elizabeth of Hungary, to amplify literary meditations based on the Bible.
169. *leeffuli*: lawfully.   *schewid*: revealed.
171. *divers*: various.
172. *swich*: such.   *take*: i.e. include.
173. *us-self*: ourselves.
175. *wole*: is willing.   *here*: hear.
176. *sonere*: sooner.
177. *set*: made.   *of . . . pris*: of lesser value.   *hope*: expect.
178. *been*: are.
179. *so . . . lever*: one who lives so virtuously.
181. *sette lest*: count, reckon, least.
182. *worthe*: worthy.
184. *dedli*: mortal.
185. *sein*: say.
186. *sothfastnesse*: truth.   *ful . . . maystrie*: a very small achievement.
187. *perfith*: perfect.
188. *on lyve*: alive.   *and*: if.

standin in the same occasions that the most sinful man stood
in, and therto he hadde had the same temptacions and that   190
same disposicion and the grace of God withdrawe from hym,
he schulde have do as evil as he, or worse. And therfore as of
his owin proprete he may holde himself as most sinful. For it
is but only of Godes goodnesse that kepith him fro the periles
that othir fallin in.   195

And also ther is anothir wey a man to holde himself as on of
the most sinful, though he fele meche grace and vertu yoven
to him, and is this: yef a man or woman for his holi levyng
falle into pride, beholding her vertues and goode dedis, and
rejoyeth in hemself with pride, wenyng that thei be not so   200
sinful as othir been ne doo not thoo evel dedes that othir
doon, and in this deliten in hemself and fallen thus in pride
and veinglorie, wilfulli holding weel be hemself, thei ben more
dispicable in the siht of God than thei that have sinnid in gret
owtward sinnes. For I likene hem to the pharise that Oure   205
Lord spekith of in the Gospel. The pharise thowte and seide
to God that he dede goode dedis and was not so sinful as the
publican and in this he hadde pride and rejoiced in himself
and therfore he was refusid of God. And the sinful publican
for his mekenesse and contricion was receyve to grace.   210
Lucifer also, he sinnid not in owtward fleschli sinnes, which
arn most abominable and reprovable in the siht of man, but he

---

189. standin: stood.   *occasions*: opportunities.
190. therto: in addition.
191. disposicion: temperament, frame of mind.
       withdrawe: withdrawn, taken away.
192–3. as(3) . . . proprete: as far as his own nature is concerned.
196. on: one.
197. meche: much.   *yoven*: given.
198. levyng: living, way of life.
200. rejoyeth: rejoices.   *wenyng*: thinking.
202. deliten in: are pleased with.
203. veinglorie: vainglory, vanity.   *wilfulli*: deliberately.
       holding . . . hemself: having a high opinion of themselves.
204. siht: sight.
205. owtward: external.   *likene*: compare.
       the pharise: the story of the Pharisee and the Publican comes from
Luke 18:9–14.
206. thowte: thought.
208. publican: tax collector.
209. refusid of: rejected by.
211. Lucifer: traditionally identified with Satan, leader of the fallen angels.
       fleschli: physical, i.e. sins such as lechery (unchastity), gluttony
(greediness), and sloth (laziness).

sinnid in pride onli, which is most reprovable in the siht of
God. And therfore he that was so faire an aungel, for his
pride become the fowlest fend of helle. 215

O, sithin that pride is so perilous that it fadith al gostli
beute and gretli displesith God, it owith mechel to ben hatid
and eschewid of every creature, to be soore aferd therof. God
yeve us grace evere to flee therfro. And I seye yow trewli, what
creature that wole hatin it and eschewen it, he must evere 220
holde himself werst of alle othir. And so I hope that ye do.
But yet I write this to remenbre bothe yow and othire
therupon and especiali to excite myself to have it weel in
mynde. And I am sekir whoso holdith himself most sinful, he
hath neythir skorn ne hatred ne disdein of noon of his 225
evyncristen for eny sinne that thei do or have doon; but thei
have pite and compassion of hem and hate the sinnes and love
the persones. And so mekenesse, who that wole takin it,
causith charite and al goodnesse.

And, sustir, bindith not yowself to seye al ovir the preieres 230
every day but seye summe on oon day and summe on anothir
day, as ye have leyser and tyme. And whoso that evir usith
mechil to seie it, schal finde therinne grace, comforth and
strengthe. I wolde ye couden the sentence withoutyn the book,
for and ye so coude, ye schulden fele mochil more comfort 235
and unyon in God to seye it so inforth, than forto seie it be

213. *reprovable*: reprehensible.
214. *he . . . aungel*: Lucifer's beauty was proverbial.
215. *fowlest fend*: ugliest devil.
216. *sithin*: since.   *fadith*: causes to fade.
217. *beute*: beauty.   *owith mechel*: ought greatly.
218. *eschewid*: avoided, shunned.   *soore aferd*: terrified.
220. *wole*: wants to.
222. *remenbre*: remind.
223. *therupon*: on the subject.   *excite*: urge.   *weel*: well.
224. *sekir*: sure.
225. *neythir*: neither.
228. *takin*: adopt.
230. *bindith . . . yowself*: do not commit yourself (i.e. by a vow); compare *A
Revelation Showed to a Holy Woman*, above, p. 174.
230. *al ovir*: right through.
232. *leyser*: leisure.
232–3. *usith mechil*: has the frequent custom.
234. *couden . . . book*: i.e. knew the words off by heart.
235. *and*: if.
236. *unyon*: union (the ultimate aim of the mystic).   *inforth*: inwardly.
236–7. *be scripture*: i.e. following the written text. These remarks throw a
most interesting light on the transition from an oral to a written culture and
on late medieval attitudes towards reading.

scripture. And farith now weel, myn goode sustir. God yeve us bothe grace in al thing to do as it is most to his worschep and plesing. Amen.

> Syke and sorwe deeply.　240
> Wepe and moorne sadly.
> Preye and thinke devoutly.
> Love and longe continualy.

Textual notes

10. derkhed and defaute] Derkhed defaute.
44. sche] ye.
87. maistiris] maistir.
90. yef ye hadde seide] yef hadde seide.
93. thei schulde] thei to.
157. ensample] emsample.
203. hemself] himself.

237. farith now weel: now farewell.
238. worschep: honour.
240–3. Syke . . . continualy: versions of these lines of verse appear in seven other ME manuscripts and may provide a clue to the origins of this text. They are found at the end of *The Mirror of Simple Souls* (all three manuscripts of which belonged to the London Charterhouse, which had close links with the Syon Bridgettines) and also in Oxford Bodley MS Laud. Misc. 330, a copy of *The Doctrine of the Heart*, a prose text specifically addressed to nuns.
240. Syke: sigh.
241. moorne: mourn.　*sadly*: solemnly.
243. longe: long, yearn.

13 Dame Eleanor Hull

Dame Eleanor Hull, daughter of Sir John Malet, a retainer of John of Gaunt, was born *c.* 1394 at Enmore in Somersetshire. She married Sir John Hull, who also served Gaunt and his son Henry Bolingbroke (later King Henry IV), *c.* 1410, and bore one son, Edward (d. 1453); she herself was in the service of Queen Joan, Henry IV's second wife. Dame Eleanor was closely associated with the rich and powerful Benedictine Abbey of St Albans. Widowed before 1421, she never remarried but lived for some time at Sopwell Priory, a house of Benedictine nuns dependent on St Albans; her lifelong friend, confessor and legal adviser, Roger Huswyff, was a lawyer who worked for St Albans Abbey and later became a priest. She died in 1460 at Cannington, near Enmore, in the small local Benedictine priory to which she had retired (see Barratt 1989: 88–90).

Dame Eleanor Hull translated, as *The Seven Psalms*, an elaborate thirteenth-century French commentary on the Latin text of the Penitential Psalms, i.e. those psalms (Psalms 6, 31, 37, 50, 101, 129 and 142) which from an early date the Church had singled out as particularly appropriate for those who had confessed their sins and been forgiven. The commentary is similar to many written and read in the monasteries of Western Europe from the twelfth century onwards; it draws heavily on St Augustine (354–430) and the twelfth-century theologian Peter Lombard (see Minnis and Scott 1988: 65–112). It is a surprising choice for a woman to translate, perhaps showing the influence of Huswyff, as in the later Middle Ages such Scriptural exegesis was the exclusive preserve of university-educated male clerics (see Smalley 1983; Evans 1984). Dame Eleanor's translation, therefore, is particularly valuable as it demonstrates the level of theological and linguistic competence that could be achieved by a woman, and shows how women could involve themselves, equally with men, in the dissemination of scholarly texts. She also translated a French collection of prayers and meditations, *Meditations upon the Seven Days of the Week*, which claims to be compiled from the writings of St Augustine, St Anselm (*c.* 1033–1109) and St Bernard (1090–1153). There are many general parallels with their authentic writings, as with texts which passed under their names in the Middle Ages, but the Old French source itself has not been located.

Comment: The first passage is part of the commentary on the first half of Psalm 31:10, 'Many are the scourges of the sinner'. The commentary amplifies in the standard medieval manner by illustrating with an exemplum each of the five types of scourge that God inflicts on the sinful. Such brief stories with a moralising intention are common in medieval Scriptural commentary and sermons, and are used by Chaucer in the *Pardoner's Tale*, *Friar's Tale* and *Summoner's Tale*. The story of the Roman martyr Boniface (d. 280) and his mistress Aglaes, used to illustrate the Fourth Scourge, was probably taken from the *Golden Legend*, compiled by Jacobus de Voragine (*c.* 1230–98: *Legenda Aurea*, pp. 316–18). This typically improbable piece of hagiography, which the translator (as far as one can tell in the absence of the original) has not censored or expurgated, demonstrates the complex interaction between courtly and mystical love in medieval culture. It treats the protagonists sympathetically, accepting both the attractions of a liaison that is presumably adulterous on the lady's part and the indisputably 'wykkyd' nature of this 'werk'. The man involved in the illicit relationship dies and the woman who survives devotes herself to a life of penance, which both expiates her guilt and perpetuates the memory of their sinful love.

The second passage, on the Name of Mary, comes from the opening section of *Meditations upon the Seven Days of the Week*. Devotion to the name of Jesus was very popular in the later Middle Ages and it was logical that a corresponding devotion to the name of Mary should develop, but in fact it was rare at this period; the Feast of the Most Holy Name of Mary was not instituted until the seventeenth century. Most of the material in this unusual meditation is taken directly from the writings of St Bernard.

The third passage comes from the Saturday meditation on the Five Joys of the Virgin, i.e. the Annunciation, Nativity, Resurrection, Ascension and Assumption. It treats the Annunciation, a subject commonly found in collections of prayers and meditations, rather more elaborately than usual. Again its source, apart from the account given in St Luke's Gospel, is St Bernard (for the Latin text, see *PL* 183: 55–87). Its main purpose is to stress the many ways in which the regular operations of the laws of nature were suspended so that Mary could bear the Son of God, by drawing on all the resources of medieval human embryology and angelology. It also provides a complete English translation of the Song of the Blessed Virgin Mary, the Magnificat – a text attributed to a woman, which has thus passed from Greek (if not from an Aramaic original) into Latin, then into Old French, to be finally translated into Middle English by another woman.

The surprising eulogy of Mary's womb in this passage complements the praise of her maternal breasts in the meditation on the name of Mary. The effect is ambiguous: the texts simultaneously exalt what all women have in common (which may well have appealed to a female translator) and stress the qualitative difference between Mary, both Virgin and Mother, and all other women. Their breasts were being eroticised and their wombs, in the writings of medieval gynaecologists, were very far from 'sweet and clean' or 'noble and exalted marriage chambers' where angels served the wedding feast of the Son of God (compare above, p. 32). The figure of Mary thus both encourages and stifles women's aspirations.

Dame Eleanor Hull's prose is competent by the standards of Middle English translation. Most of the time she firmly controls her long sentences, made up of many subordinate clauses and no doubt closely modelled on the 'style clergial' of her French original (cf. Christine de Pisan, above, p. 139; Bornstein 1977). There are no obvious gross mistranslations, her vocabulary is not excessively Gallic and she skilfully works into her own prose the Latin quotations which are an integral part of the commentary. It is the work of an honest craftswoman carrying out a religious and literary task for which she had few models. She may herself have acted as a model for Lady Margaret Beaufort (see below, pp. 301–10), another laywoman from the ruling classes who translated devotional texts from the French.

Manuscript: Cambridge University Library Kk. 1. 6, ff. 2–179ᵛ, transcribed *c.* 1450, contains both translations, which are unpublished. This is the only copy of *The Seven Psalms*; another version of the *Meditations* is found in University of Illinois MS 80.

Further reading (for full details see Bibliography): On Dame Eleanor, see Barratt 1989; on medieval Scriptural exegesis, see Smalley 1983; Evans 1984.

From *The Seven Psalms*

a) *The Legend of Saint Boniface*
(CUL MS Kk. 1. 6, ff. 45–46)

Now ys tyme that ye know whiche ys the schorge that
begynnyth and endyht in the temporal dethe of the body, that
ys the schorge of holy martiers that of ther fre wyl delyveryd
hem to dethe forto enhaunce the feythe of God and forto
amende ther awne defautys; wherfor they be now in ful pesse.   5
Among whiche was Seynt Boneface, that floryschyd in many
gracys, anamly in beaute of youthe, so that his erdly lady, that
was of hye power, had take hym into here love, the whiche
laste longe bytuene hem, nyht and day in grete ryches and
sure delyte, tyl that our Lord God behyld the lady with his   10
pytous and mercyful yen so that sche lefte here wykkyd werke
and porposyd here to do grete amendys.
    So that in a day when Boneface and sche were in ther
secrete chambrys, sche aresonyd hym and seyd, 'O my dere
love' sche seyd, 'Y cry God mercy for the and for me. Thou   15
knowyste wel our wykkyd governance and the meke soffrance
of God, that hathe kepte our bodyes from schame and hathe

2. *endyht*: ends.
3. *martiers*: martyrs.
3–4. *delyveryd hem*: gave themselves up.
4. *enhaunce*: increase.
5. *ful pesse*: consummate peace.
6–7. *floryschyd ... gracys*: was amply endowed with many good qualities.
7. *erdly*: earthly.
8. *hye power*: lofty, exalted status.
9. *laste*: lasted, endured.   *bytuene*: between.   *ryches*: abundance.
10. *sure delyte*: confident pleasure.   *behyld*: beheld, looked upon.
11. *pytous ... yen*: piteous and merciful eyes.
12. *porposyd ... amendys*: made up her mind to make generous restitution.
14. *secrete chambrys*: private apartments.   *aresonyd*: argued with.
15. *cry ... mercy*: ask God's forgiveness.
16. *governance*: behaviour.   *meke soffrance*: humble forbearance.
17. *kepte ... schame*: preserved our bodies from disgrace.

yeve tyme and space to our soulys forto purchase his lordschip
and his love. And therfor Y am avysyd, yf thou wylt assent, of
a thyng that gretly myght helpe ous and proffyt ous; and that   20
ys that we myght make a chyrche in the name of o pressyous
martyr, the whiche we schold ever worchip in erthe, that he
myght pray for ous to that blessyd Lord of hevyn. And Y schal
tel you in what maner thys schal be don and our desyrs
parformyd. Ye schul go into that cyte wher men torment the   25
true belevers of God and ye schul bye a body of one of hem
that most parfytly hathe soffryd for the love of God.'

'Madame,' he seyd, 'your plesance schal be don in this
matier, for Y schal as truly folow your good conseyl as Y have
folowyd the contrarye.' And the mercyful God beheld hym so   30
that with a fyne desyre of martredom he caste a grete syhe and
seyd to the lady pytously, 'Madame, what wold ye sey and this
synful body wold soffre this martredom for God and for the
savacyon of our soulys?'

Whan hys lady herd thys, sche smylyd and seyd, 'Hou   35
myght so yong and so fressche a body that hathe so long
custumyd veyne joye soffre so hasty a torment, wylfully, of
martredom?'

But Boneface anoon tornyd hym, with good wyl and
spessyal grace of our mercyful Lord Jhesu that myghtyly   40
mayntenyd hys good porpos, and wente his weye to the cyte
and cryed with hye voyse, 'I am,' he seyd, 'verrey crystyn,' and
that he rehercyd oft tymys. Then was he takyn and tormentyd

18. *yeve*: given.   *space*: opportunity.
      purchase . . . lordschip: obtain his benevolent patronage.
19. *Y am avysyd*: I have decided.
20. *proffyt ous*: do us good.
21. *o pressyous*: a single precious.
22. *worchip*: honour.
24–5. *desyrs parformyd*: wishes carried out.
26. *bye*: buy.
27. *parfytly*: perfectly.
28. *plesance*: pleasure.
29. *conseyl*: advice.
31. *fyne*: pure, refined.   *caste*: heaved.   *syhe*: sigh.
32. *and*: if.
37. *custumyd*: been accustomed to.   *veyne*: foolish, empty.   *hasty*: harsh.
      wylfully: voluntarily.
39. *tornyd hym*: was converted.
40. *spessyal*: special.
40–1. *myghtyly mayntenyd*: powerfully sustained, upheld.
41. *porpos*: intention.
42. *verrey crystyn*: a true Christian.
43. *rehercyd*: repeated.   *oft tymys*: many times, often.
      takyn: captured, arrested.

with so many dyvers peynys, with so grete pacyens that the
cours of his martredom was endyd so gloryously so that hys   45
body ys worchyppyd in erthe and hys sowle ful hye corownyd
in hevyn. And therfor hyt may be seyd of hym, *Multa flagella
peccatoris etc.*

And the lady also, that with a joyful sorow and with a
devoute prosessyon sche resceyvyd that holy body and   50
worchyppyd hit al here lyfe as hit aperyth, yet in thys same
dayes sche made of hym a true avokat forto acord here to the
grete mercy of God, by whom sche was byfore dyscordyd from
the pesse of Godde and made nyhe to hys wretthe. But for
sche hopyd in the pytous mercy of God, therfor he beclyppyd   55
here with his mercy and his grace and schorgyd the good
Boneface with the hasty schorgys of mercy, the whiche passyd
from hym by his gloryous dethe-soffryng.

From *Meditations Upon the Seven Days of the Week*

b) *Meditation on the Name of Mary*
(ff. 152–153)

This blessed name Marye is as mych as to sey as 'the starre of
the see' and heryth wherfor. The shipmen that costyn the see   60
ben aqueyntyd with a sterre that sitte nye the hynes of hevyn,

44. *dyvers peynys*: varied tortures.
45. *cours*: course, process.
46. *worchyppyd*: honoured, reverenced.   *corownyd*: crowned.
47–8. *Multa* . . . peccatoris: 'Many are the scourges of the sinner', Psalm
31:10 again.
50. *prosessyon*: procession.   *resceyvyd*: received.
51. *as hit aperyth*: as it seems.
51–2. *in . . . dayes*: during the same time.
52. *avokat*: advocate, spokesperson.   *acord here*: reconcile her.
53. *dyscordyd*: set at odds, alienated.
54. *pesse*: peace.   *made nyhe*: brought near.   *wretthe*: anger.
54–6. *But . . . grace*: compare Psalm 31: 10 (see above).
55. *beclyppyd*: embraced, encompassed.
57–8. *passyd from*: left.
58. *dethe-soffryng*: suffering of death.
59. *as mych as to sey*: as much as to say, means.
59–60. *starre of the see*: L. *stella maris*, a very ancient title under which the
Virgin was invoked.
60. *heryth wherfor*: hear why.   *shipmen*: sailors.   *costyn*: sail.
61. *sitte . . . hevyn*: is fixed near the height or zenith of the heavens.

after which sterre thei gyden alle her course. For by this
sterre, whan thei see hym thei knowin whether thei ben to
mych in the right syde or to mych in the left syde, or wheder
thei go to moche forward or bakward, or whether thei go wele   65
or evylle. And when thei lese this sterre by cloude or by
tempest, than wote thei note where thei gon, but ben alle
disawaried.

Alle this world is a grete see, fulle of cloudys and of
tempestys. Ther-in is no stabilnes nor no suerte, no more   70
than in the wild see. For now we be hole, now syke, now glad,
now sory, or angry, or wel plesyd, upon this see that is so fulle
of perillys. Almyghty God hath purveyd for us a bryght sterre,
feyre and clere, syttyng fulle ny to hym, that is Our Lady
Seynt Mary, by whos ensample we shold gyde alle the course   75
of our lyf, and by the remembrauns of her we may eschewe
alle perillys of synne, and by whos helpe we mowe drawe to
the porte of paradyse.

O what that ever ye be, man or woman, in religion or out of
religion, that fele yourself to perisshe in this tempestous see,   80
turne never your ye awey from this bright sterre, and yf ther

62. *after*: according.   *gyden*: steer.   *her*: their.
62–3. *hym*: i.e. the star.   *knowin*: know.
63. *ben . . . syde*: are too far to starboard.
64. *wheder*: whether, if.
65. *to moche*: too far.
65–6. *go*(2) . . . *evylle*: are navigating well or badly.
66. *lese*: lose.
67. *than*: then.   *wote thei note*: they do not know.
67–8. *alle disawaried*: completely lost.
69–70. *Alle . . . tempestys*: a traditional allegorisation of the sea (compare
Hamlet's 'sea of troubles').
70. *stabilnes*: stability.   *suerte*: security, safety.
71. *hole*: healthy.   *syke*: sick.
72. *sory*: sad.   *wel plesyd*: happy.
73. *purveyd*: provided.
74. *clere*: clear, radiant.   *fulle ny*: very close.
75. *ensample*: example.   *shold*: should.
76. *remembrauns*: memory, mindfulness.   *eschewe*: avoid, shun.
77. *perillys*: perils, dangers.   *mowe*: are able to.   *drawe to*: arrive at.
78. *porte*: port, haven.
79–94. *O . . . Marye*: this whole paragraph is a free translation of a famous
passage from St Bernard's Second Homily on the Annunciation (*Missus est
angelus Gabriel*): for the Latin text see *PL* 183: 70C–D.
79–80. *in . . . religion*: i.e. monk, nun or secular.
80. *fele . . . perisshe*: think you are about to perish.   *tempestous*: stormy.
81. *ye*: eye.   *yf*: if.

aryse ayens yow grete wynd of temptacion, yf ye be chasyd
upon the rokkys of tribulacion, behold the starre and calle
'Mary'. Yf ye be temptyd, that ye fele, to gretely of yourself,
behold the starre and calle 'Marye'. Yf ye be travaylyd with   85
covytyse, with envye or detraccion, behold the starre and calle
'Marye'. Yf anger or slouth assayle the shippe of your corage,
behold the starre and calle 'Mary'. Yf ye be sorefulle or hevy,
behold the starre and calle 'Marye'. Yf ye be dredefulle or
disawarye, behold the starre and calle 'Mary'. Yf ye be morn   90
or pensif, behold the starre and calle 'Marye'. Yf ye be
somtyme to overmyry and joyfulle, behold the starre and calle
'Mary'. Yf ye be oft grevyd with your flesshe, behold the starre
and calle 'Marye'.

This shold be do if eny wylle take us to synne, byfore that   95
we do the synne. But peraventure ye have synned and the
temptacion hathe overcome yow; now peraventure ye be falle,
in dede or in wille or in bothe. What shulle ye then do? Yit be
ye not without hope, for I shalle sey you more yit. Yf ye be
falle in grete crymes and that ye fynd your conciens fulle of   100
ordure and of fylth so that ye may not onethis soffre yourself
for the grete hidoure that ye have of the synne that ye have
don, than anone with alle your hert callyth upon the blessyd

---

82. *chasyd*: driven.
83. *rokkys*: rocks.
84. *that ... yourself*: as you think, too much (to resist) from your (own resources).
85. *travaylyd*: tormented.
86. *covytyse*: covetousness, avarice.   *detraccion*: slander.
87. *slouth*: sloth, laziness.   *assayle*: assault.   *corage*: heart, spirit.
88. *hevy*: gloomy.
89. *dredefulle*: fearful, anxious.
90. *disawarye*: lost.   *morn*: mourning, sorrowful.
91. *pensif*: thoughtful, melancholy.
92. *to overmyry*: too excessively cheerful.
93. *grevyd with*: pained by.
95. *eny wylle*: any desire.   *take*: seize.
96. *peraventure*: perhaps.
97. *ye be falle*: you have fallen.
98. *dede*: deed.   *Yit*: yet, still.
99. *sey*: tell.
100. *conciens*: conscience.
101. *ordure*: excrement, defilement.   *fylth*: filth.
     ye ... soffre: you can scarcely bear, put up with.
102. *hidoure*: disgust, revulsion.
103. *anone*: at once, promptly.

name Marye, with here blessyd surname that she put herself
to.   105
   Now here what it is: we rede that she aperyd in a tyme to
one of here servauntys where that he was in the poynt of
dethe and she askyd hym yf he knewe here and he answerd,
dredefully tremblyng, and seyd, 'Nay, lady, I knowe yowe not.'
Than she seyde to hym so swetely and so pytously as she wele   110
couthe, 'Yet am I Mary, the Moder of Mercy.' Fulle swete is
that name, but moch swetter is that surname. O, grete vertu is
in yow, glorious lady Seynt Marye. But none sitte so welle for
the herte of the synfulle caytyf as your mercy, whan it is
named. We preysyn your humylyte, your vergynyte, your hynes   115
and your dignyte, and wele we aught to do it for reson is that
we do it. But ferre above savoryth ous most your mercy, this
record we most tenderly and therof we calle most oft and
therto we fle most surely, so as the sobyng child that of alle

104. *here*: her.   *surname*: additional title.
104–5. *that . . . to*: which she gave herself.
106. *here*: hear, listen to.
      rede: read. The story comes from the life of Odo by John of Cluny,
PL 133: 72.
106. *aperyd*: appeared.
107. *where that*: when.   *in*: at.
108. *knewe*: i.e. recognised.
109. *dredefully*: fearfully.
110. *pytously*: pityingly.
110–11. *as . . . couthe*: as she knew so well how to do.
111. *the Moder of Mercy*: the twelfth century saw a new stress on Mary's
spiritual motherhood. Although St Bernard himself objected to this trend,
other Cistercians encouraged it; for instance, the twelfth-century Englishman Aelred of Rievaulx, whose works were often confused with those of
Bernard, writes movingly in one of his sermons of Mary as 'our Mother',
who feeds us with her spiritual milk (for the Latin, see *PL* 195: 323). In the
fifteenth century a new iconographic image appears to express this idea, the
so-called 'Mantle Virgin', which depicts the Virgin sheltering all men and
women beneath her cloak.
112. *moch swetter*: much sweeter.
112–19. *O . . . most surely*: this passage derives from St Bernard's sermon
on the Octave of the Assumption (for the Latin, see *PL* 183: 428D–429A)
and is interesting for its exaltation of Mary's mercy above her virginity.
113. *sitte so welle*: is so fitting.
114. *caytyf*: wretch.
115. *preysyn*: praise.   *hynes*: highness, elevation.
116. *aught*: ought.   *reson is*: it is reasonable.
117. *ferre*: far.   *savoryth ous*: smells sweetly to us.
118. *record*: remember.   *therof*: on that.
119. *fle*: flee.   *surely*: confidently.   *so as*: just like.
      sobyng: sobbing, crying.

the membres of his moder he lovyth none so moch as her   120
bryst, for ther he fyndyth his most comfort.

Yf he have hongyr or threst, or if he be angred or hurt, to
the brest is alle his refute. This do we, dere Lady, your pore
childryn, your beggers, in alle our nedes. We rennyn to the
brest of your mercy. And wherfor? For ther we fynd most our   125
socour and comfort. Ther is not on of us, lytelle nere grete,
old nere yong, yf he bethenke wele in hymself, but that he
hath fulle oft found comfort in the mercy of our swete Lady,
blessyd Seynt Marye. Ther is non that faylyth that wille, with
all here hertys wille, require here. This may we preve in   130
ourself, how rightfully she is called 'Maria' and how rightfully
she is called 'Moder of Mercy'.

c) *The Conception of Christ* (ff. 167ᵛ–168ᵛ)

Than answeryd that mekest mayde, assentyng fully to the
angelle, and seyde, 'Lo me here, the servaunt of God. Be it to
me after your saying.' And than anone conceyvyd she Goddys   135
sone in flesshe and blode in here vergynes wombe, a quykke

120. *membres*: members, limbs.
121. *bryst*: breast.   *most*: greatest.
122. *hongyr*: hunger.   *threst*: thirst.
123. *refute*: refuge, haven.
124. *beggers*: poor dependants.   *nedes*: needs, necessities.   *rennyn*: run.
126. *socour*: succour, aid.   *on*: one.   *nere*: nor.
127. *yf . . . hymself*: if he searches his soul carefully.
129. *faylyth*: fails.   *wille*: is willing.
129–30. *with . . . wille*: with all the will, intention, of their hearts.
130. *require here*: ask her (for help).   *preve*: test.
131. *rightfully*: rightly.
135–44. *And . . . persone*: it was generally believed in the Middle Ages that human life did not begin at the moment of conception. Philosophers and theologians distinguished a first stage of forty days, during which the vital organs developed and the limbs were formed; only after six weeks was the embryo animated, endowed with a soul ('ensouled'), and made capable of movement ('quickened'). The point being made in this passage is that in the special case of Christ these laws of nature were suspended and that at the very moment of conception the embryo within the Virgin's womb was perfectly formed (though tiny) and ensouled. See Needham 1959: 75–6; Hewson 1975: 167–9.
135. *anone*: at once.
136. *quykke*: quickened.

childe, God and manne. For also sone as she assentyd to the
angelle, all the Holye Trynyte, Fader and Sone and Holy
Goste, made and formyd of noght the soule of Jhesu Cryste
and in the wombe of that purist vyrgyne clothyd it with here   140
most puryst flesshe and bloode with alle the parfyt membrys
parfytly of his body. At one tyme was that blessyd soule made
and that blessyd body formyd and everyche of hem, bothe
God and man, joynyd in o persone, wherfor ther was never so
lytylle a childe quykke. For other childryn that bene   145
conceyvyd be not anone formyd perfytly in body, nere quykke
in soule, but after grete while and many wokys encresyth tylle
it be performyd. And than is the soule made and the body
with that soule quyknyd. But so was it not of that yong childe
so swete, for alle at o tyme he was conceyvyd and performyd   150
in body and made yn soule and quyknyd, and in everyche of
hem perfyte God and perfyt man in o persone.

Ha, right swete lady, maydyn and moder of the Sone of
God, holy Mary, who may ymagyn or think hou ye were then
fulfyllyd of joye and more than fulfilled with joy, whan ye bare   155
in your right swete and clene wombe the Sone of Allmyghty
God with the Fader and the Holy Gost, he that is alle the joy
of angelys and of seyntys and seyntys! Who may thynke the joy
and the feste that was at that hevynly and erthely maryage,
where the Sone of God, kyng of hevyn and of erthe and of alle   160

137. *also sone*: as soon.
139. *formyd of noght*: created out of nothing.
141. *parfyt membrys*: perfectly formed limbs.
143. *formyd*: (fully) formed.
    everyche of hem: each of them (i.e. the soul and the fully formed body).
144. *in o persone*: in a single being, person.   *wherfor*: for which reason.
145. *lytylle*: little, tiny.
146–7. *quykke in soule*: quickened with a soul.
147. *after grete while*: after a long time.
    many . . . encresyth: it grows for many weeks.
    tylle . . . performyd: until it is fully formed.
150. *alle . . . tyme*: completely at a single moment.
151–2. *in*(2) . . . *hem*: in both of them (i.e. body and soul).
153. *Ha*: Ah.
154. *ymagyn*: imagine, envisage.
155. *fulfyllyd of*: filled with.   *bare*: bore, carried.
156. *clene*: pure.
158. *seyntys and seyntys*: this odd phrase probably results from a literal
translation of the F., which may have read *seints et seintes*, 'male and female
saints'.
159. *feste*: feast.
160–1. *alle . . . theryn*: all that is contained there.

the contentys theryn, emperour of angelys, humbled hymselfe
to that noble and gloryous lady as forto wedde in her our
kynde, the whiche he toke to hym in that chambre that was
moste clene and pure and beste arayed with chastyte and
vergynyte and with alle vertuys. For it was most syttyng and   165
most reson that that chambre that sholde receyve so hye and
so worthy a kyng as parfyt God and Goddys sone, lorde and
maker of alle thyng, that it sholde be clene and feyre and fulle
of beaute. For not only he come not into that noble and holy
chambre forto dwelle o day, ner o weke, nere o monyth, but   170
forto holde the hye feste of that maryage nine monthis with
grete solempnyte.

What hert myght thynk the joy that there was where alle the
Trynyte helde the fest of this weddyng bytwene the Sone of
God and of Holy Chirche, at which hye and noble fest alle the   175
angelles of hevyn servydyn by ordor after the nine ordyrs? For
ye shulle undyrstond that of every ordor of angelys of hevyn
ther were in grete nombre byfore the Lorde, the sone of God,
forto make grete joy of this weddyng bytwene hym and Holy

162–3. as . . . kynde: to be united in her with our humanity.
163. toke to hym: adopted.

chambre: chamber, room, i.e. the Virgin's womb. A sermon attributed
to St Augustine plays with the idea of the Virgin's womb as the wedding
chamber within which Christ is betrothed to humanity (for the Latin, see
PL 39: 1986C); here the private nuptial bedroom where a marriage is
consummated has become the great hall where the wedding feast is publicly
held.
164. beste arayed: best adorned, decked out.
165. vertuys: virtues.   *syttyng*: suitable, fitting.
166. reson: reasonable.
169–70. For . . . monyth: i.e. not only did he come there to stay for more
than a single day, week or month.
171. holde: keep, celebrate.   *nine monthis*: for nine months.
174–5. this . . . Chirche: as the Church is traditionally defined as the
mystical Body of Christ, the union of Christ and his physical body, which
takes place when he is conceived as a human child in the Virgin's womb,
symbolises the marriage or union between Christ and his Church.
176. servydyn: served.   *by ordor*: according to their order.

after . . . ordyrs: a sixth-century treatise, the *Celestial Hierarchies* of the
pseudo-Dionysius, was the source of the medieval tradition that there were
nine orders, or ranks, of angels: seraphim, cherubim, thrones, dominions,
powers, virtues, principalities, archangels and angels. Normally, only the
two lowest orders had dealings with human beings.
177. of(1): from, out of.
178. in grete nombre: in large numbers.

Chirche, and namely sythe that therby shold be reformyd and   180
restoryd the falle of angelys. Than be alle thes resons so grete
and merveylous joy was in the herte of that most blessyd
vergyne and moder of God that it was merveyle that here
herte myght susteyne it and that it had not brostyn for joy.
Wherefor she not withholde here but that she shewyd the joy   185
of herte in that swete song of Magnificat, that never in alle
here lyfe at o tyme she spak nere sang so myche, as ferre as
we may fele by Holy Writte.

And this song is thus moche to sey in Englysshe, that whan
ye here it, ye may have the more devocyon in Our Lady: 'Mi   190
soule,' seythe that blessyd Vergyne, 'magnyfyeth our Lorde
and my sperit joyeth in God my savyour, for that he hath
beholde the humylite of his servaunt. Alle generacyons shalle
sey that I am blessyd, for he that is alle myghty hathe done to
me grete thingys, and holy is his name. And his mercy   195
strecchyth from generacyon in generacion dredyng hym. He

180. namely sythe: especially since.
   therby: by that means (i.e. the Incarnation).
   reformyd: formed anew.
181. falle: (the consequences of) the Fall of the Angels; it was commonly
believed that God created human beings to fill up in heaven the gaps left by
the defection of Satan and his followers, the fallen angels.
181. be: because of.
183. it was merveyle: it was a miracle.
184. susteyne: sustain, bear.   *brostyn*: burst.
185. not . . . shewyd: did not restrain herself from showing.
186. that(1) *. . . Magnificat*: in the Gospel narrative Mary composed the
Magnificat ('My soul doth magnify the Lord') when she visited her cousin
Elizabeth; by ignoring this and telescoping events this text creates a
fascinating juxtaposition of physical and poetic fecundity.
186–8. that(2) *. . . Writte*: it is certainly true that Luke 1:46–55 is the
longest speech the Virgin makes in the Gospels. The potentiality of the
Virgin as a model for women poets and prophets seems not to have been
exploited in the Middle Ages, though she sometimes revealed poems to
visionaries (St Godric's lyrics, preserved in Early Middle English, were
dictated to him in visions by the Virgin).
189. is . . . sey: is as follows.
190. here: hear. The Magnificat was regularly sung as the canticle at
Vespers, the evening service attended every day by monks and nuns, and by
many devout lay people such as Margery Kempe.
191. magnyfyeth: magnifies, extols.
192. sperit: spirit.   *joyeth*: rejoices.
193. beholde: beheld, looked upon.   *humylite*: lowliness.
   generacyons: generations.
196. dredyng: that fear.

hathe made myghty workis with his arme and hathe dispysyd
the prowde with the thought of his herte. He hathe put doun
the proude from the segis and lyfte up the humble of hertys.
He hathe fulfyllyd the hongry with godys and lefte the riche   200
voyde and veyne. He hathe receyvyd Israel his childe and
remembryd hym of his mercy, as he hathe spokyn in
prophesye to our fadrys, Abraham and his sede that comyn
after hym in worldes of worldes.'

Textual notes

40. *myghtyly*] myghtly.
82. *ayens yow*] ayens.
101. *fylth*] feyth.   *onethis*] onthis.
129. *wille*] wille that.
130. *all here hertys*] all hertys.
138. *Holye*] hole.
144. *joynyd*] and joynyd.
195. *his name*] name.
196. *generacion . . . generacyon*] gernacion.

197. *myghty workis*: great works.   *dispysyd*: scorned.
198. *with . . . herte*: 'in the conceit of their heart' in the Douai Rheims
translation.
198. *put doun*: turned out.
199. *segis*: seats, thrones.   *lyfte up*: lifted up, exalted.
200. *godys*: good things.
201. *voyde and veyne*: empty and hollow.
    receyvyd: received, accepted.
202. *remembryd hym*: remembered, been mindful of.
203. *sede*: seed, descendants.
204. *in . . . worldes*: for ever and ever (a literal translation of the Latin
liturgical formula *in saecula saeculorum*).

14 Juliana Berners

The closing words of *The Book of St Albans*, a compendium of three texts on hunting, hawking and heraldry printed in 1486, attribute one, *The Boke of Hunting*, to 'Dam Julyans Barnes'. There has been much discussion of the identity of this woman, now conventionally known as Dame Juliana Berners. According to the antiquary John Bale, writing in 1549, she had been alive in 1460, while William Burton (1575–1645), in a note that he wrote before 1612 in his copy of *The Book of St Albans*, now in the Cambridge University Library, identified her more precisely as 'the Lady Julian Berners, daughter of Sir James Berners, of Berners-Roding, in Essex, Knight, and Sister to Richard Lord Berners . . . Lady Prioresse of Sopwell Nunnery neere St Albons'.

Further independent corroboration of Dame Juliana's existence is provided by Chauncy in his *History of Hertfordshire* (1700). Therefore, even though the fitful records of Sopwell Priory (see above, p. 219) do not record any prioress of that name, the identification is not totally without foundation. The priory was associated with at least one literary women; the translator Dame Eleanor Hull lived there from time to time during the 1420s. It is ironic that she, a laywoman, might have been working on her translations of religious texts not long before one of the nuns, if not the prioress herself, started to versify this practical little poem on a purely secular subject.

A prioress could very well have composed *The Book of Hunting*. It is not an original composition but rather a versification of two prose treatises: William Twiti's *L'Art de Venerie* (c. 1327; see *William Twiti: The Art of Hunting*, pp. 36–8), originally written in Anglo-Norman, of which two Middle English prose translations survive; and Gaston de Foix's *Livre de Chasse*, which Edward Duke of York, younger son of Edward III, translated as *The Master of Game* at the very beginning of the fifteenth century. The poem did not therefore require any personal knowledge of, or even interest in, hunting. It might appropriately be compiled by someone engaged in the elementary education of upper-class children, as the subjects covered include what one might now call natural history, domestic science, and etiquette as well as the sport itself. Nor did the fifteenth-century printer of *The Book of St Albans* find it inherently implausible that a woman should have written this poem; he no doubt knew that medieval women took part in hunts, particularly in hare coursing and rabbiting. It has recently been argued, however, that Dame Juliana Berners should not be connected with *The Book of Hunting* at all, but was rather the compiler of the miscellaneous material, of the sort often preserved in commonplace books, found at the ends of both *The Book of Hawking* and *The Book of Hunting* (see Hands 1975).

Comment: It is interesting that a woman should have composed, or at least been credited with composing, a textbook on such a practical subject. This suggests that medieval expectations of the breadth of a woman's knowledge and areas of expertise were perhaps higher than we today allow. The text itself again shows the medieval woman writer as a transmitter of traditional wisdom, a compiler and adapter of the ideas of others, usually men.

The first extract comes from the part of the poem which draws on Twiti's *Art of Hunting*. Significantly it takes the form of an instructive dialogue between a mother and son, in which the mother mediates the traditional wisdom ascribed to the great hunter Sir Tristram. The maternal role here is clearly analogous to, and provides a validation for, the role of the (possibly female) compiler. This passage, like much of the poem, is concerned with classification and nomenclature, the sort of knowledge young gentry needed in order to be socially acceptable. It goes on to demonstrate the medieval fascination with 'unnatural natural history' in its discussion of the androgynous hare and his/her idiosyncrasies, while in the last section we are reminded of the practical function of hunting in which women had a vested interest: to keep the larder stocked.

The second extract comes from that part of the poem which draws on *The Master of Game*; it again takes the form of a dialogue, this time between master and man. The passage reverts to the subject of the hare, particularly its habits of excretion, which are conscientiously if somewhat improbably recorded. If the translator was indeed a woman, this passage indicates that medieval women were not expected to be squeamish about natural functions (a conclusion that could also be drawn from the Trotula texts; see above, pp. 29–39). It should also remind us that in the Middle Ages, still a predominantly oral culture, verse was often used for purely utilitarian and educational purposes, as it was easier to remember than prose.

Copy text: *The Book of St Albans*, published by the so-called 'Schoolmaster of St Albans' in 1486 (STC 3308); facsimile edition with Introduction by William Blades (1901), and with Introduction and Notes by Rachel Hands (1975). *The Book of Hunting* itself (IMEV 4064), without the attribution to Juliana Berners, is also found in Oxford Bodley MS Rawlinson poet. 143, ff. 1–11, and in Lambeth Palace MS 491B, ff. 287–294ᵛ (see Jacob 1944; Hands 1967).

Further reading (for full details see Bibliography): On the textual tradition of the poem, see Binns 1950; Hands 1967; Jacob 1944.

From *The Book of Hunting*

a) *Hunting Terminology*
(sigs ei^r–v)

Bestys of venery

Wheresoevere ye fare by fryth or by fell,
My dere chylde, take hede how Tristram dooth you tell.
How many maner beestys of venery ther were,
Lystyn to yowre dame and she shall yow lere.   5
Fowre maner beestys of venery there are:
The first of theym is the hert; the secunde is the hare;
The boore is oon of tho,
The wolff, and not oon moo.

Bestys of the chace   10

And where that ye cum in playne or in place,
I shall yow tell which be beestys of enchace.
Oon of theym is the bucke, another is the doo,
The fox and the martron and the wilde roo.
And ye shall, my dere chylde, other bestys all,   15
Where-so ye hem fynde, 'rascall' ye shall hem call,
In fryth or in fell
Or in forest, I yow tell.

Note here the aage of an hert

1. venery: hunting.
2. Wheresoevere . . . fell: wherever you go, over forest or hill.
3. Tristram: Sir Tristram, in Arthurian legend the nephew of King Mark and lover of Isolde, was also noted for his skill as a hunter and was regarded as the source of traditional wisdom on the subject.
4. maner . . . venery: kinds of game animals, i.e beasts hunted by coursing.
5. Lystyn: listen.   *dame*: i.e. mother.   *lere*: teach.
7. theym: them.   *hert*: hart.
8. boore: boar.   *oon of tho*: one of those.
9. moo: more.
11. where . . . cum: wherever you go.
12. beestys of enchace: i.e. animals hunted with dogs.
13. doo: doe.
14. martron: marten, polecat.   *roo*: roe-deer.
16. rascall: rascal, i.e. animals not hunted as game.
19. aage: age.

And forto speke of the hert, iff ye will it lere,   20
Ye shall hym a 'calfe' call at the fyrst yere.
The secunde yere a 'broket' so shall ye hym call.
The therde yere a 'spayad', lerneth thus all.
The fowrith yere a 'stagge' call hym by any way.
The fithe yere a 'grete stagge' youre dame bide yow say.   25
The sixte yere call ye hym an 'hert'.
Doth so, my childe, wylis ye been in quart.

b) *The Hare*
(sigs eiij^{r-v})

Now forto speke of the hare, my sonnys, secureli,
That beest kyng shall be calde of all venery.
For all the fayre spekyng and blawyng, leif sere,   30
Commyth of sechyng and fyndyng of the hare.
For, my leif chylder, I take it on honde,
He is the mervellest beest that is in ony londe.
For he fymaes and crotis and roungeth evermoore
And beerith talow and gris, and above-teeth hath be-foore. 35
And otherwhile he is male, and so ye shall hym fynde,
And otherwhile female and kyndelis by kynde.
And when he is female and kyndelis hym within,
In three degrees he hem berith or he with hem twyn:

22. broket: young male deer with small horns.
23. spayad: male deer in its third year.
24. fowrith: fourth.
27. wylis ... quart: while you are in good health.
28. secureli: certainly, truly.
29. That ... venery: that animal should be called the king of all game
animals.
30. fayre spekyng: beautiful terminology (of the hunt).
    blawyng: blowing (of the hunting horns).   *leif sere*: dear sir.
31. sechyng: tracking.
32. chylder: children.   *take ... honde*: undertake, guarantee.
33. mervellest: most wonderful.
34. fymaes: casts droppings.   *crotis*: voids excrement in pellets.
    roungeth: chews the cud.
35. beerith ... gris: has suet (peculiar to ruminating animals) and fat.
    above-teeth: upper teeth.
36. otherwhile: sometimes.
37. kyndelis by kynde: gives birth by course of nature.
38. kyndelis ... within: (there are) young inside him.
39. degrees: stages.
    or ... twyn: before s/he parts with them (by giving birth).

Too rough and too smoth, who will hem se,   40
And too knottis also that kyndelis will be
When he is female
So tell I my tale.

The rewarde for howndys

When yowre houndes by strencith hath done her to dede,   45
The hunter shall rewarde hem then with the hede,
With the shulderis and the sides and with the bowellis all
And all thyngis within the wombe save onli the gall;
The paunche also,
Yeve hem noon of thoo.   50
Wich rewarde when oon the erth it is dalt
With all goode hunteris the 'halow' it is calt.
Then the loynes of the hare loke ye not forgete,
Bot bryng hem to the kechyn for the lordis meete.
And of this ilke hare   55
Speke we no mare.

40–1. Too ... be: i.e. the hare bears two offspring at a time, and they go
through three stages of development – rough, smooth and unformed lumps
of flesh.
41–2. knottis ... female: lumps of flesh that will become offspring when the
hare is in his/her female phase.
44. howndys: hounds.
45. strencith: force.   *done ... dede*: killed her.
47. sides: flanks.
48. wombe: stomach, abdomen.
49. paunche: internal organs, viscera.
50. Yeve ... thoo: don't give them any of that.
51. oon: on.   *dalt*: shared out.
52. halow: hallow, i.e. the parts of a hare given to the hounds for a reward.
    calt: called.
53. loynes: loins.   *loke*: be careful.
54. kechyn: kitchen.   *meete*: food.
55. ilke: same.
56. mare: more.

c) *More about the Hare*
(sig. fij^r)

Why the hare fumays and croteis

'Yit, mayster, wolde I wete whi that men sayn
That the haare fumays and croteys booth playn,
And all other maner beestys that huntid be   60
Femyon or fenon, as we wele hit se.'
'That shall I weell tell the,' quod the mayster then,
'Forwhy that he femays and crotis weell I ken.
He femaith for he beryth talow, this is no lees,
And he croteis, men sayn, for he beerith grees   65
And roukis on his houghis when he lettis it go
And beestys of sich kynde fynde we no moo.'
'How mony beestis femayen, mayster, fayn I wolde lere,
And how many fenon, that ware goode to here.'
'All this to tell,' quod the mayster, 'I holde hit bot light: 70
All beestis that beere talow and stonde upright
Femayen when thay do, so say as I the kenne,
And all oder fenon that rowken downe thenne.'

Textual notes

46. *hem*] hym.
70. *light*] lihgt.

58. *Yit*: yet.   *wolde I wete*: I would like to know.
59. *fumays*: void dung while standing upright.
61. *Femyon or fenon*: void their excrement (either) upright or squatting.
62. *quod*: said.
63. *Forwhy*: why.   *ken*: know.
64. *beryth*: carries (within himself).   *talow*: suet (see above, note to l. 35).
    lees: lie.
65. *grees*: fat, adipose tissue.
66. *roukis*: squats.
    houghis: hocks (the joint between the true knee and the fetlock).
    it: i.e. the excrement.
67. *beestys . . . kynde*: animals of such a nature.
68. *fayn*: gladly.
72. *kenne*: tell.
73. *oder*: other.   *rowken*: squat.

15 Some Paston Letters

The Paston Letters and Papers, which date from 1425 to the early sixteenth century, are an extensive collection of letters to and from male and female members of the Paston family, together with associated documents such as wills. The first member of this family of Norfolk gentry whose letters are preserved was William Paston I (1378–1444), a successful lawyer who increased the originally modest family landholdings by purchase. He also married an heiress, Agnes Berry (*c.* 1400–79), who survived her husband to dominate the family for many years. She bore at least five children, the eldest of whom, John Paston I (1421–66), studied at Cambridge and at the Inner Temple (for law students) and married another heiress, Margaret Mautby (*c.* 1420–84). She brought lands in Norfolk and Suffolk to the marriage and bore seven children: John II (1442–79), John III (1444–1504), Edmond (*c.* 1450–before 1504), Margery (*c.* 1448–*c.* 1479), Anne (*c.* 1455–94/5), Walter (*c.* 1457–79) and William (1459–1504).

Margaret Paston also introduced her husband to her relative Sir John Fastolf, a childless widower and immensely wealthy veteran of the Hundred Years' War. John Paston became Fastolf's confidant, trustee of some of his estates, and one of the executors of his will. But Paston also claimed that a few days before Fastolf's death in 1459 he had made a 'nuncupative', i.e. oral, will. This new will made Paston solely responsible for carrying out Fastolf's cherished plan of founding a college of priests and poor men at Caister, one of Fastolf's principal manors. (This college had no educational purpose; its only function was to pray for the souls of Fastolf and his family.) In order to endow the college, Fastolf left John Paston valuable lands in Norfolk, including the Manor of Caister itself, for which Paston was supposed to make a cash payment of four thousand marks.

John Paston immediately took possession of the Norfolk manors and their revenues but not surprisingly the other executors of the original will, including William Waynflete, Bishop of Winchester, disputed the validity of the nuncupative will. The dispute dragged on for many years and overshadowed the lives of the whole family; John Paston I died in 1466 in his mid forties, partly as a result of the stress (he was imprisoned several times), but his sons continued to hold the disputed manors. In 1469, which was a bad year altogether for the family, the Duke of Norfolk purchased the Manor of Caister from one of the other executors, besieged it, and finally took it by force, killing two family retainers in the process. In 1470 John Paston II made a compromise agreement with Waynflete: Paston gave up all the Fastolf inheritance except for Caister and two other Norfolk manors; no more was to be said of the four thousand marks still owed the estate; and Waynflete took over responsibility for founding the college. He provided for this obligation in his own new foundation of Magdalen College, Oxford.

Comment: The first group of letters concerns the marriages or proposed marriages of the children of Margaret and John Paston I and vividly illustrates the emotional and financial complications of matrimony in the Middle Ages. Both Johns put off marrying until they were in their thirties (although John III had written to his elder brother in 1470, 'I pray get us a wyf somwhere'); John Paston II died unmarried in 1479 but fortunately by then his brother John III was married to Margery Brews. This was a love match encouraged by both mothers which nearly came to grief over money, because of the close-fistedness of Margery's father or the uncooperativeness of John's elder brother, depending on one's point of view. Of the sisters, Margery made a most unsuitable alliance with Richard Calle, the Pastons' bailiff, in defiance of her family, friends and the local bishop, while Anne was married off to William Yelverton, the son of another of Fastolf's executors. The second set of letters comes from those written to the Pastons by a wide cross-section of women from outside the family itself. All the writers use writing unself-consciously for a variety of practical purposes in a way that indicates a thoroughly literate mentality. They are familiar with the idea that written records are valuable, that writing can have practical effects, and that it is a substitute for 'presence' (the Abbess of Denny, a strictly enclosed nun, is particularly revealing on this).

None of the women's letters, except for the Duchess of Suffolk's, is indisputably written in their own hand. There is, however, good reason to believe that Agnes Paston, the mother of John Paston I, wrote one of her surviving letters, and part of another for her husband, in a clear and expert hand. Elizabeth Clere may well have written all her own letters, and other women sign their own names or add brief notes. But we need not conclude that the women were technically illiterate; they may just have been too busy or, in the case of the Abbess of Denny, too grand to write their own letters and preferred to use scribes just as people today might use the services of a typist. The men, too, who wrote out some of their letters themselves, more often used scribes.

Like modern letters, medieval letters relied heavily on conventional phraseology of the 'How are you? I hope you are well' kind. Some of these formulae are surprisingly close to their modern equivalents, but others are hard to render literally. Even more so than elsewhere in this anthology, some of the glosses to these extracts attempt to convey the flavour and the gist of what must often have been very informal, colloquial Middle English, rather than to offer close, accurate translations.

Manuscripts: All the texts are edited from the original letters, which have been bound together to make up a number of manuscript compilations.

Further reading (for full details see Bibliography): For introductions to the Pastons, see Bennett 1968 (for long the standard scholarly monograph); Barber 1981 (written in a popular style). For recent, more specialised discussions of gender-related issues in the letters, see Haskell 1973; Maddern 1988.

Margaret Paston's Children and their Marriages

a) From Cecily Daune to John Paston II
(BL MS Add. 34889, f. 166)*

[between 1463 and 1468]†

To the right worshipfull sir and, with my faithful hert
and service full entyerly beloved gode maistir,
Sir John Paston

Right worshipfull sir, and with my faithfull herte and service
full entyerly beloved gode maistir, in my most humble wyse I   5
recommaund me unto your goode maistership. Pleace it the
same to wite that I thenke right longe to I have verrey knolege
of your welfare, the which undirstonde wil be to me right
grete comfort. And that causeth me to write unto you as nowe,
and also to late you wite that I herde reperte ye shulde be   10
wedded unto a doughtir of the Duchez of Somirset, which

---

* Davis, II, 389–90 (see Bibliography, Primary Texts). Nothing is known
of Cecily Daune, the author of this enigmatic letter, other than what can be
deduced from the letter itself. She is hard to place socially; apparently a
low-status dependant, given her request for 'livery', she none the less signs
her letter herself and her formal, respectful style, salted with well-chosen
proverbial wisdom, suggests a woman of some education.
† [*between 1463 and 1468*]: unless otherwise stated, Davis's datings of the
letters have been adopted; see his edition for their justification.
1–3. To ... Paston: the superscription, the equivalent of the modern
address, was always written on the back of the letter. Medieval letters did
not have envelopes but were simply folded and sealed with wax.
1. worshipfull: honourable.   *with*: by.
2. full entyerly: completely.
5. wyse: manner, fashion.
5–6. I ... maistership: I commend myself to Your Honour.
6–7. Pleace ... wite: I should like you to know.
7. thenke: think.   *to*: until.   *verrey knolege*: true knowledge.
8. the ... undirstonde: which when it is known to me.
9. as nowe: right now.
10. late ... wite: let you know.   *herde reperte*: hear (a) report.
    shulde: were to.
11. doughtir ... Somirset: a daughter of the Duchess of Somerset. Some
time before 1470 (when their first child was born) John Paston II's uncle
William, who was only six years older than his nephew, did marry Lady

matir, and I spake with you, I couth enforme your maistirship
that were to longe to write as nowe. But I shal and do pray
God dayly to sende you such one unto your worldes make that
wil drede and faithfully unfeyned love you above alle othir   15
erthely creatures. For that is most excellent richesse in this
worlde, as I suppose. Fore erthely goodes bene transitory and
wedding contynues for terme of lyfe, which with som folke is a
full longe terme. And therfore, sire, savyng your displeasire,
me semez wedding wolde have goode avysement.   20

Moreovir, sir, like it your maistirship to undirstond that
wyntir and colde weders draweth negh and I have but fewe
clothez but of your gift, God thanke you. Wherefore, sir, and
it like you, I besech your gode maistirship that ye will
vouchsafe to remembre me your servaunte with som lyverey,   25
such as pleaseth you, ayens this wyntir, to make me a gown to
kepe me from the colde wedders; and that I myght have it,
and such answere as ye pleace in the premisses, sente unto me
be the bringere herof.

And I schal contynuwe youre oratrix and pore servaunte,   30

Anne Beaufort, younger daughter of Edmund, 2nd Duke of Somerset (d.
1455); possibly Cecily Daune had heard a garbled version of that intended
marriage.

11–12. which matir: (concerning) this matter.
12. and: if.
12–13. couth ... nowe: could tell Your Honour something which it would
take too long to write now.
14. such ... make: such a person to be your wife in this world.
15. drede: fear, respect.   *unfeyned*: genuinely.
17. erthely goodes: worldly possessions (the implication is that the main
attraction of the match must be the lady's money).
18. for ... lyfe: all one's life.
19. savyng ... displeasire: i.e. without offence.
20. me semez: (it) seems to me.
     wolde ... avysement: should have careful consideration.
21. like ... undirstond: may it please Your Honour to know.
22. weders: weather.   *draweth negh*: draw near, are coming on.
     but fewe: only a few.
23. but of: except by.   *God ... you*: may God give you thanks.
23–4. and ... you: if it pleases you.
25. lyverey: 'the uniform garb granted by a king, nobleman, bishop, etc., to
a vassal, retainer or servant; also, a single item of dress so granted' (*MED*).
26. ayens: in preparation for.
28. such ... premisses: such an answer as you wish to give on the aforesaid
matters.
29. be: by.   *bringere herof*: bearer of this (letter).
30. contynuwe: continue.
     oratrix: female petitioner, woman who prays for you.

and hertely pray to God for your prosperite, whom I besech
have you, right worshipfull sir, and with my faithful herte and
service full entierly beloved gode maistir, in his blessed
governaunce. Writen at Hellowe the thridde day of Novembre.

Cicile Daune   35

b) Margaret Paston to her son John Paston II (BL MS Add. 34889, ff. 83ᵛ–84ʳ)*

[1469, 10 or 11 September]

... On Fryday the bysschope sent fore here be Asschefeld
and othere that arn ryth sory of here demenyng. And the

31–2. whom ... you: to whom I pray to keep you.
34. governaunce: care.   *Hellowe*: Hellow, in Lincolnshire.
    thridde: third.
35. Cicile Daune: in a different hand but the same ink: presumably her
signature.
* Davis, I, 342–4. Margery Paston, who was aged about twenty-one, had
fallen in love with the family's bailiff, Richard Calle. Calle had tried to get
her brothers to support the proposed marriage earlier in the year (Davis I,
541) and John III had had to write to his elder brother to deny indignantly
the implication that he approved (Calle 'shold never have my good wyll
forto make my sustyr to selle kandyll and mustard in Famlyngham').
Margery and Richard contracted a clandestine marriage – or thought they
had. Margery's family hoped, not to dissolve the marriage, but to establish
that no marriage in fact existed, that Margery was not 'bound' but still 'free
to chose'. The Bishop of Norwich was called in to investigate, as marriage
was a sacrament rather than merely a civil contract and therfore fell into the
Church's jurisdiction. His position was somewhat delicate. He would
naturally like to encourage women to obey their families and as a member
of the ruling class himself would be well aware of the shock Margery had
given the Pastons' social standing; but as a bishop his primary concern
would be whether or not a valid marriage – however undesirable – had
been contracted. In the Middle Ages it was possible to contract a valid
marriage without the presence of a priest or any other witness, if the right
form of words were used. As in this case there were no witnesses, the truth
could be elicited only by the careful questioning of the two parties. (See
further Haskell 1973: 567–8.)
    Margaret does not mince her words: her anger, outrage and pain still
leap off the page in a torrent of complex syntax and vigorous colloquialisms.
Her daughter's character, too, comes through strongly – her determination
and wit in an awkward and embarrassing situation.
36. the bysschope: the Bishop of Norwich, Walter Lyhert (1446–72).
    here: her.   *be Asschefeld*: by (through) Ashfield.
37. othere: others.   *ryth ... demenyng*: really unhappy about her behaviour.

bysschop seyd to here ryth pleynly, and put here in
rememberawns how sche was born, wat kyn and frenddys that
sche had, and xuld have mo yf sche were rulyd and gydyd   40
aftyre them; and yf sche ded not, wat rebuke and schame and
los yt xuld be to here, yf sche were not gydyd be them, and
cause of foresakyng of here fore any good ore helpe ore
kownfort that sche xuld have of hem; and seyd that he had
hard sey that sche loved scheche on that here frend were not   45
plesyd wyth that sche xuld have, and therefore he bad here be
ryth wel avysyd how sche ded, and seyd that he woold
wndyrstond the worddys that sche had seyd to hym, wheythere
yt mad matramony ore not.

And sche rehersyd wat sche had seyd and seyd, yf thoo   50
worddys mad yt not suhere, sche seyd boldly that sche wold
make yt suerhere ore than sche went thens. For sche sayd
sche thowthe in here conschens sche was bownd, watsoevere
the worddys wern. Thes leud worddys gereveth me and here
grandam as myche as alle the remnawnte. And than the   55
bysschop and the schawnselere bothe seyd that there was
neythere I nere no frend of hers wold reseyvere.

38. ryth pleynly: really plainly.
38–9. put ... rememberawns: reminded her.
39. wat kyn: what (kind of) family, relatives.
40. xuld ... mo: and should have (still) more.   *gydyd*: guided.
41. aftyre them: according to their wishes.   *ded*: did.
42. los: loss.
43. cause ... here: a reason for her being abandoned.
43–4. fore ... hem: as far as any material help or comfort that she would
have (otherwise) from them.
45. hard sey: heard (it) said.   *scheche on*: such a one.   *frend*: friends.
46. plesyd ... have: i.e. did not wish her to marry.   *bad*: bade, commanded.
47. ryth ... ded: think really carefully what she was doing.
47–8. woold wndyrstond: wished to understand.
48. worddys: words.   *hym*: i.e. Richard Calle.
48–9. wheythere ... not: (as to) whether it constituted marriage or not.
50. rehersyd: repeated.   *wat*: what.   *thoo*: those.
51. suhere: sure, secure.
52. suerhere: more secure.   *ore than*: before.   *thens*: thence, from there.
53. thowthe: thought.   *conschens*: conscience.   *bownd*: bound.
    watsoevere: whatever.
54. wern: were.   *leud*: foolish.   *gereveth*: grieve, distress.
54–5. here grandam: her grandmother (probably Agnes Paston, Margaret's
mother-in-law).
55. as(1) ... remnawnte: as much as all the rest.
56. schawnselere: chancellor (of the diocese), i.e. the chief executive officer.
56–7. there ... reseyvere: neither I nor any of her friends would receive her.

And than Calle was exameynd aparte be hymsylfe, that here
worddys and hys acordyd, and the tyme and where yt xuld a
be don. And than the bysschop sayd that he supposyd that   60
there xuld be fownd othere thynggys ageyns hym that mythe
cause the lettyng thereof, and therefore he sayd he wold not
be to hasty to geve sentens thereupon, and sayd that he wold
geve overe day tyl the Wodynsday ore Thursday aftyre
Mykylmes, and so yt tys delayyd. They woold an had here wyl   65
parformyd in haste, but the bysschop seyd he woold non
otherewyse than he had sayd.

I was wyth my moder at here plase wan sche was exameynd
and wan I hard sey wat here demenyng was, I schargyd my
servantys that sche xuld not be reseyved in myn hows. I had   70
yeven here warnyng, sche mythe a be ware afore yf sche had a
be grasyows. And I sent to on ore too more that they xuld not
reseyve here yf sche cam. Sche was browthe ageyn to my
place fore to a be reseyved, and Ser Jamys tolde them that
browthe here that I had schargyd hem alle, and sche xuld not   75

58. *exameynd*: examined, questioned.
   aparte . . . hymsylfe: separately on his own.
58–60. *that . . . don*: (with the result) that her words and his coincided, and
when and where it had been done.
61–2. *xuld . . . thereof*: i.e. there might well be other things discovered in
his disfavour (for instance the existence of a previous marriage) that could
cause the hindering of it (the validity of the marriage).
63. *to*: too.   *geve sentens*: give his opinion, judgement.
64. *geve . . . day*: adjourn.   *Wodynsday*: Wednesday.
65. *Mykylmes*: Michaelmas, the Feast of St Michael and All Angels (30
September).
65. *yt tys delayyd*: it is delayed, postponed.   *woold an*: would have.
   here wyl: their will (to live together as man and wife).
66. *parformyd in haste*: carried out quickly.   *woold*: would (act).
66–7. *non otherewyse*: in no other way.
68. *moder*: i.e. mother-in-law.   *plase*: place (Agnes lived in Norwich).
   wan: when.   *sche*: i.e. Margery.
69. *hard . . . was*: heard it said how she had behaved.
   schargyd: charged, instructed.
70. *reseyved*: received, admitted.
71. *yeven*: given.
71–2. *sche . . . grasyows*: she could have paid attention earlier if she had
been good.
72. *sent*: sent (word).   *on . . . too*: one or two.
73. *browthe ageyn*: brought back.
74. *fore . . . reseyved*: to have been admitted.
   Ser Jamys: James Gloys, Margaret's chaplain; Margaret's sons disliked
him and felt he had too much influence over their mother.

be reseyved. And soo my lord of Norwych hath set here at Rogere Bestys to be there tyle the day before-sayd. God knowyth fule evel ageyn hys wyle and hys wyvys, yf they durst do otherewyse. I am sory that they arn acumyrd wyth here, but yet I am better payed that sche is there fore the whyle than 80 sche had ben in othere place, because of the sadnes and god dysposysion of hymsylfe and hys wyfe, fore sche xal not be soverd there to pleye the brethele.

I pray yow and requere yow that ye take yt not pensyly, fore I wot wele yt gothe ryth nere yowr hart, and so doth yt to myn 85 and to othere. But remembyre yow, and so do I, that we have lost of here but a brethele and set yt the les to hart. Fore and sche had be good, watsoevere sche had be yt xuld not a ben os it tys, fore and he were ded at thys owyre sche xuld nevere be at myn hart as sche was. As fore the devors that ye wrete to 90 me of, I suppose wat ye ment, but I scharge yow upon my blyssyng that ye do not, nere cause non othere to do, that xuld offend God and yowr conschens. Fore and ye do ore cause

76. *my . . . Norwych*: the Lord Bishop of Norwich.   *set*: placed.
76-7. *at . . . Bestys*: at Roger Best's. Best was a grocer and a prominent Norwich citizen, twice mayor.
77. *tyle*: until.
78. *fule . . . wyvys*: very much against his and his wife's wishes.
78-9. *yf . . . otherewyse*: if they dared to act otherwise.
79. *acumyrd*: lumbered.
80. *better payed*: more pleased.   *fore . . . whyle*: in the meantime.
81-2. *sadnes . . . dysposysion*: level-headedness and suitable attitude.
82. *xal*: shall.
83. *soverd*: suffered, allowed.   *pleye the brethele*: play the fool.
84. *requere*: request.   *pensyly*: sadly.
85. *wot wele*: well know.   *yt . . . hart*: i.e. it really hurts you.
86. *remembyre yow*: remember.
87. *of here*: in her.   *but a brethele*: just a good-for-nothing.
     set . . . hart: take it less to heart.   *and*: if.
88-9. *watsoevere . . . tys*: i.e. whatever she was would not have been as bad as this.
89. *and he*: if he (i.e. Richard Calle).   *ded . . . owyre*: dead this very hour.
89-90. *sche . . . was*: i.e. I would never feel as fond of her as I did. When Margaret made her will thirteen years later she did in fact leave a small legacy to Margery's eldest boy. She left nothing to Margery herself who was probably already dead.
90. *devors*: divorce, i.e. annulment.   *wrete*: wrote.
91. *I . . . ment*: I understand what you intended.
91-2. *upon . . . blyssyng*: on (pain of losing) my blessing.
92. *nere*: nor.
92-3. *that . . . God*: (anything) that would cause offence to God.
93. *and*(2): if.

fore to be do, God wul take vengawns thereupon and ye xuld
put yowrsylfe and othere in gret joparte. Fore wott yt wele,   95
sche xal ful sore repent here leudnes hereaftyre, and I pray
God sche mute soo. I pray yow, fore myn hartys hese, be ye of
a good cownfort in alle thynggys. I trust God xal helpe ryth
wele, and I pray God so do in alle owr maters. I wuld ye toke
hed yf there were any labore mad in the kort of Cawntyrbery   100
fore the leud matere foresayd.

But yf the Duke be purveyd fore, he and hys wyse kownsel
xalle lese thys cuntre. Yt tys told me that he sethe that he wul
not spare to do that he is purposyd fore no duke in Ynglond.
God helpe at nede.   105

94. wul . . . thereupon: will take his revenge for it.
95. joparte: jeopardy, danger.   *wott yt wele*: know well, i.e. mark my words.
96. sche . . . hereaftyre: she will bitterly regret her foolish behaviour in the
future.
97. mute: may.   *hartys hese*: heart's ease, peace of mind.
97–8. be . . . cownfort: take heart.
99. owr maters: our affairs (apart from Margery's delinquent behaviour,
there was serious trouble brewing at Caister – see Headnote).
100. labore mad: exertions being made.
    kort . . . Cawntyrbery: the (ecclesiastical) court of the archdiocese of
Canterbury.
101. fore . . . foresayd: in connection with the foolish business just
mentioned (i.e. presumably attempts to obtain an annulment).
102. But . . . fore: unless something is done about the Duke (John
Mowbray, 4th Duke of Norfolk, about to beseige the Pastons at Caister).
102. wyse kownsel: sage advice (ironic).
103. xalle . . . cuntre: will ruin this country.   *Yt . . . me*: I am told.
    sethe: says.
103–4. wul . . . purposyd: won't refrain from doing what he intends.
104. fore . . . Ynglond: for any duke in England (George, Duke of Clarence,
was trying to mediate between the Pastons and the Duke of Norfolk).
105. God . . . nede: Heaven help us!

c) Margaret Paston to her younger son John Paston III (BL Add. MS 34889, f. 107)*

[Probably 1470, 6 July]

To John Paston the yongere be this delivered in hast

I grete you wele and send you Goddes blyssyng and myn, letyng you wete that sith ye departed my cosyn Calthorp sent me a letter compleynyng in his wrytyng that forasmych as he cannot be payd of his tenauntes as he hat be before this tyme, 110 he purposith to lesse his howshold and to leve the streytlyere, wherfore he desireth me to purvey for your suster Anne. He seth she waxeth hygh and it were tyme to purvey here a mariage.

I marveyll what causeth hym to write so now: owthere she 115 hath displeased hym or ell he hath takyn here wyth summe diffaught. Therefore I pray you comune wyth my cosyn Clere at London and wete how he is disposyd to here-ward, and

* Davis, I, 348.
106. yongere: younger.
107. grete you wele: greet you warmly.
108. wete: know.   *sith*: since.
    my cosyn Calthorp: Sir William Calthorp (d. 1494), a relative of Margaret's husband, in whose household her daughter Anne was living. The usual method of educating girls of the gentry or aristocracy was to send them away from home to a household of similar or, preferably, higher status to their parents'. Anne is, as it were, being expelled from school for unspecified reasons.
109. compleynyng . . . wrytyng: lamenting in his letter.   *forasmych*: in that.
110. of: by.   *tenauntes*: tenants.   *hat be*: has been.
111. purposith . . . streytlyere: intends to diminish his household establishment and live more economically.
112. purvey: make (other) arrangements.
113. seth: says.
    waxeth hygh: is growing tall (Anne must have been about fifteen) or, possibly, is getting above herself.
113–14. were . . . mariage: would be time to arrange a marriage for her.
115. marveyll: am astonished.   *owthere*: either.
116. ell: else.
116–17. takyn . . . diffaught: caught her out in some wrong-doing.
117. comune wyth: talk to.
    my cosyn Clere: either the son or husband of Margaret's close friend and relative Elizabeth Clere.
118. wete . . . here-ward: get to know how he feels about her.

send me word, for I shall be fayn to send for here and wyth
me she shall but lese here tyme, and wythought she wull be   120
the better occupied she shall oftyn tymes meve me and put me
in gret inquietenesse. Remembre what labour I had wyth your
suster. Therfore do your parte to help here forth that may be
to your wurchep and myn.

Item, remembre the bill that I spake to you of to gete of   125
your brothere of such money as he hath receyvid of me sith
your faderes disseas. Se your unkyll Mautby if ye may, and
send me summe tydynges as sone as ye may.

God kepe you. Wretyn the Fryday next before Sent
Thomas of Caunterbery, in hast.   130

Be your moder

---

119. fayn: obliged.
120. she . . . tyme: she will simply waste her time.
    wythought: without, i.e. unless.   *wull*: will.
121. meve: annoy.
121–2. put . . . inquietenesse: cause me great anxiety.
122. labour: trouble.
122–3. your suster: i.e. Margery Calle, who had finally married Richard by
the end of 1469.
123. help . . . forth: help her on, give her a helping hand.
123–4. may . . . myn: (it) may do both of us credit.
125. Item: moreover.   *bill*: note, record.   *gete of*: get from.
126. your brothere: John Paston II; Margaret felt that he was extravagant.
    sith: since.
127. faderes disseas: father's death (John Paston I had died in 1466).
    unkyll Mautby: probably John's great-uncle, Margaret's uncle Edward
Mautby, as Margaret herself was an only child.
128. summe tydynges: some news.
129–30. Sent . . . Caunterbery: i.e. the Feast of the Translation of St
Thomas à Becket, 7 July.
131. Be: by.

d) Two letters from Dame Elizabeth Brews to John Paston III (British Library MS Add. 27445, f. 105, and MS Add. 43490, f. 22)*

[1477, February]

Unto my ryght wurschypffull cosyn John Paston be thys letture delyvered etc.

Ryght wurschypfull cosyn, I recommande me unto yowe etc. And I send myn husbonde a bill of the mater that ye knowe   135
of, and he wrote another bill to me agayn towchyng the same mater; and he wold that ye schuld go unto my maistresse yowr modur and asaye if ye myght gete the hole twenty pound into yowr handes, and then he wolde be more gladd to marye wyth yowe and will gyffe yowe an hundred pound. And cosyn, that   140
day that sche is maryed my fadur will gyffe hyr fifty merk.

But and we acorde I schall gyffe yowe a grettur tresure, that is a wytty gentylwoman, and if I sey it, bothe good and vertuos. For if I schuld take money for hyr, I wold not gyffe hyr for a thousend pound. But, cosyn, I trust yowe so meche   145
that I wold thynke hyr wele besett on yowe and ye were

---

* Davis II, 435–6. Dame Elizabeth Brews was the mother of Margery (see next), whom John Paston III was considering marrying. Her letters are written by Thomas Kela, a family servant.
134. cosyn: cousin; in ME the term is wide and covers any relative by blood, marriage or spiritual affinity.
135. send: sent.   *bill*: note.
136. agayn: back.   *towchyng*: touching, concerning.
137. wold: wanted.
137–8. my ... modur: my lady your mother.
138. asaye: try.   *hole*: whole.
139–40. more ... yowe: more happy to conclude a marriage agreement with you.
140. gyffe: give.
141. sche: i.e. Margery.
    my fadur: i.e. Gilbert Debenham, retainer of the Duke of Norfolk.
    merk: marks; a mark was worth 13s 4d, two-thirds of a pound.
142. and ... acorde: if we come to an agreement.
    grettur tresure: greater treasure.
143. a wytty gentylwoman: an intelligent, well bred woman.
    and if: even though.
144. schuld: were to.   *I(2) ... hyr*: I would not give her away.
146. wele besett: appropriately bestowed.
146. and: if.

worthe meche more. And, cosyn, a lytyll aftur that ye were
gon, come a man fro my cosyn Derby and broght me wurde
that suche a chance fell that he myght not com at the day that
was set, as I schall let yowe undyrstond more pleynly when I   150
speke with yowe etc. But, cosyn, and it wold plese yowe to
com agayn what dey that ye will set, I dare undyrtake that they
schall kepe the same day, for I wold be glad that, and myn
husbond and ye myght acorde in thys maryage, that it myght
be my fortune to make an ende in thys mater betwene my   155
cosyns and yowe, that yche of yowe myght love other in
frendely wyse, etc.

And cosyn, if thys byll please not yowr entent, I pray yowe
that it may be brent etc. No more unto yowe at thys tyme, but
almyghty Jesus preserve yowe etc.   160

Be yowr cosyn Dame Elizabeth Brews

[1477, about 9 February]

To my wurschypfull cosyn John Paston be this bill
delyveryd etc.

Cosyn, I recommande me unto yowe, thankyng yowe hertely
for the grette chere that ye made me and all my folkys the last   165
tyme that I was at Norwych. And ye promysyd me that ye wold
never breke the mater to Mergery unto suche tyme as ye and I
were at a poynt. But ye hafe made hyr suche advokett for yowe
that I may never hafe rest nyght ner day for callyng and cryeng
uppon to brynge the saide mater to effecte etc.   170

And cosyn, uppon Fryday is Sent Volentynes Day, and

149. suche ... fell: i.e. it so happened.
152. what: whatever.   *undyrtake*: guarantee.
155-6. my(1) ... *yowe*(1): my good fortune to conclude this matter between
my family and you.
156. yche: each.   *other*: each other.
156-7. in ... wyse: in a friendly way.
158. if ... entent: if this note does not suit you.
159. brent: burnt.
165. grette chere: splendid hospitality.   *folkys*: people.
167. breke: broach.
167-8. unto ... poynt: until such time as you and I had agreed.
168. advokett: advocate, spokesperson.
169-70. for ... uppon: because of her begging and beseeching.
171. Sent Volentynes: Saint Valentine's.

every brydde chesyth hym a make; and yf it lyke yowe to com
on Thursday at nyght, and so purvey yowe that ye may abyde
ther tyll Monday, I trusty to God that ye schall so speke to
myn husbonde, and I schall prey that we schall bryng the   175
mater to a conclusyon, etc. For cosyn, it is but a sympill oke
that is cut down at the firste stroke; for ye will be resonabill, I
trust to God, whech hafe yowe ever in hys mercyfull kepyng
etc.

> Be yowr cosyn Dame Elizabeth Brews   180
> otherwes schall be called be Goddys grace.

e) Two letters from Margery Brews, later Paston, to John Paston III (BL MS Add. 43490, ff. 23–4)*

[1477, February]

Unto my ryght wele-belovyd Voluntyn John Paston,
squyer, be this bill delyvered, etc.

Ryght reverent and wurschypfull and my ryght wele-beloved
Voluntyne, I recommande me unto yowe full hertely, desyring   185
to here of yowr welefare, whech I beseche Almyghty God long

---

172. *brydde*: bird.   *chesyth ... make*: chooses a mate for himself.
     yf ... yowe: if you would like.
173. *purvey yowe*: arrange.   *abyde*: stay.
174. *trusty*: trust.
176. *but ... oke*: only a feeble oak tree.
177. *resonabill*: open to reason.
178. *whech hafe*: may He keep.
181. *otherwes ... called*: who shall be called something else (i.e. 'mother'
     rather than 'cousin').

* Davis, I, 662–3.
Margery Brews was the daughter of Sir Thomas Brews and his wife
Elizabeth (see above). Her letters, like her mother's, are in the hand of
Thomas Kela, but she initials the first one herself.
182. *Voluntyn*: Valentine, 'a person of the opposite sex chosen on
Valentine's Day as a sweetheart, lover or special friend for the ensuing year'
(*MED*).
184. *wurschypfull*: honourable.
185. *full hertely*: with all my heart.
186. *here*: hear.   *yowr welefare*: your welfare, how you are.

forto preserve unto hys plesure and yowr hertys desyre. And
yf it please yowe to here of my welefare, I am not in good
heele of body ner of herte, nor schall be tyll I here from yowe.

For ther wottys no creature what peyn that I endure,   190
And forto be deede I dare it not discure.

And my lady my moder hath labored the mater to my
fadure full delygently, but sche can no more gete than ye
knowe of, for the whech God knowyth I am full sory. But yf
that ye loffe me, as I tryste verely that ye do, ye will not leffe   195
me therfor. For if that ye hade not halfe the lyvelode that ye
hafe, forto do the grettyst labure that any woman on lyve
myght I wold not forsake yowe. And yf ye commande me to
kepe me true where-ever I go, iwyse I will do all my myght
yowe to love and never no mo. And yf my freendys say that I   200
do amys, thei schal not me let so forto do. Myn herte me
byddys evermore to love yowe truly over all erthely thing. And
yf thei be never so wroth, I tryst it schall be bettur in tyme
commyng.

187. unto . . . plesure: to His will.   *hertys desyre*: heart's desire.
188. yf . . . welefare: if you want to hear how I am.
189. heele: health.   *tyll*: until.
190–1. For . . . discure: there is no indication in the MS that these lines are
verse; Margery is perhaps quoting a familiar rhyming tag rather than trying
to write poetry herself.
190. wottys: knows.   *what . . . endure*: what pain it is that I suffer.
191. forto be deede: even on pain of death.   *discure*: disclose, reveal.
192–3. labored . . . delygently: pursued the matter (of the marriage
settlement) with my father very assiduously.
193. no more gete: cannot get any more (money).
195. loffe: love.   *tryste verely*: confidently believe.   *leffe*: leave.
196. therfor: for that reason.
196–7. if . . . hafe: (even) if you didn't possess half the money you do.
197. grettyst labure: greatest toil, exertion.   *on lyve*: alive.
198–204. And . . . commyng: Davis prints these sentences as six lines of
extremely rough verse – they can be made to rhyme but they certainly do
not scan – but they are written as prose in the manuscript.
199. kepe me true: remain faithful.   *iwyse*: indeed.
200. never no mo: never anyone else.
201. do amys: am acting wrongly.
     thei . . . . do: they won't prevent me from doing so.
202. byddys: bids, commands.   *over*: above.
203. yf . . . wroth: however angry they may be.   *tryst*: trust, am confident.
203–4. tyme commyng: time to come.

No more to yowe at this tyme, but the Holy Trinite hafe   205
yowe in kepyng. And I besech yowe that this bill be not seyn
of non erthely creature safe only yourselfe etc. And thys lettur
was indyte at Topcroft wyth full hevy herte etc.

Be your own M.B.

To my ryght wele-belovyd cosyn John Paston, swyere,   210
be this lettur delyveryd etc.

Ryght wurschypffull and wele-belovyd Volentyne, in my moste
umble wyse I recommande me unto yowe etc. And hertely I
thanke yowe for the letture whech that ye sende me be John
Bekurton, wherby I undyrstonde and knowe that ye be   215
purposyd to com to Topcroft in schorte tyme, and wythowte
any erand or mater but only to hafe a conclusyon of the mater
betwyx my fadur and yowe. I wolde be most glad of any
creature on lyve so that the mater myght growe to effect. And
theras ye say, and ye com and fynde the mater no more   220
toward then ye dyd afortyme, ye wold no more put my fadur

205. *at ... tyme*: for now.
205–6. *Holy ... kepyng*: may the Holy Trinity guard you.
206–7. *besech ... yourselfe*: please don't let anyone in the world except you
see this letter. The clerk Thomas Kela actually wrote it but he was an old
and trusted family retainer who became so emotionally involved in the
protracted negotiations that he wrote himself to John Paston III to say that
both he and Margery's mother were working hard to forward the match ('I
am yowr man and my good will ye schall hafe in worde and dede').
208. *indyte*: composed.   *Topcroft*: Sir Thomas Brews' residence in Norfolk.
    full ... herte: with a very heavy heart.
    etc.: probably meaningless here.
210. *cosyn*: cousin (not necessarily implying close kinship if any).
    swyere: squire.
212–13. *moste ... wyse*: most humble fashion.
214. *sende*: sent.   *be*: by.
215–16. *be purposyd*: intend.
216. *in ... tyme*: shortly.
216–18. *wythowte ... yowe*: on no other business but to bring to a
conclusion the negotiations between my father and you.
219. *on lyve*: alive.   *so that*: if only.   *growe to effect*: come to fruition.
220. *theras*: in that.   *and*(1): if.
220–1. *no more toward*: no further advanced.
221. *afortyme*: before.
221–3. *ye*(2) ... *afture*: you would no longer want to put my parents to any
expense or trouble in that matter for a considerable time (i.e. ever).

and my lady my moder to no cost ner besenesse for that cause
a good wyle afture, weche causyth myn herte to be full hevy;
and yf ye com and the mater take to non effecte, then schuld I
be meche more sory and full of hevynesse.   225

And as for myselfe, I hafe don and undyrstond in the mater
that I can or may, as Good knowyth. And I let yowe pleynly
undyrstond that my fader wyll no more money parte wythall in
that behalfe but an hundred pound and fifty marke, whech is
ryght far fro the acomplyshment of yowr desyre. Wherfor, yf   230
that ye cowde be content wyth that good and my por persone,
I wold be the meryest mayden on grounde. And yf ye thynke
not yowrselfe so satysfyed, or that ye myght hafe mech more
good, as I hafe undyrstonde be yowe afor, good, trewe and
lovyng Volentyne, that ye take no such labure uppon yowe as   235
to com more for that mater. But let it passe and never more to
be spokyn of, as I may be yowr trewe lover and bedewoman
duryng my lyfe.

No more unto yowe at thys tyme, but almyghty Jesus
preserve yowe, bothe body and sowle etc.   240

Be your Voluntyne

Mergery Brews

223. *weche*: which.
224. *and yf*: if.   *take . . . effecte*: comes to nothing.
225. *meche*: much.   *hevynesse*: sorrow, unhappiness.
226. *I . . . undyrstond*: I have done and endured.
227. *that . . . may*: as much as I know how or am able to.   *Good*: God.
227–8. *let . . . undyrstond*: I want you clearly to understand.
228–9. *wyll . . . behalfe*: refuses to part with any more money in that matter.
229. *but*: except.   *marke*: marks.
230. *ryght . . . desyre*: very far from fulfilling your wishes (John wanted 400
marks settled on Margery and a loan of £120 from his prospective father-
in-law).
231. *cowde*: could.   *good . . . persone*: amount of money and my poor self.
232. *meryest . . . grounde*: happiest girl in the world.
233–4. *or . . . good*(1): unless you could get much more money.
235–6. *that . . . more*: (I beg you) not to take the trouble to come any more.
236–7. *let . . . of*: i.e. let's forget it and say no more about it.
237. *as*: on condition that.   *trewe*: faithful.
    bedewoman: woman that prays for you, 'your humble servant'.

[Margaret Paston, whose behaviour towards her son John III contrasts
markedly with her attitude towards her daughter Margery (Haskell 1973:
469), helped the marriage on by giving the couple the Manor of Sparham,
which was hers. This annoyed John Paston II, who as the eldest son might
have expected to inherit it in due course; he had recently broken off his
own engagement. The marriage negotiations were embarrassingly protracted

Other Women Write to the Pastons

f) From Elizabeth Clere to Margaret Paston (BL MS Add. 27445, f. 24)*

[1466 or soon after]

To my worschepfull cosyn Margarete Paston be this
delyvered

Worchepful cosyn, I comaunde me to you, desiryng to here of   245
your hele and hertes ease, the wheche I beseche God sende
you. And as for my litel cosyn, your sone is a faire childe and
a mery, blissed be God.

Cosyn, the cause of my writyng at this tyme is for certeyn
evidences of Frethorp that I delyvered my cosyn your   250
husbonde forto a mad awarde betwix Rammesbury and me,
and o boke of papeer of the customs of Ormesby, and o rolle

but the combined efforts of Margery and Elizabeth Brews, old Thomas
Kela, and Margaret Paston and John III overcame the caution of Sir
Thomas and the reluctance of John II and the couple were married by the
end of the year. Margery bore her husband two sons, of whom the second,
William, grew to maturity.]

* Davis, II, 351. Written soon after the death of John Paston I in May
1466 when Margaret would be sorting through his papers and tidying up
his affairs. Elizabeth Clere was a relative and close friend of Margaret; the
four letters from her which survive, of widely different dates, are all in the
same hand which is probably her own.
245. comaunde: commend, recommend.
246. hele: health.   *hertes ease*: peace of mind.
247. my . . . cosyn: probably Margaret's youngest child, William, b. 1459.
    faire: pretty.
248. mery: cheerful.   *blissed*: blessed.
250. evidences: legal documents such as deeds, charters, etc., which could
be used to support a claim.
250. Frethorp: Freethorpe, in Norfolk.
    delyvered my cosyn: handed over to my cousin.
251. forto . . . me: so that he could arbitrate between Ramsbury and me.
252. o . . . papeer: a paper book (books were still more likely to be made of
vellum or parchment).
252. customs: manorial customary law.
    Ormesby: Ormesby St Margaret, in Norfolk.
252–3. o . . . Domysday: one roll called 'Doomsday'. A roll was a scroll
containing documents and records.

called Domysday and other certeyn evidences longyng to the
seide maner, and one dede of a tayle of Reynthorp, the
whiche I delyvered hym, and certeyn evidences of Cleydon 255
and of Burgh. And also, cosyn, your faderlawe was of councell
bothe with my moder and my moderlawe, wherfore I sopose
ther myght be lefte som evidences or copies of evidences of
my liflode, that is to seye Tacolneston, Therston, Reynthorp,
Rusteynes in Wymondham, Kesewik and Stratton, with hym. 260
Wherfore, cosyn, I beseche you hertily that whanne ye loke
among your evidences that ye wolde ley hem aparte for me, as
my very truste is that ye will, for I here sey that ye have right
weell and conciensly delyvered certeyn persones the evidences
longyng to hem and I truste veryly ye wil the same to me. 265

Cosyn, ther cam a man fro Norwiche to me and fonde be
the weye certeyn rolles and toke hem me, the wheche long to
you and not to me; wherfore I sende hem you be the bryngger
of this bille.

No more to you at this tyme, but the Holy Trinite have you 270
in his blissed kepyng.

Be your cosyn

E. Clere

253. *longyng*: appertaining.
254. *maner*: manor (of Ormesby).
   dede . . . *tayle*: deed of entail, 'the limitation of inheritance by
conditions imposed or fixed by the donor, especially by conditions
restricting inheritance to a particular class of heirs' (*MED*).
254. *Reynthorp*: Rainthorpe, in Norfolk.
255–6. *Cleydon* . . . *Burgh*: Claydon and Burgh, both in Suffolk.
256. *faderlawe*: father-in-law, i.e. William Paston I (d. 1444).
256–7. *of*(2) . . . *moderlawe*: in the confidence of both my mother and
mother-in-law.
257. *wherfore*: therefore.   *sopose*: suppose, reckon.
258–9. *of my liflode*: concerning my property.
259–60. *Tacolneston* . . . *Kesewik*: Tacolneston, Therston, Rainthorpe,
Wymondham and Keswick are all manors in Norfolk.
260. *Stratton*: either Stratton St Michael or Stratton Strawless in Norfolk.
262. *ley* . . . *aparte*: put them on one side.
263. *very truste*: complete confidence.   *here sey*: hear it said.
264. *weell*: well.   *conciensly*: conscientiously.
265. *longyng*: belonging.
266–7. *fonde* . . . *weye*: found on his way, journey.
267. *toke hem me*: brought them to me.   *long*: belong.
268. *bryngger*: bearer.
269. *bille*: note, letter.

g) From Joan Keteryche, Abbess of Denny, to
John Paston I
(Oxford Bodl. MS Gough Camb. 3, p. 227^{a-b})*

[*c.* 1461–2, 31 January]

To the right worshipfull jentilman Paiston, executure to
Syr John Fostolff   275

Jesus

Reverent and worschipfull syr, aftyre due recomendacioun
premisyd, plesythe you at the reverens of owre spouse Jesu, to

* Davis II, 265–6. Joan Keterich or Keteryche (d. 1479), sister of William
Keteryche of Landbeach, was the newly elected Abbess of Denny, an abbey
of strictly enclosed Franciscan nuns a few miles outside Cambridge,
renowned for its piety, which a generation earlier had been friendly with
Margery Kempe (see *Book of Margery Kempe*, Book 1, Chapter 84). Her
letter is written in a practised hand, presumably that of a clerk, but her
complex epistolary style, with its strongly French vocabulary (e.g.
foundatrice, inportable, recomendacioun, petyscioun, disposiscioun) and lengthy
sentences made up of many subordinate clauses, is typical of literary rather
than oral composition and presumably her own. Apparently she did not
know John Paston I personally (his surname is wrongly spelt 'Paiston' and
no Christian name is given); but she did know that he was executor of Sir
John Fastolf's will and therefore controlled a great deal of money. She had
probably also heard that under the terms of the will Paston was supposed to
found a college of priests at Caister. With considerable initiative she
suggests that he re-found Denny and outlines the financial and spiritual
advantages of such a course of action. The abbey was actually well off by
the standards of medieval women's religious houses, though it lost some of
its Cambridge lands when Henry VI took them to endow his new
foundation, King's College. But it had recently suffered a series of financial
disasters – for eighteen years between 1452 and 1470 it was embroiled in
an impoverishing legal dispute with Thomas Burgoyne (see Bourdillon
1926: 29–32; Moorman 1974: 43–5). Paston did not answer this elegant
and cultured begging letter, and most of the Fastolf inheritance ultimately
enriched Magdalen College, Oxford.
274. jentilman: gentleman, squire; John Paston I was a member of the
gentry but was never knighted.
274. executure: executor.
275. Fostolff: Fastolf.
276. Jesus: as a religious, Joan Keteryche writes the usual abbreviation of
the Holy Name (*Ihc*) at the top in the left-hand margin of her letter.
277–8. aftyre . . . premisyd: after having greeted you suitably.
278. plesythe you: may it please you.   *at the reverens of*: in reverence for.
   owre spouse Jesu: the nuns regarded themselves as brides of Christ.

qwom we be wilfully professyd, to here gracyousely owre
humble petyscioun, as nowe compellyd, eythere to compleyn   280
us, eythere ellez to suffre owre devout place falle and perysche
in owre dayis, qwyche hathe been so longe tyme wrongffully
oppressid by plee for owre beste and moste substancyal
lyvelode . . . .

[The Abbess goes on to detail their financial problems and the ruinous
lawsuit in which they are currently involved.]

Reverent syr, I, beynge ful symple and yonge of age and   285
chosyn to be abbesse of this wrongfully-oppressyd place, God
knowyth ful myche ayens my will, in my compleynt makyng to
God I was put in mynde of the goodys that been in youre
handys, and also of youre holsom and goode disposiscioun;
qwyche yave me a gret corage to make my petyscioun to you   290
for the recovere of owre pore place, besechynge youre
goodenesse to consydre how we be closyd wythinne the ston
wallys and may non odyrvyse speke wyth you but only be
wrytynge. And the ratheere socoure us for Owre Lordys love
wyth sweche goodys as we may contynue stylle the servaunt of   295

---

279. qwom: whom.   *wilfully professyd*: voluntarily vowed.
here gracyousely: graciously hear.
280. petyscioun: petition.
as nowe compellyd: i.e. we being currently compelled.
280–1. eythere . . . us: either to voice our grievances.
281. eythere . . . . perysche: or else allow our pious house to perish.
282. in . . . dayis: in our time.   *qwyche*: which (i.e. the 'devout place').
so longe tyme: for such a long time.
283–4. plee . . . lyvelode: a lawsuit over our best and most substantial
sources of income.
285. ful symple: very unsophisticated.
287. myche: much.   *ayens*: against.
287–8. in . . . God: while I was lamenting to God.
288. I . . . mynde: I was reminded.
goodys: wealth.
289. holsom . . . disposiscioun: (spiritually) healthy and virtuous character.
290. yave . . . corage: gave me considerable heart.
291. for . . . place: for the restoration of our wretched house.
292. closyd: enclosed (papal permission was required to enter the enclosure
at Denny).
293. non odyrvyse: (in) no other way.
293–4. but . . . wrytynge: except only by writing.
294. ratheere: sooner.   *socoure*: assist, aid.
295. sweche goodys: such wealth.   *as*: that.   *servaunt*: servants.

Jesu, and odyre aftyre us in lyke vyse, the qwyche we wolde
thynke to us as a newe fundacioun. And so in owre suffragys
we wolde annexe the soule of that worthi knyht Syr John
Fastolff and swyche odyre as ye will desyre unto the soule of
owre blyssid foundatrice. And, worschipful syr, it is more esy   300
as yeet to releve us up ayeen than to belde a newe place;
qwyche I truste veryli ye wolde doo yif ye knewe the blyssid
dispocissioun of my weel-disposyd modris and sustris, be
qwos goode conversacioun I trust in Jesu to have of you
summe socoure and comfort now at my moste hevy   305
begynnynge. And yif Owre Lord wolde move youre hert to see
owre pore place, I truste verily to God we schulde have you
and youris evere aftyre in goode remembraunz.

The bryngere of this symple lettre wrytin in greet hevynes
hathe experience of alle owre inportable hurtys before-   310
rehersyd, the qwyche trewly was the cause that he wold of his

296. *odyre*: others.   *lyke vyse*: similar fashion.
296–7. *the . . . us*: which we would look upon.
297. *fundacioun*: foundation, act of founding.   *suffragys*: prayers.
298. *annexe*: add.   *knyht*: knight.
299. *swyche odyre*: such others.   *will desyre*: would wish.
300. *owre blyssid foundatrice*: our blessed foundress. Denny was founded in
1342 by Mary of St Pol, Countess of Pembroke, who also founded
Pembroke College, Cambridge (see Bourdillon 1926: 18–22). She had a
great reputation for piety, so this offer is a graceful compliment to Sir John
Fastolf.
301. *as yeet*: still.   *releve . . . ayeen*: lift us up again.   *belde*: build.
302. *veryli*: truly.
302–3. *blyssid dispocissioun*: holy character.
303. *weel-disposyd*: virtuously-inclined.
    modris: mothers; former superiors would continue to have the
honorific title 'Mother'.
303–4. *be . . . conversacioun*: by whose virtuous way of life.
304. *of*: from.
305–6. *hevy begynnynge*: sorrowful beginning (of her term as abbess).
306. *wolde*: were to.   *move*: stir.
307–8. *have . . . remembraunz*: remember you and your family with
gratitude (i.e. in their prayers) for ever after.
309. *bryngere*: bearer.
    this symple lettre: a conventional gesture of humility; this letter's prose
style is in fact more sophisticated and stately than that of the other women
represented here.
309. *wrytin*: written.   *hevynes*: sorrow.
310. *inportable*: intolerable.
310–11. *before-rehersyd*: repeated earlier.
311–12. *wold . . . coostis*: was willing at his own expense.

owne coostis be messangere. Owre blyssid lord revard hym
therfore, qwyche evere preserve you and youris, body and
soule, in goodnesse for hise gret mercy.
Wrytyn at Denneye the laste day of Januere.   315

Youre pore bedewoman Jone Keteryche,
Abbesse of Denneye

h) From Elizabeth, Duchess of Suffolk, to John Paston III (BL MS Add. 43490, f. 42)*

[between 1479 and June 1483]

Onto Jon Paston in hast

Mastyr Paston, I pray yow that it may plese yow to leve yowr
logeyng for thre or fore days tyl I may be porved of anodyr,   320
and I schal do as musche to yowr plesyr. For Godys sake say

312–13. *Owre . . . therfore*: may Our Blessed Lord reward him for that.
313. *qwyche . . . preserve*: and may he ever keep.
314. *hise*: his.
315. *Januere*: January.
316. *bedewoman*: petitioner.

* Davis, II, 442. Elizabeth, Duchess of Suffolk, daughter of Richard Duke
of York and his wife Cecily, sister of Edward IV, and wife of John de la
Pole (1463–91), was a very great lady indeed. Her note, written in her own
big, untidy hand, is a splendid contrast to the studied formalities of the
Abbess of Denny. The Pastons' relationships with the various Dukes and
Duchesses of Suffolk were complex, but Elizabeth's breezy confidence that
she will get her own way – she wants John Paston to move out so that she
can temporarily occupy his lodgings in London – suggests that she and
John Paston III, at least, were on excellent terms.
318. *Onto . . . hast*: the superscription is in a different hand, not the
Duchess's.
319. *Mastyr Paston*: this abrupt opening is most unusual in the correspondence.
319–20. *I . . . days*: please leave your lodging (in London) for three or four
days (so that Elizabeth can use it herself).
320. *tyl . . . anodyr*: until I can obtain somewhere else.
321. *musche*: much.
   to yowr plesyr: to please you (i.e. some day I'll do the same for you).
   Godys: God's.
321–2. *say . . . nay*: don't refuse me.

me not nay, and I pray yow rekomaund me to my Lord
Chambyrleyn.

Yowr frend Elizabeth

Textual notes

62. sayd] say.
102. kownsel] kowsel.
155. an] and.
236. it] is.
263. will], *265. truste*],   *267. me, the wheche*], MS torn.
277. recomendacioun] recomendacoun.
286. abbesse] abbsse.
289. disposiscioun] disposiscoun.
290. petyscioun] petyscoun.
297. fundacioun] fundacoun.
304. conversacioun] conversacoun.

322–3. rekomaund ... Chambyrleyn: give my regards to the Lord
Chamberlain (William Lord Hastings, whom John Paston served from 1479
until his execution in 1483).

16 Fifteenth- and early sixteenth-century poems

Women appear to have written a number of later medieval English love poems, whose speaking voices, represented as female without irony or detachment and not overtly dramatised, may well be identical with those of the writers of the poems. Apart from one here entitled 'A Hymn to Venus', which the unique manuscript ascribes to 'Queen Elizabeth' (probably the wife of Edward IV), these poems are anonymous, like so many medieval love lyrics. Certain themes, however, emerge as typical of these women poets, such as assertions of fidelity, laments for separation over which the speaker has no control, and a stoic acceptance of abandonment that is quite unlike the unbridled despair and cries for vengeance of some of the 'women's laments' (probably written by men) of the earlier period (see Plummer 1981; Introduction, pp. 18–20).

Although this writing is all amateur, it is sometimes far from amateurish. (The distinction between specialist, expert and occasional oral poets is perhaps useful here; see Finnegan 1977: 191–8.) For instance, these poems often show an interest in technical complexities such as innovative stanza patterns, rhetorical figures and anagrams. A favourite form is the verse letter, whose popularity is doubtless connected with women's growing participation in private correspondence (see text 15, Some Paston Letters, pp. 240–61).

The only known Middle English poems explicitly ascribed to women in the surviving manuscripts come from the fifteenth and early sixteenth centuries. Two of these three poems are hymns to the Virgin; one is attributed by the fifteenth-century bibliophile and amateur scribe John Shirley to 'an holy anchoress of Mansfield', and the other is ascribed, apparently by her sister, to Eleanor Percy, Duchess of Buckingham (see footnotes to texts d and e). This coincidence of subject raises the question of how much later medieval religious poetry was written by women. Possibly some of the poems in which the Virgin laments the death of Christ, or Christ reproaches the human soul for its infidelity (see Woolf 1968: 185–219, 239–73; Gray 1972: 137–45) were composed by women, as their themes of loss and the betrayal of trust are so similar to those of women's secular poetry. In the later sixteenth and seventeenth centuries women were to write much religious poetry and also poems on the deaths of children and spouses (see Hobby 1988: 54–62 and *Kissing the Rod*, pp. 10–12) but no such poems are to be found in the medieval period.

Two allegorical dream poems of the fifteenth century which were long ascribed to Chaucer, 'The Flower and the Leaf' and 'The Assembly of Ladies' (ed. Pearsall, 3rd edn, 1980), have female narrators. There seems no good reason to doubt that they were also written by women, though not, as was originally argued, by the same woman (see Pearsall 1980: 13–20; Barratt 1987b: 1–24), and not primarily because of the interest in detailed description of clothing found in both extracts, as was seriously suggested in the past.

'The Assembly of Ladies' is an account, given by the Narrator to her interlocutor, an inquisitive Knight, of a dream in which she and a group of other ladies and gentlewomen undertake an allegorical journey at the command of Lady Loyalty in order to present her at her palace with 'bills' (written statements) of complaint about their sufferings in love. The attitudes displayed towards women's experience are similar to those of the shorter poems, particularly the stress on women's faithfulness (significantly, Lady Loyalty is the principal allegorical personification, on whose mercy the Dreamer throws herself) and the assumption of women's helplessness. In the extracts chosen, the Dreamer-Narrator's reluctance to voice her sorrow, although she expresses her constancy non-verbally through the wearing of blue, perhaps sheds some light on the general problem of the dearth of women's poetry. There are also many parallels between the underlying despair of the 'bills of complaint', particularly the Narrator's own which is reproduced here, and that of 'Unkindness Hath Killed Her' (text g). The poet's ear for sprightly dialogue (which could be compared with both Margery Kempe's and some of the Paston women's), and for the small change of women's conversation, also shows to advantage in both the passages chosen.

'The Flower and the Leaf' is a far superior and, in some ways, highly original poem; it is no surprise that it was once attributed to Chaucer. It shares the high moral tone of some of the shorter poems and of much women's prose, with its exaltation of chastity and of active virtue as ideals for women, as exemplified by Diana and her Company of the Leaf, and its rejection of the frivolity, idleness and pleasure seeking of Flora and the Company of the Flower. The Company of the Leaf is associated with faithfulness unto death in love as well as with virginity, and with bravery, which is not confined to men.

It is interesting that long after other poets had abandoned the form, women were still writing allegorical dream poems in the early seventeenth century. Elizabeth Melville, Lady Culross, published *Ane Godlie Dreame* in 1603, 'a Calvinist tract, dealing with her vision of the hell that awaits all but God's anointed' (*Kissing the Rod*, p. 32). Rachel Speght published 'Mortalities Memorandum, with a Dreame Prefixed' in 1621; her dream poem, which is an allegorical account of her life, education, controversial writings and the death of her mother, precedes a longer poem on the inevitability of death (see *Kissing the Rod*, pp. 68–78).

Further reading (for full details see the Bibliography): On the manuscript context of some of the courtly lyrics, see Boffey 1985; for a literary study of the women's poems in the Findern Manuscript, see Hanson-Smith 1979, and for a codicological study of the manuscript itself, see Harris 1983. On the poems from early sixteenth-century songbooks, see Stevens 1961.

a) *Poems from MS Rawlinson C. 813**

(i)   Evyn as mery as I make myght,
Ytt ys nott as I wolde.
For to on I have my troweth iplyght
And anoder hathe my harte yn holde.

He that hathe my trowthe iplyght,   5
He dwellyd with me a whyle.
But he that hathe my hart yn holde,
I wyll hym never begyle.

I must take as I have bake:
Therof I have my fyll.   10
Butt I must drynke as I have brewe,
Wheder ytt be good or yll.

All my harte I have here wrytton,
To sende yow yn a byll.
Ytt shal be to your understandyng   15
I have nott all my wyll.

---

* Oxford Bodley MS Rawlinson C. 813 is an early sixteenth-century collection of fifty-odd poems in several different hands. It contains an unusually high proportion of poems, often verse letters using epistolary conventions, written from a woman's point of view. Though some are extremely amateurish, the three poems selected are not only competent but also have in common implied situations and attitudes that are not altogether stereotypical.

(i) f. 58ᵛ. *IMEV* 733.1. A verse letter (see ll. 13–14) in quatrains.
3. on: one.   *have ... iplyght*: have plighted my troth.
4. hathe ... holde: possesses my heart.
9. I(1) ... bake: proverbial; compare 'I have made my bed and must lie on it.'
11. brewe: brewed.
13. wrytton: written.
14. byll: i.e. letter.
15. Ytt ... understandyng: i.e. you must understand.

(ii)   Swetharte, I love yow more fervent then my fader,
         Yet knowe I wyll youre love soo fervent ys
         In anoder place, that I dare nott desyre
         Your love ageyne, nor nought I wyll, iwysse.   20
         But I beseke Gode of your love grante yow blysse
         And preserve yn grace bothe yonge and olde.
         Grante me my love, I aske noo more, iwysse:
         Amonge your new lovers, yet remember your olde.

         Now wyll I sey as I thynke yn my harte   25
         Of yow, sweteharte, whyche I fynde soo strange,
         As on of them that wyll nott turne nor converte.
         By my assent ye shal begyne the range.
         I was not ware ye cast yow forto change
         But, for all thys, I shall doo my dever   30
         To love yow well; butt trust ye me for ever.

(iii)   Right best beloved and most in assurance
         Of my trewe harte, I me recommende
         Hartely unto you withowten vareance;

(ii) f. 63. *IMEV* 3228.5. Two stanzas of eight and seven lines.
17. fervent: fervently.   *then*: than.
18. wyll: well.
20. ageyne: in return, back.
21. I . . . blysse: I pray that God grant you joy of your love.
22. preserve . . . olde: keep (you) in his grace, as both a young man and an old.
26. whyche: whom.   *strange*: distant.
27. As . . . converte: being (myself) one of those that will not turn or change.
28. assent: consent.
    range: act of ranging about (in search of a new love).
29. ware: aware.   *ye . . . change*: you intended to change.
30. dever: duty.

(iii) ff. 71ʳ–72ᵛ. *IMEV* 2821. Another verse letter (for the formulaic phrases, e.g. 'Right best beloved', 'I me recommende', compare the Paston Letters) answering a letter from her lover, the shifty and equivocal contents of which can be easily reconstructed from this dignified response. The poem consists of nine seven-line rhyme-royal stanzas (as used by Chaucer in *Troilus and Criseyde*).
32–3. most . . . harte: (the one) most fully in possession of my loyal heart.
34. Hartely: heartily.
    withowten vareance: steadfastly.

And have receyved the whiche ye to me did send,   35
Wherby I perceyve your loving harte and minde;
Desiring you in the same soo to continewe,
And then for your grett paynes comfforte may insuye.

Thanking me for my kindnes in times paste,
Your desire is I shuld kepe in mynde   40
The purpose I was in when ye spake with me laste.
Truly, unconstant you shall me never fynde,
But ever to be trewe, feithffull and kinde,
And to you beire my trew harte withouten vareance,
Desiring you to make me noo dyssemblance.   45

Also, wher you saye that my bewtye soo sore
Shuld you inflame with persing violence,
That with extreme love of me you shuld be caught
    in snare:
I mervell therof gretly without douttance
That itt shuld have suche might or puisance,   50
For I knowe right well I was never soo bewtiouse
That I shuld you constren to be soo amerous.

Also wher you saye that absens shuld be
The grettest payne that can be devised
Unto on that is in grette extremitee   55
And with paynffull love soore tormented:
Itt is of a truthe, itt can nott be denyed
Butt that absens causeth ofte penciffenes;
Butt I suppose you be in noo suche distresse.

---

35. the whiche: (the letter) which.
38. insuye: follow.
44. beire: bear.
45. dyssemblance: dissembling, prevarication.
47. persing: piercing.
48. caught in snare: ensnared, trapped.
49. douttance: doubt.
50. itt: i.e. 'my bewtye'.   *puisance*: power.
51. bewtiouse: beautiful.
52. constren: constrain, compel.   *amerous*: amorous.
58. penciffenes: apprehension, sorrow.

Also itt is truth that throughe povertye   60
Many on dare nott putt hymselffe in prease:
Butt I take you for none of them, trulye,
Butt that you durst, if that itt did you please,
Yourselffe putt forthe, your harte forto ease.
For how shuld I your sorowez redresse   65
Butt iff that ye to me doo them pleynly expresse?

Also wher you desire me that I shuld nott shrinke,
Butt that I shuld continewe in the same mynde
That you lafte me in, soo that then you might thinke
That ther were some truthe in womans kinde: 70
Surely in the same mynde ye shall me styll fynde,
Soo that you shall nott nede me forto mistruste,
Though peraventure you have fonde some unjuste.

Itt is a trewe proverbe and off olde antiquite,
'Dispraise nott all, thoughe on have offended'.   75
Butt they be worthye prease that stydffast and
    trewe be,
And they disprease, that oderwayez have intended:
Yett say well, 'By the worst the best may be amended',
For my love ys sett uppon a perffitt gronde.
Noo dissayte in me truly shal be founde.   80

Butt I wyl be trewe, though I shuld continewe
All my hole lyffe in payne and hevynesse.
I wyll never change you for any oder newe.
Yow be my joye, my comfforte and gladnes,
Whome I shall serve with all dilligence.   85
Exyle me never from your harte soo dere,
Whiche unto my harte have sett you most nere.

61. *Many . . . prease*: many a one dare not put himself forward.
66. *Butt iff*: unless.
69. *lafte*: left.
70. *womans kinde*: women's nature.
71. *Surely*: certainly.
73. *fonde*: found.
75. *on*: one.
76. *prease*: praise.   *stydffast*: steadfast.
77. *oderwayez*: otherwise.
80. *dissayte*: deceit.
82. *hole lyffe*: whole life.
83. *I . . . . newe*: a cliché of late medieval love poetry; compare l. 497.
87. *Whiche . . . nere*: (me) who have placed you closest to my heart.

Fynally, this scedule forto conclude,
My purpose is certen according to the same,
Myndyng for your sake all fantasyez to exclude   90
Off love fayned, and the contrarye to attaine:
And by lyke usage off us shall springe the fame
Unto the presence off Venus, that Goddas eternall,
Whoo off hur goodnes grante joye to trewe lovers all.

b) *Poems from the Findern Manuscript* *

(i)   What-so men seyn,   95
       Love is no peyn
       To them, serteyn,   Butt varians.

---

88. scedule: document, list.
89. certen: certain, fixed.
90. fantasyez: fancies.
91. love fayned: pretended love.
       the contrarye: i.e. genuine, unfeigned love.
       attaine: achieve.
92. lyke usage: similar practice (i.e. on your part too).
       off ... fame: our reputation shall ascend.
93. Goddas: goddess.
94. hur: her.   *grante*: (may she) grant.

* The Findern Manuscript (CUL MS Ff. 1. 6) is a well-known collection of poetry (lyrics, metrical romances and extracts from longer poems such as Chaucer's) put together over some years by members of the Findern family of Derbyshire, their friends, relatives and servants. Some women's names appear in the manuscript ('Margery hungerford' on f. 20ᵛ, 'ffrances kruken' on f. 65ᵛ, 'Elizabet koton' and 'Elisabet frauncys' on f. 109) which may be those of scribes; several of the poems are explicitly written from a woman's viewpoint (see below) and others whose gender is not overt may well also be women's texts. See Robbins 1954; Harris 1983.

(i) f. 56ʳ. *IMEV* 3917. The verse form (two-stress four-syllable lines grouped in quatrains that are linked in pairs by the rhymes) may ultimately derive from Medieval Latin poetry (see Davies 1963: 355) and is not uncommon in Middle English. The poem is printed here as it is set out in the manuscript, which emphasises its ingenuity; it is possible to read each column as an independent poem.
95. What-so: whatever.
96. peyn: pain.
97. Butt varians: without/except for variation.

For they constreyn
Ther hertis to feyn,
Ther mowthis to pleyn   Ther displesauns;   100

(Whych is in dede
Butt feynyd drede,
So God me spede,   And dowbilnys)

Ther othis to bede
Ther lyvys to lede;   105
And proferith mede   Newfangellnys.

For when they pray
Ye shall have nay,
What-so they sey: Beware, for sham.

For every daye   110
They waite ther pray,
Wher-so they may   And make butt game.

Then semyth me,
Ye may well se
They be so fre   In evyry plase,   115

---

98. *constreyn*: compell.
99. *feyn*: feign.
100. *pleyn*: lament.   *displesauns*: suffering.
103. *So ... spede*: so help me God.   *dowbilnys*: duplicity.
104–5. *Ther ... lede*: to offer their oaths to conduct their lives.
106. *And ... Newfangellnys*: and love of novelty offers blandishments.
109. *sham*: shame.
111. *waite*: lie in wait for.   *pray*: prey.
112. *Wher-so*: wherever.
       make butt game: just treat it as a joke.
115. *fre*: noble, lavish.   *plase*: place.

Hitt were pete
Butt they shold be
Begelid, parde,   Withowtyn grase.

(ii)   My woofull hert, this clad in payn,
       Wote natt welle what do nor seyn: 120
          Longe absens grevyth me so.

       For lakke of syght nere am I sleyn,
       All joy myne hert hath in dissedeyn:
          Comfort fro me is go.

       Then thogh I wold me owght complayn   125
       Of my sorwe and grete payn
          Who shold comforte me do?

       Ther is no thynge can make me to be fayn
       Butt the syght of hym agayn
          That cawsis my wo.   130

       None butt he may me susteyn,
       He is my comfort in all payn:
          Y love hym and no moo.

116–8. Hitt ... Begelid: it would be a shame if they were not deceived.
118. parde: by God.   *Withowtyn grase*: without mercy.

(ii) f. 69ᵛ. *IMEV* 2279. Seven stanzas, each consisting of two four-stress
lines and a single three-stress line; a technical *tour de force* as only two
rhymes are used in the whole poem.
119. this: thus.
120. Wote ... seyn: does not well know what to do or say.
122. lakke: lack.   *nere*: nearly.
123. All ... dissedeyn: my heart holds all joy in contempt.
125. thogh ... complayn: even if I were to lament at all.
128. fayn: glad.
130. cawsis: causes.
131. susteyn: sustain, support.

To hym I woll be trywe and playn,
And evyr his owne in serteyn   135
  Tyll deth departe us to.

My hert shall I never fro hym refrayn;
I gave hitt hym withowte constrayn,
  Evyr to contenwe so.

(iii)   Come home, dere hert, from tarieng;   140
Kausith me to wepe, bothe weile and wring,
Also to lyve evere in distresse
So gret there may no wight expresse:
Al my joye ye torne to mournyng.

Sorowe is in myn herte digging;   145
To dethe, I trowe, he woul me bring
In woful trans withoute redresse.

Whanne I have of you sume tiding,
Gret joye I have, withoute failing,
Right as me ought with rightwisnesse;   150
But yet may not myn heveynesse
Depart frome me til your comyng.

134. trywe: true, faithful.   *playn:* open, candid.
135. serteyn: certainty.
136. departe: separate.
137. refrayn: withdraw.
138. constrayn: constraint.
139. contenwe: continue.

(iii) ff. 135–136. *IMEV* 3878. The verse form of four verse-paragraphs of thirteen lines, made up of five-line, three-line and five-line stanzas, is most unusual. In the manuscript the first verse-paragraph is written as the last, but a study of the rhymes suggests that it has been displaced. The last verse-paragraph is apparently a line short; this may well be deliberate if the fifty-one lines of the poems are meant to signify an absence of a year less a single week.
140. tarieng: lingering.
141. Kausith: (your delay) causes.   *weile:* wail.
143. there .... expresse: no one is able to express it.
144. torne: turn, convert.
146. woul: would, intends.
147. trans: trance.
150. Right ... rightwisnesse: just as I should with justice.
151. heveynesse: sorrow.

To you, my joye and my wordly pleasaunce,
I wol shrive me with dredful countenaunce
Of chiding, which your letter bereth wittenesse;   155
Therto constrained by my woful distresse,
Asking you absolucion and penaunce.

What wol ye more of me but repentaunce?
God wol himselve have therof suffisaunce:
Mercy I seke and aske aye foryevenesse.   160

By Seynt Martyn, and ye knew my grevaunce,
The whiche I suffred with long continuance,
Dreding ye were of my woos roghtlesse:
That was to me a grevous hevinesse,
Yet aske I mercy to be in pacience.   165

There may areste me no pleasance,
And our be our I fele grevaunce.
I not to whome I may complaine,
For he that may my woo restreine
Wol have of me no remembrance.   170

Sith I ame under his governaunce,
He shuld sett me suche ordinaunce
As I might have ease of my paine.

153. *wordly pleasaunce*: earthly pleasure.
154. *wol . . . me*: will make my confession.
154–5. *dredful . . . chiding*: with a bearing fearful of rebuke.
159. *suffisaunce*: enough, sufficiency.
160. *aye*: constantly.
161. *Seynt Martyn*: the point of this reference is not clear: Martin of Tours (371–97), patron of France, had been a Roman soldier which may suggest that the husband was fighting in France; Martinmas (11 November), his feast day, was traditionally the time for hiring servants and killing cattle in preparation for winter.
     and: if.
163. *Dreding . . . roghtlesse*: fearing you cared nothing for my sorrows.
166. *areste*: restrain, check.
167. *our be our*: hour by hour.   *grevaunce*: grief, sorrow.
168. *not*: do not know.
169. *may . . . restreine*: is able to diminish.
171. *Sith*: since.   *governaunce*: authority, control.
172. *sett . . . ordinaunce*: i.e. so ordain it.

Me thinkith he might have conscience
And of my woos sum suffisance,   175
Considering that I ame so plaine
To him ever, with joye or paine:
Let him have therof repentance.

Welcome be ye, my sovereine,
The cause of my joyfull peine.   180
For the while ye were away,
Myn hert seyd noght but 'walaway'.

No more I do my mirthis fayne
But in gladnesse I swym and baine:
Ye have my mornyng dreven away.   185

Of your comyng I ame so fayne
That mirthes done my sorow steine,
And make amonge theim suche afray
That reste may they with me no day.
Gladnesse ye have brought me againe.   190

174. *conscience*: awareness, consciousness.
175. *suffisance*: sufficiency, i.e. enough.
176. *plaine*: open, straightforward.
178. *repentance*: remorse, compunction.
179. *sovereine*: sovereign lord, i.e. husband.
182. *walaway*: 'alas and alack'.
183. *fayne*: counterfeit.
184. *baine*: bathe.
185. *dreven*: driven.
186. *fayne*: glad, eager.
187. *mirthes . . . steine*: joys make my sorrows turn pale.
188. *afray*: attack.
189. *reste*: remain.

(iv)   Yit wulde I nat the causer faryd amysse,
For all the good that ever Y had or schall.
Therfor Y take myn aventure, iwisse,
As sche that hath forsaken joyus all
And to all payne is bothe sojet and thralle.   195
Lo, thus I stonde withowten wordes moo,
All voyde of joy an full of payne and woo.

Now ye that bathe in myrthe and plesaunce,
Have mynde on me that was sumtyme in ease
And had the worldyl at myn oune ordynaunce,   200
Whiche now is turned into al disease.
Now glad wher sche that Fortune so cowde please,
That sche myght stonde in verry sycurnesse
Never to fele the stroke of unkyndnesse.

Departyng ys the grownde of dysplesaunce   205
Most in my hert of eny thing erthly.
I you ensure holy in remembraunce,
Within myself Y thenke hit verryly,
Wiche schall contynu with me dayly.
Syns that ye moste nedys departe me fro,   210
It ys to me a verry dedly woo.

(iv) ff. 153ᵛ–154. *IMEV* 4272.5.
191. Yit ... amysse: Yet I would not want the person who caused my sorrows to suffer.
192. good: possessions.
193. take ... aventure: accept my fate.   *iwisse*: indeed.
194. joyus: joys.
195. sojet: subject.
200. worldyl: world.
    at ... ordynaunce: under my own control.
202. glad .... please: she would be fortunate who so knew how to please Fortune.
203. verry sycurnesse: true security.
204. stroke: blow.
205. Departyng: separation.   *dysplesaunce*: discontent.
207. ensure: assure.   *holy*: wholly.
210. Syns: since.*moste nedys*: must necessarily.

c) *Queen Elizabeth's Hymn to Venus* *

Myne hert is set uppon a lusty pynne;
I praye to Venus of good continuaunce.
For I rejoyse the case that I am in:
Delyverd from sorow, annexed to plesaunce,   215
Of all comfort havyng habundaunce.
This joy and I, I trust, shal never twynne.
Myne hert is set uppon a lusty pynne.

I pray to Venus of good continuaunce,
Sith she hath set me in the wey of ease,   220
Myne hertly servyse with myne attendaunce
So to contynue that ever I may please,
Thus voydyng from all pensful disease.
Now stand I hole fer from all grevaunce;
I praye to Venus of good continuaunce.   225

---

* Oxford Bodley Rawlinson MS C. 86, ff. 155ᵛ–156. *IMEV* 2179. Most of
the manuscript is an early sixteenth-century collection of poetry, much of it
by Chaucer and Lydgate, which manifests some sort of preoccupation with
women. It contains, for instance, three Lamentations of the Virgin; the
'Complaint of Dido' extracted from the *Legend of Good Women*; two metrical
romances ('Launfal' and 'The Wedding of Sir Gawain and Dame Ragnell'),
one of which derives ultimately from a *lai* of Marie de France; Chaucer's
Clerk's Tale and *Prioress's Tale*, as well an anti-feminist attack on women's
extravagant dress. The manuscript attributes this poem to 'Quene Elyzabeth'
(see l. 254), probably Elizabeth Woodville, wife of Edward IV (the
manuscript also contains a Latin elegy on his death) and sister of Anthony
Woodville, the translator and patron of Caxton. The verse form is unparalleled elsewhere; it is an elaboration of the sestina but not only is the
first line of each rhyme-royal stanza the same as the last line; the second
line of the first stanza is the first line of the second stanza, and so on.
212. set . . . pynne: i.e. in a merry frame of mind. The origin of this phrase
is obscure but *pynne* may have the sense of '(musical) pitch'.
213. of . . . continuaunce: for her continued favour.
214. case: situation.
215. annexed: attached.
216. habundaunce: abundance, plenty.
217. twynne: part.
220. Sith: since.
221. hertly: heart-felt.   *attendaunce*: duty, homage.
223. voydyng: departing.   *pensful*: sorrowful.   *disease*: discomfort, pain.
224. hole: whole, entire.   *fer*: far.

For I rejoyse the case that I am in.
My gladnesse is such ther grevyth me no payne.
And so to serve nevyr shal I blynne.
And thogh I wolde, I may not me refrayne,
Myne herte and I so set is in certayn.　　　　　230
We shal never slake but ever new begyn;
For I rejoyse the case that I am in.

Delyverd from sorow, annexed to plesaunce,
That all my joy I set, as aught of ryght,
To please, as after my symple suffisaunce,　　　235
To me the goodlyest, most beauteous in sight;
A verry lanterne to ye, al other lyght;
Most to my comfort on her remembraunce,
Delyverd from sorow, annexed to plesaunce.

Of all comfort havyng habundaunce,　　　　　240
As whan that I thynke the goodlyhed
Of the most femyne and meke in countenaunce,
Verray myrrour and ster of womanhed;
Whos ryght good fame so large abrod doth spred.
Ful glad to me to have congnossaunce　　　　　245
Of all comfort havyng habundaunce.

This joy and I, I trust, shall never twyn,
So that I am so ferfurth in the trace
My joyes ben doubil wher other be but thyn.

228. *serve*: i.e serve Venus.　　*blynne*: cease.
231. *We*: i.e. 'my heart and I'.　　*slake*: slacken.　　*new*: anew, again.
234. *aught of ryght*: as (my) rightful possession.
235. *suffisaunce*: capacity.
236. *To . . . goodlyest*: (Venus who is) in my eyes the best.
237. *verry . . . lyght*: a true source of illumination (lantern) to all you other lights.
241. *goodlyhed*: goodliness.
242. *femyne*: feminine.
243. *ster*: (guiding) star; cf. Eleanor Hull's invocation of the Virgin as 'star of the sea' (p. 223).
244. *large abrod*: widely.
245. *Ful . . . congnossaunce*: I am very happy to know.
248. *ferfurth . . . trace*: far advanced on the way.
249. *doubil*: two-fold.　　*other . . . thyn*: others are just thin.

For I am stabely set in suche a place   250
Wher beaute cresith and ever wellyth grace
Whiche is ful famous and borne of nobil kyn.
This joy and I, I trust, shal never twyn.

Finis quod Quene Elyzabeth

d) *An Anchoress's Hymn to the Virgin**

Heille, glorious Virgyne, grounde of al oure grace.   255
Heyle, mayde and moder in virgynitee.
Heyle, whame the Sone of God cheesse for his place,
Sent frome above thane frome the Faders see.
Heyle, with thyne ere conceyvinge, sente to thee
By Gabriell, he thus to thee seyinge: 260
'Heyle, ful of grace, Marye, God is with thee.'
Heyle, with thine humble herte ther obeyinge.

Heyle, that with God so privee art and pleyne.
Of alle wymmen ay blessed mot thou be.

250. *stabely*: stably, securely.
251. *cresith*: increases.
     ever . . . grace: grace flows constantly.

* Oxford Bodley MS Ashmole 59, f. 68ʳ⁻ᵛ. *IMEV* 1046. This manuscript is
one of several autograph manuscripts compiled and transcribed by the
bibliophile and amateur scribe John Shirley (?1366–1456). It contains a
number of historical, moral and religious poems, many attributed to
Lydgate, but Shirley ascribes this poem to 'an holy Ankaresse of
Maunsffeld'. It also survives in two other MSS, BL Cotton Caligula A ii,
where it is unattributed, and BL Add. 29729, compiled by the historian
John Stowe in 1558. Stowe ascribes the whole volume, though not
specifically this poem, to Lydgate. It is certainly written in Lydgate's
elaborately aureate and easily imitable style. Five eight-line stanzas; a line is
missing from the second stanza.
257. *whame*: whom.   *cheesse*: chose.
258. *thane*: then.   *see*: seat, throne.
259. *with . . . conceyvinge*: it was a common medieval belief that the Virgin
conceived Christ (the Word of God) through the ear.
263. *privee*: intimate.   *pleyne*: open, candid.
264. *mot*: may.

Heyle, that conceyved and bere withoute peyne   265
The secounde persone in the Trynitee.
Heyle, cristal clere; heyle, closet of clennesse.
Heyle, blest bourgeon; heyle, blossome of bautee.
Heyle, chaste lylye descended frome hyenesse.

Heyle, emparyse in heven hyest estate.   270
Heyle, mayde makelesse; heyle, moder of pitee.
Heyle, qwene of comforte, of joye desolate
Whane thowe thy chylde sawe deying on a tree.
Heyle, whos uprist was shyninge unto thee.
Heyle, that oure mescheves olde hast nuwe drest.   275
Heyle, by whos mene Jhesu hathe made us free:
The fruyt of thy wombe, ever beo it eblest.

Heyle, stedfast sterre with stremis lemyng light.
Heyle, that byhelde ful clerely with thye eye
Thy sone ascendinge by his propre might,   280
Percynk the clowdes unto the heven hye,
Whane it was seyde to hem of Galylee,
'Why merveyle yee, thus lokinge up in veyne?
This lord that thus descended mightely,
As he styed up he sal come doune ageyne.'   285

---

267. *closet*: chamber, abode.   *clennesse*: purity.
268. *bourgeon*: flower.   *bautee*: beauty.
270. *emparyse*: empress.   *heven*: heaven's.
271. *makelesse*: peerless.
272. *desolate*: deprived.
273. *tree*: i.e. the cross.
274. *uprist*: resurrection; sunrise.
275. *mescheves olde*: ancient sins, misfortunes.
     nuwe drest: newly remedied.
276. *mene*: mediation.
277. *beo*: be.   *eblest*: blessed.
278. *stremis*: rays.   *lemyng light*: shining bright.
280. *propre might*: own power.
281. *Percynk*: piercing.
285. *styed up*: ascended.   *sal*: shall.

Heyle, floure of vertue which that may not fade.
Heyle, roos of ryse, mooste holsome of odour.
Heyle whome the Holy Gooste came thee to glade
In pure assumpcion up to his toure.
Heyle, comly queene, there corounde with hounour.   290
Heyle, mediatryce and meene for mankynde.
Heyle, salve to seeke, us synners sende socour,
Thees joyes fyve surmountinge in oure mynde.

e) *Eleanor Percy's Prayer**

Oratio Elionore Percie
Ducissa Buckhammie   295

287. roos of ryse: rose on the stem.   *holsome*: healthful.
289. assumpcion: (bodily) Assumption (into heaven).
   toure: tower, i.e. the heavenly city of Jerusalem.
290. corounde: crowned.
291. mediatryce: mediatrix.   *meene*: intercessor.
292. salve to seeke: balm for the sick.
293. Thees joyes fyve: the Five Joys of Mary were (as in this poem) the Annunciation, the Nativity, the Resurrection, the Ascension and the Assumption.
293. surmountinge: going over.

* BL MS Arundel 318, f. 152ʳ⁻ᵛ. Not in *IMEV*. This manuscript is a handsome Book of Hours, on the final pages of which this verse prayer, a translation of a well-known Latin hymn, 'Gaude virgo, mater Christi' (Rejoice, O Virgin, Mother of Christ), has been written out by Anne Arundel, sister of Eleanor Percy. Eleanor was the daughter of Henry Percy, Duke of Northumberland, and his wife Maud Herbert; in 1500 she married Edward Stafford, 3rd Duke of Buckingham (1478–1521), to whom she bore a son and three daughters. Her husband (who was a nephew of Elizabeth Woodville and had been the ward of Lady Margaret Beaufort) was executed on concocted charges of treason by Henry VIII; her son Henry became a leading Protestant and also translated Erasmus into English. This is a macaronic poem, i.e. written in more than one language; it consists of four four-line stanzas, the fourth line always being Latin and rhyming on -*o*; the English lines vary between four and five stresses.
294–5. Oratio . . . Buckhammie: 'the prayer of Eleanor Percy, Duchess of Buckingham' (a rhyming couplet).

Gawde, Vergine and mother beinge
To Criste Jhesu, bothe God and Kinge.
By the blissed eyare him consevinge
Gabrielis nuncio.

Gawde, Vergine off all humylytie,   300
Showinge to us thy sonnes humanitie
Whan he without paine borne was of the
In pudoris lilio.

Gawde, flower of thi lorde and sonne,
Dieng without gilte for oure redemption: 305
To thy grete joye and oure salvation
Fulgit resurrectio.

Gawde, for Criste assendid is
With all triumphe to eternall blisse;
From whens he came first, iwisse,   310
Motu fertur proprio.

Gawde, swete roose, for thy blissed ure;
Assumpte thow war with angell cure,
With joye ever more there to endure
In celi palacio.   315

Gawde, Vergine and mother of grace,
Praye to thie sonne for oure trespace,
That we may comme to that hevenli place,
Sanctorum contubernio;

296. *Gawde*: 'Rejoyce'.
298. *eyare*: ear.
299. Gabrielis nuncio: 'by Gabriel's message'.
303. In . . . lilio: 'in the lily of chastity'.
307. Fulgit resurrectio: 'the resurrection shines out'.
311. Motu fertur proprio: 'borne up by his own movement', i.e. of his own
accord.
312. *ure*: hour (of death).
313. *Assumpte*: assumed (into Heaven).
    angell cure: the care of the angels.
314. *endure*: last, continue.
315. In . . . palacio: 'in the palace of Heaven'.
317. *trespace*: trespass, sin.
319. Sanctorum contubernio: 'in the company of the saints'.

Where-as the freute of thy wombe, trulie   320
To ous most comforte, most dere ladie,
Shall still ther reigne everlastinglie
> *In perhenni gawdio.*

This praeir compiled of vertuous memorie
By the right noble duches Buckghammie,   325
Whos soule God pardon, late Elener Percie
> *Veritatis a titulo.*

f) *Two Poems from Humphrey Newton's Commonplace Book**

(i)   Beaute of you, burne, in my body abydis;
Right reufully I sike, thof I be fer you fro.
If ye be true in trouth, lof hit not slidis   330
And I schall swere the same justely also.

---

320. Where-as: where.   *freute*: fruit.
321. ous: us.
323. In . . . gawdio: 'in eternal joy'.
327. Veritatis a titulo: '?by a true title'; the manuscript reads *Verit atitulo*
which is meaningless and must be corrupt.

* Oxford Bodley MS Lat. Misc. c. 66 is 'commonplace book' (that is, a
book in which are recorded miscellaneous extracts in prose or verse to be
especially remembered or referred to) compiled by Humphrey Newton of
Pownall, Cheshire (1466–1536). It contains legal documents, miscellaneous
notes, medical treatises and some poems, most of which Newton
presumably composed himself. These two, however, are written from a
woman's viewpoint and the second one at least is perhaps too delicately
ironic about the speaker's deserted lover (presumably Newton) to have been
written by Newton himself.

(i) f. 93[va]. *IMEV* 481. A single rhyme-royal stanza; the initial letters of lines
1–5 form an anagram of BRIAN, presumably the name of the speaker's
lover.
328. burne: sir.
329. reufully: sorrowfully.   *sike*: sigh.   *thof*: though.
330. lof . . . slidis: love does not slip away.

Not ye be wroth thof I sey fayn as I wold do:
My body I wold betake into youre gentillnes
With hert intier and sperete of mekenes.

(ii)   Farewell, that was my lef so dere,   335
Fro her that loved you so well.
Ye were my lef from yere to yere:
Wheder I were yours I connot tell.
To you I have byn trew and lell
At all tymes unto this day;   340
And now I say farewell, farewelle,
I tak my lef for ever and ay.

Youre lof, forsoth, ye have not lost:
If ye loved me, I loved you, iwys!
Bot that I put you to gret cost;   345
Therfor I have you clipt and kist
Bot now, my luf, I most nedes sesse
And tak me to hym that me has tan.
Therfore tak ye another wher ye list:
I gif you good lef, sertayn.   350

Gif ye me licence to do the same.
This tokyn truly I you betak
In remenbrance of my name.

332. *Not ... wroth*: Do not be angry.
        thof ... do: even if I say what I would willingly do.
333. *betake*: entrust.
334. *intier*: whole.   *sperete*: spirit.

(ii) f. 93vb. *IMEV* 768. Three eight-line stanzas, with a variable rhyme
scheme.
335. *lef*: beloved.
339. *lell*: loyal.
342. *lef*: leave.
343. *lof*: love.   *lost*: i.e. wasted.
345. *Bot ... cost*: i.e. you have not wasted your love, except insofar as I put
you to great expense.
346. *clipt*: embraced.
347. *sesse*: cease.
348. *tan*: taken.
350. *lef*: permission.
352. *This tokyn*: i.e. this poem.

Send me a tokyn for my sake.
Wheder it be send erly or late,   355
I shall it kepe for old qwayntance.
And now to Crist I you betake,
To save and kepe in whert and sance.

g) *Unkindness Hath Killed Her**

Grevus ys my sorowe
Both evyne and moro.   360
Unto myselffe alone
Thus do I make my mowne
    That unkyndnes haith kyllyd me
    And putt me to this peyne.
    Alas, what remedy   365
    That I cannot refreyne.

Whan other men doyth sleype
Thene do I syght and weype,
All ragius in my bed,
As one for paynes neyre ded,   370

356. *for . . . qwayntance*: for the sake of long-standing friendship.
357. *betake*: commend, entrust.
358. *kepe . . . sance*: keep you safe and well.

* BL MS Sloane 1584, ff. 85–7. *IMEV* 1018. This manuscript is a priest's
handbook written out by John Gysborn, a Premonstratensian canon of
Coverham in Yorkshire (see Boffey 1985: 129), which contains a number of
theological and medical treatises as well as a few lyrics. An early sixteenth-
century printed book, *The Gude and Goodlie Ballatis* (ed. Mitchell, pp.
151–7), contains a sacred parody of this poem, in which the speaker is
Christ and the lover the rejecting human soul. Fourteen stanzas of four
three-stress lines with an integrated four-line refrain.
359. *Grevus*: grievous, bitter.
360. *evyne . . . moro*: by night and day.
362. *mowne*: moan.
363. *haith*: hath.
366. *refreyne*: abstain, forbear.
367. *men*: people.   *doyth sleype*: do sleep.
368. *weype*: weep.
369. *ragius*: passionate.
370. *neyre*: nearly.

That unkyndnes have kyllyd me
And putt me to this payne.
Alas, what remedy
That I cannott refreyne.

My harte, ytt have no reste,   375
Butt styll with peynes oppreste,
And yett of all my smart
Ytt grevith moste my harte
    That unkyndnes shuld kyll me
    And putt me to this payne.   380
    Alas, what remedy
    That I cannott refreyne.

Wo worth trust untrusty.
Wo worth love unlovyd.
Wo worth hape unblamyd.   385
Wo worth fautt unnamyd:
    Thus unkyndly to kyll me
    And putt me to this payne.
    Now, alas, what remedy
    That I cannott refrayne.   390

Alas, I lyve to longe;
My paynes be so stronge.
For comforth have I none.
God wott I wold fayne be gone
    For unkyndnes haith kyllyd me   395
    And putt me to this payne.
    Alas, what remedy
    That I cannott refrayne.

Iff ony wyght be here
That byeth love so dere,   400
Come nere, lye downe by me
And weype for company.
    For unkyndnes haith kyllyd me

377. *smart*: sufferings.
383. *Wo worth*: woe betide.   *untrusty*: untrustworthy.
385. *hape unblamyd*: uncensured mishap.
386. *fautt*: fault.
399. *ony wyght*: any person.
400. *That . . . dere*: who pays so high a price for love.

And putt me to this payne.
Alas, what remedy   405
That I cannott refrayne.

My foes whiche love me nott
Bevayle my deth, I wott.
And he that love me beste
Hymeselfe my deth haith dreste.   410
　　What unkyndnes shuld kyle me
　　If this ware nott my payne?
　　Alas, what remedy
　　That I cannott refreyne.

My last wyll here I make.   415
To God my soule I betake
And my wrechyd body
As erth in a hole to lye
　　For unkyndnes to kyle me
　　And putt me to this payne.   420
　　Alas, what remedy
　　That I cannot refreyne.

O harte, I the bequyeth
To hyme that is my deth.
Yff that no harte haith he,   425
My harte his schal be,
　　Thought unkyndnes haith kyllyd me
　　And putt me to this payne.
　　Yett yf my body dye,
　　My hertt cannot refrayne.   430

Placebo, dilexi:
Com weype this obsequye.
My mowrnarus, dolfully
Come weype this psalmody

---

408. Bevayle: bewail.
410. dreste: arranged, prepared.
416. betake: bequeath.
431. Placebo, dilexi: 'I shall please [the Lord in the land of the living]',
Psalm 114: 9, and 'I have loved [because the Lord will hear the voice of my
prayer]', Psalm 114: 1. These words open the Vigils of the Dead.
432. obsequye: service for the dead.
433. mowrnarus: mourners.
434. psalmody: psalm singing.

Of 'Unkyndnes haith kyllyd me   435
And putt me to this payne.
Behold this wrechid body
That your unkyndnes haith slayne.'

Now I besych all ye,
Namely that lovers be,   440
My love my deth forgyve
And soffer hyme to lyve
    Thought unkyndnes haith kyllyd me
    And putt me to this payne.
Yett haid I rether dye   445
For his sake ons agayne.

My tombe, ytt schal be blewe,
In tokyne that I was trewe.
To bringe my love frome doute,
Itt shal be writtyn abowtte   450
    That unkyndnes haith kyllyd me
    And putt me to this payne.
Behold this wrechid body
That your unkyndnes haith slayne.

O lady, lerne by me: 455
Sley nott love wylfully.
For fer love waxyth denty.
And thus it shal nott be
    Unkyndnes to kyle me
    Or putt love to this payne.   460
I ware the better dye
For loves sake agayne.

440. *Namely*: in particular.
441. *My . . . forgyve*: forgive my beloved for my death.
442. *soffer*: allow.
446. *ons agayne*: once more.
447. *blewe*: blue (the traditional colour of constancy, as in the phrase 'true blue').
448. *trewe*: loyal.
450. *writtyn abowtte*: inscribed around.
457. *fer . . . denty*: distant love grows scarce, rare.
459. *kyle*: kill.
461. *ware*: were, would be.

Grevus is my soro,
Butt deth ys my boro.
For to myselfe alone   465
Thus do I make my mone
    That unkyndnes haith kyllyd me
    And passyd is my payne.
    Prey for this ded body
    That your unkyndnes haith slayne.   470
                                        Amen.

h) *A Carol**

Wolde God that hyt were so
As I cowde wysshe bytuyxt us too.

The man that I loved al ther best
In al thys contre, est other west,   475
To me he ys a strange gest.
What wonder est thow I be woo?

When me were levest that he schold duelle,
He wold noght sey onys farewelle.
He wold noght sey ones farewell   480
When tyme was come that he most go.

464. *boro*: pledge, guarantor.
468. *passyd*: past, gone.

* CUL MS Add. 5943, f. 178ᵛ. *IMEV* 3418. In the manuscript feminine
pronouns have been written between the lines in appropriate places so that
the poem can be adapted to a male speaker and the gender roles reversed.
The argument of this carol is somewhat obscure but it seems not to present
a standard literary situation. Six four-line stanzas with burden or refrain
and a variable rhyme scheme.
473. *cowde*: could.   *bytuyxt*: between.
474. *al ther best*: best of all.
475. *est*: east.   *other*: or.
476. *gest*: lover, man.
477. *est*: is it.   *thow*: though.
478. *me . . . duelle*: I most wanted him to stay.
479. *onys*: once.

In places ofte when I hym mete
I dar noght speke but forth I go.
With herte and eyes I hym grete:
So trywe of love I know no mo.   485

As he ys myn hert love,
My dyrward dyre, iblessed he be,
I swere by God that ys above:
Non hath my love but only he.

I am icomfortyd in every syde;   490
The colures wexeth both fres and newe;
When he ys come and wyl abyde
I wott ful wel that he ys trywe.

I love hym trywely and no mo;
Wolde God that he hyt knywe.   495
And ever I hope hyt schal be so.
Then schal I chaunge for no new.

483. *forth I go*: I go off, away.
485. *So . . . mo*: I know of no others as loyal in love (as I).
486. *hert*: heart's.
487. *dyrward dyre*: precious beloved.
490–3. *I . . . trywe*: the sense of this stanza is unclear; it could mean that
she is constantly reassured (falsely) that her lover is faithful but she will
believe it only when he comes to remain with her.
490. *icomfortyd*: reassured.
491. *colures*: tricks, ruses.   *wexeth*: grow.   *fres*: fresh, bright.
492. *ys . . . abyde*: has come and is willing to stay.
497. *chaunge . . . new*: exchange (him) for a new lover: a poetic cliché in
late medieval and early Tudor verse (Huttar 1965: 170–2); cf. above, l. 83.

i) *Two Early Tudor Lyrics from the Fairfax Manuscript* *

(i) My wofull hart in paynfull weryness
Which hath byn long plungyng with thought unseyne,
Full lyk to drowne in wawis of distress   500
Saffe helpe and grace of my lord and soverayne,
Is now be hym so comfortid agayne
That I am bownde above all erthly thyng
To love and dred hym as my lord and kyng.

(ii) Yowre counturfetyng with doubyll delyng   505
Avaylyth nothyng: and wote ye why?
For ye with your faynyng hath such demyng
To make a belevyng: nay, nay, hardely.
Hit were to grete pite that women truly
Hade so grete foly that cowde nott tell,   510
When that ye do lye, then speke ye so swetely
And thynk the contrary: thus knowe we well.

* The Fairfax Manuscript, BL MS Add. 5465, is an early Tudor songbook
(see Stevens 1961: 3–4). Both these poems appear as two-part songs with
musical settings. As the manuscript is connected with the Court, the
references in the first poem to 'my lord and soverayne' and 'my lord and
kyng' may well be quite literal and not necessarily imply a female speaker.

(i) ff. 8, 9. *IMEV* 2279. A single rhyme-royal stanza.
499. plungyng: sinking.   *unseyne*: unspoken.
500. Full lyk: very likely.
501. Saffe: i.e. were it not for.
502. be: by.
503. bownde: bound, constrained.

(ii) ff. 22ᵛ, 23ᵛ. *IMEV* 4281.5.
505. counturfetyng: counterfeiting.
   doubyll delyng: double-dealing, action marked by duplicity.
507. faynyng: pretence.
   hath ... demyng: make such a judgment, i.e. think.
508. make a belevyng: cause (people) to believe.
   hardely: indeed, assuredly.
509. to ... pite: too great a pity.

j) *A Song from Ritson's Manuscript**

O blessed Lord, how may this be,
That Y am thus in hevinesse?
And yet Y have do my besynesse   515
Ever to plese hym with all my myghth
Bothe erly, late, by day and by nyghth.

k) *One Last Word about Love**

He that wil be a lover in every wise,
He muste have thre thingis whiche Jeame lackith.
The first is goodlyhede at poynt devise;   520
The secunde is manere, which manhoode makith;
The thryd is goode, that no woman hatith.
Marke well this, that lovers wil be
Muste nedys have oone of thes thre.

l) From 'The Flower and the Leaf'*

[The Narrator, unable to sleep, has gone for a walk in the
early morning. Sitting in a beautiful arbour, she listens first to
a goldfinch and then to a nightingale.]

* Ritson's Manuscript (BL MS Add. 5665), f. 69ᵛ. *IMEV* 2393.5. This
manuscript is another Tudor songbook (see Stevens 1961: 5–6). This poem
is written out as a two-part song. A single five-line stanza.
514. hevinesse: sorrow.
515. do ... besynesse: done my utmost.
516. myghth: might, power.

* BL MS Royal 18 A vi, f. 22. *IMEV* 1170. This manuscript contains
several medical (including gynaecological) treatises as well as this amusingly
cynical poem which satirises both the young man's shortcomings and the
low expectations women have of their lovers. A single rhyme-royal stanza.
520. goodlyhede ... devise: perfect beauty.
521. manere: (good) manners.
    manhoode: gentlemanliness; cf. the proverb 'Manners maketh man'.
522. goode: money.
523. that ... be: (those) that wish to be lovers.

* 'The Flower and the Leaf' does not survive in manuscript and the only
independent witness to the text is Thomas Speght's 1598 edition of
Chaucer (which also prints 'The Assembly of Ladies'). His 1602 edition

(i)   And as I sat, the birds harkening thus,   525
Me thought that I heard voices sodainly,
The most sweetest and most delicious
That ever any wight, I trow trewly,
Heard in their life; for the armony
And sweet accord was in so good musike   530
That the voice to angels most was like.

At the last, out of a grove even by,
That was right goodly and pleasant to sight,
I sie where there came singing lustily
A world of ladies; but to tell aright   535
Their great beauty, it lieth not in my might,
Ne their array; neverthelesse I shall
Tell you a part, though I speake not of all.

In surcotes white of velvet wele sitting
They were clad, and the semes echone,   540
As it were a maner garnishing,
Was set with emerauds, one and one,
By and by, but many a rich stone
Was set on the purfles, out of dout,
Of colors, sleves, and traines round about,   545

makes some minor changes but there is no reason to think them authoritative, so the extracts here have been prepared from the 1598 edition but incorporate some conjectural emendations by later editors. It is interesting that Rachel Speght, who composed her own allegorical dream poem in the early seventeenth century (see above, p. 263), was either Thomas Speght's daughter or niece.

528. *wight*: creature.   *trow*: believe.
529. *armony*: harmony.
530. *accord*: concord.
532. *even*: right.
534. *sie*: saw.   *lustily*: cheerfully.
535. *world*: multitude.
539. *surcotes*: outer coats or garments, 'commonly worn by people of rank of both sexes' (*OED*).
539. *sitting*: suitable, fitting.
540. *semes echone*: each of the seams.
541. *maner garnishing*: kind of decoration.
542. *emerauds*: emeralds.   *one and one*: i.e. in rows.
543. *By and by*: one by one.
544. *purfles*: fur trimming, embroidered border.
545. *sleves*: sleeves.

As great pearles round and orient,
Diamonds fine and rubies red,
And many another stone, of which I went
The names now, and everich on her head
A rich fret of gold, which without dread   550
Was full of stately rich stones set.
And every lady had a chapelet

On her head, of leves fresh and greene
So wele wrought, and so mervelously,
That it was a noble sight to sene: 555
Some of laurer, and some ful pleasantly
Had chapelets of woodbind, and sadly
Some of agnus castus were also
Chapelets fresh; but there were many of tho

That daunced and eke song ful soberly.   560
But all they yede in manere of compace,
But one there yede in mid the company,
Soole by herselfe, but all followed the pace
That she kept, whose heavenly-figured face
So pleasant was, and her wele-shape person,   565
That of beauty she past hem everichon

---

546. *orient*: shining, brilliant.
548. *went*: lack.
550. *fret*: ornamental hair-net, headband or diadem.
     dread: doubt.
552. *chapelet*: garland, circlet.
554. *wrought*: made.
556. *laurer*: laurel.
557. *woodbind*: honeysuckle.   *sadly*: soberly.
558. *agnus castus*: a Mediterranean shrub, traditionally regarded as preserving chastity.
559. *tho*: those.
561. *yede*: went, walked.   *manere . . . compace*: a circular formation.
562. *one*: this lady is later revealed to be Diana, goddess of chastity.
     mid: the middle.
563. *Soole*: sole, alone.
564. *heavenly-figured*: fashioned by heaven
565. *wele-shape*: beautifully formed.
566. *past*: surpassed.

And more richly beseene by manyfold
She was also in every maner thing;
On her head, full plesaunt to behold,
A crowne of gold, rich for any king,   570
A braunch of agnus castus eke bearing
In her hand, and to my sight trewly
She lady was of the company.

[This group of ladies of the Company of the Leaf is joined by
nine knights with their retinues. The Company of the Flower
arrive, and are first scorched by the sun and then soaked in a
downpour. The Company of the Leaf rescues them, and both
groups go off amiably together. The Narrator, who has
observed all that has passed, gets up to leave.]

(ii)   I drest me forth, and happed to mete anon
Right a faire lady, I you ensure,   575
And she come riding by hirselfe alone
All in white, with semblance ful demure.
I saluted her and bad her good aventure
Must her befall, as I coud most humbly,
And she answered, 'My doughter, gramercy'.   580

'Madam,' quod I, 'if that I durst enquere
Of you, I would faine of that company
Wit what they be that past by this arbere.'
And she ayen answered right friendly,
'My faire doughter, all tho that passed hereby   585
In white clothing, be servants everichone
Unto the Leafe, and I myselfe am one.'

567. beseene: adorned.   *manyfold*: far.
571. eke: also.
574. drest me: went.   *happed*: chanced.   *anon*: straight away.
575. Right a faire: a really beautiful.   *ensure*: assure.
577. semblance: appearance.   *demure*: dignified, poised.
578–9. bad . . . befall: i.e. wished her well.
580. gramercy: many thanks.
582. faine: gladly.
583. Wit: know.   *arbere*: arbor, shady retreat.
584. ayen: back.

'Se ye not her that crowned is,' quod she,
'All in white?' 'Madame,' quod I, 'yis.'
'That is Diane, goddes of chastity,   590
And for bicause that she a maiden is
In her hond the braunch she bereth this,
That "agnus castus" men call properly,
And all the ladies in her company

Which ye se of that hearb chaplets weare,   595
Be such as han kepte alway her maidenhede.
And all they that of laurer chaplets beare
Be such as hardy were and wan by deed
Victorious name which never may be dede.
And all they were so worthy of ther hond,   600
In her time, that none might hem withstond.'

'And tho that weare chapelets on ther hede
Of fresh woodbind, be such as never were
To love untrue in word, thought, ne dede,
But aye stedfast, ne for plesance ne fere,   605
Though that they shuld their harts all to-tere,
Would never flit, but ever were stedfast
Till that their lives there asunder brast.'

[The Lady goes on to explain that the Company of the Flower
is composed of those who love idleness. When she asks the
Narrator to which group she lends her allegiance, she asserts
her loyalty to the Company of the Leaf and is dismissed with
the Lady's blessing.]

589. *yis*: yes.
595. *hearb*: plant.
596. *han kepte*: have preserved.
598. *hardy*: brave. Some of the ladies wore laurel chaplets (see l. 597).
     wan: won.
600. *worthy . . . hond*: brave in their actions.
601. *withstond*: resist.
605. *aye*: always.   *plesance*: pleasure.   *fere*: fear.
606. *all to-tere*: completely tear to pieces.
607. *flit*: waver.
608. *brast*: burst.

m) From 'The Assembly of Ladies'*

[The Narrator tells a knight of her dream in which she is summoned by Perseverance to present herself, dressed in blue, at the Palace of Lady Loyalty, together with her friends (women only) to present their grievances. She sets off, accompanied by Diligence.]

(i)   Than parted we at spryngyng of the day,
       And furth we went a soft and esy pase.   610
       Til at the last we were on oure journay
       So fer onward that we myght se the place.
       'Nowe lete us rest,' quod I, 'a litel space,
       And say we as devoutly as we can
       A Pater Noster for Seynte Julyan.'   615

       'With al myn hert,' quod she, 'I gre me wele.
       Moche better shul we spede whan we have done.'
       Than taryed we and sayde it every dele.
       And whan the day was fer gon after none,
       We sawe a place, and thider come we sone,   620
       Whiche rounde about was closid with a wal,
       Semyng to me ful like an hospital.

* 'The Assembly of Ladies' was printed by Thynne in his 1532 edition of Chaucer, and also printed by Speght in 1598 (see note to 'The Flower and the Leaf'). But unlike 'The Flower and the Leaf' it is extant in three fifteenth-century manuscripts: BL MS Add. 34360 (A), Cambridge Trinity College MS R. 3. 19, and Longleat MS 258. Pearsall bases his edition on MS Add. 34360 (A), which has also been followed here. In the Textual Notes, T refers to the readings common to Thynne's edition and the Trinity College and Longleat manuscripts.

(i) BL MS Add. 34360 ff. 40ᵛ–41.
609. spryngyng . . . day: dawn.
610. pase: i.e. speed.
612. fer onward: far advanced.
613. space: period of time.
615. Seynte Julyan: St Julian was the patron saint of hospitality.
616. gre me: agree.
617. spede: fare, progress.
618. taryed: lingered.   *every dele*: completely.
621. closid: enclosed.
622. hospital: hospice, place where pilgrims are received.

There fonde I oon had brought al myn array,
A gentilwomman of myn acqueyntaunce.
'I have mervaile,' quod I, 'what maner wey   625
Ye had knowlache of al this governaunce!'
'Yis, yis,' quod she, 'I herd Perseveraunce,
How she warned youre felawes everichone,
And what array that ye shal have upon.'

'Now, for my love,' quod I, 'I yow pray,   630
Sith ye have take upon yow al this peyne,
That ye wold helpe me on with myne array,
For wite ye wele, I wold be go ful fayne.'
'Al this prayer nedith nat, certeyne,'
Quod she ageyne. 'Com of, and hie yow soone   635
And ye shal se how wele it shal be done.'

'But this I dowte me gretely, wote ye what,
That my felaws bien passed by and gone.'
'I waraunt yow,' quod she, 'that ar they nat!
For here they shul assemble everichon.   640
Natwithstandyng, I counseil yow anone,
Make ye redy and tarye ye no more.
It is non harme though ye be there afore.'

---

623. oon: one (who).   *array*: clothing.
625. what ... wey: i.e. how.
626. governaunce: business.
628. warned: advised.   *felawes*: fellows, companions.
629. have upon: have on, i.e. wear.
631. Sith: since.
633. wite ... wele: know well.   *wold ... fayne*: would gladly be gone.
634. nedith nat: is not necessary.
635. ageyne: back, in return.   *Com of*: come on.   *hie yow*: hurry.
637. dowte me: am afraid.   *wote ye*: do you know.
639. waraunt: guarantee, promise.
640. everichon: each one.
641. counseil: advise.
643. though: even if.   *afore*: before, in advance.

So than I dressid me in myn array
And asked hir if it were wele or noo?   645
'It is,' quod she, 'right wele unto my pay;
Ye dare nat care to what place so ever ye goo!'
And while that she and I debated soo,
Com Diligence, and sawe me al in bliew.
'Suster,' quod she, 'right wele broke ye your niewe!'   650

[At the palace, the Dreamer meets Discretion and Acquaintance (Friendship), and is welcomed by Countenance (Self-
Possession).]

(ii)   Than Contenaunce asked me anone,
'Yowre felawship, where bien they now?' quod she.
'Forsoth,' quod I, 'they bien comyng echeone,
But in certeyne I knowe nat where they be.
At this wyndow whan they come ye may se.   655
Here wil I stande, awaityng ever among,
For wele I wote they wil nat now be long.'

Thus as I stode, musyng ful busily,
I thought to take heede of hir array.
Hir gowne was bliew, this wote I verily,   660
Of goode facion and furred wele with gray,
Upon hir sleve hir worde, this is no nay,
The whiche saide thus, as my penne can endite,
'A moy que je voy,' writen with lettres white.

646. *unto . . . pay*: to my satisfaction.
647. *dare . . . care*: need not worry.
648. *debated*: discussed.
649. *Com*: came.   *bliew*: blue (clothing).
650. *broke*: use, i.e. wear.   *niewe*: new (clothing).

(ii) f. 41ᵛ.
652. *felawship*: group of friends.
661. *goode facion*: excellent workmanship.   *gray*: grey fur.
662. *worde*: motto.   *this . . . nay*: there is no denying.
663. *endite*: write, record.
664. *A . . . voy*: 'What I see is mine', i.e. 'Mistress of all I survey'.

Than ferforth as she com streyght unto me,   665
'Yowre worde,' quod she, 'fayne wold I that I knewe.'
'Forsoth,' quod I, 'ye shal wele know and se.
And for my word, I have none, this is trewe;
It is inough that my clothyng be blew,
As here before I had comaundement,   670
And so to do I am right wele content.'

[The Dreamer's companions all present their complaints,
which she repeats, to Lady Loyalty. The knight to whom she
is narrating her dream then asks:]

(iii) 'Ye have rehersed me these billis alle,
But now late se somwhat of youre entente.'
'It may so happe peraventure ye shal.'
'Now, I pray yow, while I am here present.'   675
'Ye shal, parde, have knowlache what I ment.
But thus I say in trowth and make no fable,
The case itsilf is inly lamentable

And wele I wote that ye wil thynk the same
Like as I say, whan ye han herd my bil.'   680
'Now, goode, telle on, I hate yow, be Seynt Jame.'
'Abide a while, it is nat yit my wil.
Yet must ye wite, bi reason and bi skil,
Sith ye knowe al that hath be done afore.
And thus it sayde, without any more: 685

---

669. *inough*: enough, sufficient.

(iii) ff. 47ᵛ–48
672–84. *Ye . . . afore*: on the interpretation of this passage, see Barratt
1987b: 19–20.
672. *rehersed*: repeated, recited.
       billis: formal pleas, petitions or statements.
673. *late . . . entente*: let (me) see something of your mind or intention.
674. *happe*: happen, chance.
676. *parde*: by God, i.e. indeed.   *knowlache*: knowledge.
677. *make . . . fable*: am not inventing a story.
681. *goode*: good (lady).   *hate*: command.   *Jame*: James.
683. *skil*: reason.
684. *afore*: before.
685. *it*: i.e. her 'bill'.

"Nothyng so lief as death to come to me
For fynal end of my sorwes and peyne.
What shuld I more desire, as seme ye?
And ye knewe al aforne it, for certeyne
I wote ye wold, and for to telle yow pleyne,   690
Without hir help that hath al thyng in cure,
I can nat thynk that it may long endure.

And for my trouth, preved it hath bien wele
(To sey the soth, it can be no more)
Of ful long tyme, and suffred every dele   695
In pacience and kept it al in store;
Of hir goodenesse besechyng hir therfor
That I myght have my thank in suche wise
As my desert deservith of justice." '

[Lady Loyalty graciously receives all the petitions and promises to hold a full parliament later. The ladies set out to leave, and the Dreamer tells how she awakes.]

Textual notes

125. complayn] complan.
230. in certayn] certayn.
258. see] place.
287–8. Heyle . . . glade] these two lines appear in reverse order.

686. lief: welcome.
688. seme ye: you think.
689. And: if.   *aforne*: before, i.e. that preceded.
690. pleyne: plainly.
691. hir: her, i.e. Lady Loyalty.   *cure*: (her) care.
692. it: i.e. the Narrator's life.
693. trouth: integrity, loyalty.   *preved*: proved, tested.   *bien*: been.
694. can . . . more: is capable of no further (proof).
695. Of . . . tyme: for a very long time.   *dele*: bit.
696. kept . . . store: stored it all up.
697. hir: again, the reference is to Lady Loyalty, whose assistance is thus invoked indirectly.
698. thank: requital.
699. desert: merit.   *of justice*: i.e. in fairness.

288. *to glade*] glade.
327. Veritatis] Verit.
336. *Fro*] & fro.
337. *yere to yere*] yere.
356. *qwayntance*] qwayntenance.
450. *writtyn*] writtynge.
458. *And . . . be*] conjectural emendation, no lacuna in MS.
539. *In*] The.
553. *leves*] not in S; Skeat's conjectural emendation, adopted by Pearsall.
589. *yis*] yes S.
598. *wan by deed*] manly indeed S; Pearsall's conjectural emendation.
632. *with*] T.
659. *hir*] T, theyr A.
664. *A*] T, O A.
666. *worde*] T, A omits.
667. *Forsoth*] T, Ferforth A.   *se*] T, she A.
686. *as*] T.
689. *knewe*] L, Th; knowe A, Tr.

17 Lady Margaret Beaufort

Lady Margaret Beaufort (1443–1509), Countess of Richmond and Derby, mother of Henry VII and grandmother of Henry VIII, was the great-granddaughter of John of Gaunt and his third wife (formerly his mistress) Katherine Swynford. The Lady Margaret married Edmund Tudor, Henry VI's half-brother, in 1455 and bore him one child. Edmund died when she was still very young and she remarried twice, strictly for reasons of political convenience, bearing no more children, and eventually took a vow of chastity (see further Routh 1924; Simon 1982). Her son Henry claimed the throne in 1485 through his Beaufort mother, not through his Tudor father (the Tudors were descended from Catherine de Valois, widow of Henry V, and her second husband Owen Tudor).

The Lady Margaret had an intimidating reputation for orthodox piety, like most of the Lancastrians: Henry IV had persecuted the Lollards and Henry V had founded Syon, the Bridgettine monastery, and Sheen, a Carthusian monastery. (Their servants, too, such as Dame Eleanor Hull, were often equally pious.) She also promoted learning, patronising the early printers Caxton and Wynkyn de Worde (see Keiser 1987b), and the humanist scholar John Fisher. Fisher became her confessor and under his influence she founded two colleges at Cambridge and established professorships of Divinity (i.e. theology) at both the ancient universities. The Dutch humanist Erasmus held the Cambridge chair at one time and the Lady Margaret's interest in *The Imitation of Christ* also indicates the humanist side of her piety (see below). But her popularisation of *The Mirror of Gold to the Sinful Soul*, a text firmly in the medieval tradition of contempt for the world, and her knowledge of French rather than Latin link her with the medieval tradition of learned women such as Dame Eleanor, rather than with the Greek and Latin learning soon to be demonstrated by Margaret Roper, daughter of Sir Thomas More, and, most spectacularly, by Lady Margaret's great-granddaughter Queen Elizabeth (see Hogrefe 1977: 209–33).

The Lady Margaret made two translations of popular devotional texts, neither aimed specifically at a female audience. Both are conscientious and fairly accurate, though sometimes over-literal. Her first, made in 1503, was from a French version (probably the one published in 1488) of Book IV of the *De Imitatione Christi* (*The Imitation of Christ*), traditionally ascribed to Thomas à Kempis (1380–1471). *The Imitation* was a key text in the spiritual movement known as the *devotio moderna* ('modern devotion'), which reacted against late medieval mysticism, scholastic philosophy, religious formalism and intellectual speculation about the Godhead. It stressed devotion to Christ, particularly in his Passion and in the Eucharist, self-knowledge, disciplined meditation, and the prayerful reading of the Bible, and it formed the humanist piety of Erasmus. The Lady Margaret also sponsored William Atkinson's translation of the first three books of *The Imitation* and was thus responsible for introducing into England a devotional classic whose simple piety has been continuously popular since the fifteenth century with Catholics and Protestants alike in numerous translations.

A year or two later she translated from the French the originally Latin *Speculum Aureum* (*The Mirror of Gold*). First published as part of *Specula omnis status humanae vitae* (*The Mirrors of Every Estate of Human Life*) in 1495, and sometimes attributed to Denis the Carthusian, it was probably the work of another Carthusian monk, James of Gruytroede (c. 1400–75), a prolific but unoriginal writer out of touch with contemporary theological and spiritual thought. This tissue of commonplaces was printed many times during the fifteenth and sixteenth centuries. Its choice by the Lady Margaret is an indication of the continued coexistence of essentially conservative religious attitudes, even in circles influenced by humanism.

Comment: The first passage is the final chapter of Book IV of *The Imitation*. It is significant that the Lady Margaret chose this book, which is concerned with the Sacrament of Christ's Body and Blood, to translate herself. Her choice locates her squarely in the medieval female tradition of devotion to the Eucharist (see Bynum 1987; above, p. 96). This final chapter is the strongly anti-speculative climax of the whole treatise but is not gratuitously anti-intellectual: speculation about the Eucharist, which easily fell into heresy in the Middle Ages, was both difficult and dangerous.

The passages from *The Mirror of Gold* illustrate the traditional attitudes of that text, with which the Lady Margaret seems to have been quite content to associate herself. Contempt for the world, the body (especially the female body) and its pleasures was pervasive throughout the Middle Ages. That a woman, the most exalted in the land, should choose to translate this text indicates the degree to which such attitudes continued to be internalised.

Copy texts: *The Imitation of Christ* was first published by Pynson in 1503 (*STC* 23954.7, 23955); the text here has been prepared from the BL copy (C. 21. c. 5) of the latter. *The Mirror* was first published by Richard Pynson, probably in 1506 (*STC* 6894.5); the text here is based on the copy in the Bodleian Library.

Further reading (for full details see Bibliography): For a brief factual account of the Lady Margaret's life, see Routh 1924, and for a more popular and imaginative treatment, Simon 1982; on her influence on the printing policies of Caxton and de Worde, see Keiser 1987b. On the *devotio moderna* and *The Imitation of Christ* see Raitt 1987: 176–93; Oberman 1981: 45–56; on Erasmus, see Bainton 1969.

From *The Imitation of Christ*
a) Submit Reason to Faith
(sig. civ^v–v^r)

It behoves the to kepe the from to curyous inquysicyon of the
right profounde sacrament, if thou wylt nat be confounded in
thy proper vice and drowned in the deppeth of opynyons. For
he that wyll inquyre of the hye magestye of God, he shall
anone be oppressed and thrust downe from the glory of the   5
same. God may open more than man may understande. The
devoute and meke inquisicyon of trouth is alwey redy to be
doctryned and taught. And if thou study to goo by the holy,
true and entyer sentences of holy faders, it is nat reprovable
but well to be praysed. And that symplenesse is well to be   10
praysed, that leveth the wayes of dyfficultyes and questyons,
and goeth by the playne and ferme pathe of the commaundementes of God. Many hath lost their devocyon in sechynge so
besily the hye inspekable thynges.

It is ynoughe to demaunde of the, fast feyth, pure and clene   15
lyfe, and nat the hye and subtyll profounde mysteries of God;
for if thou may nat comprehende and understande that that is
within the, howe mayst thou thanne understande thynges that
be above the? Submytte the than mekely unto God and all thy
understandynge to the feyth of Holy Churche, and the light of   20
true scyence shall be gyven unto the, as shall be to the moost

1. *to*(2) . . . *of*: too elaborate inquisitiveness about.
2. *sacrament*: i.e. the Eucharist, concerning which there were numerous
controversies in the late Middle Ages.
2–3. *confounded . . . vice*: bogged down in your own viciousness.
3. *deppeth*: depth.   *opynyons*: theories.
4. *inquyre of*: investigate, pry into.
5. *anone*: immediately.
6. *may*: is able to.
   open: reveal. But the L. text here reads *operari*, 'work, perform'; possibly
the F. translator read *aperire*, 'open'.
7. *inquisicyon of*: enquiry into.
8. *doctryned*: instructed.
9. *entyer sentences*: sound authoritative teachings.   *reprovable*: reprehensible.
10. *symplenesse*: simplicity.
13. *devocyon*: faith.   *sechynge*: seeking.
14. *besily*: inquisitively.   *inspekable*: unspeakable, ineffable.
21. *scyence*: knowledge.

necessary and profytable. Some be greatly tempted wyth the feyth of that holy sacrament, but that is nat to be reputed unto theym, but rather unto that cursed ennemye the fende. And for that lette nat thy good wyll nor dyspute nat in thy   25 thoughtes, nor answere nat to the doubtes that the ennemye of hell bryngeth before the, but fermly trust in the wordes of God and byleve in sayntes and holy prophetes, and than shall that cursed ennemye sone fle from the.

It is often profytable that the servauntes of God suffre and   30 susteyne suche assaultes. For the ennemye tempteth nat the myscreauntes and unfeythfull people, nor also the great synners that he suerly holdeth and possedeth; but he tempteth, travayleth and tormenteth in dyvers maners the goode, faythful and crysten creatures. And therfore kepe the   35 alweyes with meke, true feyth and doubte the nought but come unto thys holy sacrament wyth lowly reverence. And that thou mayst nat understande, commytte it unto Almyghty God, for he shall nat disceyve the. But he shall be disceyved that to moche trusteth in hymselfe. God walked wyth the symple   40 people and shewed hymselfe openly unto the meke. He gave understandynge unto them that were pore in spyrite. And he hydde hys grace and secretes from theym that were proude, hygh and curyous. For the humayne reason may lightly erre and be disceyved, but the true feyth may never dysceyve nor   45 fayle. All reason and naturall inquysicyon ought to folowe feythe, wythoute farther reasonynge. Faste feyth and true love surmounteth all curyous inquisicyon, pryncipally in thys mater, and marvelously openeth to understandynge in secrete maner of this holy and right excellent sacrament.   50

O eternall God and wythoute mesure of myght and bounte, whiche hast made the infynyte greate and wonderfull thynges

22. *wyth*: concerning.
23. *reputed unto*: held against.
24. *fende*: fiend.
25. *lette*: hinder.
32. *myscreauntes*: unbelievers.   *unfeythfull*: faithless.
33. *suerly*: surely, securely.   *possedeth*: possesses.
34. *travayleth*: troubles.
36. *doubte . . . nought*: do not fear.
37. *that*: that which.
44. *hygh*: haughty.   *curyous*: inquisitive.   *humayne*: human.
    lightly: easily.
47. *farther*: further, i.e. beyond the bounds of faith.
48. *surmounteth*: surpasses, excels.
51. *wythoute . . . bounte*: i.e. immeasurably powerful and good.

in the heven and erthe, whiche none is sufficyent to enquyre, understande or fynde the secretes of thy so marvelous werkes; and therfore they be called inestimable, for mannys reason nouther may nor can comprehende thy werkys. To whome, gode Lorde Almyghty, be gyven laude and praysynge wythouten ende. Amen.

From *The Mirror of Gold to the Sinful Soul*

b) *On Human Indignity*
(sigs Aiii^v–iv^r)

The prophete Jeremie, consideringe the freylte and myserie of mankynde by maner of lamentacion in writyng, saith thus: 'Alas I, poore creature, wherfore was I borne out of the wombe of my moder to se the labour and sorowe of this world and to consume my dayes in confusion?' Alas, if this holy man Jeremie, the whiche almighty God sanctified in the wombe of his moder, he himself said and profered so piteous wordes; what may I say that am engendred and conceyved in the wombe of my moder by synne?

And to that purpose saith Saint Barnard: 'Study to know thyself, for that is the thinge moost avayllable and more praysable to thy weale, to knowe thyself, then it shuld be to knowe the course of sterres, the strengeth of herbes or the compleccion of all men, the naturis of beestes or the science of all erthly thinge. For in that knowleige thou knowest not what to thy soule is profitable.'

55. *inestimable*: unappraisable, incomprehensible.
57. *laude*: praise.
59. *Jeremie*: Jeremiah.   *freylte*: frailty.
61–3. *Alas . . . confusion*: Jeremiah 20: 18: 'Why came I out of the womb, to see labour and sorrow, and that my days should be spent in confusion?'
65. *profered*: put forth.
66. *engendred*: begotten.
68–74. *Study . . . profitable*: from a popular medieval text commonly attributed to St Bernard, the *Meditationes Piissimae* (*PL* 184: 485). 'Know thyself' was also a humanist maxim but with a very different application; here true self-knowledge leads, not to a conviction of the dignity of humankind, but to a full appreciation of its wretchedness.
69. *avayllable*: beneficial, helpful.
70. *praysable*: laudable.   *weale*: welfare.   *then*: than.
71. *course*: path, movement.   *strengeth*: powers.
72. *compleccion*: constitution, nature.   *science*: knowledge.

Nowe consider and beholde, thou mortall and miserable   75
man, what was of the byfore thy nativitie, and what is it of the
nowe sythe thou was borne, and what shal be of the to the
houre of thy deth, and what shal be of the after this mortall
lyfe. Certainly thou haste been frome thy begynnynge a thynge
vile, stinkynge, detestable and abhomynable, conceyved in   80
fylthe rotennes of flesshe and stynkynge fylthy concupiscence
and in th'embracement of stinkyng lechery and, that worse is,
conceyved in the unclene spottes of synne. And yf thou
beholde and consyder well what mete thou art norisshed with
in thy moders wombe, truly noon other but with corrupt and   85
infect blod, as well is knowen by many phylosophers and other
great clerkes. And after thy nativite thou that haste ben
norisshed of so foule and vile nature in thy moders wombe, as
bifore is said, thou art also ordeined to wepinges and criynges
and to many other miseries in the exile of this sorowfull   90
worlde and, that that is more grevous, thou art also subjecte to
thy deth, the whiche every true Cristen man ought daily to
remembre and thinke upon.

Behold then and consider in thy lyf that amonge all thing
that almighty God hath created and fourmed, man is made of   95
the most foule and abhomynable mater, that is to know of the
slyme of th'erth, the which erth is the lest worthy of al other
elimentis. God hath made the planetes and sterres of the
nature of the fyre; the windes and birdes of the ayre; the
fisshes of the water; the men and other beestes of the erth.   100

76. *what . . . the*: what there was of you.   *nativitie*: birth.
77. *sythe*: since.
79–83. *Certainly . . . synne*: these terms of abuse may seem extreme but are
entirely typical of medieval treatments of the *contemptus mundi* ('contempt
for the world') theme.
81. *fylthe*: filthy.
82. *th'embracement*: the embrace.
83. *conceyved . . . synne*: i.e. conceived in a state of original sin. Cf. also
Psalm 50: 7: 'For behold I was conceived in iniquities; and in sins did my
mother conceive me'.
84. *mete*: food.
85–6. *corrupt and infect*: rotten and infected, i.e. menstrual, as the L. text
makes clear, adding here several lines on the supposed disastrous effects on
plants and animals of menstrual blood.
86. *phylosophers*: scientists.
89. *ordeined*: doomed, destined.
96. *that . . . know*: that is to say.
98. *elimentis*: elements (the four traditional elements of earth, air, fire and
water).

Now consider then the thinges of olde antiquite and thou
shalt finde thyself most foule and when thou shalt knowe the
other bodies which of the fire hath ben made and brought
forth, thou shalt among al other cretours repute thyself right
vile and miserable and thou shalt not, will or may say or   105
thinke thyself semblable to celestiall thinges, or shal be bold to
preferre thyselfe byfore the thingis erthely. But yf thou wilt
company thyselfe with any creatour, acompany the to brute
beestis and thou shalt fynde thyselfe to theym moost
semblable and lyke. For so saith the wyse Salamon, 'Man and   110
brute beestes semblably be comen of the erth and to th'erthe
they shall retourne.' Knowe then howe noble thou art in this
worlde and take hede that the beaute, the praysinge of people,
the strengeth and the heate of youthe, the riches and
th'onours of the worlde, may not kepe the frome knowinge of 115
the vilite of thy birth.

c) *The Perils of Lust* (sigs Bi–ii)

Lechery is enmy to all vertues and to alle goodnes and for that
saithe Boice in his thirde Boke of Consolacion that he is
happy that lyveth withoute lechery, for lechery is a swete
sykenes and bringith a man to dethe or ever he perceyve it, as 120
witnessith Valerie in his ninth boke; the whiche Valerie also in

101. of old antiquite: from time immemorial.
104. cretours: creatures.   *repute*: think, reckon.
106. semblable: similar.
107. preferre thyselfe: put yourself before.
108. company thyselfe: associate.
110–12. Man . . . retourne: Ecclesiastes 3: 20: 'And all things go to one
place: of earth they were made, and into earth they return together.'
113. praysinge of people: i.e. popularity.
114. heate: fervour.
115. th'onours: the honours.
116. vilite: vileness.
117–42. not found in the L. text.
118. Boice: Boethius.
    thirde . . . Consolacion: third book of the Consolation [of Philosophy].
120. or . . . it: before he ever notices it.
121. Valerie: Valerius Maximus; the passage cited is possibly the opening of
Book IV of *Factorum et dictorum memorabilium libri novem*, 'Blandum etiam
malum luxuria', i.e. 'Lechery too is an enticing vice.' On Valerius
Maximus (much used by Christine de Pisan) see p. 137.
121–6. Valerie . . . lechery: Valerius Maximus tells this story of Sophocles,
not Josephus (the first-century Jewish historian), in Book IV, III, Ext. 2.

his fourthe boke telleth howe Josephus in his age demaundide
of on yf he were not lecherous? And he answered, 'I praye
the, speke to me of somme other thinge. For as I am advised,
I have had a greate victorie, that I maye by age eschewe   125
lechery.' For by lechery alle evyllis commythe and to that
creature alle goode thinges be troubled.

Alas, what was the cause of the distruccion of the people of
Sichen but for violacion of Digne, the doughter of Jacob, the
whiche wolde goo to see to the daunces and there ravisshed,   130
as it apperith in the Booke of Jenesie in the twenty-third
chapitour? We rede also of many, that is to saye, moo then
fifty thousande were slayne bycause of the lecherye comytted
with the woman of Levite, as it apperith in the twentieth
chapitour of the Booke of Jugis. And a man was slayne for the   135
lechery of Absolon his brother, for so moche that he had
defouled Thamar his suster, as it apperith in the secounde
Boke of Kingis in the tenth chaptour. Abnar by his lechery

122. age: i.e. old age.
122–3. demaundide of on: asked someone.
124. am advised: consider.
125. eschewe: avoid.
126–7. to . . . creature: by that creature, i.e. Lechery.
129. Sichen: Sichem, son of Hemor the Hevite.
   Digne: i.e. Dinah, daughter of Leah and Jacob, the tragic story of
whose rape in Genesis 34 was used throughout the Middle Ages to warn
women against the dangers of curiosity, lust and appearing in public.
130. wolde . . . daunces: this detail is not in the Bible, which simply says
Dinah 'went out to see the women of that country', but it helps to imply
that her behaviour was culpably frivolous.
130. ravisshed: (was) raped.
131–2. Booke . . . chapitour: the reference is wrong (see above).
132. moo: more.
133–4. lecherye . . . Levite: this appalling story, the moral of which is far from
clear, is found in Judges 19 and 20. The Levite's concubine or wife was
raped and killed by 'the sons of Belial' in place of the Levite himself
(provoking Milton's notorious lines 'the hospitable door / Exposed a
matron to avoid worse rape' in *Paradise Lost*, I, 504–5); in the subsequent
war 83,000 men died on both sides. In this text, however, there is no
indication that the woman was an unwilling partner in 'lecherye', and no
mention of her own death.
137. defouled: defiled.
   Thamar: the story of Thamar, daughter of David; her rape by David's
eldest son (her half-brother) Amnon, and the vengeance of her full brother
Absalom is found in 2 Kings 13 (again the reference is given incorrectly).
138–41. Abnar . . . chaptour: this passage is confused. Isboseth was not the
father of Abner but the son of Saul; Abner was the ruler of Saul's
household. Isboseth reproached Abner for sleeping with Saul's concubine,

knewe the concupiscens of his fader Hisboseth, but within
shorte while after they were both slayne, as it apperith in the   140
secounde Boke of Kynges in the fourthe chaptour. What was
the cause of the Diluvye but lechery?

d) *Ubi Sunt?* (sig. Evi^v)

Yf thou wolde knowe what is the joye, might, dignite, honours
and riches of the worlde, understande and herken the
prophete Baruc in his thirde chapitour, the which   145
demaundeth in this maner: 'Where be the princes of the
people, that had seignyorie and dominacion of the bestis of
th'erth, and that played and disported with the birdes of
heven? Where be the men that gadereth golde and silver, and
affye them in their treasour, never satisfied with gettynge?   150
Iwys, they be all passed and deed and discended into hell and
other be come in their placis, whiche nowe joye and use of
their goodes that they leste.' And where be the grate clerkes
and the oratours, or where be the great dyners in excesse and
superhaboundaunce of meates, or they that have put their   155

and in anger Abner defected to David, but was soon killed by Joab, see 2
Kings 3. Again the reference is incorrect, but 2 Kings 4 does record the
subsequent murder of Isboseth by his own men. The connection of either
man's death with Saul's, or Abner's own, lechery is extremely tenuous.

139. his fader Hisboseth: i.e. Isboseth's father (Saul); probably a misunderstanding of the F. construction.
142. Diluvye: the Flood, caused by lechery because 'the sons of God seeing
the daughters of men, that they were fair, took to themselves wives of all
which they chose' (Genesis 6: 2) and angered God by procreating giants.
143–66. A classic expression of the popular *ubi sunt* ('where are they?')
topos, which is so pervasive in medieval literature, e.g. in the Old English
poems 'The Wanderer' and 'The Seafarer', in Middle English lyrics such
as 'Where beth they, beforen us weren?' (*Medieval English Lyrics*, p. 56; see
also pp. 40–1 and 311–12) and in François Villon's famous poem 'Où sont
les neiges d'antan?' ('Where are the snows of yesteryear?').
146–53. Where . . . leste: Baruch 3: 16–19.
147. seignyorie: lordship, power.
150. affye them: put their trust in.
151. Iwys: truly.
153. leste: lost.   *clerkes*: learned men.
154. dyners: this would appear to mean 'diners, those who feast', but *OED*
does not record this meaning before the nineteenth century.
155. superhaboundaunce of meates: superfluity of food.

pleasaunce to norisshe horses, palfreys and suche other? And
where be the popes, emperours, kynges, dukes, princes,
marques, erles, barons, noble burgeis, marchauntes, laborers
and folkes of all estates? They be all in powder and rottennes,
and of the most greate ther is noo more but a lytell memorye   160
uppon their sepulcre in lettres conteyned. But goo see in their
sepulcres and tombes and loke and thou canst wel knowe and
truly juge whiche is thy mayster and whiche is the verlet,
whiche bones be of the pore and wiche be of the riche?
Devide, yf thou maye, the laborer from the kinge, the feble   165
frome the strong, the faire from the foule and deformed!

Textual notes

40. myghtyly] myghtly.
82. ayens yow] ayens.
101. fylth] feyth.   *onethis*] onthis.
129. wille] will that.
130. all here hertys] all hertys.
138. Holye] hole.
144. joynyd] and joynyd.
195. his name] name.
196. generacion . . . generacyon] gernacion.

156. norisshe: rear.
157. popes: in the Bodley copy this word has been erased, evidence that the
text was still being read after Henry VIII's break with Rome.
158. burgeis: magistrates, counsellors.
159. powder: dust.
160–1. lytell . . . conteyned: i.e. a brief epitaph carved on their tombs.
162. and(3): if.
163. verlet: servant.
165. Devide: distinguish.   *maye*: can.

Bibliography

Primary texts

Introduction

The Ancrene Riwle, trans. by M.B. Salu, London, 1963.

The Book of Fayttes of Armes and of Chyualrye, ed. by A.T.P. Byles, EETS os 189, London, 1932, corr. edn 1937.

The Book of Margery Kempe, ed. by S.B. Meech and H.E. Allen, EETS os 212, London, 1940.

Christine de Pizan: The Book of the City of Ladies, trans. by E.J. Richards, London, 1983.

The Early English Carols, ed. by R. Greene, Oxford, 1977.

The English Register of Godstow Abbey, Part I, ed. by A. Clark, EETS os 129, London, 1905.

Early Middle English Verse and Prose, ed. by J.A.W. Bennett and G.V. Smithers, 2nd edn, rev., Oxford, 1974.

English Lyrics of the XIIIth Century, ed. by Carleton Brown, Oxford, 1932.

Hoccleve's Works: The Minor Poems, ed. by F.J. Furnivall and I. Gollancz, EETS es 61 and 73, London, rev. repr. 1970.

The Latin Poems of Richard Ledrede OFM, ed. by E. Colledge, Toronto, 1974; includes the ME poems of the Red Book of Ossory.

The Letters of Abelard and Heloise, trans. with an Introduction by B. Radice, London, 1974.

The Lyrics of the Red Book of Ossory, ed. by R.L. Greene, Oxford, 1974.

Medieval English Lyrics, ed. by R.T. Davies, London, 1963.

Middle English Prose for Women: The 'Katherine Group' and 'Ancrene Wisse', ed. by B. Millett and J. Wogan-Browne, Oxford, 1990.

The Moral Proverbs of Christine . . . trans. by the Earl Rivers, and reprinted from the original edn of William Caxton, AD 1478, with introductory remarks by William Blades, London, 1859.

The Myroure of Oure Ladye, ed. by J.H. Blunt, EETS es 19, London, 1873.

311

A Pre-Conquest English Prayer Book, ed. by B.J. Muir, Henry
  Bradshaw Society 103, 1988.
The Riverside Chaucer, ed. by L.D. Benson, Boston, 1987.

1 Middle English Trotula texts

Aristotle: Generation of Animals with an English translation by A.L.
  Peck, London, 1942.
*Medieval Woman's Guide to Health: The First English Gynecological
  Handbook*, ed. by B. Rowland, Kent, Ohio, 1981.

2 Marie de France

The Auchinleck Manuscript, Introduction by Derek Pearsall and I.C.
  Cunningham, London, 1977; facsimile edn with bibliography.
The Lais of Marie de France, trans. with an Introduction by Glyn S.
  Burgess and Keith Busby, Harmondsworth, Middlesex, 1986.
Marie de France: Lais, ed. by A. Ewert, Oxford, 1944; edn of the
  OF text.
Margaret Wattie, *The Middle English Lai le Freine*, Smith College
  Studies in Modern Languages 10, 3 (1929); full edn of the ME.

3 Mechtild of Hackeborn and Gertrude the Great

The Book of Ghostly Grace, ed. by T.A. Halligan, Pontifical Institute
  for Medieval Studies, Studies and Texts 46, Toronto, 1979.
*Gertrud the Great of Helfta: The Herald of God's Loving-Kindness Books
  One and Two*, trans. with an Introduction and notes by A. Barratt,
  The Cistercian Fathers Series 35, Kalamazoo, 1991.
Pearl, Cleanness, Patience, Sir Gawain and the Green Knight, ed. by
  A.C. Cawley and J.J. Anderson, 2nd. edn, London, 1976.

4 Marguerite Porete

Marguerite Porete: Le Mirouer des Simples Ames, ed. by R. Guarnieri,
  and *Margaretae Porete: Speculum Simplicium Animarum*, ed. by
  P. Verdeyen, S.J. *CCCM* 69, Turnholt, 1986; edns of the OF and
  L. versions.
Doiron, M. (1968), '*The mirrour of simple souls*: A Middle English
  translation', *AISP*, Vol. v, pp. 247–355; edn of the ME based on
  Cambridge St John's College MS.
The Mirror of Simple Souls, trans. by Clare Kirchberger, London,
  1927; a modernisation of the MS Bodley 505 text, made before
  Porete's authorship was known.

5 St Elizabeth of Hungary

Oliger, P.L. (1926), 'Revelationes B. Elisabeth: Disquisitio Critica cum Textibus Latino et Catalaunensi', *Antonianum*, Vol. i, pp. 24–83; written in L.; prints one of the L. versions and also the Catalan translation.

'The Revelacions of Saynt Elysabeth the kynges doughter of hungarye' in *Lyf of Saint Katherin of Senis*, printed by Wynkyn de Worde, ?1492 (*STC* 24766), ff. 91ᵛ–6, ed. by C. Horstmann (1886), *Archiv*, Vol. lxxvi, pp. 392–400.

6 Bridget of Sweden

The Liber Coelestis of St Bridget of Sweden, ed. by R. Ellis, EETS os 291, 1987.

The Revelations of Saint Birgitta, ed. by W.P. Cumming, EETS os 178, 1929.

'*The Rewyll of Seynt Sauioure*' *and Other Middle English Brigittine Legislative Texts*, Vol. 2, ed. by James Hogg, Salzburger Studien zür Anglistik und Amerikanistik 6, Salzburg, 1978 (facsimile edns of MSS CUL Ff. 6. 33 and St John's College Cambridge 11).

7 Catherine of Siena

Catherine of Siena: The Dialogue, trans. and Introduction by Suzanne Noffke, O.P., New York, 1980.

I, Catherine: Selected Writings of Catherine of Siena, ed. and trans. by K. Foster and M.J. Ronayne, London, 1980.

The Orcherd of Syon, ed. by P. Hodgson and G.M. Liegey, EETS os 258, 1966.

8 Julian of Norwich

A Book of Shewings to the Anchoress Julian of Norwich, ed. by E. Colledge and J. Walsh, 2 vols, Toronto, 1978; critical edn of both versions.

Julian of Norwich's Revelations of Divine Love, ed. by Frances Beer, MET 8, Heidelberg, 1978; edn of the Short (Carthusian) Version.

A Revelation of Love, ed. by M. Glasscoe, Exeter, 1978; edn of the Long (Benedictine) Version.

9 Christine de Pisan

The Book of Fayttes of Armes and of Chyualrye, ed. by A.T.P. Byles, EETS os 189, London, 1932, corr. edn, 1937.

The Epistle of Othea translated from the French text of Christine de Pisan by Stephen Scrope, ed. by Curt F. Bühler, EETS os 264, London, 1970.

The Epistle of the Prison of Human Life ..., ed. and trans. by J.A. Wisman, Vol. 21, Series A, Garland Library of Medieval Literature, New York and London, 1984; useful bibliography.

Le Livre du Corps de Policie, ed. by Robert H. Lucas, Geneva, 1967.

The Middle English Translation of Christine de Pisan's 'Livre du Corps de Policie', ed. by Diane Bornstein, MET 17, Heidelberg, 1977.

The Moral Proverbs of Christine ... translated by the Earl Rivers, and repr. from the original edn of William Caxton, AD 1478, with introductory remarks by William Blades, London, 1859; the first book by a woman printed in England.

Aristotle: The Nicomachean Ethics, with an English translation by H. Rackham, London, rev. edn 1947, repr. 1968.

Disticha Catonis, ed. by M. Boas, Amsterdam, 1952.

Jacobus de Voragine: Legenda Aurea, ed. by Th. Graesse, 2nd edn, Leipzig, 1850.

Seneca: Moral Essays, with an English trans. by John W. Basore, 3 vols., London and Cambridge, Mass., 1928–35, repr. 1958.

Valerius Maximus: Factorum et dictorum memorabilium libri novem, ed. by C. Kempf, Leipzig, 1888.

10 A Revelation of Purgatory

Pearl, ed. by E.V. Gordon, Oxford, 1953.

The Thornton Manuscript (Lincoln Cathedral MS 91), Introductions by D.S. Brewer and A.E.B. Owen, London, 1975, repr. with rev. introductions, 1977; facsimile edn of this important MS.

Yorkshire Writers: Richard Rolle of Hampole and his Followers, ed. by C. Horstmann, 2 vols, London, 1895–6, Vol. i, pp. 383–92; edn of the Thornton MS version.

11 Margery Kempe

The Book of Margery Kempe, ed. by S.B. Meech and H.E. Allen, EETS os 212, London, 1940.

The Book of Margery Kempe: A Modern Version, ed. by W. Butler-Bowden, Oxford, 1936, repr. 1944; the first appearance of *The Book* in print, with minimal modernisation.

The Book of Margery Kempe, trans. by B. Windeatt, London, 1985; excellent modern version with useful notes and Introduction.

14 Juliana Berners

The Boke of Saint Albans by Dame Juliana Berners with an Introduction by William Blades, London, 1901; facsimile of the 1486 edn.

English Hawking and Hunting in 'The Boke of St Albans', ed. by Rachel Hands, Oxford, 1975; facsimile of the 1486 edn, with substantial Introduction and notes.

Julians Barnes: Boke of Huntyng, ed. by Gunnar Tilander, *Cynegetica* 11, Karlshamn, 1964.

William Twiti: The Art of Hunting, ed. by Bror Danielsson, *Cynegetica Anglica* 1, Stockholm, 1977.

15 Some Paston Letters

Paston Letters, selected and edited with Introduction, notes and glossary, by N. Davis, Oxford, 1958; a selection in the original ME for students.

The Paston Letters and Papers, ed. by N. Davis, 2 vols, Oxford, 1971, 1976; the standard edition, containing all the known documents.

The Paston Letters: A Selection in Modern Spelling, ed. with an Introduction by N. Davis (Oxford, 1963, corr. edn 1983). Minimal modernisation; useful Introduction, notes on the various members of the family and a helpful list of dates.

16 Fifteenth- and early Sixteenth-century poems

The Findern Manuscript: Cambridge University Library MS Ff. 1. 6, Introduction by Richard Beadle and A.E.B. Owen, London, 1977; facsimile edn.

'*The Floure and the Leafe*' and '*The Assembly of Ladies*', ed. by D.A. Pearsall, 3rd edn, Manchester, 1980.

The Gude and Goodlie Ballatis, ed. by A.F. Mitchell, Scottish Text Society 39, Edinburgh, 1897.

Kissing the Rod: An Anthology of Seventeenth-Century Women's Verse, ed. by G. Greer, S. Hastings, J. Medoff, and M. Sansone, London, 1988.

Medieval English Lyrics, ed. by R.T. Davies, London, 1963.

Padelford, F.M. (1908), 'Liedersammlungen des XVI. Jahrhunderts, besonders aus der Zeit Heinrichs VIII. IV. 7. The Songs of Rawlinson MS C. 813', *Anglia*, Vol. xxxi, pp. 309–97; complete edn of all the Rawlinson poems.

Robbins, R.H. (1950), 'The Poems of Humfrey Newton, Esq., 1466–1536', *PMLA*, Vol. lxv, pp. 249–81.

—— (1954), 'The Findern Anthology', *PMLA*, Vol. lxix, pp. 610–42; first edn of many of the lyrics, including all the women's poems; discussion of the manuscript and the female scribes.

17 Lady Margaret Beaufort

The Earliest English Translation . . . of the De Imitatione Christi, ed. by J.K. Ingram, EETS es 63, London, 1893.

Secondary works

Ancelet-Hustache, J. (1928), 'Vie d'Elisabeth de Hongrie Vièrge de l'Ordre des Prêcheurs (?1294–1336)', in *La Vie Mystique d'un Monastère de Dominicaines au Moyen Age*, Paris.

Armstrong, K. (1986), *The Gospel According to Woman: Christianity's Creation of the Sex War in the West*, London.

Atkinson, C.W. (1983), *Mystic and Pilgrim: The Book and the World of Margery Kempe*, Ithaca.

Barber, R.W. (1981), *The Pastons, a Family in the Wars of the Roses*, London.

Bainton, R. (1969), *Erasmus of Christendom*, New York.

Barratt, A. (1987a), 'Flying in the Face of Tradition: A New View of "The Owl and the Nightingale" ', *University of Toronto Quarterly*, Vol. lvi, pp. 471–85.

—— (1987b), ' "The Flower and the Leaf" and "The Assembly of Ladies": Is There a (Sexual) Difference?', *Philological Quarterly*, Vol. lxvi, pp. 1–24.

—— (1989), 'Dame Eleanor Hull: A Fifteenth Century Translator' in R. Ellis (ed.), *The Medieval Translator: The Theory and Practice of Translation in the Middle Ages*, Cambridge, pp. 87–101.

—— (1990), ' "I Am Rose" Restored', *Notes and Queries*, Vol. ccxxxv, p. 270.

—— (1992), '*The Revelations of St Elizabeth of Hungary:* Problems of Attribution', *The Library*.

—— (forthcoming) 'The Virgin and the Visionary in the Revelations of St Elizabeth', *Mystics Quarterly*.

Barron, W.R.J. (1987), *English Medieval Romance*, London and New York.

Belsey, C. (1980), *Critical Practice*, London and New York.

Bennett, H.S. (1968), *The Pastons and Their England*, Oxford.

Benton, J.F. (1985), 'Trotula, Women's Problems, and the Professionalization of Medicine in the Middle Ages', *Bulletin of the History of Medicine*, Vol. lix, pp. 30–53.

Binns, A.L. (1950), 'A Manuscript Source of *The Book of St Albans*', *BJRL*, Vol. xxxiii, pp. 15–24.

Boffey, J. (1985), *Manuscripts of English Courtly Love Lyrics in the Later Middle Ages*, Cambridge.

Bornstein, D. (1977), 'French Influence on Fifteenth-century English Prose as Exemplified by the Translation of Christine de Pizan's *Livre du corps de policie*', *Medieval Studies*, Vol. xxxix, pp. 369–86; on Christine's *style clergial*.

Bourdillon, A.F.C. (1926), *The Order of Minoresses in England*, Manchester; a detailed study of medieval English Franciscan nuns.

Bradley, Sister R. (forthcoming), 'Julian of Norwich' in *The Garland Encyclopaedia of Medieval England*.

Bullock-Davies, C. (1965), 'Marie, Abbess of Shaftesbury, and her Brothers', *EHR*, Vol. lxxx, pp. 314–22; on the identity of Marie de France.

Butkovich, A. (1972), *Revelations: Saint Birgitta of Sweden*, Los Angeles.

Bynum, C.W. (1982), 'Women Mystics in the Thirteenth Century: The Case of the Nuns of Helfta' in *Jesus as Mother*, Berkeley and Los Angeles, pp. 170–262.

—— (1987), *Holy Feast and Holy Fast: The Religious Significance of Food to Medieval Women*, Berkeley, Los Angeles and London.

Campbell, P.G.C. (1925), 'Christine de Pisan en Angleterre', *Revue de littérature comparée*, Vol. v, pp. 659–70; on Christine's literary and personal connections with England – still useful.

Carpenter, C. (1987), 'The Religion of the Gentry of Fifteenth-century England', in Daniel Williams (ed.), *England in the Fifteenth Century: Proceedings of the 1986 Harlaxton Symposium*, Woodbridge, Suffolk, pp. 53–74; on late medieval attitudes towards Purgatory.

Colledge, E. and Guarnieri, R. (1968), 'The Glosses by M.N. and Richard Methley to "The Mirror of Simple Souls"', *AISP*, Vol. v, pp. 357–82.

Crawford, P. (1985), 'Women's Published Writings 1600–1700' in M. Prior (ed.), *Women in English Society 1500–1700*, London and New York, pp. 211–82.

Curtayne, A. (1929), *Saint Catherine of Siena*, London.

Davis, G. and Joyce, B.A. (1989), *Personal Writings by Women to 1900: A Bibliography of American and British Writers*, London.

Dronke, P. (1961), 'The Rawlinson Lyrics', *Notes and Queries*, New Series, Vol. viii, pp. 245–6.

—— (1976), *Abelard and Heloise in Medieval Testimonies*, Glasgow.

—— (1984), *Women Writers of the Middle Ages*, Cambridge.

Eccles, A. (1982), *Obstetrics and Gynaecology in Tudor and Stuart England*, Kent, Ohio.

Ellis, R. (1982), ' "Flores ad fabricandum ... coronam": An Investigation into the Uses of the Revelations of St Bridget of Sweden in Fifteenth-century England', *Medium Aevum*, Vol. li, pp. 163–86.

—— (1990), 'Margery Kempe's Scribe and the Miraculous Books' in H. Phillips (ed.), *Langland, the Mystics and the Medieval English Religious Tradition*, Woodbridge, Suffolk, pp. 161–75.

Evans, G.R. (1984), *The Language and Logic of the Bible: The Earlier Middle Ages*, Cambridge.

Farmer, D.H. (1978), *The Oxford Dictionary of Saints*, Oxford.

Fawtier, R. and Canet, L. (1948), *La double expérience de Catherine Benincasa*, Paris.

Ferrante, J.M. (1984), 'The French Courtly Poet: Marie de France' in K.M. Wilson (ed.), *Medieval Women Writers*, Athens, Georgia and Manchester, pp. 64–89.

Finnegan, Sister Mary Jeremy (1980), 'Catherine in England: *The Orchard of Syon*', *Spirituality Today*, Vol. xxxii, pp. 13–24.

Finnegan, R. (1977), *Oral Poetry: Its Nature, Significance, and Social Context*, Cambridge.

Flanagan, S. (1989), *Hildegard of Bingen: A Visionary Life*, London and New York.

Fleming, J.V. (1971), 'Hoccleve's "Letter of Cupid" and the "quarrel" over the *Roman de la Rose*', *Medium Aevum*, Vol. xl, pp. 21–39.

Fox, J.C. (1910), 'Marie de France', *EHR*, Vol. xxv, pp. 303–6.

—— (1911), 'Marie, Abbess of Shaftesbury', *EHR*, Vol. xxvi, pp. 317–26.

Glasscoe, Marion (1989), 'Visions and Revisions: A Further Look at the Manuscripts of Julian of Norwich', *Studies in Bibliography*, Vol. xlii, pp. 103–20.

Gray, D. (1972), *Themes and Images in the Medieval English Religious Lyric*, London.

Green, M. (1989), 'Women's Medical Practice and Health Care in Medieval Europe', *Signs: Journal of Women in Culture and Society*, Vol. xiv, pp. 434–73.

Halligan, T.A. (1974), 'The *Revelations* of St Matilda in English: "The Booke of Gostlye Grace" ', *Notes and Queries*, New Series, Vol. xxi, pp. 443–6.

Hands, R. (1967), 'Juliana Berners and *The Boke of St. Albans*', *Review of English Studies*, Vol. xviii, pp. 373–86.

Hanson-Smith, E. (1979), 'A Woman's View of Courtly Love: The Findern Anthology', *Journal of Women's Studies in Literature*, Vol. i, pp. 179–94.

Hardesty, N.A. (1982), *Great Women of Faith*, Nashville, Tenn.

Harris, K. (1983), 'The Origins and Make-up of Cambridge University Library MS Ff. 1. 6', *Transactions of the Cambridge Bibliographical Society*, Vol. viii, pp. 299–333.

Haskell, A.S. (1973), 'The Paston Women on Marriage in Fifteenth-century England', *Viator: Medieval and Renaissance Studies*, Vol. iv, pp. 459–71.

Hewson, M.A. (1975), *Giles of Rome and the Medieval Theory of Conception*, London.

Hirsh, J.C. (1975), 'Author and Scribe in *The Book of Margery Kempe*', *Medium Aevum*, Vol. xliv, pp. 145–50; argues that Margery's scribe was largely responsible for the shaping of *The Book*.

—— (1989), *The Revelations of Margery Kempe: Paramystical Practices in Late Medieval England*, Leiden; a thoughtful study of the exact nature of Margery's mysticism.

Hobby, E. (1988), *Virtue of Necessity: English Women's Writings 1649–88*, London.

Hodgson, P. (1942), '*The Orcherd of Syon* and the English Mystical Tradition', *Proceedings of the British Academy*, Vol. l, pp. 229–49.

Hogrefe, P. (1977), *Women of Action in Tudor England*, Ames, Iowa.

Huttar, C.A. (1965), ' "Forsake Me Neuer for No New": A Note on Wyatt's Poetic Diction', *Notes and Queries*, Vol. ccx, pp. 170–2.

Jacob, E.F. (1944), 'The Book of St Albans', *BJRL*, Vol. xxviii, pp. 1–22.

Keiser, G. (1987a), 'St Jerome and the Brigittines: Visions of the Afterlife in Fifteenth-century England' in Daniel Williams (ed.), *England in the Fifteenth Century*, Woodbridge, Suffolk, pp. 143–52; one of the few studies of *A Revelation of Purgatory*.

—— (1987b), 'Lady Margaret Beaufort and the Economics of Devotionalism' in M. Glasscoe (ed.), *The Medieval Mystical Tradition in England: Exeter Symposium IV*, Cambridge, pp. 9–26.

Kirshner, J. and Wemple, S.F. (eds) (1985), *Women in the Medieval World*, Oxford and New York.

Knowles, D. (1955), *The Religious Orders in England: Vol. II, The End of the Middle Ages*, Cambridge.

—— (1961), *The Religious Orders in England: Vol. III, The Tudor Age*, Cambridge.

Lagorio, V.M. and Bradley, R. (1981), *The 14th-century English Mystics: A Comprehensive, Annotated Bibliography*, New York and London. Very useful; interprets the term 'mystics' widely. Sections on Mechtild, Porete, Bridget, Catherine, Julian and Margery.

Lamb, H.E. (1985) 'The Cooke Sisters: Attitudes towards Learned Women in the Renaissance' in M.P. Hannay (ed.), *Silent but for the Word: Tudor Women as Patrons, Translators, and Writers of Religious Works*, Kent, Ohio, pp. 107–125.

Legge, M.D. (1963), *Anglo-Norman Literature and Its Background*, Oxford.

Le Goff, J. (1984), *The Birth of Purgatory*, trans. by A. Goldenhammer, London.

Lerner, R.E. (1972), *The Heresy of the Free Spirit in the Later Middle Ages*, Berkeley, Los Angeles and London.

Loomis, L.H. (1942), 'The Auchinleck Manuscript and a Possible London Bookshop of 1330–1340', *PMLA*, Vol. lvii, pp. 595–627.

Lucas, R.H. (1970), 'Mediaeval French Translations of the Latin Classics to 1500', *Speculum*, Vol. xlv, pp. 225–53.

Maddern, P. (1988), 'Honour among the Pastons: Gender and Integrity in Fifteenth-century English Provincial Society', *Journal of Medieval History*, Vol. xiv, pp. 357–71; stresses the difference between male and female concepts of 'honour'.

Mary Denise RSM, Sister (1958), 'The Orchard of Syon: An Introduction', *Traditio*, Vol. cxiv, pp. 269–93.

Mary Jeremy, Sister (1962), *Scholars and Mystics*, Chicago.

Mehl, D. (1968), *The Middle English Romances of the Thirteenth and Fourteenth Centuries*, London.

Miller, R.P. (ed.) (1977), *Chaucer: Sources and Backgrounds*, New York.

Millett, B. and Wogan-Browne, J. (eds) (1990), *Medieval English Prose for Women*, Oxford.

Minnis, A.J. (1984), *Medieval Theory of Authorship*, London.

Minnis, A.J. and Scott, A.B. with the assistance of David Wallace (1988), *Medieval Literary Theory and Criticism c. 1100–c. 1375: The Commentary Tradition*, Oxford.

Moorman, J.R.H. (1974), *The Franciscans in England*, Oxford; deals briefly with the Franciscan nuns of Denny.

Needham, J. (1959), *A History of Embryology*, 2nd edn, Cambridge.

Oberman, H.A. (1981), *Masters of the Reformation: The Emergence of a New Intellectual Climate in Europe*, Cambridge.

Ogilvie-Thomson, S.J. (1980), 'An edition of the English Works in MS. Longleat 29 excluding *The Parson's Tale*', 4 vols, unpublished Oxford DPhil thesis; includes an annotated edn of the Longleat MS version of 'A Revelation Showed to a Holy Woman', collated with the other two manuscripts, with useful notes.

Ong, W. (1967, repr. 1981), *The Presence of the Word: Some Prolegomena for Cultural and Religious History*, Minneapolis, Minn.

Orme, N. (1973), *English Schools in the Middle Ages*, London.

—— (1984), *From Childhood to Chivalry*, London and New York.

Parker, R. (1984), *The Subversive Stitch: Embroidery and the Making of the Feminine*, London.

Pelphrey, B. (1989), *Christ Our Mother: Julian of Norwich*, London; a recent study, primarily from a theological point of view.

Petroff, E.A. (ed.) (1986), *Medieval Women's Visionary Literature*, New York and Oxford; anthology of translated texts with authoritative Introduction and comprehensive bibliography.

Plummer, J.F. (1981), 'The Woman's Song in Middle English and its European Backgrounds' in J.F. Plummer (ed.), *Vox Feminae: Studies in Medieval Women's Songs*, Kalamazoo, pp. 135–54.

Pollard, W. (1987), 'Mystical Elements in a Fifteenth-century Prayer Sequence: "The Festis [*sic*] and the Passion of Oure Lord Ihesu Crist"' in M. Glasscoe (ed.), *The Medieval Mystical Tradition in England: Exeter Symposium IV*, Cambridge, pp. 47–61.

Power, E. (1922), *Medieval English Nunneries c. 1275 to 1535*, Cambridge; still the standard account.

Raitt, J. (ed.) (1987), *Christian Spirituality: High Middle Ages and Reformation*, New York.

Riehle, W. (1981), *The Middle English Mystics*, trans. by B. Standring, London.

Robbins, R.H. (1942), 'Two Middle English Satiric Love Epistles', *Modern Language Review*, Vol. xxxvii, pp. 415–21; a pair of abusive poems, one purporting to be written by a woman.

Rousselle, A. (1988), *Porneia: On Desire and the Body in Antiquity*, trans. by F. Pheasant, Oxford.

Routh, E.M.G. (1924), *Lady Margaret: A Memoir*, Oxford.

Shahar, S. (1983), *The Fourth Estate: A History of Women in the Middle Ages*, trans. by Chaya Galai, London and New York.

Simon, L. (1982), *Of Virtue Rare: Margaret Beaufort, Matriarch of the House of Tudor*, Boston, Mass.

Smalley, B. (1983), *The Study of the Bible in the Middle Ages*, 3rd edn, Oxford; the standard introduction to medieval Scriptural exegesis.

Southern, R.W. (1953, repr. 1959), *The Making of the Middle Ages*, London.

Stevens, J. (1961), *Music and Poetry in the Early Tudor Court*, London.

—— (1973), *Medieval Romance: Themes and Approaches*, London.

Tatlock, J.S.P. (1933), 'Muriel: The Earliest English Poetess', *PMLA*, Vol. xlviii, pp. 317–21.

Utley, F.L. (1944), *The Crooked Rib*, Columbus, Ohio; concerned mainly with anti-feminist writings.

Verdeyen, P. (1986), 'Le procès d'inquisition contre Marguerite Porete et Guiard de Cressonessart', *Revue d'histoire ecclésiastique*, Vol. lxxxi, pp. 47–94.

Watkin, E.I. (1979), *On Julian of Norwich and in Defence of Margery Kempe*, Exeter.

Webster, R. (1990), *Studying Literary Theory: An Introduction*, London.

Willard, Charity C. (1984), *Christine de Pizan: Her Life and Works*, New York; the most comprehensive study of Christine in English.

Wilson, K.M. (ed.) (1984), *Medieval Women Writers*, Athens, Georgia, and Manchester; collection of translated extracts with useful Introductions and bibliographies.

Woolf, R. (1968), *The English Religious Lyric in the Middle Ages*, Oxford.

Index